U. S. Supreme Court

U. S. SUPREME COURT

Volume 1

Abington School District v. Schempp —
Fundamental rights

Edited by
Thomas Tandy Lewis
St. Cloud State University

SALEM PRESS, INC.
Pasadena, California   Hackensack, New Jersey

Frontispiece: *Associate Justice Samuel A. Alito, Jr. (left) with recently installed Chief Justice John Roberts on the steps of the Supreme Court building immediately after Alito's investiture on February 16, 2006.* (AP/Wide World Photos)

Essays originally appeared in *Encyclopedia of the U.S. Supreme Court* (2001). New essays and other materials have been added.

∞ The paper used in these volumes conforms to the American National Standard for Permanence of Paper for Printed Library Materials, Z39.48-1992 (R1997).

Library of Congress Cataloging-in-Publication Data

The U.S. Supreme Court / edited by Thomas Tandy Lewis.

v. cm. – (Magill's choice)

Includes bibliographical references and indexes.

ISBN 978-1-58765-363-6 (set : alk. paper)

ISBN 978-1-58765-364-3 (vol. 1 : alk. paper)

ISBN 978-1-58765-365-0 (vol. 2 : alk. paper)

ISBN 978-1-58765-366-7 (vol. 3 : alk. paper)

1. United States Supreme Court–History. I. Lewis, Thomas T. (Thomas Tandy) II. Title: United States Supreme Court.

KF8742.U5 2007

347.73'2609–dc22

2006037878

PRINTED IN CANADA

Contents

Contents

Contents

Publisher's Note

Within the vast framework of the federal system of American government, the U.S. Supreme Court stands out as a uniquely powerful institution. Although it has only nine unelected members, it alone can overturn the actions of every other branch of government, at all levels. Any decision by any elected executive officer—from a small-town mayor to the president of the United States—any legislation enacted by any elected body—from a city council to the Congress of the United States—can be invalidated by the Supreme Court. By contrast, only two methods exist to overturn unpopular Court decisions: The Court can reverse its own rulings, or the Congress or state conventions can initiate the long and difficult process of constitutional amendment. Since the Court was created in 1789, it has reversed itself many times; however, opponents to its decisions have managed to get the Constitution amended only a handful of times. There is no other institution quite like the Supreme Court—in the United States or anywhere else in the world.

What limits are there to the power of this very special institution? What impact has it actually had on the nation's constitutional history? What manner of people have sat on its benches and how did they get there? How does the Court actually function? These and many other questions are the subject matter of *The U.S. Supreme Court.* Adapted from Salem Press's *Encyclopedia of the U.S. Supreme Court* (2001), this Magill's Choice set concentrates more narrowly on the history and key issues that the Court itself has faced. It is designed to meet the growing need among students and members of the general public for clear, concise, authoritative, and up-to-date information about the Court.

CONTENT AND FORMAT

The 395 topics treated in individual essays in these volumes have been selected, formatted, and written with the needs of nonspecialist readers in mind. Emphasis throughout the set is on clear explanations of subjects, supported by illuminating graphics and more than 150 illustrations. Essays range in length from 250 to 3,000 words and contain several distinct component parts. All essays open with specially formatted top-matter sections, whose content varies according to essay type. The core of every essay is a clear discussion of its subject, whose relevance to the Supreme Court is constantly stressed. Essays of 1,000 or more words append brief lists of recommended readings, and essays of 2,000 or more words provide annotated discussions of the recommended readings. All essays are signed by their authors, whose names and affiliations are listed in the list of contributors at the front of volume 1.

Essay topics are thoroughly linked by cross-references. A Categorized List of Entries following the appendix section at the back of volume 3 groups related essays under broad subject headings. Despite these aids, each essay is written to stand on its own as much as possible. Essay top matter is presented in a concise, ready-reference format that provides the most essential information at a glance. Top matter in each of the essays on individual justices, for example, opens with its subject's full name, brief identification, full birth- and death-date information, and a summary statement of the justice's significance in Court history. The top matter in these essays also adds exact dates of the justices' Court service and identifies the presidents who appointed them.

In the more than two centuries since the Court first convened, it has passed down thousands of decisions in individual cases. Many of its decisions contain broad rulings that have become part of the law of the land. Indeed, some decisions—such as *Brown v. Board of Education* (1954) on school desegregation, *Miranda v. Arizona* (1966) on protection against self-incrimination, and *Roe v. Wade* (1973) on abortion rights—have materially affected the lives of tens of millions of Americans. Court cases are thus part of U.S. constitutional history, and it is impossible to understand the workings of the Supreme Court without a study of them.

The U.S. Supreme Court has essays on 126 of the most important decisions the Court has made. The cases appear within the text under the names by which they are most commonly known, such as *Brown v. Board of Education*. To ensure precise identification in top matter, case names are followed by the standard citations given in *United States Reports*. Essay top matter also provides the dates on which the Supreme Court passed down the decisions, concise summaries of issues involved, and brief statements of the cases' significance. The bodies of the essays themselves are mostly brief; they emphasize how the cases fit into constitutional history and touch on details that illuminate the workings of the Court and the opinions of its justices. In addition, an appendix of Notable Supreme Court Rulings in volume 3 summarizes data on more than six hundred court cases, and additional references to cases—including many not covered in either individual essays or the appendix table—can be found in the Court Case Index that precedes the general Subject Index.

The U.S. Supreme Court also contains essays on broad types of law, such as administrative law, antitrust law, bankruptcy law, and civil law, as well as individual pieces of legislation and clauses and amendments to the U.S. Constitution. Top matter on essays on these subjects provides, as appropriate, the dates when the laws were passed, brief descriptions of the laws, and summaries of their significance. Closely related to essays of this type are articles on broad issues, such as abortion, affirmative action, capital punishment, capitalism, and censorship. These essays examine how the Court has treated important issues throughout its history. Emphasis here, as in the set as a whole, is on the Court itself. For example, the essay on affirmative action is not so much a history of the concept as it is an examination of the role that the Supreme Court played in its development and application. *The U.S. Supreme Court* also contains essays on specific historical events and eras, such as the Civil Rights movement, the Civil War, the Cold War, Reconstruction, and World War II.

The mechanics of how the Supreme Court works and procedural matters of it and of the court system generally are covered in many essays. Included in this broad category are such subjects as staff positions; basic terminology, such as "Briefs," "Cert pool," and "Certiorari"; and broad concepts related to the Court's powers and practices, such as "Judicial powers," "Rules of the Court," and "Workload." Readers are also encouraged to consult the Glossary at the end of the third volume.

SPECIAL FEATURES

In addition to the set's reader-friendly alphabetical arrangement of articles, *The U.S. Supreme Court* offers a number of features to help users find the information they seek. At the end of every article is a list of from three to ten alphabetically arranged cross-references to related articles. The Categorized List of Entries at the end of volume 3 offers lists of articles under forty-three subject headings, ranging from "Abortion" to "War and the Military." Following that appendix are the Court Case Index, Photo Index, and general Subject Index.

Volume 3's appendix section also includes the complete text of the U.S. Constitution and its amendments, an annotated Bibliography, a table of court cases, and a table summarizing information on the justices' careers. The history of the Court is condensed in the Time Line, which provides dates of justices' nominations, confirmations, and oaths of office, as well as many details on legislation and other relevant facts.

ACKNOWLEDGMENTS

The U.S. Supreme Court takes most of its articles from Salem Press's award-winning three-volume *Encyclopedia of the U.S. Supreme Court* (2001). It contains about one-third of the encyclopedia's original essays, which account for about one-half of the encyclopedia's original text. In addition to updating the content and Further Reading notes in the original encyclopedia articles, it completely replaces more than fifty outdated articles and adds twenty-six entirely new articles.

A work such as this would not be possible without the contributions of the nearly 150 scholars who wrote the essays. We therefore wish to reiterate our thanks to those contributors. We especially wish to thank the Editor, Professor Thomas Tandy Lewis of St. Cloud State University, whose deep expertise in the subject, desire to update the set's content, and attention to detail have helped to make this publication a substantially improved and much expanded work. Finally, we extend our thanks to Professor William Dunlop for his helpful suggestions.

Contributors

Nobuko Adachi
Illinois State University

Bethany Andreasen
Minot State University

John Andrulis
Western New England College

Paula C. Arledge
Northeast Louisiana University

Gayle R. Avant
Baylor University

Charles F. Bahmueller
Center for Civic Education

Carl L. Bankston III
Tulane University

Paul Bateman
Southwestern University School of Law

Bernard W. Bell
Rutgers Law School

Sara C. Benesh
University of New Orleans

Alvin K. Benson
Utah Valley State College

Milton Berman
University of Rochester

Steve D. Boilard
Sacramento, California

Michael W. Bowers
University of Nevada at Las Vegas

Timothy S. Boylan
Winthrop University

Saul Brenner
University of North Carolina at Charlotte

Beau Breslin
Skidmore College

Richard A. Brisbin, Jr.
West Virginia University

Joseph V. Brogan
La Salle University

Fred Buchstein
John Carroll University

Edmund J. Campion
University of Tennessee

Bradley C. Canon
University of Kentucky

Christine R. Catron
St. Mary's University

H. Lee Cheek, Jr.
Brewton-Parker College

Bradley Stewart Chilton
University of North Texas

Jim D. Clark
Richland College

Thomas Clarkin
Lake Hills, Texas

Douglas Clouatre
Kennesaw State University

Alisa White Coleman
University of Texas at Arlington

Susan Coleman
West Texas A&M University

Michael L. Coulter
Grove City College

Edward R. Crowther
Adams State College

Rebecca Davis
Georgia Southern University

Frank Day
Clemson University

Gordon Neal Diem
Advance Education and Development Institute

Steven J. Dunker
Northeastern State University

William V. Dunlap
Quinnipiac University School of Law

Philip A. Dynia
Loyola University

Robert P. Ellis
Worcester State College

Kevin Eyster
Madonna University

Daryl R. Fair
College of New Jersey

Michael P. Federici
Mercyhurst College

John E. Finn
Wesleyan University

Alan M. Fisher
California State University at Dominguez Hills

John Fliter
Kansas State University

Michael Flynn
Nova Southeastern University Law School

Carol G. Fox
East Tennessee State University

Robert P. George
Princeton University

Phyllis B. Gerstenfeld
California State University at Stanislaus

Evan Gerstmann
Loyola Marymount University

Richard A. Glenn
Millersville University

Robert Justin Goldstein
Oakland University

Nancy M. Gordon
Amherst, Massachusetts

Robert F. Gorman
Southwest Texas State University

Lewis L. Gould
University of Texas at Austin

Diana R. Grant
California State University at Stanislaus

William C. Green
Morehead State University

Steven P. Grossman
University of Baltimore School of Law

John Gruhl
University of Nebraska at Lincoln

Timothy L. Hall
University of Mississippi

Diane Andrews Henningfeld
Adrian College

John R. Hermann
Trinity University

Mark L. Higgins
Wayne State College

L. Lynn Hogue
Georgia State University College of Law

Barbara Holden-Smith
Cornell University School of Law

Eric Howard
Los Angeles, California

Harvey Gresham Hudspeth
Mississippi Valley State University

John C. Hughes
Saint Michael's College

Robert Jacobs
Central Washington University

Bruce E. Johansen
University of Nebraska at Omaha

Alan E. Johnson
Brecksville, Ohio

Dale W. Johnson
Southern Wesleyan University

Herbert A. Johnson
University of South Carolina School of Law

Ronald Kahn
Oberlin College

Thomas M. Keck
University of Oklahoma

Robert Keele
The University of the South

Marshall R. King
Maryville University at St. Louis

David J. Langum
Cumberland School of Law of Samford University

Contributors

James E. Lennertz
Lafayette College

Paul Lermack
Bradley University

David W. Levy
University of Oklahoma

Thomas Tandy Lewis
St. Cloud State University

Lester G. Lindley
Nova Southeastern University

Matthew Lindstrom
Siena College

Janet Alice Long
Pasadena, California

James J. Lopach
University of Montana

William Shepard McAninch
University of South Carolina School of Law

Siobhan McCabe
Siena College

Dana P. McDermott
Martinsburg, West Virginia

Priscilla H. Machado
United States Naval Academy

Thomas C. Mackey
University of Louisville

Kelly J. Madison
California State University at Los Angeles

Eduardo Magalhaes III
Simpson College

Patrick Malcolmson
St. Thomas University

David E. Marion
Hampden-Sydney College

John Austin Matzko
Bob Jones University

Albert P. Melone
Southern Illinois University at Carbondale

Joseph A. Melusky
St. Francis College

Kurt X. Metzmeier
University of Kentucky College of Law

Ken Millen-Penn
Fairmont State College

Andrea E. Miller
Glendale, California

Mark C. Miller
Clark University

Wayne D. Moore
Virginia Polytechnic Institute and State University

William V. Moore
College of Charleston

Robert P. Morin
California State University at Chico

Sharon K. O'Roke
Oklahoma City University School of Law

William Osborne
Florida International University

William D. Pederson
Louisiana State University

Nis Petersen
New Jersey City University

Oliver B. Pollak
University of Nebraska at Omaha

Steven J. Ramold
University of Nebraska at Lincoln

John David Rausch, Jr.
West Texas A&M University

Stephen F. Rohde
Los Angeles, California

Francine Sanders Romero
University of Texas at San Antonio

William G. Ross
Cumberland School of Law of Samford University

Paul F. Rothstein
Georgetown University School of Law

Kurt M. Saunders
California State University at Northridge

Sean J. Savage
Saint Mary's College

Rose Secrest
Signal Mountain, Tennessee

Gregory N. Seltzer
Villa Julie College

Elizabeth Algren Shaw
Cleveland, Ohio

Christopher Shortell
Los Angeles, California

R. Baird Shuman
University of Illinois at Urbana-Champaign

Christopher E. Smith
Michigan State University

Chuck Smith
West Virginia State College

Jane Marie Smith
Slippery Rock University

Bes Stark Spangler
Peace College

Arthur K. Steinberg
Livingstone College

Glenn L. Swygart
Tennessee Temple University

Donald G. Tannenbaum
Gettysburg College

Steven C. Tauber
University of South Florida

G. Thomas Taylor
University of Maine

Jeffrey E. Thomas
Kansas City School of Law at University of Missouri

Susan L. Thomas
Hollins University

David Trevino
Ohio Northern University

Dean Van Bibber
Fairmont State College

Joanne LeBlanc Verity
Edmond, Oklahoma

Theodore M. Vestal
Oklahoma State University

Dean Wagstaffe
Florida International University

Spencer Weber Waller
Brooklyn Law School

Annita Marie Ward
Salem-Teikyo University

Bradley C. S. Watson
Saint Vincent College

Marcia J. Weiss
Point Park College

Lou Falkner Williams
Kansas State University

Richard L. Wilson
University of Tennessee at Chattanooga

Michael Witkoski
Columbia, South Carolina

Philip R. Zampini
Westfield State College

Editor's Introduction

This encyclopedic guide to the U.S. Supreme Court is designed provide students and general readers with a user-friendly source for obtaining dependable information about all aspects of the Court, with an emphasis on two themes: the Court's role in the U.S. political system and its changing interpretations of the U.S. Constitution. Not primarily designed for lawyers and specialists in the law, this set is has been written with a general audience in mind, especially the patrons of public, school, and university libraries. Academic courses in political science, history, and sociology frequently refer to the decisions of the Court, including their political and social impacts. Sometimes students or lay readers want simply to look up particular topics to acquire a basic overview. Students who need to write research papers will find in this guide an introductory summary of the Supreme Court as well as directions about where to go for additional information.

Most of the articles in these three volumes originated in Salem Press's *Encyclopedia of the U.S. Supreme Court* (2001). Although it has been only six years since that work was went to press, the Court has issued a large number of significant decisions. For example, in its controversial late 2000 *Bush v. Gore* ruling, the Court ordered an end to the recount of Florida's disputed ballots in the presidential election, thus assuring that George W. Bush would be the next president. Other noteworthy recent rulings include *Grutter v. Bollinger* (2003), which approved affirmative action programs in university admissions policies, *Lawrence v. Texas* (2005), which vetoed the criminalizing of homosexual practices, and *Roper v. Simmons* (2005), which prohibited executions of persons who commit murder while minors. New entries on these and about twenty other cases have been written for this set. Moreover, many topical entries from the encyclopedia have been updated, and there are several new topical entries. A noteworthy addition in the appendix section is an alphabetical listing with short summaries of more five hundred of the Court's rulings.

THE COURT AND THE U. S. POLITICAL SYSTEM

Justice Oliver Wendell Holmes once called the Supreme Court a "storm centre" of political controversy. For more than two hundred years, the Court has maintained a major role in the country's political system, and its decisions have affected the lives of all Americans. For example, any person studying the history of race relations could not obtain a valid perspective without taking into account the Court's decisions on issues such as slavery, restrictive immigration policies, the establishment of racial segregation following the Reconstruction era, the promotion of civil rights after World War II, interpretations of Native American treaties, and attempts to draw legislative districts that enhance minority representation. Other compelling issues handled by the Court include the rights of criminal defendants, religious liberty, separation of church and state, attempts to regulate pornography, the right to express unpopular ideas, and the institutional powers of Congress and the president. When the Court announces important decisions, it is no accident that newspapers throughout the country give the events large headlines on their front pages.

The U.S. system of constitutional government is a product of many influences and historical developments. The British tradition of limited government, or constitutionalism, gradually evolved since the medieval period. The Magna Carta of 1215, for example, required that even England's king had to follow the established "law of the land," and the English Bill of Rights of 1689 required that government must respect a listing of rights and liberties. These developments merged with the English common law, often defined as incremental judge-made law, which included the practice of *stare decisis* (literally, "let the decision stand"), meaning that judicial precedents are legally binding unless they are overturned by legislative statutes or later court rulings. The common law provided English and American judges with much more power than the continental European system of civil law that was based almost exclusively on codified statutes. During the late eighteenth century, American lawyers often referred to the famous *Dr. Bonham's Case* of 1610, in which Sir Edward Coke had asserted that parliamentary acts were invalid if they contradicted "the common right and reason" of the common law. However, the supremacy clause of the U.S. Constitution's Article VI, which explicitly recognizes the written Constitution as the "supreme Law of the Land," was a significant departure from the English tradition of parliamentary supremacy.

From the time that the U.S. Constitution was written in 1789, informed observers have discussed the great powers of the American judiciary, particularly the powers of its highest court. In *The Federalist* No. 78, Alexander Hamilton praised the judiciary as the "least dangerous branch" and wrote that the "interpretation of the laws is the proper and peculiar province of the courts." In addition, he observed that because the Constitution would become the nation's highest law after it was ratified, whenever "an irreconcilable variance" between the Constitution and a legislative statute arose, judges would naturally give preference to the Constitution. In effect, Hamilton was making a theoretical argument in favor of the doctrine of judicial review, the ultimate source of the Court's political power, as later articulated in the famous case of *Marbury v. Madison* (1803), when the Court finally struck down part of congressional statute as unconstitutional. This power contributed to Alexis de Tocqueville's emphasis on the role of the judiciary in *Democracy in America* (1835), in which he wrote that "scarcely any political question arises in the United States that is not resolved, sooner or later, into a judicial question."

Emphasizing the constitutional separation of political powers into three branches, proponents of judicial restraint frequently argue that the role of the Supreme Court should be limited to rendering decisions in judicial cases and not include making laws, which is the proper role of Congress and the state legislatures. Although strong arguments have been made for judicial restraint, it is important to recognize the differences between the broad concept of *law* and the narrower concept of *legislation* (or statutes). Case law provides the building blocks of the common law, which has been particularly important in the constitutional law of the Anglo-American legal tradition. Both the U.S. Constitution and legislative statutes, moreover, frequently must be interpreted in order to be enforced. Article III of the Constitution declares that the Supreme Court has final appellate jurisdiction over a large variety of cases and controversies, especially those related to the Constitution and federal legislation. During the early nineteenth century. the Supreme Court utilized the practice of *stare decisis* to develop judicial doctrines. During the twentieth century, the number of significant doctrines increased. A good example was the doctrine of "selective incorporation," or the application of the fundamental rights of the first eight amendments to the states by way of the due process clause of the Fourteenth Amendment.

Many of the Court's most important opinions have dealt with the topic of federalism—the relationship between the national government and the individual states. Under the leadership of Chief Justice John Marshall (1801-1835), the Court's nationalistic interpretations of Article I, Section 8 endorsed expansive powers of Congress pursuant to its authority to regulate commerce and to pass legislation "necessary and proper" to its enumerated powers. Under Marshall's successor, Roger Brooke Taney, the Court moved to limit the powers of the national government, a perspective called "dual federalism," which is based on the notion that coequal state and national governments were autonomous within their respective spheres. Following the Civil War (1861-1865), the Court recognized the indissolubility of the Union, but it soon interpreted the Fourteenth Amendment narrowly while emphasizing the states' police powers under the Tenth Amendment, thereby continuing the paradigm of dual federalism. With the New Deal era, however, the nationalist view again became triumphant, with the Court in *United States v. Darby Lumber Co.* (1941) holding that the Tenth Amendment put no limits on congressional power. However, the pendulum again turned during the Rehnquist Court (1986-2005), especially in *Printz v. United States* (1997), when the Court enunciated a doctrine of "dual sovereignty," which can be viewed as a middle position between the *Darby* ruling and the earlier doctrine of dual federalism. While it is impossible to predict the future of federalism, it is reasonable to expect that the Court will continue to define and redefine the proper roles and powers of the states.

International wars and fears of domestic violence have frequently resulted in restrictions on the individual liberties guaranteed in the Constitution. This was particularly true during the two World Wars of the early twentieth century. The dramatic terrorist attacks on the United States of September 11, 2001, also had such an effect. On October 25, 2001, Congress enacted an omnibus law of some 342 pages, entitled the USA Patriot Act, which expanded the authority of law enforcement officials to monitor telephone and Internet conversations and to detain aliens on mere suspicion. The American Civil Liberties

Union and other libertarian groups alleged that the complex law undermined several constitutional guarantees, especially the Fourth Amendment's rules concerning probable cause and search warrants. Then, on November 13, President George W. Bush issued a military order which authorized military tribunals for trials of noncitizens accused of terrorism without jury trials and other established requirements of due process. however, the Supreme Court ruled that the aliens held in the U.S. base at Cuba's Guantanamo Bay had the right to petition for habeas corpus relief in federal courts. In *Hamdan v. Rumsfeld* (2006), the Court overturned as unconstitutional the administration's plans to hold trials of those suspected of war crimes in military commissions.

CONSTITUTIONAL INTERPRETATIONS

The Constitution is written in the standard English language, with only a few terms—such as "bill of attainder" and "Letters of Marque and Reprisal"—that are not easily recognizable by most English-speaking citizens. Indeed, a large number of provisions in the Constitution are quite straightforward, not requiring any complex theory of interpretation. For example, when the document states that U.S. presidents must be at least thirty-five years old, no one questions what is meant by "years," and scholars do not debate the original intent of the Constitution's Framers by asking whether the spirit of the requirement would be satisfied by a mature person who is thirty-three years old. In contrast, other portions of the Constitution are rather ambiguous and susceptible to a variety of interpretations, which is why Chief Justice Charles Evans Hughes once stated, "We are under a Constitution, but the Constitution is what the judges say it is."

An illustration of Hughes's statement is the Eighth Amendment's clause prohibiting cruel and unusual punishment. In interpreting this clause, Justice Tom C. Clark and others have argued that it prohibits only those punishments that are both cruel and unusual, while many justices have thought that cruelty alone is the main criteria of a punishment's constitutionality. Moreover, the word "unusual" might be taken to refer to a punishment that is not often utilized often, or it might mean that the punishment is not part of the legal code in most jurisdictions. A more complex question is whether one should understand the phrase to mean those kinds of punishments that were considered cruel and usual when the amendment was written and ratified, or whether the phrase should be interpreted, in the words of former Chief Justice Earl Warren, according to "the evolving standards of decency that mark the progress of a maturing society." A related issue is whether a justice may legitimately take into account the subjective notion of natural law, the content of which is largely a consequence of an individual's moral intuitions and cultural conditioning. There is also the question of whether the Eighth Amendment should continue to apply only to the federal government, as it did from 1791 until 1962, or whether the Supreme Court was justified in applying the amendment to the states by incorporating it into the meaning of due process in the Fourteenth Amendment. Justices have wrestled with all of these interpretative questions in their decisions.

When justices grapple with the meanings of words such as "cruel and unusual," the use of the term "strict constructionism" tends to be inappropriate. However, the focus on controversial questions, such as the constitutionality of the death penalty, obscures the fact that most people who have thought about the Eighth Amendment actually agree on numerous issues. Almost every American, for example, would agree that the prohibition on cruel and unusual punishment prohibits the inflicting of unnecessary pain and suffering. Almost everyone would agree that a grossly disproportionate punishment, such as the use of capital punishment for a minor theft, would be cruel and unusual. Contrary to the assertions of some proponents of postmodernism, words and phrases are not completely indeterminate, for they necessarily express a restricted range of denotations and connotations. Extreme forms of judicial activism, moreover, appear to be incompatible with the very notion of constitutional democracy. Even if one accepts the premise of a "living Constitution," the constitutional separation of government into three equal branches seems to imply that the judiciary does not have unlimited discretion or a total monopoly in defining the meanings of the document. After all, Article I of the Constitution begins with the statement, "All legislative powers herein granted shall be vested in a Congress." Also, Justice Hugo L. Black and others have observed that there would be no need for a process of constitution amendments if the judges possessed absolute authority to act as Platonic guardians in making judgments without reference to reasonable meanings of the constitutional text.

Clauses prohibiting the deprivation of "life, liberty, or property, without due process of law" that are found in both the Fifth and Fourteenth Amendments, have been particularly susceptible to alternative readings. During the twentieth century, the Court gradually held that procedural due process includes a mandate that the states' criminal procedures must be consistent with the fundamental rights found in the Bill of Rights. Much more contentious is process, , the doctrine of substantive due process—the principle that government cannot deprive persons of substantive rights in an arbitrary manner or without an adequate justification. From 1898 until 1937, a probusiness Court applied this doctrine primarily to economic liberties, requiring government to respect a broad "right of contract," thereby overturning many laws designed to protect employees. However, the Court also applied the doctrine to protect some noneconomic rights, including the requirement that states honor the substantive rights of the First Amendment. With *Griswold v. Connecticut* (1965), the Court began ruling that the due process clause protected a right to privacy (later called "liberty interests"), which pertains particularly to intimate family and sexual relationships. The reasoning of *Griswold* was subsequently extended to a host of related matters, including the rights to terminate unwanted pregnancies, to refuse unwanted medical treatment, and to engage in homosexual practices in a private home. Reasonable people can disagree about whether such broad constructions of the due process clause are justifiable.

The Constitution says almost nothing about the standards and methods that judges should use in making interpretations. It does not say whether or not justices should look to the intent of the Constitution's original Framers, just as it does not indicate whether the justices should look to the literal text or to the broader spirit of the document. Many jurists have asserted that the enigmatic Ninth Amendment implies some recognition for the concept of natural law, while other think the amendment refers to unwritten rights under common law or to states' rights. The Constitution never explicitly indicates whether the Court's constitutional and statutory interpretations should respect the practice of *stare decisis*, although it is perhaps relevant that the Seventh Amendment requires the courts to utilize the "rules of the common law" when examining judgments in suits at common law in federal courts. Even the most vociferous critics of the original understanding perspective of constitutional interpretation must acknowledge that much of the language in the constitution, such as references to jury trials and due process, does not make sense apart from the Framers' understanding of what such terms meant at the time they created the Constitution.

Anyone who thinks that the law is dull should study the work of the Supreme Court. Each case that comes before the Court has its own unique story, with human beings engaged in a conflict over competing interests and values, often involving both constitutional and moral principles. To take just one example, the case of *Gideon v. Wainwright* (1963), in which the Court interpreted the Sixth Amendment as requiring government to provide legal counsel for poor criminal defendants, it is difficult to imagine how any novelist could create a more fascinating story. During the history of the Court, moreover, a surprising number of brilliant and interesting people have served as justices. Many of their legal opinions are recognized as significant works of political and legal philosophy, sometimes written in an attractive literary style.

Thomas Tandy Lewis
St. Cloud State University

U. S. Supreme Court

Abington School District v. Schempp

CITATION: 374 U.S. 203

DATE: June 17, 1963

ISSUE: School prayer

SIGNIFICANCE: This decision reaffirmed the Supreme Court's 1962 ruling that made it unconstitutional for public schools to sponsor prayers or Bible readings.

Writing for an 8-1 majority, Justice Tom C. Clark reiterated the Supreme Court's position in *Engel v. Vitale* (1962) that the government could not promote religion by sponsoring public school prayers or Bible readings. In *Abington*, the American Civil Liberties Union helped the Schempps challenge a Pennsylvania law requiring public schools to begin each day by reading Bible verses. In the companion case, *Murray v. Curlett* (1963), nationally known atheist Madalyn Mur-

After the Supreme Court banned school prayer, teachers found other ways to start to begin the school day. Here, an elementary school teacher in Pittsburgh reads from a book called The School Day Begins. *(Library of Congress)*

1

ray (later O'Hair) attacked a Baltimore city statute providing for a daily reading in the city schools of the Lord's Prayer or a passage from the Bible. Unlike the situation in *Engel*, the government did not write the prayer and used the readings without comment, but the Court still found both laws an impermissible promotion of religion.

Although two new justices participated in *Abington*, the outcome remained the same as *Engel*. Justice Potter Stewart wrote the Court's lone dissent, arguing that the free exercise clause should be given preferred status to avoid inherent conflicts with the establishment clause. The Court sought to minimize criticism by having Clark, a politically moderate southern Presbyterian, write the Court's opinion and Justices Arthur J. Goldberg (Jewish) and William J. Brennan, Jr. (Roman Catholic) write strong concurrences, but widespread public criticism continued from religious groups against the Court for interfering with religion.

Richard L. Wilson

SEE ALSO Clark, Tom C.; *Engel v. Vitale*; *Epperson v. Arkansas*; Religion, establishment of; *Wallace v. Jaffree*.

Abortion

DESCRIPTION: Intentional expulsion or removal of the fetus from the womb except for the purpose of accomplishing a live birth or removing a dead fetus from the womb.

SIGNIFICANCE: With its controversial decision in *Roe v. Wade* (1973), the Supreme Court declared that women had the right to have an abortion, which it later interpreted to prohibit laws that unduly burdened a woman's ability to choose an abortion until the third trimester of pregnancy.

Scarcely any constitutional issue provoked more controversy in the last half of the twentieth century than the issue of whether the U.S. Constitution protected a woman's right to obtain an abortion. On some issues during this period, such as racial segregation, the Supreme Court was able to guide the country toward an ultimate consensus. However, on the issue of abortion, the Court was unable to accomplish such closure. The two major political parties partially defined themselves by reference to their respective attitudes toward this question, often using the abortion issue as a litmus test for their evaluation of potential Supreme Court justices. Protesters marked the anniversary of the Court's original abortion decision with vigils in front of the Court. Legislators, both federal and state, proposed an endless series of laws that would restrict or at least discourage abortions. In the last decade of the twentieth century, the Court stood by its original declaration that the right to abortion was protected by the Constitution. Nevertheless, the Court redefined the standard to be used in evaluating laws relating to abortion with the effect of increasing the ability of state and federal lawmakers to regulate in this controversial area.

BEFORE THE RIGHT TO ABORTION

Prior to the nineteenth century, laws regulating abortions were virtually unknown because the procedure was extraordinarily dangerous and this danger operated as a deterrent, making abortion-banning laws largely superfluous. However, improved medical techniques in the nineteenth century made abortions more common and prompted state lawmakers to prohibit them. By the middle of the twentieth century, abortion, except when necessary to protect the pregnant woman's life, was illegal everywhere in the United States.

Beginning in the middle of the twentieth century, however, the Supreme Court determined that not all state laws bearing on issues of procreation were immune from constitutional scrutiny. In *Skinner v. Oklahoma* (1942), the Court determined that a state law providing for compulsory sterilization of certain habitual criminals amounted to an unconstitutional discrimination in violation of the Fourteenth Amendment's equal protection clause. The Court concluded that certain rights were sufficiently fundamental to require the government to demonstrate an overwhelmingly persuasive justification before depriving selected people of these rights. Though the Constitution nowhere specifically enumerates a right to procreation, the Court nevertheless concluded that this right was sufficiently fundamental to require strict scrutiny of the sterilization law. Finding no

3

compelling purpose served by the law, the Court declared it unconstitutional.

Two decades later, the Court again turned to a consideration of whether the Constitution protected individuals from state laws that intruded into matters relating to procreation. *Griswold v. Connecticut* (1965) called upon the Court to determine the constitutionality of a state law prohibiting use of contraceptives. By the early 1960's this kind of law was extraordinarily rare, prompting Justice Potter Stewart to characterize it as "exceedingly silly," but its constitutional infirmity was not immediately apparent. Justice William O. Douglas, though, writing for the Court, concluded that the right to use contraceptives lay within a zone of privacy protected by penumbras of various constitutional provisions. Other justices argued in concurring opinions that the right to use contraceptives was a species of the liberty protected from undue deprivations by the Fourteenth Amendment's due process clause. Justices Hugo L. Black and Stewart dissented. Black, in particular, challenged the majority's willingness to use the due process clause to scrutinize the reasonableness of laws affecting rights not specifically enumerated in the Constitution. He accused the majority of resurrecting the same form of substantive due process employed by the Court earlier in the century in cases such as *Lochner v. New York* (1905), which invalidated what the Court viewed as unreasonable restrictions on the freedom of contract.

THE ABORTION RULING

The Court's holding in *Griswold* suggested that the Constitution protected a zone of privacy relating to matters of procreation, though the justices remained divided in their views of precisely where to root this right of privacy in the Constitution's text. Such controversy as the case engendered, however, was mostly abstract because an overwhelming majority of states had long since abandoned laws against the use of contraceptives. When the Court turned to the subject of abortion in *Roe v. Wade* (1973), however, it confronted prohibitions against abortion that were still in force in a majority of the states. The decade before *Roe* had seen some change in state laws relating to abortion. The 1962 Model Penal Code, drafted by the American Law Institute and followed by some states, allowed for abortions in cases involving rape or serious birth defects. A few states—New York, Alaska, and Hawaii—had repealed their antiabortion laws. However, a majority of states retained significant restrictions on the ability of women to obtain abortions, and in *Roe*, the Court swept aside virtually all these laws.

Justice Harry A. Blackmun, writing for the majority, concluded that the right of privacy previously recognized in cases such as *Griswold* was broad enough to encompass a woman's right to an abortion. He located the constitutional right of privacy in the Fourteenth Amendment's due process clause, which protected against deprivations of life, liberty, or property without due process of law. Finding the right to abortion fundamental, he determined that the government could not abridge the right without satisfying a strict review, which entailed demonstrating that the abridgment was necessary to serve some compelling governmental interest and that it was the least restrictive means of achieving that interest.

Using this formulation, Blackmun turned to the interests purportedly served by state abortion regulations: protecting the health of the pregnant woman and protecting the potential life of the unborn fetus. Blackmun suggested that no consensus existed as to when human life began and that, in any event, the fetus was not a "person" entitled to constitutional protection. Dividing pregnancy into three trimesters, Blackmun concluded that in the first trimester of pregnancy, neither a state's interest in the health of the pregnant woman nor its interest in the potential life of a fetus justified restrictions on abortion. In the second trimester, though, he found abortions sufficiently dangerous to the health of the pregnant woman to justify such regulations as necessary to protect the woman's health. Finally, after viability, in the third trimester, Blackmun reasoned that the state's interest in the potential life of the fetus was sufficiently weighty to justify a prohibition against all abortions except those necessary to preserve the life or the health of the pregnant woman. The abortion right thus established by *Roe* was virtually absolute during the first three months of pregnancy, subject only to regulations designed to protect the woman's health during the second three months, and subject to prohibition to protect the fetus during the last three months.

RESPONSES TO THE RULING

Though the Court's decision in *Roe* was widely hailed in some quarters of American life, criticism of the Court's decision was immediate and vociferous. Some legal scholars argued that the Court substituted its judgment on a controversial issue for the judgment of political majorities without constitutional justification. They agreed with Justice Black's claim in *Griswold* that the Court's use of the due process clause to evaluate the reasonableness of laws affecting rights not specifically protected by the Constitution resurrected in liberal political garb the same spirit that had inspired conservative justices to invalidate laws restricting the unenumerated right to contract in the first part of the twentieth century. Scholars supportive of the result in *Roe* argued that the Court's reasoning was correct. The problem with cases such as *Lochner*, they argued, was not that they protected unnamed fundamental rights, but that they designated the right to contract as fundamental. In contrast, they agreed with the Court that the right of privacy, including the right of a woman to choose to have an abortion, was indeed fundamental and should be protected from unreasonable legislative interference.

The Court's decision in *Roe* prompted the emergence of a right-to-life movement dedicated to overturning it, whether by constitutional amendment, legislative action, or reconstitution of the Court itself. Politicians opposed to the Court's ruling responded by proposing legislation and a constitutional amendment that would declare the fetus a "person" and therefore subject to constitutional protection. Neither the legislation nor the amendment succeeded in gaining passage, however. Opponents of the decision eventually turned their attention to the composition of the Court that had rendered the decision in *Roe* and, especially during the 1980's, attempted to screen nominees to the Court as to whether they approved or disapproved of *Roe*'s reasoning. This effort also produced only limited success. In the meantime, legislatures—especially at the state level—passed a variety of legislation that did not entirely prohibit abortions but placed a variety of obstacles in the paths of women seeking to exercise their right to seek an abortion. It remained to be seen after *Roe* whether such regulations would pass constitutional muster.

POST-*ROE* ABORTION REGULATIONS

In the fifteen years immediately after the *Roe* decision, abortion regulations generally found a cool welcome in the Court. Relying on the trimester scheme announced in *Roe*, the Court generally invalidated all laws that restricted the ability of women to obtain an abortion before the last trimester of pregnancy. For example, the Court declared laws requiring a spouse's consent to an abortion unconstitutional in *Planned Parenthood of Central Missouri v. Danforth* (1976). Restrictions on various abortion techniques were also invalidated, as were requirements that abortions be performed in hospitals as opposed to clinics. Moreover, the Court was initially hostile to laws designed to discourage abortions, such as those requiring a waiting period before a woman obtained an abortion or those requiring physicians to provide specific counsel to patients about the dangers of the abortion procedure.

The Court upheld a few forms of abortion regulation. It sustained the constitutionality of laws requiring parental consent when the woman seeking an abortion was a minor as long as the law also provided a means for the minor to obtain the consent of a judge rather than her parents. More significantly, the Court held that the right to an abortion did not include the right to have an abortion financed at public expense. In *Harris v. McRae* (1980), the Court upheld the constitutionality of the Hyde Amendment (1976), a federal law that prevents the use of Medicaid funds to pay for abortions except where necessary to save the pregnant woman's life. A majority of the Court, in an opinion by Justice Stewart, distinguished between laws that impeded a woman's right to seek an abortion and laws that simply declined to facilitate that right. According to the Court, although the federal or state governments could not take away a woman's right to an abortion, they nevertheless need not subsidize it.

A CONSERVATIVE TURN

During President Reagan's two terms of office in the 1980's, he made it a priority to nominate justices to the Court who would favor overruling *Roe v. Wade*. He partially achieved this purpose by appointing Justice William H. Rehnquist—one of the original dissenters in *Roe*—as chief justice upon the retirement of Chief Justice Warren E.

Burger. Late in his second term, President Reagan attempted to appoint Robert H. Bork, an outspoken critic of *Roe*, to fill the seat on the Court vacated by Justice Lewis F. Powell, Jr., only to have the Senate reject the nomination. Nevertheless, Reagan's other nominees—Sandra Day O'Connor, Antonin Scalia, and Anthony M. Kennedy—were all viewed as representing some measure of dissatisfaction with the decision in *Roe*.

By the close of the 1980's, some reconsideration of *Roe* seemed imminent. In *Webster v. Reproductive Health Services* (1989), a majority of the Court appeared to reject a rigid view of the trimester analysis of *Roe* by upholding a requirement that fetuses be tested for viability after twenty weeks of pregnancy. Under *Roe*, twenty weeks, being within the second trimester, fell within a period when the state's interest in the potential life of the fetus was insufficient to justify any impediment to a woman's abortion right. Four justices were prepared to overrule *Roe* explicitly on this point. Justice O'Connor concurred in the result but was unwilling to repudiate *Roe*'s trimester approach completely.

In the wake of the decision in *Webster*, observers of the Court speculated that a majority of the justices were poised to revisit *Roe*. Four justices remained solidly behind the precedent—William J. Brennan, Jr., Thurgood Marshall, John Paul Stevens, and Blackmun—and dissented vigorously from the holding in *Webster*. Standing on the opposite side were Chief Justice Rehnquist and Justices Scalia, Kennedy, and Byron R. White. Justice O'Connor stood in the middle—apparently willing to reconsider at least some aspects of *Roe v. Wade*. In the years immediately following *Webster*, President George H. W. Bush added two more justices to the Court to replace staunch defenders of *Roe*. Justice David H. Souter took the seat formerly held by Brennan, and Justice Clarence Thomas filled the seat vacated by Marshall. These appointments seemed likely to tip the balance against continued adherence to the principles of *Roe v. Wade*.

THE REVOLUTION THAT WAS AND WAS NOT

In 1992 a Court largely reconstituted from its composition at the time of *Roe* considered a cluster of abortion regulations in *Planned Parenthood of Southeastern Pennsylvania v. Casey*, including a require-

Abortion protestors at a rally outside the Supreme Court building on the thirty-third anniversary of the Roe v. Wade *decision in January, 2006. (AP/Wide World Photos)*

ment that women seeking an abortion wait at least twenty-four hours after being given information by a physician about the nature of the abortion procedure, the fetus's developmental stage, and alternatives to abortion. The Court also considered a requirement that married women notify their husbands of their intent to have an abortion. The widely anticipated decision of the Court proved to frustrate many predictions about its likely result, while satisfying neither those who wished to abolish the constitutional right to abortion nor those who wished to defend abortion against all government restrictions on the procedure.

Three justices joined to write the opinion: O'Connor, Kennedy, and Souter. The first major element of their opinion was to reaffirm the basic holding of *Roe v. Wade* that the Constitution guaranteed the right to abortion. With an eye to the profound political controversy still surrounding abortion nearly two decades after *Roe*, the justices argued that adherence to the core of the Court's previous holding was necessary to sustain the Court's legitimacy and to prevent it from appearing to bow to political pressure. They were joined in this reaffirmation of *Roe* by Justices Blackmun and Stevens. However, the Court's opinion, while not overruling *Roe*, nevertheless substantially revised the formulation originally adopted by the Court in *Roe*. Instead of the trimester scheme, which prevented laws from interfering with a woman's choice to have an abortion except to protect her health after the first trimester and to protect the fetus after the second trimester, the Court focused on whether a particular law amounted to an undue burden on the right to abortion. Under this formulation, some regulations of abortion might be undertaken throughout a pregnancy. Applying this new test, a majority of the Court found that the twenty-four-hour waiting period was not an undue burden, but that the spousal notification was an unconstitutional burden on a woman's right to an abortion.

The state of Nebraska enacted a statute making it a felony to perform a "partial birth abortion" except when the procedure was necessary to save the woman's life. The procedure, also called dilation and extraction (D & X), was defined as the partial vaginal delivery of "a living unborn child before killing the child." A physician who did the procedures, Dr. Leroy Carhart, brought suit seeking a declaration that the law was unconstitutionally vague and that it placed an undue burden on him and his female patients. In the resulting case of *Stenberg v. Carhart* (2000), the Supreme Court agreed, by a 5-4 margin, with Carhart's complaint. Delivering the opinion for the court, Justice Stephen G. Breyer wrote that the Nebraska law "violates the U.S. Constitution, as interpreted by *Casey* and *Roe*." The most basic defect of the law was that it did not allow for exceptions to protect the health of the woman. Because anyone performing an abortion procedure must fear criminal prosecution, Breyer concluded that the law resulted in "an undue burden upon a woman's right to make an abortion decision."

In a strong dissent, Justice Antonin Scalia wrote that it was "quite simply absurd" to assert that the Constitution prohibits the states from banning "this visibly brutal means of eliminating our half-born posterity." In 2003, Congress enacted a federal Partial Abortion law similar to the Nebraska statute struck down in *Carhart*. Since the decision was based on a 5-4 vote, the replacement of Justice Sandra Day O'Connor on the Court by Samuel Alito in 2006 raised the possibility of a different outcome in a future case.

Timothy L. Hall
Updated by the Editor

FURTHER READING

The Ethics of Abortion: Pro-Life v. Pro-Choice, edited by Robert M. Baird and Stuart E. Rosenbaum (Amherst, N.Y.: Prometheus, 2001), provides a reasoned appraisal of the conflicting views of the pro-life and pro-choice sides in the abortion debate. Kathlyn Gay's *Abortion: Understanding the Debate* (Berkeley Heights, N.J.: Enlow Publishers, 2004) is a contemporary analysis of the competing positions relating to the moral and legal status of abortion. N. E. H. Hull and Peter Charles Huffer's *Roe v. Wade: The Abortion Rights Controversy in American History* (Lawrence: University Press of Kansas, 2001) tries to locate the *Roe v. Wade* decision in the context of broader social changes in American society. *Abortion: The Supreme Court Decisions*, edited by Ian Shapiro (Indianapolis, Ind.: Hackett, 1995), collects the major legal decisions defining the current constitutional law concerning abortion.

For further background, readers may consult *The Abortion Controversy: A Documentary History*, edited by Eva R. Rubin (Westport, Conn.: Greenwood, 1994), which includes both Supreme Court materials and other important political documents relating to abortion, and *Abortion: A Reference Handbook*, by Marie Costa (2d ed., Santa Barbara, Calif.: ABC-Clio, 1996), which offers a variety of background information concerning the abortion controversy, including a chronology of abortion laws from ancient times to the present, biographies of those involved in the abortion debate, and a variety of statistics concerning abortion.

A variety of sources treat the historical context of the Court's abortion decisions. *Liberty and Sexuality: The Right to Privacy and the Making of "Roe v. Wade,"* by David J. Garrow (New York: Macmillan, 1994), is a sweeping history of the cases and controversies leading up to the Court's decision. *"Roe v. Wade": The Untold Story of the Landmark Supreme Court Decision That Made Abortion Legal*, by Marian Faux (New

York: Macmillan, 1988), focuses more specifically on the trial and appeal of *Roe* itself. *Rehnquist Justice: Understanding the Court Dynamic*, edited by Earl M. Maltz (Lawrence: University Press of Kansas, 2003), *The Most Activist Supreme Court in History: The Road to Modern Judicial Conservatism*, by Thomas M. Keck (Chicago: University of Chicago Press, 2004), and *A Court Divided: The Rehnquist Court and the Future of Constitutional Law*, by Mark Tushnet (New York: W. W. Norton, 2005), touch on more recent Court decisions regarding abortion.

The interplay between the Court and other social actors may be explored in Lee Epstein and Joseph F. Kobylka's *The Supreme Court and Legal Change: Abortion and the Death Penalty* (Chapel Hill: University of North Carolina Press, 1992), which emphasizes the role that legal arguments played in constitutional cases involving abortion and the death penalty, and in Neal Devins's *Shaping Constitutional Values: Elected Government, the Supreme Court, and the Abortion Debate* (Baltimore, Md.: Johns Hopkins University Press, 1996), which explores the relationship between the Court and politics with respect to the abortion controversy. *Abortion: The Clash of Absolutes*, by Harvard Law School professor Laurence H. Tribe (New York: Norton, 1992), presents a summary of the constitutional issue from the standpoint of a position protective of abortion rights.

Mary Ann Glendon's *Abortion and Divorce in Western Law* (Cambridge, Mass.: Harvard University Press, 1987) provides an international perspective on the issue of divorce by comparing the Court's treatment of the issue with the results of decisions in the courts of other nations. Finally, *Wrath of Angels: The American Abortion War*, by James Risen and Judy L. Thomas (New York: Basic Books, 1998), is an illuminating account of the abortion protest movement inaugurated by the Court's decision in *Roe v. Wade*.

SEE ALSO Birth control and contraception; Blackmun, Harry A.; *Buck v. Bell*; Due process, substantive; Fourteenth Amendment; *Griswold v. Connecticut*; Judicial scrutiny; Nominations to the Court; *Planned Parenthood of Southeastern Pennsylvania v. Casey*; *Roe v. Wade*.

Adamson v. California

CITATION: 332 U.S. 46
DATE: June 23, 1947
ISSUE: Incorporation doctrine
SIGNIFICANCE: Reaffirming that the Fifth Amendment privilege against self-incrimination was not applicable to the states, the Supreme Court reiterated that the due process clause of the Fourteenth Amendment incorporated only those procedural rights considered essential to a fair trial.

When tried for murder, Admiral D. Adamson did not testify, because of his prior criminal record. The district attorney, as permitted by applicable state law at the time, told the jury that Adamson's refusal to testify was a good reason to infer his guilt. The Supreme Court had earlier permitted this practice in *Twining v. New Jersey* (1908). After Adamson was convicted, his attorney argued that permitting the prosecutorial comment was a violation of the Fifth Amendment. A 5-4 majority of the Court upheld the conviction, based on the long-standing doctrine that the Fourteenth Amendment did not require the states to honor all the privileges and protections of the Bill of Rights.

Adamson is notable primarily because of Hugo L. Black's long dissent, which used historical data to argue for the "total incorporation" of the entire Bill of Rights into the Fourteenth Amendment. Justice Felix Frankfurter's concurring opinion defended the alternative theory of "selective incorporation." Although subsequent Courts have never accepted Black's perspective, the privilege against self-incrimination was made binding on the states in *Malloy v. Hogan* (1964). This privilege was interpreted to prohibit prosecutorial comment on a defendant's failure to testify in *Griffin v. California* (1965).

Thomas Tandy Lewis

SEE ALSO *Barron v. Baltimore;* Constitutional interpretation; Fifth Amendment; Fourteenth Amendment; Incorporation doctrine; *Palko v. Connecticut.*

Adarand Constructors v. Peña

CITATION: 515 U.S. 200
DATE: June 12, 1995
ISSUE: Affirmative action
SIGNIFICANCE: The Supreme Court required lower courts to use the
standards of "strict scrutiny" when examining any preferences
based on race.

The Federal Highway Division provided premiums to general contractors for awarding contracts to firms owned by members of racial
minorities recognized as having experienced social and economic
disadvantages. Although the Adarand Constructors company was the
lowest bidder for one construction project, the award was made to a
Hispanic-owned company. Adarand sued, claiming that this race-
based preference violated the Fifth Amendment guarantee of equal
protection. In *Richmond v. J. A. Croson Co.* (1989), the Supreme Court
had required "strict scrutiny" on racial classifications at the state and
local levels, but it had applied "intermediate scrutiny" for federal
programs in *Metro Broadcasting v. Federal Communications Commission*
(1990). The court of appeals used the more lenient standard and upheld the government's policy.

However, the Supreme Court overturned the lower court's decision. Speaking for a 5-4 majority, Justice Sandra Day O'Connor held
that all racial classifications must be analyzed under the strict scrutiny
standard, which required such classifications to be "narrowly tailored
measures that further compelling governmental objectives." Contra-
dicting what many authorities had written, O'Connor denied that
strict scrutiny would always be "fatal in fact." Although the *Adarand*
decision did not end all affirmative action, it did increase the probability that federal programs involving preferences would be challenged and invalidated.

Thomas Tandy Lewis

SEE ALSO Affirmative action; Equal protection clause; Judicial scrutiny; *Regents of the University of California v. Bakke.*

Advisory Opinions

DESCRIPTION: Judicial decisions issued about a hypothetical case, usually at the request of the legislative or executive branch, to determine the constitutionality of proposed legislation.

SIGNIFICANCE: The Supreme Court stated that the federal courts will not issue advisory opinions but will rule only on actual cases and controversies.

Advisory opinions allow legislatures and executive officials to determine issues of constitutionality before proposed legislation is enacted. Although these opinions are commonly issued by some state and many foreign courts, the U.S. Supreme Court stated that the federal courts will rule only on actual controversies and not on hypothetical issues.

The prohibition on advisory opinions from U.S. federal courts dates from very early in U.S. history. On July 18, 1793, President George Washington sought an advisory opinion from the Supreme Court regarding the interpretation of the 1778 Franco-American Treaty. On August 8, 1793, the justices of the Court wrote a letter to formally decline to provide the requested advice, citing separation of powers concerns. Chief Justice John Jay stated that the justices were "judges of a court in the last resort" and should refuse to issue opinions except as a result of normal litigation undertaken by real parties in an actual conflict.

This ruling reinforced the independence of the federal courts and reaffirmed the attorney general's role as legal adviser to the president. However, this prohibition does not apply to the states, and some state constitutions do allow the state courts to issue advisory opinions.

Mark C. Miller

SEE ALSO Constitutional interpretation; Jay, John; Judicial review; National security; Separation of powers; Standing.

Affirmative Action

DESCRIPTION: Programs of governmental agencies or private institutions designed to provide members of racial and ethnic minorities and women with access to opportunities in education and employment.

SIGNIFICANCE: Because of discrimination against women and minority members, governmental agencies, businesses, and educational institutions gave them special opportunities, which some people criticized as discriminating against nonminority members. A divided Supreme Court struggled with the question of when such programs are acceptable.

Affirmative action is a highly controversial means of pursuing equal access to resources in education and employment. Although the term affirmative action first appeared in an official document in an executive order issued by President Lyndon B. Johnson in 1965, affirmative action did not emerge as a government policy until the 1970's. In *Griggs v. Duke Power Co.* (1971), the Supreme Court ruled that discrimination could be judged to exist when business practices resulted in limiting opportunities for minorities, even if there had been no evidence of intent to discriminate on the part of the employer. This altered the definition of discrimination, making it a matter of built-in racial bias.

Duke Power Company required either a high-school diploma or a passing grade on a general intelligence test for a job in its power plant. Fewer black applicants than white applicants passed this test. The plaintiffs argued that in this case, educational credentials and test results had no direct relevance to job performance, so no justification existed for a job requirement that disproportionately affected members of the minority race. The Court, under Chief Justice Warren E. Burger, found that employment practices that exclude African American job seekers and are not related to job performance are indeed discriminatory.

The concept of built-in discrimination established by *Griggs* helped lay the groundwork for political efforts to dismantle unintended barriers to full participation in American society. Affirmative action, according to the official government definition, involved ac-

16

tion to overcome past or present barriers to equal opportunity. Two of the most obvious ways of overcoming such barriers were establishing quotas of minority members or women to be hired or admitted to educational programs and creating set-asides, positions reserved for minority members or women. These remedies, however, met with challenges by those in groups not benefiting from affirmative action, who charged that they were suffering from officially sanctioned discrimination.

In 1971 a Jewish man named DeFunis applied for admission to the University of Washington Law School but was rejected. The law school followed a practice of dividing its applicants into two categories, minority group members and majority group members, using lower standards for admitting minority group members. If DeFunis had been black, American Indian, or Latino, his test scores and grades would have gained him entry. He sued, claiming that his rights to equal legal protection, guaranteed by the Fourteenth Amendment, had been violated.

DeFunis v. Odegaard came before the Court in 1974. However, DeFunis had been admitted to the law school after a lower court found in his favor, and the school had said that he would be allowed to graduate, regardless of the Court's ruling. The Court ruled the case moot because a ruling would not affect the outcome for the plaintiff, and it dismissed the appeal. Justice William O. Douglas wrote a dissent expressing his view that DeFunis had indeed been denied equal protection under the law.

INCREASING CHALLENGES

Although the Court did not have to rule on preferential treatment of protected categories of people in the DeFunis case, challenges to affirmative action increased through the 1970's. One of the objections was the claim that affirmative action violated Title VII of the Civil Rights Act of 1964, which forbids discrimination on the basis of race. Many critics maintained that preferential treatment of minority group members could be viewed as discrimination against those who were not minority group members. In *United Steelworkers of America v. Weber* (1979), the court ruled that Title VII's prohibition against racial discrimination does not condemn all private, voluntary race-conscious affirmative action plans. Kaiser Aluminum and Chemical Corporation and the United Steelworkers Union maintained a training program. As long as the percentage of African Americans among Kaiser's plant employees was less than the percentage of African Americans in the local workforce, half of the openings on this program were reserved for African Americans. Brian Weber, a white man who had not been allowed to enter the training program, sued, claiming that he had been a victim of racial discrimination.

Justice William J. Brennan, Jr., writing for the majority of justices, maintained that Congress had not intended Title VII to prohibit private, voluntary efforts to overcome long-established patterns of racial discrimination in employment. In addition, the Fourteenth Amendment did not apply in this case because it did not involve any governmental actions. Whites, in Brennan's view, were not handicapped by the policy regarding the training program because no whites were fired and whites still had opportunities for advancement.

The best-known challenge to affirmative action to come before the Court was *Regents of the University of California v. Bakke* (1978). Alan Bakke was a white man who had been denied admission to the University of California medical school at Davis. In 1972 the thirty-two-year-old Bakke was a Marine Corps veteran who had served in Vietnam and an engineer at a research center of the National Aeronautics and Space Administration (NASA) near Palo Alto, California. While working at NASA, he decided to become a medical doctor. He took classes to prepare himself for medical school and served as a volunteer in a local hospital emergency room.

Despite high scores on the Medical College Admissions Test and strong letters of recommendation, Bakke was rejected by the University of California and ten other schools to which he applied. Bakke wrote to the chairman of admissions at the University of California, Davis, requesting reconsideration, charging that racial minority members who were less qualified than he had been admitted through a special admissions program. Bakke reapplied for early admissions in 1973 and prepared to sue if he was again rejected. In the summer of 1974 Bakke's suit was officially filed in Yolo County Superior Court.

Bakke became one of the most celebrated court cases of the decade. It provoked national debate over affirmative action and brought wide attention to the practice of setting aside places in businesses or educational institutions for minority members. The California Supreme Court found that Bakke had suffered racial discrimination. In November, 1976, the Board of Regents of the University of California voted to appeal the decision to the Supreme Court.

Four justices, led by Justice Brennan, voted not to hear the case. Five chose to hear it, however, and it went on the Court docket. Ultimately, the Court reached a split decision. Four justices concluded that the University of California had clearly violated both the equal protection clause of the Fourteenth Amendment and the Civil Rights Act of 1964. Four other justices disagreed and wanted to uphold the legality of taking race into consideration for education or employment. The swing vote, Justice Lewis F. Powell, Jr., essentially divided his decision. He sided with the four who maintained that the minority set-aside program at Davis was unconstitutional; however, he also stated that although racial quotas were unacceptable, race could be taken into consideration. The majority opinion, written by Brennan, incorporated Powell's ambivalence. It stated that it was constitutional to take race into account to remedy disadvantages resulting from past prejudice and discrimination, but that race alone could not be the basis for making decisions about opportunities in employment or education.

AFTER *BAKKE*

Many legal scholars believe that *Bakke* established an unclear precedent. Although it did uphold the basic principle of affirmative action, it also left the door open for challenges to specific affirmative action policies. As a part of the 1977 Public Works Employment Act, Congress set aside 10 percent of all federal appropriations for public works contracts for minority contractors and subcontractors. This legislation came before the Court in *Fullilove v. Klutznick* (1980). Once again, a controversial issue split the members of the Court.

One of the differences between *Fullilove* and earlier affirmative action cases was that it involved the actions of Congress, which may act with greater power and authority than a private employer or a local school board and is also charged with seeking the present and future welfare of the nation. Chief Justice Burger's opinion, joined by Justices Powell and Byron R. White, recognized this, stating that Congress has the power to act to remedy social evils and that there was a compelling governmental interest in seeking to counteract the deep-rooted disadvantages of minority contractors. Thurgood Marshall, joined by Justices Brennan and Harry A. Blackmun, wrote a concurring opinion arguing that the actions of Congress were constitutional because the set-aside provision was related to the congressionally approved goal of overcoming racial inequality. Justices Potter Stewart, William H. Rehnquist, and John Paul Stevens disagreed. Stewart and Rehnquist maintained that an unconstitutional practice could not be constitutional simply because it came from Congress rather than from a lesser source and that the set-aside involved distributing governmental privileges based on birth. Stevens objected to the governmental favoring of some groups over others and pointed out that those who were likely to benefit most were the least disadvantaged members of minority groups, such as successful black or Hispanic businesspeople. Thus, although *Fullilove* established once more the principle of affirmative action, it also made it clear that there were fundamental disagreements on the principle, even among the justices.

Two major issues emerged from the *Fullilove* decision. One was the concept that affirmative action policies undertaken by the government merit a special deference because of the constitutional authority of Congress to make laws. The second was that because affirmative action is a means of pursuing governmental policies, agencies and organizations must be able to demonstrate that their affirmative action programs serve a compelling governmental interest. This second point placed the burden of justifying affirmative action programs on those seeking to establish the policies. Those seeking to pursue affirmative action policies must be able to demonstrate that these policies are narrowly designed to compensate for past discrimination or to bring about a clearly defined goal. For this reason, the Court decided in *Mississippi University for Women v. Hogan* (1982) that a college could not deny men entry into a nursing program on the grounds that this was intended to compensate women for past discrimination. On the other hand, when past discrimination could be clearly demonstrated, affirmative action policies were deemed acceptable. A requirement in Alabama that one black state trooper be promoted for every promotion of a white state trooper was upheld by the Court in *United States v. Paradise* (1987) because it could be demonstrated that underrepresentation of African Americans at high ranks was caused by past discrimination by the Alabama Department of Public Safety. In *Richmond v. J. A. Croson Co.* (1989), however, the Court ruled that the Richmond city government's minority business utilization plan failed to provide appropriate statistical data showing systematic underrepresentation of minority-owned businesses. Therefore, the Court found that the plan was not narrowly tailored to remedy the effects of prior discrimination and failed to demonstrate a compelling government interest for awarding a certain percentage of contracts to minority-owned businesses.

Both the concept of the special status of Congress and of the legitimacy of affirmative action for compelling governmental interests were upheld in *Metro Broadcasting v. Federal Communications Commission* (1990), in which a majority of justices ruled that minority preference policies of the Federal Communications Commission were acceptable because they met both criteria.

LIMITS ON AFFIRMATIVE ACTION

During the 1990's, there were a number of public challenges to affirmative action, notably in the Texas and California systems of higher education, where controversial laws passed in 1997 made it illegal to give preferential treatment to members of protected groups. Affirmative action proponent Marshall left the Court in 1991, and new justices appointed by Presidents Ronald Reagan and George H. W. Bush—including Sandra Day O'Connor, Anthony M. Kennedy, Antonin Scalia, and Clarence Thomas—appeared to be largely unsympathetic to affirmative-action-style policies.

In his book on affirmative action and the Court, Lincoln Caplan observed that in the middle to late 1990's Chief Justice Rehnquist and Justices O'Connor, Kennedy, Scalia, and Thomas never voted to uphold an affirmative action program based on race. Thomas, the only African American among these justices, was the strongest and most open opponent of the preferential treatment of minorities, which he derided as "racial paternalism." The limiting of affirmative action appeared in *Adarand Constructors v. Peña* (1995), in which the Court expanded the idea that programs had to serve a compelling interest. Affirmative action programs, the court ruled, must be observed with the strictest scrutiny and must be necessary to meet a compelling state interest.

By the end of the twentieth century, many observers were predicting that the Court would make a ruling that would end affirmative action. This perception made some defenders of affirmative action policies reluctant to bring cases before the Court. This happened, for example, in the case of Sharon Taxman. Taxman, a white teacher, had been laid off from her job by the school district of Piscataway, New Jersey, in 1991. The school district needed to reduce its teaching force and had to choose between Taxman and an equally qualified black teacher. Because black teachers were underrepresented in the district, the school system used its voluntary affirmative action program to decide between the two teachers. Taxman sued, claiming racial discrimination. The case was poised to go to the Court in late 1997. Fear that a Court ruling in favor of Taxman would further weaken affirmative action led civil rights groups to support the Piscataway School Board's decision to pay Taxman a $433,000 settlement in November, 1997, rather than risk an unfavorable Court decision.

At the beginning of the twenty-first century, many legal experts were expecting that the Supreme Court might reverse the controversial *Bakke* decision and declare affirmative action to be unconstitutional in the admissions policies of colleges and universities. The Court of Appeals for the Fifth Circuit had recently stuck down the use of race-based preferences at the University of Texas law school, and the Supreme Court had declined the opportunity to review the case. Persons interested in the fate of affirmative action programs were focusing their attention on two lawsuits challenging the admissions practices of the University of Michigan. Both decisions were announced on June 23, 2003.

In the case of *Gratz v. Bollinger*, the Court held, by a 6-3 vote, that the policy used for selecting undergraduate students violated both the Fourteenth Amendment and the Civil Rights Act of 1964. Writing for the majority, Justice Sandra Day O'Connor explained that the awarding of automatic preferences without any individualized evaluation of students did not withstand strict scrutiny, which required a narrowly tailored approach to achieving a compelling interest. In the case of *Grutter v. Bollinger*, however, the Court voted five to four to uphold the more moderate use of racial preferences used by the law school. Speaking for the majority, O'Connor emphasized that the law school had not automatically given minority applicants extra points— as in the policy for undergraduates—but had evaluated each student individually, taking race into account as one of many variables. She found that this approach was narrowly tailored to achieve diversity (also called a "critical mass" of minority students), which she and four other justices accepted as a compelling state interest.

Despite the *Grutter* decision, the long-term future of affirmative action programs was by no means assured. In 2005, Justice O'Connor announced her retirement and Chief Justice William H. Rehnquist died of cancer. John Roberts became the new Chief Justice, and Samuel Alito took O'Connor's seat. Both new justices were not expected to be strong supporters of race-conscious policies. Four of the remaining justices—John Paul Stevens, Ruth Bader Ginsburg, Stephen G. Breyer, and David Souter—had consistently supported all such policies. Two justices—Justices Antonin Scalia and Clarence Thomas—had predictably been firm opponents, and they usually had gained the support of Justice Anthony Kennedy. It appeared likely, therefore, that the continuation of affirmation action programs would depend on the views of Roberts and Alito.

Carl L. Bankston III
Updated by the Editor

FURTHER READING

A useful general overview of the Supreme Court's handling of affirmative action issues can be found in Michael J. Klarman's *From Jim Crow to Civil Rights: The Supreme Court and the Struggle for Racial Equality* (New York: Oxford University Press, 2004). Girardeau A. Spann's *The Law of Affirmative Action: Twenty-Five Years of Supreme Court Decisions on Race and Remedies* (New York: New York University Press, 2000) and Lincoln Caplan's *Up Against the Law: Affirmative Action and the Supreme Court* (New York: Twentieth Century Fund Press, 1997) are useful introductions to the role of the Supreme Court in the American debate over affirmative action that also offer explanations of the practices and consequences of affirmative action programs. Terry Anderson's *The Pursuit of Fairness: A History of Affirmative Action* (New York: Oxford University Press, 2004) provides the most comprehensive and interesting historical study of the topic. Greg Stohr's *A Black and White Case: How Affirmative Action Survived Its Greatest Legal Challenge* (Princeton, N.J.: Bloomberg Press, 2004) gives well-written, detailed accounts of *Grutter v. Bollinger* and *Gratz v. Bollinger* within their historical contexts.

A great deal has been written on the *Bakke* case. Timothy J. O'Neill's *"Bakke" and the Politics of Equality: Friends and Foes in the Classroom of Litigation* (Middletown, Conn.: Wesleyan University Press, 1981) is a detailed study of the case and of the political forces on both sides. Readers who want to know about the *Bakke* case should consult *Behind "Bakke": Affirmative Action and the Supreme Court* (New York: New York University Press, 1988) by Bernard Schwartz. Andrew Kull's *The Color-Blind Constitution* (Cambridge, Mass.: Harvard University Press, 1992) attempts to discover the history of the argument that the Constitution prohibits racial classifications by agencies of the government. The last chapter, "Benign Racial Sorting," is particularly useful to those interested in the arguments surrounding affirmative action issues.

Dinesh D'Souza's *Illiberal Education: The Politics of Race and Sex on Campus* (New York: Free Press, 1991), a work strongly opposed to affirmative action, presents a view of affirmative action policies in universities before these began to be scaled back. *The Shape of the River: Long-Term Consequences of Considering Race in College and University Admissions* (Princeton, N.J.: Princeton University Press, 1998), by William G. Bowen and Derek C. Bok, provides a positive view of affirmative action in higher education. For overviews of the Rehnquist Court's handling of affirmative action cases, see *Rehnquist Justice: Understanding the Court Dynamic*, edited by Earl M. Maltz (Lawrence: University Press of Kansas, 2003), and *A Court Divided: The Rehnquist Court and the Future of Constitutional Law*, by Mark Tushnet (New York: W. W. Norton, 2005).

SEE ALSO *Adarand Constructors v. Peña*; Employment discrimination; Equal protection clause; Fourteenth Amendment; Gender issues; *Gratz v. Bollinger/ Grutter v. Bollinger*; *Griggs v. Duke Power Co.*; Race and discrimination; *Regents of the University of California v. Bakke*; School integration and busing; Thomas, Clarence.

Age Discrimination

DESCRIPTION: Inequality of opportunities, services, or treatment based on age, most often affecting older persons.

SIGNIFICANCE: The Supreme Court has examined numerous allegations of age discrimination under both the equal protection clause of the Fourteenth Amendment and the Age Discrimination in Employment Act of 1967 and the latter's amendments.

During the 1970's, a number of older government workers went to court alleging employment discrimination in violation of the equal protection clause of the Fourteenth Amendment. In reviewing these cases, the Supreme Court decided that age was not a suspect category, and therefore the Court applied minimal judicial scrutiny (also called the rational basis test), which placed a high burden of proof on the plaintiffs. Based on this test, the legal challengers had very little chance of success. In contrast, if classifications had been based on race, the Court would have applied strict scrutiny and required the classification to be narrowly tailored to achieve a compelling state interest. If the classification had been based on gender, the Court would apply intermediate scrutiny—a more difficult hurdle than for race but much less difficult than for age.

The Age Discrimination in Employment Act (ADEA) of 1967 originally applied only to the private-sector. It provided legal protection for employees over forty years old from age discrimination in hiring, compensation, discharge, promotion, or conditions of employment. The statute allowed employers to set age limits when it could be shown that such limits are justified by a "bona fide occupational qualification reasonably necessary to the normal operation of the particular business" (BFOQ). The ADEA has been amended several times.

In 1974, Congress extended the ADEA to most public-sector employees. An amendment of 1986 eliminated the upper age of seventy. Another amendment in 1990 included several complex provisions, including a requirement that employers pay older employees the same fringe benefits as younger workers.

The ADEA is enforced primarily by the Equal Employment Opportunity Commission (EEOC). Before filing lawsuits, complainants must file claims with either the EEOC or state commissions on human rights. The EEOC attempts to resolve disputes through voluntary compliance before taking legal action. Employees are not required to wait for the EEOC to make final determinations before filing claims.

MANDATORY RETIREMENT

Plaintiffs suing for age discrimination under the Fourteenth Amendment have seldom been able to overcome the difficult hurdle of minimal scrutiny. In the first important case relating to this matter, *Massachusetts Board of Retirement v. Murgia* (1976), the Supreme Court reviewed a constitutional challenge to a state statute mandating the retirement of police officers at the age of fifty. Based on the premise that old age did not define "a discrete and insular minority," the justices quickly concluded that the appropriate test was whether there was a rational basis (or justification) for the law. In view of the physical and cognitive demands of police work, they answered in the affirmative. In *Vance v. Bradley* (1979), the Court reviewed another challenge under the equal protection clause, this time a requirement that foreign service officers retire at the age of sixty. Again, based on the rational-basis test, the Court upheld the policy as reasonable.

Plaintiffs challenging retirement policies under the ADEA had a somewhat better chance of prevailing, for here the standard was whether the policy was a bona fide occupational qualification (BFOQ). In its first ADEA case, *United Airlines v. McMann* (1977), the Supreme Court held that the BFOQ standard justified a policy of mandating that airline pilots retire at the age of sixty. Another influential BFOQ precedent was *Western Air Lines v. Criswell* (1985), when the Court unanimously overturned a policy requiring the involuntary retirement of flight engineers (who did not operate sensitive flight controls) at the age of sixty. *Criswell* established the assessment of a BFOQ with a two-pronged test: first, whether the ages limit is reasonably necessary to protect public safety; second, whether individual decisions about retirement age would be more appropriate than a uniform age limit for all employees.

In *TWA v. Thurston* (1985), the Court unanimously found that the airline company violated the ADEA when it refused to give the same opportunities for job transfer to retiring pilots as it gave to younger disabled pilots. However, the Court denied the pilots' claim for double damages, which required evidence of a "willful violation" of the ADEA. The Court held that a violation would only be classified as "willful" when an employer demonstrates a "reckless disregard" for what the ADEA requires.

OTHER EMPLOYMENT CASES

The Supreme Court explored the issue of whether business decisions are actually "pretexts" for age discrimination in *Hazen Paper Co. v. Biggins* (1993). This case involved a sixty-two-year-old man who had been dismissed only a few weeks before his pension was to become vested. Assuming that the employer fired Biggins to save having to pay into the employee's pension fund, the Court found that the firing did not violate the ADEA because there was no evidence that the employer had fired him because of his age as such. The indirect, empirical correlation between age and pension status was not sufficient to prove age discrimination. The *Biggins* decision made it much more difficult for plaintiffs to win judgment awards under the ADEA.

In *Gilmer v. Interstate/Johnson Lane Corporation* (1991), the Court held that an employee who signed an agreement to arbitrate employment disputes may not proceed with an ADEA lawsuit but must instead submit the dispute to an arbitrator. The issue before the Court in *McKennon v. Nashville Banner* (1995) was whether an employee who was discharged in violation of the ADEA is barred from relief if the employer subsequently finds enough evidence of misbehavior to justify a firing. The Court ruled that such after-the-firing evidence does not block all relief under the ADEA, but that it might limit the amount of the award.

In *O'Connor v. Consolidated Coin Caterers* (1996), the Court unanimously held that age discrimination may occur whenever a person over forty years old is fired, regardless of whether the replacement is older or younger than forty. However, the Court rejected a "reverse discrimination" claim in *General Dynamics Land Systems v. Cline* (2004), allowing an employer to provide better health care to older workers than younger workers. The Court found no evidence of congressional intent "to stop an employer from favoring an older employee over a younger one."

In *Smith v. City of Jackson* (2006), the Court first considered an ADEA case alleging a disparate impact claim, based on the theory that an employment practice unintentionally discriminated against older workers. Smith and other local police officers had claimed that a salary scale had a negative effect on officers older than forty. After reviewing the case, the Court responded with two unanimous rulings. Under its first ruling the ADEA authorized suits based on a disparate impact of a policy. However, the Court also ruled that the ADEA allowed policies with discriminatory results if the policies were based on "reasonable factors" other than age, which meant that the employer did not have to justify its policy by the demanding "business necessity" standard, which would have been necessary if the disparate impact had been based on race or gender. Under the more lenient rule, not surprisingly, the police officers failed to win their case.

FEDERALISM ISSUES

Advocates of states' rights disliked the 1974 amendment that made the ADEA binding on state governments, as they believed it was inconsistent with the Tenth and Eleventh Amendments. In *Equal Employment Opportunity Commission v. Wyoming* (1983), however, the Court voted five to four to uphold the constitutionality of the amendment. Justice William Brennan explained that the amendment was a legitimate application of Congress's power to regulate interstate commerce. Speaking for the four dissenters, Chief Justice Warren Burger based his argument on states' residual powers under the Tenth Amendment.

By the 1990's, the justices on the Supreme Court had become more amenable to claims of states' rights. While reviewing Missouri's requirement that state judges retire at the age of seventy in *Gregory v.*

Ashcroft (1991), the Court held, by a 5-4 margin, that the requirement violated neither the Fourteenth Amendment nor the ADEA. In addition to emphasizing the state's Tenth Amendment right to determine the qualifications of high state officials, the Court declared that the ADEA did not apply to policy-making officials such as state judges.

The case of *Kimel v. Florida Board of Regents* (2000) involved several older employees of a state university who had sued the board of trustees under the ADEA. In a 5-4 opinion, the Supreme Court ruled that because of the states' immunity under the Eleventh Amendment, Congress had no constitutional power to authorize private individuals to sue a state except as a means to enforce the Fourteenth Amendment. Reasserting that age discrimination under the Fourteenth Amendment is decided by the rational basis test, Justice Sandra Day O'Connor argued that in passing the 1974 amendment, Congress had attempted to "rewrite" the Court's Fourteenth Amendment jurisprudence, which is unconstitutional. She added, however, that public employees in most states could still bring age discrimination lawsuits under state laws.

Thomas Tandy Lewis

FURTHER READING

Coni, Nicholas. *Aging: The Facts.* New York: Oxford University Press, 1992.

Equal Employment Opportunity Commission. *Age Discrimination.* Washington, D.C.: Government Printing Office, 1998.

Gregory, Raymond. *Age Discrimination in the American Workplace.* Piscataway, N.J.: Rutgers University Press, 2001.

Hushbeck, Judith C. *Old And Obsolete: Age Discrimination and the American Worker, 1860-1920.* New York: Garland Press, 1989.

Lindemann, Barbara, and David Kadue. *Age Discrimination in Employment Law.* Washington, D.C.: BNA Books, 2003.

MacNicol, John. *Age Discrimination: An Historical and Contemporary Analysis.* New York: Cambridge University Press, 2006.

Nichols, Barbara, and Peter Leonard, eds. *Gender, Aging and the State.* New York: Black Rose Books, 1994.

SEE ALSO Employment discrimination; Equal protection clause; Gender issues; Race and discrimination.

Samuel A. Alito, Jr.

IDENTIFICATION: Associate justice (January 31, 2006-   )
NOMINATED BY: George W. Bush
BORN: April 1, 1950, Trenton, New Jersey
SIGNIFICANCE: As a judge of the Court of Appeals for the Third Circuit for sixteen years, Alito established a reputation as a hardworking, highly competent, and generally conservative judge. When he replaced the moderate swing voter, Justice Sandra Day O'Connor, on the Court, most observers expected that his tenure would move the Court in a more conservative direction.

The mother of Samuel A. Alito, Jr., mother was a schoolteacher and his father, having left Italy as a child, was a teacher before becoming New Jersey's director of legislative services. During his youth, Alito was studious and ambitious. In 1972, he received his bachelor's degree from Princeton's School of Public and International Affairs. While an undergraduate, he was an active member of the university's Army Reserve Officer Training Corps (ROTC) program. He then attended the Yale Law School, where he served as editor of the *Yale Law Journal* and completed his J.D. degree in 1975.

After his graduation, Alito worked as law clerk for a judge of the Third Circuit, while also finding time to serve in the Army Reserve as second lieutenant of Signal Corps. From 1981 to 1987, he held several high positions in the Department of Justice, in which he enthusiastically defended the conservative policies of President Ronald Reagan. Over the next three years Alito served as U.S. attorney for the District of New Jersey and prosecuted many organized crime and drug trafficking cases. In 1990, he became an appellate judge on the Third Circuit, a position he still held when President George W. Bush named him to replace Justice Sandra Day O'Connor on October 31, 2005.

ALITO'S JURISPRUDENCE

At the time of Alito's nomination, the Supreme Court was frequently polarized between liberal and conservative justices, especially on the controversial issues of abortion, affirmative action, the establishment clause, and criminal procedures. Because Justice O'Connor sometimes voted with the four more liberal members of the Court, liberal groups feared that the addition of Alito would likely move the Court in a right-wing direction. Organizations devoted to abortion rights were particularly hostile to Alito's nomination. Conservative groups, in contrast, generally applauded Bush's choice. The nonpartisan American Bar Association ranked Alito as "well qualified," the organization's highest rating.

When journalists and organizations searched for materials about Alito's judicial philosophy, they discovered a paper trail of complexity. As a student at Princeton, Alito had led a student conference that called for curbs on domestic spying and had urged for an end to discrimination against homosexuals. Shortly after graduation, however,

Samuel A. Alito, Jr. (AP/ Wide World Photos)

he had joined the conservative Concerned Alumni of Princeton (CAP), which published articles expressing reactionary views about race and gender. Liberals were especially concerned to learn that he had referred approvingly his CAP membership when applying for a job in the Reagan administration. It was not clear, however, whether he had mentioned this organization out of conviction or because he thought it would help his chances of employment.

As a judge on the Third Circuit, Alito had to follow the binding precedents established by the Supreme Court, and in this capacity it was difficult to know his views on those precedents. When examining abortion cases, for example, he tended to find that many restrictions did not place an "undue burden" on women's rights to abortions. In 1991, Alito was the only judge of the Third Circuit to dissent in *Planned Parenthood of Southeastern Pennsylvania v. Casey*, when the majority overturned a law requiring women seeking abortions to notify their husbands. Alito had tended to take a narrow view of the congressional powers under the commerce clause. He had also tended to take a conservative view on law-and-order issues. Dissenting in *Doe v. Groody* (2004), he argued that the qualified immunity of police officers should have protected them from civil suit for having strip-searched a mother and daughter when carrying out a valid search of the residence, a opinion that earned him the nickname "Strip-Search Sammy" from his critics.

Although Alito is generally classified as conservative, some commentators have said that he is not easy to label. In the area of free speech rights, his record tended to be left of center. In the case of *Saxe v. School District*, for example, he argued that schools have no right to punish students for vulgar language if it is not disruptive. Alito had the reputation of tending to make case-by-case decisions and to avoid pronouncing doctrines. However, legal commentators did not agree about the substance of his judicial philosophy. Conservative law professor Douglas Kmiec, for example, called him a "judge's judge" who approached cases "with impartiality and open-mindedness." In contrast, criminal lawyer Lawrence Lustberg described him as "an activist conservatist judge" who almost always favored the prosecution and narrowly interpreted the rights of criminals and prisoners.

Alito's Senate confirmation hearings were held from January 9 until January 13, 2006. In contrast to the earlier hearings for John Roberts, several Democratic senators were very aggressive in their questions of the nominee. Some of them refused to believe that he had not been committed to the views of the Concerned Alumni of Princeton. They did their best to portray him as an extremist on issues of abortion, federalism, and government surveillance of citizens. They were especially critical of his theory of the "unitary executive," which apparently disagreed with Supreme Court precedents on the independent regulatory agencies.

Like almost all other candidates to the Court, Alito said that the need to maintain impartiality kept him from revealing how he would decide cases likely to come before the Supreme Court, especially on the delicate issue of abortion. Concerning the principle of *stare decisis*, Alito emphasized its importance to the stability of the U.S. legal tradition, and he said that precedents should be upheld except for "extraordinary" reasons. He also indicated that he did not have any agenda to make wholesale changes in the Court's jurisprudence. He further said that his membership in the Roman Catholic Church would not directly affect his positions in particular cases.

On January, 2006, the Senate Judiciary Committee endorsed Alito's nomination by a 10-8 vote that followed party lines. When debate began in the full Senate, Senator John Kerry called for a filibuster, but the senators approved a cloture vote to end debate on January 30. The next day the Senate endorsed Alito's nomination by a 58-42 margin. Shortly thereafter, he was sworn in by Chief Justice Roberts.

By February of the same year, Alito was participating in the court's decisions. Having joined the Court in mid-term, he had not heard the arguments of many cases and thus was not able to vote. On May 1, he delivered his first written opinion in the case *Holmes v. South Carolina*, for which the justices unanimously upheld a law that severely limited the rights of a criminal defendant to introduce evidence that a third party committed the crime. In *Garcetti v. Ceballos*, for example, Alito provided the fifth vote in holding that employers might discipline whistle-blowers without violating their constitutional rights. In *Hudson v. Michigan* (2006), he again provided the fifth vote in allowing the use of criminal evidence when the police did not "knock and announce" before entering a private home. In *Hamdan v. Rumsfeld* (2006) he joined with the minority that wanted to approve the use of special military commission to try alleged war criminals. In general, he voted to defend private property rights, presidential prerogatives, flexibility for police in law enforcement, and other positions considered to be right-wing.

During his first half term, Alito usually joined with Antonin Scalia and Clarence Thomas, who were usually recognized as the two most conservative justices. A quantitative study found that he agreed with Thomas in 83 percent of the cases, whereas he voted with the more liberal justice, John Paul Stevens, in only 23 percent of the cases. In decisions made with 5-4 votes, he was on the same side as the four more conservative members 15 percent more often than Justice O'Connor had been. Some observers referred to Justice Alito as "Scalito," a nickname reflecting the alleged similarities between his views and those of Justice Scalia. At that point in his judicial career, however, no one could be certain whether that nickname would continue to be accurate.

Thomas Tandy Lewis

FURTHER READING

Allen, Mike, et al. "How Alito Looks Under the Lens," *Time*, November 14, 2005, 28-32.

Dworkin, Ronald. "The Strange Case of Judge Alito," *New York Review of Books*, February 23, 2006, 31-36.

Gunther, Marc. "Judging Alito," *Fortune*, January 16, 2006, 133-134.

Taylor, Stuart, and Evan Thomas. "Keeping It Real," *Newsweek*, November 14, 2005, 22-28.

SEE ALSO Abortion; *Hamdan v. Rumsfeld*; *Hudson v. Michigan*; Nominations to the Court; O'Connor, Sandra Day; Roberts, John; Scalia, Antonin; Senate Judiciary Committee; Thomas, Clarence.

Allgeyer v. Louisiana

CITATION: 165 U.S. 578 (1897)
DATE: March 1, 1897
ISSUE: Freedom of contract
SIGNIFICANCE: The Supreme Court first used the freedom of contract doctrine to overturn a state law as unconstitutional.

In order to regulate insurance businesses, Louisiana prohibited its residents from entering into most types of insurance contracts with companies located outside the state. Allgeyer and Company was fined $1,000 for making such a contract with a New York firm. By a 9-0 vote, the Supreme Court ruled that the law unconstitutionally violated the liberty of citizens to enter into business contracts without unwarranted interference by the state. Writing for the Court, Justice Rufus W. Peckham explained that his opinion was based on the concept that substantive economic liberties were protected by the due process clause of the Fourteenth Amendment. Further, having earlier ruled that insurance was not a form of commerce, the Court could not base the decision on the issue of state jurisdiction.

Although *Allgeyer* recognized the authority of states to regulate private companies, it insisted that states must justify the reasonableness of all such regulations. Freedom of contract was to be the rule, with exceptions allowed only when clearly necessary to protect the safety, health, or welfare of the public. Through the next four decades, the *Allgeyer* precedent provided a theoretical basis for overturning numerous laws that regulated terms of employment—such as laws requiring maximum working hours or minimum wages. The Court finally stopped giving special protection for the freedom of contract doctrine in *West Coast Hotel Co. v. Parrish* (1937).

Thomas Tandy Lewis

SEE ALSO Capitalism; Contract, freedom of; Due process, substantive; Field, Stephen J.; Fourteenth Amendment; *Lochner v. New York*; *Munn v. Illinois*; Peckham, Rufus W.; *West Coast Hotel Co. v. Parrish*.

Americans with Disabilities Act

DATE: July 26, 1990

DESCRIPTION: The Americans with Disabilities Act (ADA) is a wide-ranging civil rights statute that prohibits numerous kinds of discrimination against persons with physical or mental handicaps in both public and private sectors. The statute emphasizes two major forms of discrimination: in employment and in physical barriers to buildings, transportation, and public services.

SIGNIFICANCE: The ADA has been somewhat successful in improving the economic opportunities for disabled persons, but its greatest impact has been to force both government and private businesses to improve physical access to buildings and transportation facilities. Because of the subjective nature of the legislation's language, the Supreme Court's interpretations of key terms and concepts have frequently determined whether lawsuits are successful.

Often described as the world's first comprehensive law designed to protect persons with disabilities from invidious discrimination, the ADA was modeled after the Civil Rights Act of 1964. Its origins go back to the Rehabilitation Act of 1973, which had a provision prohibiting discrimination in federal programs against an "otherwise qualified individual" solely because of a handicap. In the presidential election of 1988, both major candidates endorsed the principle of providing additional protections. After the election, Congress and President George H. W. Bush agreed on a broad statute that is divided into five parts: Title I deals with employment discrimination; Title II covers access to government buildings and services; Title III covers a vast array of nongovernmental facilities and services; Title IV deals specifically with hearing-impaired persons; and Title V deals with a variety of technical matters.

The ADA defines a disability as "a physical or mental impairment that substantially limits a major life activity." The judgment about whether a particular condition is a "disability" is made on a case by case basis. The statute requires "reasonable accommodations" to facilitate full participation of disabled persons, but it exempts mea-

36

sures that cause "undue hardship." For employment purposes, a person must be "otherwise qualified" to perform a job, and employers are not required to hire or promote a disabled person who is less competent or qualified than another candidate. The meanings and applications of the ADA's rather vague terms are primarily the responsibility of federal agencies, whose decisions are subject to judicial review. In addition, private plaintiffs in many instances may sue and receive compensation for violations.

SUPREME COURT DECISIONS

The U.S. Supreme Court has often upheld the rights of disabled persons to facilities and services under Titles II and III. In *Bragdon v. Abbot* (1998), for example, the Court ruled five to four that infection with the human immunodeficiency virus (HIV) is a disability that entitles its victims to ADA protection, thereby requiring dentists and other caregivers to provide services to such persons unless a "direct threat" can be demonstrated. In another case involving a medical impairment, *Pennsylvania Department of Corrections v. Yeskey* (1998), when a prison inmate was denied participation in a rehabilitation program because of a history of hypertension, the Court ruled unanimously that the ADA's protections extended to prisoners as well as other citizens. When Casey Martin, a professional golfer who suffered from a degenerative circulatory disorder, was denied use of a golf cart in a tournament, the Court ruled in his favor in *PGA Tour v. Martin* (2001). Justice John Paul Stevens explained that the accommodation of a golf cart would not "fundamentally alter the nature" of the game. In *Spector v. Norwegian Cruise Line* (2006), the Court held that foreign-flag cruise ships must provide services for persons with disabilities while sailing in American waters.

In employment cases under Title I, the Supreme Court has defined the word "disability" very narrowly. The key case was *Sutton v. United Air Lines* (1999), which involved two women who were refused consideration for employment by a commercial airline company because of their myopic vision, even though their vision was correctable with glasses. When reviewing the case, the Supreme Court found that the condition of the two women was not covered by Title I for three reasons: their condition did not substantially limit any life activity;

the statute covered only conditions requiring an individualized assessment; and Congress had described the act as protecting only forty-three million Americans with severe disabilities. Reaffirming the ruling in *Murphy v. United Parcel Services* (1999), the Court found that the ADA did not cover an employee with high blood pressure that was treatable with medication. The definition of disability in *Sutton* and *Murphy* greatly limited the number of people qualified to bring suit under the statute.

Other decisions by the Supreme Court have also disappointed advocates of disability rights. *Barnes v. Gorman* (2002) was a complex case about a paraplegic man who was awarded punitive damages for the serious injuries suffered while being transported by the police. Since Congress had not provided clear direction about the matter, the Court looked to parallel provisions in the Civil Rights Act of 1964, concluding that punitive damages may not be awarded in a private cause of action brought under the ADA. Disability rights activists were equally unhappy with the outcome of *U.S. Airways v. Barnett* (2002), a case in which seniority rules appeared to conflict with the rights of a disabled employee. The Court decided that whenever it was necessary for a disabled employee to be transferred to an alternative position within an organization, the ADA did not give the disabled person any right to a special privilege in taking over the position rather than another employee who was entitled to that position under a seniority system.

Early in the twenty-first century, the Supreme Court was badly divided on the issue of whether the ADA contradicts the sovereign immunity of the states under the Eleventh Amendment. In *Board of Trustees of the University of Alabama v. Garrett* (2001), two public employees sought money damages under Title I, charging that the employer had not made reasonable accommodations to their disabilities. By a 5-4 vote, the Court held that the Eleventh Amendment barred Congress from authorizing money awards for failure to comply with Title I. However, in *Tennessee v. Lane* (2004), when two persons with disabilities sued Tennessee under Article II for not providing access to the upper floors of the state courthouse, the Court, by a 5-4 margin, ruled in favor of the plaintiffs. Recognizing that access to a court of law is a fundamental right, the Court held that Congress had the authority under the Fourteenth Amendment to protect such rights under the ADA.

Thomas Tandy Lewis

FURTHER READING

Jones, Nancy Lee. *The Americans with Disabilities Act (ADA): Overview, Regulations and Interpretations.* New York; Novinka Books, 2003.

Switzer, Jacqueline Vaughn. *Disabled Rights: American Disability Policy and the Fight for Equality.* Washington D.C.: Georgetown University Press, 2003.

SEE ALSO Affirmative action; Age discrimination; Eleventh Amendment; Employment discrimination; Fourteenth Amendment; Gender issues; Race and discrimination.

Antitrust Law

DESCRIPTION: Set of statutes regulating economic competition by prohibiting anticompetitive agreements, monopolization, attempted monopolization, conspiracies to monopolize, and mergers and acquisitions that may tend to substantially injure competition.

SIGNIFICANCE: After the Sherman Antitrust Act was passed in 1890, the Supreme Court defined the scope of antitrust law and interpreted its wording and intent, delineating the permissible bounds of business behavior.

The Sherman Antitrust Act of 1890 was a broad statute prohibiting various forms of attempted and actual monopolies and agreements that restrained trade. The act allowed people who suffered injuries to their business and property to recover three times their actual damages, plus attorney fees and costs. One of the principal purposes of antitrust laws was to give the federal courts jurisdiction to create a federal common law of competition.

INTERPRETING THE ANTITRUST ACTS

In the early 1900's, the Supreme Court engaged in a long-running battle to define the scope of the interstate and foreign commerce

U.S.
SUPREME
COURT

TOBACCO
TRUST

DECISION
OF
SUPREME
COURT

STANDARD
OIL CO.

Berryman

WAITING FOR HIS —

This 1911 editorial cartoon suggests that tobacco trusts might be next to be censured by the Supreme Court, after the oil industry. (Library of Congress)

subject to the Sherman Antitrust Act and to define the act's key words. The Court's early interpretations focused on whether the act prohibited all restraints of free trade or only those that were unreasonable under the common law. It also considered what, if anything, constituted a reasonable restraint of trade.

In *Standard Oil Co. v. United States* (1911), the Court adopted the rule of reason, under which only agreements that unreasonably restrained competition were unlawful under the Sherman Act. The uncertainty of the rule of reason led to great criticism of the Court by both defenders and critics of the antitrust laws. The *Standard Oil* deci-

40

sion also prompted Congress, in 1914, to enact the Clayton Act, which listed more specific types of antitrust offenses, and to create the Federal Trade Commission, a federal agency with the power to prohibit "unfair methods of competition."

The Court began to define categories of offenses that were per se unreasonable and hence illegal under the ruling reached in *Standard Oil*. Virtually all price-fixing agreements were unlawful if it could be proved that an agreement between competitors had been reached as to the price of goods or services being bought or sold by those firms. It would be no defense that the firm operated in an industry where competition produced unusual or even harmful results, that the competitors had agreed on a "reasonable" price, or even that the firms lacked the power to raise prices pursuant to their agreement.

This trend condemning price-fixing agreements culminated in *United States v. Socony-Vacuum Oil Co.* (1940), which held that all price agreements between competitors were per se unlawful under the Sherman Act. The Court subsequently extended per se treatment to a wide variety of both horizontal and vertical agreements (agreements between manufacturers of similar products and between manufacturers and suppliers or distributors, respectively). Per se rules were created or modified to condemn agreements between competitors as to the territories or customers they served in *Timken Roller Bearing Co. v. United States* (1951), maximum- and minimum-price agreements between competitors in *Arizona v. Maricopa County Medical Society* (1982), maximum- and minimum-price agreements between sellers and their customers in *Albrecht v. Herald Co.* (1968), certain types of group boycotts in *Klor's v. Broadway-Hale Stores* (1959), so-called tying agreements that required a customer to take one product or service in order to obtain another in *United States v. Northern Pacific Railway Co.* (1958), and most nonprice vertical agreements between sellers and their customers limiting the territory or manner in which goods or services could be sold in *United States v. Arnold, Schwinn and Co.* (1967). In each of these cases, the Court cited the effect on consumers and competitors and the leading economic thinking of the times to justify the use of per se rules that did not permit the defendant to argue that its particular agreement might, on balance, promote, rather than injure, competition.

During this same period, the Court also struggled with the concept of how the Sherman and Clayton Acts applied to mergers and acquisitions. Neither act had proved effective in stemming the tide of mergers that periodically swept the nation. In 1950 Congress passed the Celler-Kefauver Act, which eliminated most of the technical loopholes in the Clayton Act and made it clear that the antitrust laws prohibited any merger or acquisition that had the tendency to injure competition. Beginning with the *Brown Shoe Co. v. United States* decision in 1962, the Court held in an unbroken string of victories for the government that virtually any quantitatively substantial merger would violate the antitrust laws if the government could show that the market shares of the merging firms and overall industry concentration would increase as a result of the merger or acquisition.

AN ECONOMIC ANALYSIS

The increasing severity of these court-made antitrust rules in the 1950's, 1960's, and early 1970's led to a backlash of scholarly criticism focused on the negative economic effects of the Court's antitrust jurisprudence. Prominent law and economics scholars such as Richard Posner and Robert H. Bork, each of whom later became influential judges, argued that the Court's antitrust decisions were inconsistent with what they argued was the principal purpose of the antitrust laws—to increase wealth, consumer welfare, and economic efficiency.

The Court quickly proved receptive to this economically oriented style of antitrust analysis. In the area of agreements between competitors, the Court retained the basic per se rule against hard-core price-fixing agreements but showed an increasing willingness to look under the surface of agreements to determine whether the agreement contained any plausible procompetitive justification that merited further inquiry. In a number of cases, including *National Society of Professional Engineers v. United States* (1978), *Broadcast Music v. Columbia Broadcasting System* (1979), and *National Collegiate Athletic Association v. Board of Regents of the University of Oklahoma* (1984), the Court ultimately condemned anticompetitive agreements between competitors relating to price but only after the type of searching inquiry that would not be possible under a true rule of per se illegality. At the same time, the Court quickly condemned agreements between competitors relating to price in *Federal Trade Commission v. Superior Court Trial Lawyers Association* (1990) or territory in *Jay Palmer et al. v. BRG of Georgia et al.* (1990), if they lacked a plausible procompetitive justification, regardless of the precise test or label being utilized by the Court.

Other per se rules were modified to require a showing of substantial market power before the practice would be condemned as per se unreasonable. For example, the Court modified the per se rule in both tying cases (*Jefferson Parish Hospital Dist. No. 2 v. Hyde*, 1984) and group boycotts (*Northwest Wholesale Stationers v. Pacific Stationery and Printing Co.*, 1985) to require the plaintiff to prove that the defendant enjoyed substantial market power before any liability be imposed. It is difficult to characterize such rules as per se liability because they recognize that these arrangements are not inevitably anticompetitive under all circumstances and typically require the proof of the relevant product and geographic market and the defendant's power within that market, all complicated factual issues that the original per se rule was designed to avoid.

VERTICAL AGREEMENTS

The most significant changes were in vertical restraints dealing with the distribution of products and services. In *Continental T.V. v. GTE Sylvania* (1977), the Court held that all vertical restraints, other than those dealing with price, would be judged under the full rule of reason, weighing the pro- and anticompetitive effects of the arrangements before rendering judgment under the antitrust laws. As a practical matter, the vast majority of such restricted distribution systems became lawful as a result of this decision.

Although vertical agreements dealing with price were nominally per se unreasonable, they became very difficult to prove. The Court in *Business Electronics Corp. v. Sharp Electronics Corp.* (1988) narrowed the definition of vertical price-fixing agreements subject to the per se rule, leaving everything else subject to the more generous *Sylvania* rule of reason approach. In *Monsanto Co. v. Spray-Rite Service Corp.* (1984), the Court narrowed the type of evidence that plaintiffs could show to demonstrate unlawful vertical price fixing. In *Atlantic Richfield Co. v. USA Petroleum Co.* (1990), the Court limited who could sue for unlawful vertical price fixing. Finally, in *State Oil Co. v. Khan*

(1997), the Court reversed one of its earlier precedents and held that maximum vertical price fixing would be treated under the full rule of reason because it was not inevitably anticompetitive and had the potential to help consumers in certain cases.

After *Sylvania*, the Court generally restricted antitrust liability by increasing the substantive and procedural hurdles necessary for either the government or private plaintiffs to prevail. Notable decisions include *Brooke Group Ltd. v. Brown and Williamson Tobacco Corp.* (1993), which limited liability for predatory pricing to those situations in which the defendant has both priced below some appropriate measure of cost and has the ability in the real world to recoup any losses and actually exercise monopoly power following the demise of its competitors. Few plaintiffs were able to prevail under this demanding standard.

Although the center of antitrust activity shifted from the courts to the enforcement agencies, the Court remained actively involved in shaping antitrust law and policy. It continued the trend of shrinking the categories of offenses that are per se unlawful in *NYNEX Corp. v. Discon* (1998) and of narrowly interpreting exemptions and immunities to the antitrust laws, while ensuring that state and local governments could regulate or avoid competition without undue interference from the federal antitrust laws. Despite a general trend toward limiting federal legislative and regulatory power over the economy, the Court preserved the antitrust laws as the preeminent use of the commerce clause, holding that the antitrust statutes extend to the full limit of the power of Congress over both interstate and foreign commerce.

The Court is the final arbiter of the legality of business behavior that affects competition as was intended by Congress in 1890. The precise rules and the tests used by the courts changed over the years in line with the current political and economic thinking. Antitrust law always looked toward economics as a source of wisdom although not as the only factor in deciding the evolution of the legal rules that set the ground rules for the market. The Court uses antitrust law as a flexible instrument determining the bounds between lawful competition and unlawful collusion or exploitation of market power to the detriment of competition and competitors.

Spencer Weber Waller

FURTHER READING

A good starting point is *Antitrust Law and Economics in a Nutshell*, by Ernest Gellhorn, William E. Kovacic, and Stephen Calkins (St. Paul, Minn.: West Publishing, 2004), a handy and authoritative guide to the essentials of antitrust law. For an overview of the history of the antitrust laws see Rudolph J. R. Peritz's *Competition Policy in America, 1888-1992* (New York: Oxford University Press, 1996) and Hans B. Thorelli's *The Federal Antitrust Policy* (Baltimore, Md.: Johns Hopkins University Press, 1955). For the leading treatises on antitrust doctrine and the Court decisions discussed in this article, see Philip Areeda and Donald Turner's *Antitrust Law* (3 vols., Boston: Little, Brown, 1978) and *Antitrust Law Developments* (4th ed., 2 vols., Chicago: American Bar Association, 1997).

The classic economic analyses of the antitrust laws can be found in Robert H. Bork's *The Antitrust Paradox: A Policy at War with Itself* (2d ed., New York: Free Press, 1993) and Richard A. Posner's *Antitrust Law* (2d ed. Chicago: University of Chicago Press, 2001). The leading analysis of the application of U.S. antitrust law to international business is Spencer Weber Waller's *James R. Atwood and Kingman Brewster's Antitrust and American Business Abroad* (3d ed., New York: Clark Boardman Callaghan, 1997).

SEE ALSO Commerce, regulation of; *Debs, In re*; Progressivism; Rule of reason.

Appellate Jurisdiction

DESCRIPTION: Power given to the Supreme Court by Article III, section 2, of the U.S. Constitution, as further defined by federal statute, to review and revise the final decisions of the highest state courts and to review cases from the U.S. Court of Appeals.

SIGNIFICANCE: The Court's appellate jurisdiction was an important factor in the uniformity and development of law in the United States and is the primary mechanism by which the supremacy clause of the U.S. Constitution is given effect.

The Supreme Court's power, including its appellate jurisdiction, originates in the U.S. Constitution. As one of the three coordinate branches of the federal government, it is the judicial arbiter of the Constitution, exercising appellate authority for this purpose over both state and federal courts. Without the Court's appellate jurisdiction, the Framers' concern for the rule of law and the supremacy of the Constitution and the statutes passed pursuant to it would have no practical effect.

All federal courts, including the Supreme Court, are courts of limited jurisdiction. As such, the federal courts are limited to hearing only certain types of cases under constitutional and statutory limits. Article III, section 2, of the U.S. Constitution limits federal court jurisdiction to cases arising under the Constitution, the laws of the United States, and treaties. It also extends jurisdiction to cases affecting ambassadors and consuls and to cases of admiralty and maritime jurisdiction. The Constitution also extends jurisdiction to controversies to which the United States is a party, controversies between two or more states, controversies between citizens of different states (known as diversity jurisdiction), and controversies between a state or its citizens against a foreign state or its citizens.

The Constitution also differentiates between the original and appellate jurisdiction of the Court. Original jurisdiction is the power of a court to hear and determine a matter before any other court does. The Supreme Court has this power with regard to cases affecting ambassadors, consuls, and those in which a state is a party. The remaining jurisdiction of the Court is appellate. Although Congress may not expand or curtail the Court's original jurisdiction, the Constitution left the nature and scope of the Court's appellate jurisdiction largely undefined. This flexibility resulted in many significant changes in the way in which the Court exercised its power to review and revise lower court decisions.

Traditionally, appellate jurisdiction has two purposes. The first is error correction. On appeal, rulings can be examined to ensure that they are correct and that the procedures that safeguard the substantial rights of the litigants were followed. The second purpose is to announce, clarify, and harmonize the rules of decision employed in a legal system. This is known as development of the law. Thus, appellate jurisdiction is concerned not only with the impact of a decision on a particular set of litigants but also with the impact on the affairs of persons other than the parties to the case it is deciding. In a system in which there are two levels of appeal, the error correction function is usually left to the first appellate level, and the law development function is left to the appellate court of last resort. In the United States, the Supreme Court's role has gradually changed from that of error correction to that of law development.

CONGRESSIONAL REGULATION

Congress did not waste much time enacting its first major legislation dealing with the federal judiciary. In the same year in which the Constitution was ratified, Congress passed the Judiciary Act of 1789. This act provided for basic appellate jurisdiction and created a three-tier judiciary staffed by Supreme Court justices and district court judges. The act established a circuit court consisting of one district court judge and two Supreme Court justices who would literally "ride the circuit" to hear cases and appeals from district court decisions. It also provided for appellate jurisdiction in the Supreme Court over civil cases from the circuit court in which the amount in controversy was in excess of two thousand dollars. (The Supreme Court did not have jurisdiction to hear appeals in criminal cases until 1889.) The act also gave the Court appellate jurisdiction to reexamine and "reverse or affirm" a final decision from the highest state court in which a decision in the suit could be had, where the validity of a federal law or a right was drawn into question and the decision was against validity.

During the United States' first century, the Court was virtually the only federal appellate court. The Court was required to rule on all appeals brought from lower federal courts as well as those brought from state courts under the Judiciary Act of 1789. The only way to gain appellate review in the Court under the Judiciary Act of 1789 was by "writ of error" (later known as appeal). Under this method, sometimes called a "writ of right," the Court was obligated to hear an appeal once it determined it had jurisdiction over the subject matter. As the United States grew, the caseload of the Court began to swell. Data available starting in 1880 shows the number of cases filed in the

Court increased tenfold. If the obligatory writ of right or appeal system had prevailed, the Court would certainly have had trouble managing such a caseload.

APPEALS OF RIGHT CURTAILED

The Court acknowledged the significant power Congress has to expand or contract its appellate jurisdiction in *Daniels v. Chicago and Rock Island Railroad Co.* (1866). This does not mean, however, that the members of the Court have no influence over Congress when it comes to legislation affecting the Court's appellate jurisdiction. Indeed, members of the Court actually had a hand in drafting one of the major pieces of legislation affecting the Court's appellate jurisdiction in the twentieth century. Under the Judiciary Act of 1925, the appeal of right was significantly curtailed and was replaced by what was eventually to become virtually the only avenue of appeal to the Court, the writ of *certiorari*. The groundwork for this shift from direct appeals to discretionary appeals was laid in 1891, when Congress created a new level of courts between the circuit and district courts and the Supreme Court. The Judiciary Act of 1891 provided for Supreme Court review over decisions of the new appeals court if the appeals court judges certified a case to the Court or the Court granted review by writ of *certiorari*. Automatic appeal was still allowed, however, in cases involving constitutional questions, treaties, jurisdictional questions, capital crimes, and conflicting laws.

Continuing this trend, the Judiciary Act of 1925 limited the appeal of right for cases from the appeals courts to those in which the appeals court held a state law invalid under the Constitution or federal laws. Appeals of right remained, however, for appeals from district courts in a small number of categories: antitrust, appeals by the United States under the Criminal Appeals Act, suits to enjoin enforcement of state laws, and suits to enjoin enforcement of Interstate Commerce Commission orders. This act and subsequent statutes that further limited the availability of appeals of right to the Court reflected an important shift in the philosophical view of the Court's function. Instead of error correction, the Court was to focus its efforts on cases raising issues of broad public interest.

By 1988, the trend of limiting appeals of right was nearly complete.

CIRCUITS OF THE COURTS OF APPEALS

Circuit	Covered areas
First	Maine, New Hampshire, Massachusetts, Rhode Island, Puerto Rico
Second	New York, Vermont, Connecticut
Third	Pennsylvania, New Jersey, Delaware, Virgin Islands
Fourth	West Virginia, Maryland, Virginia, North Carolina, South Carolina
Fifth	Texas, Louisiana, Mississippi
Sixth	Ohio, Michigan, Kentucky, Tennessee
Seventh	Wisconsin, Illinois, Indiana
Eighth	Minnesota, North Dakota, South Dakota, Nebraska, Iowa, Missouri, Arkansas
Ninth	Washington, Montana, Idaho, Oregon, Nevada, California, Arizona, Alaska, Hawaii, Northern Marianas, Guam
Tenth	Wyoming, Utah, Colorado, Kansas, Oklahoma, New Mexico
Eleventh	Florida, Georgia, Alabama
D.C.	District of Columbia

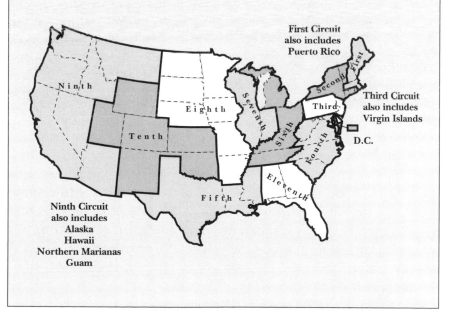

First Circuit also includes Puerto Rico

Third Circuit also includes Virgin Islands

Ninth Circuit also includes Alaska Hawaii Northern Marianas Guam

In the 1988 Act to Improve the Administration of Justice, Congress virtually eliminated the Court's nondiscretionary appellate jurisdiction. Today, the right of appeal exists only in cases that are required to be determined by a district court of three judges. The vast remainder of the Court's appellate jurisdiction is through the writ of *certiorari*, which is granted or denied at the discretion of the Court.

STANDARDS FOR GRANTING *CERTIORARI*

A review on writ of *certiorari* is granted "only when there are special and important reasons," according to the Supreme Court's rule 17. The rule goes on to list the types of reasons that may be considered by the Court in deciding whether to grant *certiorari* in a particular case. Some of the types of reasons justifying *certiorari* to a court of appeals are where a court of appeals decides a matter in conflict with another court of appeals, where a court of appeals has decided a matter in conflict with the decision of a state's highest court, and where an appeals court has drastically departed from the usual course of judicial proceedings. *Certiorari* is also justified when the court of appeals or a state's highest court has decided an important question of federal law that has never been decided by the Supreme Court or has decided a federal question in a way that conflicts with previous Court decisions. However, the rule makes it clear that the Court retains the discretion to deny *certiorari* even in cases that fall within these categories. A less formal rule employed by the Court in making *certiorari* decisions is the rule of four. Under this rule, a case is accepted for full review only if four members of the Court feel that it merits such consideration. However it is employed, this power to select the cases over which the Court will exercise its appellate jurisdiction gives the Court considerable influence over the speed and direction of the law's development.

In fact, the percentage of cases that the Court selects for appellate review fell steadily in the second half of the twentieth century. From the 1980's to the 1990's, the percentage of cases in which *certiorari* was granted dropped from around 10 percent to around 3 percent. For example, 2,441 petitions for *certiorari* were filed in 1992, and only 83 were granted.

The cases accepted for review also can reflect certain social trends.

In 1933 cases involving due process made up only 5.2 percent of total cases accepted for review, whereas in 1987 those cases amounted to 29.6 percent of the Court's docket. A similar trend can be seen in the increase in cases involving federal rights. Those cases represented about 1 percent of total cases in 1933, but nearly 11 percent in 1987. Other policy areas in which growth can be seen are equality, government benefits, and separation of governmental powers. The percentage of cases involving foreign affairs, federal regulation, economic regulation, state regulation, and internal revenue has steadily decreased.

Sharon K. O'Roke

FURTHER READING

Two good sources with which to begin any study of appellate jurisdiction are David C. Frederick's *Supreme Court and Appellate Advocacy* (St. Paul, Minn.: West Group, 2003) and Sara Catherine Benesh's *The U.S. Court of Appeals and the Law of Confessions Perspectives on the Hierarchy of Justice* (New York: LFB Scholarly Publications, 2002). Frederick's book includes a foreword by Justice Ruth Bader Ginsburg. One of the best sources for a summary of the appellate jurisdiction of the Court, as well as reprints of source documents such as the U.S. Constitution, the Judiciary Acts, and Supreme Court rules is Congressional Quarterly's *Guide to the United States Supreme Court*, edited by David G. Savage (4th ed., Washington, D.C.: Congressional Quarterly, 2004).

An excellent primer on appellate jurisdiction in general is Robert J. Martineau's *Appellate Practice and Procedure* (St. Paul, Minn: West Publishing, 1987). Statistical information on the Court and its decisions can be found in *The Supreme Court Compendium*, written by Lee Epstein, Jeffrey A. Segal, Harold J. Spaeth, and Thomas G. Walker (3d ed. Washington, D.C.: CQ Press, 2003). The Federal Judicial Center has several helpful publications, in particular, *Creating the Federal Judicial System* by Russell R. Wheeler and Cynthia Harrison (3d ed., Federal Judicial Center, 2005). In-depth information about the historical background of the Court's appellate jurisdiction, including reproduction of some source materials in the Framers' own hands, can be found in Julius Goebel, Jr.'s *History of the Supreme Court* of the United States: Antecedents and Beginnings to 1801 (New York: Macmillan, 1971).

SEE ALSO *Certiorari*, writ of; Circuit riding; Diversity jurisdiction; Judiciary Act of 1789; Oral argument; Review, process of.

Ashcroft v. Free Speech Coalition

CITATION: 535 U.S. 234
DATE: April 16, 2002
ISSUE: Child pornography
SIGNIFICANCE: The Supreme Court held that Congress has no constitutional authority to outlaw computer-generated depiction of children that is sexually oriented but not legally obscene.

The Child Pornography Prevention Act of 1996 (CPPA) criminalized all forms of child pornography, including computer-generated images that portray minors engaged in sexually explicit conduct. The act did not make any distinction between indecency and obscenity. The Free Speech Coalition, an adult entertainment commercial group, alleged in court that the statute was overly broad and vague, thereby restraining works protected by the First Amendment. The Court of Appeals agreed and held that the CPPA was unconstitutional because it banned material that was neither obscene according to the test under *Miller v. California* (1971), nor produced with the exploitation of children as in *New York v. Ferber* (1882).

The Supreme Court upheld the lower court's ruling. Writing for a 6-3 majority, Justice Anthony M. Kennedy found that the CPPA did not meet *Miller's* definition of obscenity because of its lack of reference to community standards. The CPPA lacked the support of *Ferber,* moreover, because it punished expression even though its production was not based on crime or the victimization of anyone. The *Ashcroft* opinion reaffirmed that when sexually oriented expression is neither obscene nor the product of sexual abuse, it falls under the protection of the First Amendment. Finally, Kennedy wrote that the potential misuse of material by pedophiles did not justify the statute, since almost all forms of expression are subject to abuse by some individuals.

Thomas Tandy Lewis

SEE ALSO First Amendment; Kennedy, Anthony M.; *New York v. Ferber*; Obscenity and pornography; Speech and press, freedom of.

Freedom of Assembly and Association

DESCRIPTION: The right of the people to gather peaceably and to associate with anyone they desire.

SIGNIFICANCE: The Supreme Court has generally upheld the freedom of assembly and association, although it has upheld time, place, and manner restrictions on demonstrations, picketing, and similar gatherings.

The First Amendment to the Constitution (1791) prohibits Congress from making any law that limits "the right of the people peaceably to assemble," but the Constitution does not mention freedom of association. Freedom of association has been inferred, however, from freedom of assembly, and the guarantees of the Bill of Rights, of which the First Amendment is part, have been inferred to apply to the states. Therefore, subject to the interpretation of the Supreme Court, all laws, whether state or federal, that unduly restrict freedom of assembly and association are unconstitutional.

The only explicit restriction on these freedoms is the word "peaceably"; mobs and other groups intent on violence or destruction of property lie outside constitutional protection, as do picketers who physically oppose those who wish to cross picket lines. The freedoms also impinge on trespassing laws that protect the rights of private owners of property, resulting in issues of legal interpretation. Additionally, the Court has upheld laws requiring the licensing of parades and other large assemblies that, although taking place in public areas, may disrupt traffic or otherwise place an undue burden on local authorities. The Court has made further distinctions between public and private places. Quasi-public or quasi-private places, such as college campuses and privately owned areas open to the general public, have been defined regarding the limitations of the right of assembly. How such limitations are to be interpreted and applied have been and continue to be the subject of litigation that is often controversial.

INTERPRETATIONS

The general standard that the Court applies to the question of the right of assembly is the same that it applies to speech: time, place, and manner. For example, the noisy demonstration that is legal in a park outside a public library may be considered illegal if it takes place inside the library. As the Court stated in *United States Postal Service v.*

COURT RULINGS EXPANDING PROTECTED AREAS FOR ASSEMBLIES		
Date	Court case	Protected areas
1937	Hague v. Congress of Industrial Organizations	Public streets and meeting halls
1963	Edwards v. South Carolina	State capitol steps
1965	Cox v. Louisiana	Streets, sidewalk near courthouse or State Capitol
1972	Chicago Police Department v. Mosley	Streets, sidewalk near school
1972	Chief, Capitol Police v. Jeanette Rankin Brigade	Lafayette Park, Washington, D.C.
1975	Southeastern Promotions v. Conrad	Municipal Auditorium
1982	United States v. Grace	Steps of U.S. Supreme Court Building
1987	Board of Airport Commissioners of Los Angeles v. Jews for Jesus	Central Airport Terminal could not be declared "First Amendment Free Zone" to prohibit solicitations and canvassing
1988	Boos v. Barry	Streets, sidewalks within 500 feet of embassy

Greenburgh Civic Associations (1981): "The First Amendment does not guarantee access to property simply because it is owned or controlled by the government." This statement should be compared, however, with one from *Hague v. Congress of Industrial Organizations* (1939), that whether streets or parks are publicly or privately owned, "they have immemorially been held in trust for the use of the public for purposes of assembly and discussing public questions." The conflict between these two statements is to be resolved by examination of the intent that the government has in limiting the assembly in question. In *Perry Education Association v. Perry Local Educators' Association* (1983), the Court stated that the government may "reserve a forum for its intended purposes as long as the regulation is reasonable and not an effort to suppress expression merely because public officials oppose the speaker's view." *Perry* concerned a dispute between two teachers' unions. Under the employment contract, Perry Educational Association (PEA) had access to the interschool mail system and teacher mail boxes. The bargaining agreement also provided that access rights to the mail facilities were not available to any rival union. A rival union, Perry Local Educators' Association, filed suit, contending that PEA's preferential access to the internal mail system violated the First Amendment. The Supreme Court ruled that the PEA's contract provision did not violate the First Amendment.

Freedom of association—in particular, political association, including membership in communist organizations—has been examined in similar ways. In such cases as *Yates v. United States* (1957), the Court explicitly rejected the idea that membership in a group indicates guilt by association. Communist groups are not the only ones whose memberships were subject to government scrutiny. In *National Association for the Advancement of Colored People v. Alabama* (1958), for example, the National Association for the Advancement of Colored People was able to enforce its right to free and private association, in particular to keep its membership rolls out of the hands of Alabama officials. Such protection, however, does not extend to groups that a government can demonstrate are engaged in illegal activities. The Court has upheld the careful application of federal antigang laws that make it a crime to belong to a group engaged in criminal enterprise.

COURT RULINGS RESTRICTING THE RIGHT OF ASSEMBLY

Date	Court case	Areas designated as restricted
1963	Edwards v. South Carolina	Sidewalks adjoining public buildings
1966	Adderley v. Florida	Special access
1972	Flower v. United States	Army bases
1976	Greer v. Spock	Military bases
1990	United States v. Kokinda	U.S. Post Office property sidewalks
1992	International Society for Krishna Consciousness v. Lee	Airports
1994	Madison v. Women's Health Center	Outside abortion clinics

Private organizations that discriminate according to sex, race, or other criteria have defended themselves on First Amendment grounds, with varying degrees of success. In general, the Court has placed greater emphasis on laws against discrimination than on the right to association, especially regarding large associations that have few restrictions on membership. In *Roberts v. United States Jaycees* (1984), the Court reasoned that the Jaycees lacked the distinctive characteristics, such as small size, identifiable purpose, selectivity in membership, and perhaps seclusion from the public eye that might afford constitutional protection to the organization's exclusion of women. In *Rotary International v. Rotary Club of Duarte* (1987), the Court upheld a California law that prevented Rotary International from excluding women from membership, and in *New York State Club Association v. City of New York* (1988), the Court upheld a New York City law prohibiting discrimination based on race, creed, sex, and other categories in places "of public accommodation, resort, or amusement." The court held that the law applied to clubs of more than 400 members providing regular meal service and supported by nonmembers for trade or business purposes.

A landmark case touching on freedom of association is *Griswold v. Connecticut* (1965). Griswold gave medical advice to married people regarding birth control and was convicted of breaking a Connecticut law prohibiting the use of birth control and the giving of medical advice about birth control. The Supreme Court declared the Connecticut law an unconstitutional violation of the right of privacy. The Constitution makes no mention of such a right, but in *Griswold* the Court reasoned that such a right flowed from the right to association. Put broadly, the government did not have the authority to tell people what they could talk about with whom. Thus the "right to be left alone is the beginning of all freedoms" could be inferred to freedom of association.

Abortion clinic protests, specifically the tactics employed by those opposed to abortion to prevent entrance to clinics, have generated various cases touching on freedom of assembly. In *Bray v. Alexandria Clinic* (1993), for example, the Court held that picketers in front of an abortion clinic did not violate the rights of those accessing the clinic to equal protection of the law because the picketers' methods did not rise to the level of "hinderance" considered illegal. On the other hand, the convictions of abortion clinic protesters who are too aggressive in their methods, particularly those that rise to physical confrontation, have been upheld in various courts.

In the controversial case of *Boy Scouts of America v. Dale* (2000), however, the Court held, by a 5-4 vote, that the Boy Scouts' constitutional rights to free speech and free association included the right to refuse gay scout leaders, even in states that had laws banning discrimination based on sexual orientation. Speaking for the Court, Chief Justice William H. Rehnquist affirmed that the rights of "expressive association" trumped the state's interest in prohibiting discrimination. In contrast to the *Roberts* and *Rotary International* decisions, Rehnquist concluded that forcing the Boy Scouts to accept gay scout leaders would require significant changes in the message that the organization wished to convey and the values that it sought to instill in its members. The presence of gay leaders would "force the organization to send a message, both to the young members and the world, that the Boy Scouts organization accepts homosexual conduct as a legitimate form of behavior." Rehnquist emphasized that governments did not have the authority to decide the moral and religious values of a private organization. The dissenters, however, argued that the states' antidiscrimination statutes should apply to the Boy Scouts, because the literature of the organization did not explicitly indicate that the organization viewed homosexual behavior as inherently immoral.

Eric Howard
Updated by the Editor

FURTHER READING

Abernathy, M. Glenn. *The Right of Assembly and Association.* Columbia: University of South Carolina Press, 1981.

Bresler, Robert J. *Freedom of Association: Rights and Liberties Under the Law.* Santa Barbara, Calif.: ABC-Clio, 2004.

Gutmann, Amy, ed. *Freedom of Association.* Princeton, N.J.: Princeton University Press, 1998.

Murphy, Paul L. *Rights of Assembly, Petition, Arms, and Just Compensation.* New York: Garland, 1990.

Rohde, Stephen F. *Freedom of Assembly.* New York: Facts on File, 2005.

Shiffrin, Steven H., and Jesse H. Choper. *The First Amendment: Cases, Comments, Questions.* St. Paul, Minn.: West Publishing, 1996.

SEE ALSO Bill of Rights; *Boy Scouts of America v. Dale*; *Brandenburg v. Ohio*; *DeJonge v. Oregon*; First Amendment; *Griswold v. Connecticut*; *National Association for the Advancement of Colored People v. Alabama*; States' rights and state sovereignty; Time, place, and manner regulations.

Automobile Searches

DESCRIPTION: The inspection by police and other government agents of the interiors of motor vehicles to look for evidence of unlawful activity.

SIGNIFICANCE: Starting with its 1925 ruling, the Supreme Court made it progressively easier for police and other government agencies to engage lawfully in searches of motor vehicles by interpreting the search and seizure requirements of the Fourth Amendment in a manner that clearly distinguishes the search of a vehicle from that of a residence or a container.

The framers of the Fourth Amendment were concerned about protecting people from unlawful government searches and seizures of their "houses" and "effects" when they drafted the amendment in the late eighteenth century. When the automobile became prominent in U.S. society more than a century later, the Supreme Court had to decide how the words and principles of the Fourth Amendment should be applied to searches of cars and other motor vehicles.

Beginning with its decision in *Carroll v. United States* (1925), the Court has consistently held that where there is probable cause that an automobile contains evidence of a crime, the police may search that vehicle without a search warrant. Unlike houses, automobiles are mobile and therefore the police may not have time to obtain a warrant before the vehicle and any evidence contained within it disappear, the Court reasoned. As the Court applied the warrant requirement of the Fourth Amendment differently to automobiles than to houses, almost inevitably the question arose as to whether the search of a motorhome would be treated as that of a house or an automobile. In *California v. Carney* (1985), the Court held that in most cases, the potential mobility of a motorhome obviates the need for the police to obtain a search warrant.

Searches of effects, such as containers, generally are subject to the same warrant requirement that applies to house searches. The Court was thus confronted with the question of whether to require the police to obtain a warrant before searching a container located in an automobile. In a series of cases culminating in *California v. Acevedo* (1991), the Court held that when the police have probable cause that a container in an automobile contains criminal evidence or that the evidence is located somewhere in the automobile and can fit into the container, they may search the container without obtaining a warrant.

The Court has also authorized police searches of automobiles in situations in which there was no probable cause that there was criminal evidence within the automobile. After lawfully arresting the occupant of a vehicle, the police may search the passenger area of that vehicle, including the glove compartment or items within the passenger area. According to the Court's decision in *New York v. Belton,* (1981), such a search is permissible to prevent the arrested person from grabbing a weapon or disposing of evidence. Additionally, when police properly impound a vehicle, they are allowed to search all parts of the vehicle in order to inventory its contents, as the Court held in *South Dakota v. Opperman* (1976). In *United States v. Di Re* (1999), the Court held that officers who stopped a driver for a traffic violation and saw evidence of drugs were allowed to search everything in the automobile and the private effects of a passenger.

Steven P. Grossman

FURTHER READING

Bloom, Robert M. *Searches, Seizures, and Warrants.* Westport, Conn.: Praeger, 2003.

Dash, Samuel. *The Intruders: Unreasonable Searches and Seizures from King John to John Ashcroft.* New Brunswick, N.J.: Rutgers University Press, 2004.

Hall, John Wesley. *Search and Seizure.* 3d ed. Charlottesville, Va.: LEXIS Law Publishing, 2000.

Quick, Bruce D. *Law of Arrest, Search, and Seizure: An Examination of the Fourth, Fifth, and Sixth Amendments to the United States Constitution.* Rev. ed. Bismarck, N.D.: Attorney General's Office, Criminal Justice Training and Statistics Division, 1987.

Regini, Lisa A. "The Motor Vehicle Exception: When and Where to Search." *FBI Law Enforcement Bulletin* 68, no. 7 (July, 1999): 26-32.

Savage, David G. "Privacy Rights Pulled Over: Cops Get More Power to Search Personal Effects in Vehicles." *American Bar Association Journal* 85 (June, 1999): 42-44.

Stephens, Otis H., and Richard A. Glenn. *Unreasonable Searches and Seizures: Rights and Liberties Under the Law.* Santa Barbara, Calif.: ABC-Clio, 2004.

SEE ALSO Exclusionary rule; Fourth Amendment; *Hudson v. Michigan*; Police powers; Privacy, right to; Search warrant requirement; States' rights and state sovereignty; *Whren v. United States.*

Bad Tendency Test

DESCRIPTION: A test first applied by the Supreme Court in 1919 according to which speech that had a "tendency" to incite unlawful acts was not constitutionally protected.

SIGNIFICANCE: Throughout much of the twentieth century, the Court used the bad tendency test broadly to restrict speech critical of the U.S. government or its policies.

Although usually associated with *Debs v. United States* (1919), the bad tendency test actually has its genesis in *Schenck v. United States* (1919). In that case, the Supreme Court decided that Charles Schenck, a leader of the Socialist party, was guilty of a conspiracy to violate the 1917 Espionage Act by distributing flyers denouncing the draft. As part of the opinion in *Schenck*, Justice Oliver Wendell Holmes made it clear that not all speech can or should be protected, by invoking the now-famous example of a person yelling "fire" in a crowded theater. Drawing the line between protected and unprotected speech, however, has proven difficult. In *Schenck*, the Court established the following test for determining whether speech should be protected:

> The question in every case is whether the words used are used in such circumstances and are of such a nature as to create a clear and present danger that they will bring about substantive evils that Congress has a right to prevent.

As applied, this test was far less protective of free speech than the term "clear and present danger" might suggest. No showing of present danger was required in *Schenck* or subsequent cases. The Court held that if the "tendency and intent" of the speech was to encourage illegal action, then the speech was not protected by the First Amendment. Furthermore, the Court was often willing to *assume* a bad tendency and intent if the speech was critical of the government or its policies. The bad tendency test was notoriously applied just weeks after *Schenck* in *Debs v. United States*, when the perennial presidential candidate Eugene Debs was convicted of conspiracy for telling a crowd that he was sympathetic toward those who were trying to obstruct the draft. He was sentenced to ten years in prison for the crime.

Almost immediately, the test came under fire, with Justice Holmes dissenting against the test's application in *Abrams v. United States* (1919). His was a lone voice, however, and the bad tendency test continued to be applied. For example, in *Gitlow v. New York* (1925), *Whitney v. California* (1927), and *Dennis v. United States* (1951), members of either the Socialist or Communist Parties were convicted of breaking the law because they were found to have advocated illegal action by distributing flyers or assembling in groups.

Although the Court employed various First Amendment tests after *Debs*, it did not begin to seriously move away from the substance of the bad tendency test until *Yates v. United States* in 1957. In *Yates*, the Court reversed the conspiracy convictions of fourteen "second-string" Communist Party officials, drawing a line between advocacy of an abstract principle and advocacy of action. Even so, it was not until 1969, in *Brandenburg v. Ohio*, that the Court finally abandoned the bad tendency test completely and developed the modern, highly protective standard for freedom of speech.

Evan Gerstmann
Christopher Shortell

FURTHER READING

Chafee, Zechariah, Jr. *Free Speech in the United States.* Cambridge, Mass.: Harvard University Press, 1941.

Downs, Donald. *Nazis in Skokie.* Notre Dame, Ind.: University of Notre Dame Press, 1985.

Greenawalt, Kent. *Speech, Crime and the Uses of Language.* New York: Oxford University Press, 1989.

Kersch, Ken I. *Freedom of Speech: Rights and Liberties Under the Law.* Santa Barbara, Calif.: ABC-Clio, 2003.

SEE ALSO *Brandenburg v. Ohio;* Espionage acts; *Gitlow v. New York;* Holmes, Oliver Wendell; *Schenck v. United States.*

Bail

DESCRIPTION: Money posted by persons accused of crimes as security for their appearance at trial. The U.S. Constitution offers guarantees against excessive bail, which were interpreted and generally upheld by the Supreme Court.

SIGNIFICANCE: Because of the unfairness of subjecting an unconvicted person to a long, indefinite period of imprisonment, the Court has attempted to ensure that the accused is not unreasonably detained. Denial of bail or excessive bail is also thought to be an unreasonable impediment of the accused person's right to prepare a defense.

The use of bail has been a part of the Anglo-American criminal justice system since the English Bill of Rights of 1689 gave protections against excessive bail. The founders of the American republic counted the right to a just bail among the essential liberties. The Eighth Amendment to the U.S. Constitution guarantees that "excessive bail shall not be required." A stronger expression of the contemporary feeling about bail is found in the Northwest Ordinance of 1787, which declared that "all persons shall be bailable, unless for capital offenses, where the proof shall be evident, or the presumption great."

In 1895 the Supreme Court first affirmed the importance of a right to reasonable bail in *Hudson v. Parker*. Writing for the majority, Justice Horace Gray noted that a key principle of the U.S. justice system was "the theory that a person accused of a crime shall not, until he has been finally adjudged guilty . . . be absolutely compelled to undergo imprisonment or punishment." However, an earlier decision, *McKane v. Durston* (1894), limited the scope of this decision by ruling that the Eighth Amendment's bail provision did not apply to state courts.

The Court in *Stack v. Boyle* (1951), a case involving twelve Communist Party leaders accused of conspiracy, was concerned that excessive bail hampered the accused's right to a vigorous defense. The Court held that "the traditional right to freedom before conviction permits the unhampered preparation of a defense. Unless the right to bail is preserved, the presumption of innocence, secured after centuries of struggle, would lose its meaning." The Court determined that the purpose of bail is to "serve . . . as assurance of the presence of an accused. Bail set at a figure higher than an amount reasonably calculated to fulfill this purpose is excessive under the Eighth Amendment." However, the next year, in *Carlson v. Landon* (1952), the Court in a 5-4 vote found that not all detentions were subject to bail, and Congress had the power to define cases in which bail was not allowed. The *Carlson* case was a civil case involving the detention of aliens before a deportation hearing.

PREVENTIVE DETENTION

Traditionally, the sole justification for jailing an accused but otherwise presumed innocent person before trial was to assure that the individual did not flee. It was generally not believed to be proper to deprive people of their liberty on the grounds that they may commit future crimes when they have not been convicted of a crime. The constitutional protection of the rights of the accused person has clashed in recent years with the desire by federal authorities to "preventively detain" persons accused of federal crimes to prevent them from engaging in criminal activities. One concern is the fear that members of criminal organizations freed on bail might harass and intimidate witnesses, thereby corrupting the judicial process.

The rise of international terrorism and drug trafficking led Congress to pass the Bail Reform Act of 1984, which allows a federal judge to consider preventive detention of a person accused of a federal crime if he or she finds that "no conditions or combination of conditions will reasonably assure the appearance of the [defendant] as required and the safety of any person before trial." The act allows a federal prosecutor to ask a judge to hold a defendant without bail indefinitely if the prosecutor can make a showing that the person poses a threat to others.

THE ACT EXAMINED

The constitutionality of the Bail Reform Act was determined by the Court in *United States v. Salerno* (1987). *Salerno* involved two defendants indicted for racketeering and denied bail under the provisions of the act. One of the accused was alleged by prosecutors to be the "boss" of the Genovese crime family and the other a high-ranked "captain." The crimes included several counts of extortion and conspiracy to murder. The Court examined whether the bail reforms violated the defendant's constitutional right to be free from excessive bail, but it rejected the claim that *Stack* applied to the case. Limiting the scope of *Stack*, the Court found that the right to bail had never been considered absolute and that persons accused of capital crimes and at risk of flight had long been subject to bail restrictions and upheld the act. The Court noted that although "in our society liberty is the norm, and detention prior to trial or without trial is the carefully limited exception," the Bail Reform Act fell "within that carefully limited exception." The Court determined that the "numerous procedural safeguards" adequately protected against abuse of the act.

Kurt X. Metzmeier

FURTHER READING

Duker, William F. "The Right to Bail: A Historical Inquiry." *Albany Law Review* 42 (1977): 33-120.

Goldkamp, John S. "Danger and Detention: A Second Generation of Bail Reform." *Journal of Criminal Law and Criminology* 76 (Spring, 1985): 1-74.

Metzmeier, Kurt X. "Preventive Detention: A Comparison of Bail Refusal Practices in the United States, England, Canada, and Other Common Law Nations." *Pace International Law Review* 7 (Spring, 1996): 399-438.

Singer, Richard G. *Criminal Procedure II: From Bail to Jail.* New York: Aspen, 2005.

SEE ALSO Bill of Rights; Counsel, right to; Eighth Amendment; Gray, Horace.

Baker v. Carr

CITATION: 369 U.S. 186
DATE: March 26, 1962
ISSUE: Reapportionment
SIGNIFICANCE: The Supreme Court ruled for the first time that legislative malapportionment was not a political question but an issue that could be considered by the courts.

Justice William J. Brennan, Jr., wrote the 6-2 majority opinion in this landmark case, ignoring warnings from Justices Felix Frankfurter and John Marshall Harlan II that the Supreme Court was entering a political thicket with this decision. The Court overturned *Colegrove v. Green* (1946) and ruled that the federal courts had jurisdiction to hear legislative reapportionment cases regarding states such as Tennessee, which had not reapportioned its legislative seats in more than sixty years.

Baker did not actually reapportion any districts, nor did it set forth standards for states to follow. The one person, one vote principle, not enunciated until *Gray v. Sanders* (1963), was not applied to congressional redistricting until *Wesberry v. Sanders* (1964) nor applied to all legislative houses including the state senates until *Reynolds v. Sims* (1964). These cases opened the door to a flood of litigation over the next two decades as citizens in urban areas filed suit to force rural-dominated legislatures to reapportion themselves.

The long-term impact of this decision was to correct a situation that apparently could not be corrected by the ordinary political process. As more Americans moved to urban areas, rural areas became underpopulated and overrepresented in state legislatures. In most states, rural domination was so great that the legislature had a majority of rural representatives who blocked any realistic chances of reapportioning their states. Because state legislatures also draw congressional district lines, this malapportionment extended to the national level. Reapportionment had historically been regarded as a political question beyond the reach of the federal courts, but this decision reversed that legal standard.

Richard L. Wilson

FURTHER READING

Hasen, Richard L. *The Supreme Court and Election Law Judging Equality from "Baker v. Carr" to "Bush v. Gore."* New York: New York University Press, 2003.

SEE ALSO Brennan, William J., Jr.; *Bush v. Gore*; Clark, Tom C.; Gerrymandering; Guarantee clause; Political questions; Representation, fairness of; *Reynolds v. Sims*; Warren, Earl.

Henry Baldwin

IDENTIFICATION: Associate justice (January 11, 1830-April 21, 1844)
NOMINATED BY: Andrew Jackson
BORN: January 14, 1780, New Haven, Connecticut
DIED: April 21, 1844, Philadelphia, Pennsylvania
SIGNIFICANCE: As a justice, Baldwin supported states' rights and viewed slaves as property, without civil rights.

After receiving a Doctor of Laws degree from Yale University in 1797, Henry Baldwin studied under Alexander J. Dallas in Philadelphia and was admitted to the bar. He then headed west to Ohio, getting only as far as Pittsburgh, where he settled, becoming a distinguished citizen. People there considered him intelligent, energetic, and witty.

In 1805 he moved to Crawford County in northwestern Pennsylvania, where he ran for Congress and, in 1817, became a member of the U.S. House of Representatives. He supported high tariffs and dis-

Henry Baldwin. (Max Rosenthal/Collection of the Supreme Court of the United States)

agreed vehemently with rural Jeffersonians. Suffering from ill health, Baldwin resigned from the House in 1822.

By 1828 his health had improved, and he served as adviser to Andrew Jackson, subsequently elected president and, in 1829, inaugurated for the first of his two terms. Jackson rewarded Baldwin's support when the death of Bushrod Washington created a vacancy on the Supreme Court. Jackson passed over several promising jurists to nominate Baldwin, who was easily confirmed.

Baldwin recounted his philosophical outlook as a justice in *A General View of the Origin and Nature of the Constitution and Government of the United States* (1837). In this booklet, he portrayed himself as moderate. He was a notable dissident in Chief Justice John Marshall's Court. Baldwin supported states' rights, favoring interstate commerce unfettered by federal regulation. Although he voted with pronorthern justices on matters involving slavery, he nevertheless viewed slaves as property lacking the civil rights of America's white citizens. In cases that tested the right of the federal government to overrule the sovereignty of individual states, he consistently supported the rights of states to make and enforce their own laws. This attitude explains in part his stand regarding the ownership of slaves.

Baldwin's spirited dissent in *Ex parte Crane* (1831) objected to strengthening the power of federal courts to issue writs of *mandamus*, orders issued by superior courts to lower courts. He was convinced that the Court, through judicial and political sensitivity, could determine which powers belonged to the individual states and which to the federal government.

As he aged, Baldwin became increasingly irascible, often disturbing the much-heralded equanimity of the Marshall Court. In 1831 Baldwin dissented in seven cases, a record unparalleled in the Marshall Court. Baldwin's eccentricity eventually became an embarrassment. He sometimes resorted to violent behavior, presumably stemming from an obsessive-compulsive disorder. Plagued for years by financial difficulties, Baldwin died in 1844, penniless and paralyzed, in Philadelphia.

R. Baird Shuman

FURTHER READING

Abraham, Henry Julian. *Justices and Presidents: A Political History of Appointments to the Supreme Court.* 4th ed. New York: Oxford University Press, 1999.

Bader, William H., and Roy M. Mersky, eds. *The First One Hundred Eight Justices.* Buffalo, N.Y.: William S. Hein, 2004.

Clinton, Robert, Christopher Budzisz, and Peter Renstrom, eds. *The Marshall Court: Justices, Rulings, and Legacy.* Santa Barbara, Calif.: ABC-Clio, 2007.

Huebner, Timothy S. *The Taney Court: Justices, Rulings, and Legacy.* Santa Barbara, Calif.: ABC-Clio, 2003.

Wagman, Robert J. *The Supreme Court: A Citizen's Guide.* New York: Pharos Books, 1993.

SEE ALSO Grier, Robert C.; Marshall, John; Separation of powers; States' rights and state sovereignty; Washington, Bushrod.

Bankruptcy Law

DESCRIPTION: Federal statutes that allow consumers and businesses unable to meet their financial obligations to discharge their debts and start over economically. Article I, section 8, clause 4, of the U.S. Constitution (1789) stipulates that Congress shall establish "uniform Laws on the subject of Bankruptcies throughout the United States."

SIGNIFICANCE: The Supreme Court hears appeals on issues that began in bankruptcy courts and applies bankruptcy court rules.

Business and personal finance is beset with a degree of unpredictability. Under capitalism, private individuals, public institutions, small businesses, partnerships, and major corporations sometimes face changes in the marketplace, technology, and consumer preferences that decrease income and profits, creating financial crises. Congress, in response to economic downturns, increasingly complex commercial transactions, expanding credit, and a larger number of entrepreneurships, produced major bankruptcy legislation in 1800, 1841, 1867, and 1898.

A 1970 joint resolution of Congress created the Bankruptcy Commission, with members appointed by the president, chief justice, and Congress. In 1978 Congress passed the Bankruptcy Reform Act, which, with subsequent amendments, created laws that balanced creditor and debtor interests. The nine chapters in the code occupy nearly five hundred pages in *Bankruptcy Code, Rules, and Forms* (St. Paul, Minn.: West Publishing, 1999), and the ten chapters on rules fill nearly three hundred pages. After its passage, more than sixty bankruptcy cases have been decided by the Supreme Court.

Bankruptcy court, district court, bankruptcy appellate panel, and court of appeals judges may differ in their interpretations of legislative history, legislation, rules, and the plain meaning of the text. Some court watchers believe sufficient scope exists for judges to engage in policy making while ostensibly interpreting the text of bankruptcy laws. Most bankruptcy cases reach the Supreme Court because of conflicting results on substantially identical facts reached by the various courts of appeals. The Court, seeking uniformity within the federal system, usually makes narrow decisions.

The constitutionality of the 1978 bankruptcy laws was raised in *Northern Pipeline Construction Co. v. Marathon Pipe Line Co.* (1982). Before 1978, the bankruptcy court employed semijudicial referees. The 1978 code created Article I nontenured judges, whose salaries could be reduced and who served for renewable fourteen-year terms but gave them Article III powers, which the Court held unconstitutional.

DEFINITIONS AND PROCEDURES

Bankruptcy legislation, particularly chapter 11, has historically been concerned with businesses and corporations. In the twentieth century, personal consumer bankruptcies, chapter 7 and 13, became far more numerous than business cases. The Court in *Local Loan Co. v. Hunt* (1933) stated that honest debtors should have "a new opportunity in life and a clear field for future effort." *Toibb v. Radloff* (1991) and *Johnson v. Home State Bank* (1991) expanded bankruptcy relief. In the 1990's the Court chipped away at the debtor-favorable 1978 bankruptcy laws and began to favor creditors, a trend paralleled by various legislative changes.

Grogan v. Garner (1991) established a preponderance of the evidence test for determining fraud rather than a clear and convincing evidence test, an issue visited again in *Field v. Mans* (1995). *Union Bank v. Wolas* (1991) reiterated the plain language approach to interpreting statutes. Although "willful and malicious injury" is not dischargeable, the court in *Kawaauhau v. Geiger* (1998) distinguished between intentional and reckless torts. Deadlines, like statutes of limitation, are very important. *Barnhill v. Johnson* (1992) set the standard for computing a ninety-day period on the writing of a check, *Taylor v. Freeland and Kronz* (1992) dealt with trustee objections to exemptions, and *Pioneer Investment Services Co. v. Brunswick Associates Ltd. Partnership* (1993) dealt with deadlines for filing proofs of claim.

PROPERTY

The bankrupt debtor generally does not pay more for property than it is worth. Creditors dislike this and assert that mortgages in real estate should be treated differently than liens on cars, equipment, jewelry, and other consumer items. Lien stripping was the subject of *Dewsnup v. Timm* (1992) and *Nobelman v. American Savings Bank* (1993). *BFP v. Resolution Trust Corp.* (1994) established that when a property is sold at a noncollusive sale, such as an auction, it is presumed to satisfy the requirement of "reasonably equivalent value." Even if it sells for much less than its appraisal, the sale is not a fraudulent conveyance (transfer of ownership of property). In *Associates Commercial Corp. v. Rash* (1997), the Court in distinguishing between retail and wholesale value of property, settled on replacement value. Secured claims, debts with collateral, are to be paid interest (adequate protection) according to *United Savings Association of Texas v. Timbers of Inwood Forest Associates* (1988), *United States v. Ron Pair Enterprises* (1989), and *Rake v. Wade* (1993).

In *United States v. Whiting Pools* (1983), the Court held that property seized by the Internal Revenue Service before the bankruptcy filing was property of the estate, and in *Patterson v. Shumate* (1992) it determined that Employee Retirement Income Security Act-qualified pension funds were not property of the estate.

OTHER ISSUES

The federal system, the balance between state and federal government, increasingly protects governments from being sued without their permission. *Hoffman v. Connecticut Department of Income Maintenance* (1989), *United States v. Nordic Village* (1992), and *Seminole Tribe v. Florida* (1996) expanded the immunity and authority of governments and limited the ability of debtors and the trustees to bring government agencies into the bankruptcy. The trend in sovereign immunity cases appears to detract from the bankruptcy court status as a national forum for debt resolution.

The wide range of Court decisions indicates the pervasiveness of economic issues and the bankruptcy court's role in American economic life. The Court has made decisions regarding taxes, transportation and common carriers, the absolute priority rule (an important creditor protection in devising chapter 11 reorganization plans), and family law regarding property settlements in divorces.

Public and legislative dissatisfaction with Court decisions may result in corrective legislation. In *Pennsylvania Department of Public Welfare v. Davenport* (1990), the Court held that criminal restitution could be discharged (and therefore, not paid), and Congress passed the Violent Crime Control and Law Enforcement Act of 1994, making restitution nondischargeable. When *Christians v. Crystal Evangelical Church* (1997) threatened religious liberty and tithing, Congress passed the Religious Liberty and Charitable Donation Protection Act of 1998.

Before 2005, individual retirement accounts (IRAs) were not usually classified as pension plans. They were therefore not exempt from bankruptcy estates. In the highly publicized 2005 case of *Rousey v. Jacoway*, however, the Supreme Court unanimously held that because IRAs were contracts conferring "a right to receive payment on account of age," they were exempt from bankruptcy whenever the assets were "reasonably necessary for the support of the debtor and any dependent." Although the decision was greeted with enthusiasm in many places, it turned out to have almost no practical impact. This was because a few weeks after the Court issued the ruling, Congress enacted the Bankruptcy Abuse Prevention and Consumer Protection Act (BAPCA), which among its many provisions, exempted most IRAs and other retirement funds from bankruptcy estates.

In *Central Virginia Community College v. Katz* (2006), the Supreme Court examined the relationship between federal bankruptcy law and the states' right to sovereign immunity, which is the privilege of a state not to be sued without its consent. The case involved a court-appointed supervisor of a bankrupt estate who filed a federal lawsuit to collect debts from a tax-supported college (an "arm of the state"). Virginia forcefully affirmed that the suit violated its sovereign immunity. The Court responded in a 5-4 decision that states have no right to sovereign immunity in bankruptcy cases. Speaking for the majority, Justice John Paul Stevens observed that Article I of the Constitution explicitly empowers Congress to enact bankruptcy legislation, and from this he reasoned that ratification of Article I implies the state's consent to abrogate sovereignty in this sphere of the law. *Katz* represents the Court's only decision that has ever allowed Congress to use its Article I powers to authorize persons to sue the states.

Oliver B. Pollak
Updated by the Editor

FURTHER READING

Epstein, David G., et al. *Bankruptcy: Twenty First Century Debtor-Creditor Law.* St. Paul, Minn.: Thomson/West, 2005.

Frey, Martin, Phyllis Frey, and Sidney Swinson. *An Introduction to Bankruptcy Law.* 5th ed. Clifton Park, N.Y.: Thomson/Delmar, 2004.

Gross, Karen. *Failure and Forgiveness, Rebalancing the Bankruptcy System.* New Haven, Conn.: Yale University Press, 1997.

Skeel, David. *Debt's Dominion: A History of Bankruptcy Law in America.* Princeton, N.J.: Princeton University Press, 2003.

SEE ALSO Contracts clause; Douglas, William O.; Eleventh Amendment; Trimble, Robert.

Philip P. Barbour

IDENTIFICATION: Associate justice (May 12, 1836-February 25, 1841)

NOMINATED BY: Andrew Jackson

BORN: May 25, 1783, Barboursville, Virginia

DIED: February 25, 1841, Washington, D.C.

SIGNIFICANCE: During his five years on the Supreme Court, Barbour supported states' rights over the authority of the federal government.

Philip P. Barbour began practicing law in 1802. He was elected to Congress in 1814, where he served as Speaker of the House from 1821 to 1823. In *Cohens v. Virginia* (1821), he unsuccessfully argued before the Supreme Court that a defendant had no right of appeal from a state court to a federal court. He left Congress in 1825, served as a state judge, then returned to Congress in 1827. In 1829 he unsuccessfully introduced a bill requiring five out of seven Supreme Court justices to agree in constitutional cases. In 1830 he was appointed a federal judge by President Andrew Jackson.

Philip P. Barbour. (George Healy/Collection of the Supreme Court of the United States)

Jackson nominated Barbour to the Court on December 28, 1835. He was confirmed by the Senate on March 15, 1836, and took the oath of office on May 12. During his relatively brief career on the Court, he usually agreed with the majority as it turned away from supporting the power of the federal government over the states. In *New York v. Miln* (1837), a case involving the power of a state over ships entering harbors from other states or nations, he wrote that "the authority of a state is complete, unqualified and exclusive." His few dissents from the majority came in cases that involved restrictions of states' rights.

Rose Secrest

SEE ALSO Appellate jurisdiction; Review, process of; States' rights and state sovereignty; Taney, Roger Brooke.

Barnes v. Glen Theatre

CITATION: 501 U.S. 560
DATE: June 21, 1991
ISSUE: Expressive conduct
SIGNIFICANCE: While reaffirming that nude dancing is expressive conduct protected by the First Amendment, the Supreme Court nevertheless upheld a state's general ban on complete nudity in public places.

In *Schad v. Borough of Mount Ephraim* (1981), the Supreme Court held that nonobscene nude dancing was a protected form of expression that could not be entirely prohibited throughout an entire community. Indiana's public decency statute prohibited complete nudity in all public places. Two adult-entertainment establishments in South Bend, Indiana, wanted to feature "totally nude dancing," but the decency statute required that the dancers wear pasties and G-strings.

Although the Court upheld the law by a 5-4 majority, Chief Justice William H. Rehnquist spoke for a plurality when he argued that the law was not expressly designed to prevent erotic expression and that the law only placed an incidental limitation on expression. The statute, he wrote, was essentially a time, place, and manner regulation, in keeping with the test set forth in *United States v. O'Brien* (1968). Observing that nudity had historically been proscribed by common law, he concluded that a ban on nudity furthered the state's substantial interest in protecting public morality and public order. In a concurrence, Justice David H. Souter argued that the law legitimately prevented secondary effects of nude dancing, such as prostitution.

Justice Byron R. White's dissent argued that the very purpose of the law was to prohibit the expression of a nonobscene erotic message; therefore, the law should be scrutinized with the compelling state interest test.

Thomas Tandy Lewis

SEE ALSO Obscenity and pornography; Rehnquist, William H.; Speech and press, freedom of; Vietnam War; White, Byron R.

Barron v. Baltimore

CITATION: 32 U.S. 243
DATE: February 16, 1833
ISSUES: Incorporation doctrine; property rights
SIGNIFICANCE: The Supreme Court held that the Bill of Rights did not protect citizens from actions by their state governments, a ruling that stood largely unaltered until the 1920's.

The First Amendment begins with the word "Congress," apparently making the federal government its only target, but none of the other amendments in the Bill of Rights include this language. John Barron, a Baltimore businessperson, sought to test the possibility that the Fifth Amendment in the Bill of Rights might protect him from actions of the Maryland state government.

The city of Baltimore repaired the streets and dumped the leftover construction materials into the water near the wharf Barron owned, raising the bottom of the bay so much that ships could no longer dock there, depriving Barron of his property interest in his livelihood without due process or just compensation. Barron sued Baltimore to recover damages, but Baltimore was a subunit of Maryland, whose constitution, unlike the U.S. Constitution, did not provide a guarantee against eminent domain.

Because Barron could not succeed in Maryland courts, he turned to the federal courts. However, the Supreme Court ruled that the Fifth Amendment applied only to the federal government and not to the states and that therefore Barron was not entitled to protection against state action under this amendment. After *Barron*, the courts applied this ruling consistently. Although the passage of the Fourteenth Amendment would seem to have reversed this decision, the Court did not initially agree, essentially continuing *Barron* in force until justices holding different views began to serve on the Court in the 1920's. Gradually, the incorporation doctrine effectively overturned the principles set out in *Barron*.

Richard L. Wilson

SEE ALSO Bill of Rights; Double jeopardy; Due process, procedural, Due process, substantive; Federalism; Incorporation doctrine; *Kelo v. City of New London*; Marshall, John; Takings clause.

Batson v. Kentucky

CITATION: 476 U.S. 79
DATE: April 30, 1986
ISSUE: Jury composition
SIGNIFICANCE: The Supreme Court ruled that the equal protection clause of the Fourteenth Amendment forbids a prosecutor from using peremptory challenges to remove potential jurors because of their race.

James Batson, an African American, was indicted for second-degree burglary. When the judge conducted a *voir dire* examination (preliminary check of suitability and qualifications) of the potential jurors, the prosecutor used his peremptory challenges to remove all four African Americans from the panel, resulting in an all-white jury. The Supreme Court had refused to disturb the same development in

Swain v. Alabama (1965). After Batson's conviction, nevertheless, his lawyers asserted that the process of jury selection violated his rights to equal protection and to a jury drawn from a cross section of the community.

By a 7-2 majority, the Court accepted Batson's claim. Speaking for the majority, Justice Lewis F. Powell, Jr., remanded the case and instructed the trial court to require the prosecutor to justify the exclusion of members of the defendant's race from the jury. If the prosecutor were unable to give a racially neutral explanation, Batson's conviction would have to be reversed. Powell's opinion formulated a framework for future *voir dire* proceedings. The basic idea is that a pattern of exclusion based on race creates an inference of discrimination. Once such an inference is established, the prosecutor has the burden of showing that the peremptories are not discriminatory. Emphasizing that the Constitution does not guarantee a right to peremptory challenges, Powell wrote that potential jurors may not be eliminated simply because of the assumption that people of a particular race might be more sympathetic to a particular defendant. Thus, Powell's opinion requires color-conscious rather than color-blind procedures in jury selection, and it tends to encourage the use of racial quotas.

The *Batson* principles have been significantly expanded. In *Powers v. Ohio* (1991), the Court held that criminal defendants may object to race-based peremptory challenges even if the defendant and the excluded jurors do not belong to the same race. Later that year, in *Edmondson v. Leesville Concrete Co.*, the Court applied the *Batson* framework to the selection of juries in civil trials. In *Georgia v. McCollum* (1992), the Court decided that the *Batson* ruling applies to defense attorneys. In *J. E. B. v. Alabama* (1994), moreover, the Court held that the equal protection clause prohibits discrimination in jury selection on the basis of gender.

Thomas Tandy Lewis

SEE ALSO Due process, substantive; Fourteenth Amendment; Gender issues; Jury, trial by; Powell, Lewis F., Jr.; Race and discrimination.

Bill of Attainder

DESCRIPTION: Any law that punishes a person or group without a trial.
SIGNIFICANCE: The U.S. Constitution prohibits Congress from passing bills of attainder. The Supreme Court determined that Congress was also barred from passing bills of pains and penalties,
which convey punishments short of death for seditious acts.

Bills of attainder, along with bills of pains and penalties, were employed by the British Parliament in the sixteenth and seventeenth
centuries. A bill of attainder condemned people to death without
due process and often denied their heirs the right to inherit any
properties they owned. A bill of pain and penalties sentenced people
to punishments short of the death penalty, such as banishment or seizure of their possessions, again without a trial. During the American
Revolution, some states passed bills of attainder or bills of pains and
penalties against people disloyal to the American cause.

Many of the Framers of the U.S. Constitution found bills of attainder objectionable, because they viewed it to be the role of the courts,
judging individual cases, rather than the legislature, to determine
punishment. James Madison, in *The Federalist* (1788) No. 44, found
bills of attainder to be "contrary to the first principles of the social
compact." Article I, section 9, clause 3, of the U.S. Constitution prohibits the federal government from passing bills of attainder. Article I, section 10, clause 1, prohibits the states from doing the same.
The Supreme Court interpreted these clauses as covering bills of
pains and penalties as well and grouped the two under the term "bill
of attainder." In modern usage, bills of attainder refer to legislative
acts that punish a person or group without a trial.

In *Calder v. Bull* (1798), the Court stated that the prohibition
against ex post facto laws (such as bills of attainder) dealt only with
civil and not criminal cases. Given the due process clause and the Bill
of Rights, the distinction between civil and criminal law is not applicable to modern jurisprudence. However, the Court's early interpretation was not an uncommon sentiment among the Founders.

In the twentieth century, attainder became an issue in cases in
which legislation was passed to impose punishment of any kind on in-

dividuals or members of specific groups rather than to regulate for a legitimate purpose. Legislators must scrutinize bills carefully to avoid legislation being found a bill of attainder. For example, the Court held, in *United States v. Lovett* (1946), that appropriation bills cannot speak of denying funds to "subversives" because such a designation reflects punishment through an ex post facto conviction and is a denial of due process. Attainder violates due process because it predetermines guilt. In *Beazell v. Ohio* (1925), the court stated that statutory ex post facto changes in trial procedures or the application of the legal rules are a violation of due process and constitutional violation.

In *United States v. Brown* (1965), the Court invalidated a federal statute banning Communist Party members from becoming officers in a union in order to minimize the danger of politically motivated strikes that would possibly harm the national economy. The Court found the law a bill of attainder and therefore in violation of the Constitution. It argued that the determination of whether a specific person's activities were dangerous conduct was to be made by the judiciary, not by Congress. In making the law, the Court said, Congress erred by attributing the undesirable trait (likelihood to cause a political strike) to members of a specific group, the Communist Party. The Court ruled that the bill of attainder clause was intended as a "safeguard against legislative exercise of the judicial function or more simply—trial by legislature."

Arthur K. Steinberg

FURTHER READING

Abraham, Henry Julian, and Barbara A. Perry. *Freedom and the Court: Civil Rights and Liberties in the United States.* 8th ed. Lawrence: University Press of Kansas, 2003.

Chaffee, Zechariah. *Three Human Rights in the Constitution of 1787.* Lawrence: University of Kansas Press, 1956.

Galligan, Denis J. *Due Process and Fair Procedures: A Study of Administrative Procedures.* New York: Oxford University Press, 1996.

Lee, Francis Graham. *Equal Protection: Rights and Liberties Under the Law.* Santa Barbara, Calif.: ABC-Clio, 2003.

Melusky, Joseph A., and Keith A. Pesto. *Cruel and Unusual Punishment: Rights and Liberties Under the Law.* Santa Barbara, Calif.: ABC-Clio, 2003.

Perry, Richard L., ed. *Sources of Our Liberties: Documentary Origins of Individual Liberties in the United States Constitution and Bill of Rights.* New York: Associated College Presses, 1959.

SEE ALSO *Calder v. Bull;* Due process, procedural; Jury, trial by; Separation of powers; War and civil liberties; World War II.

Bill of Rights

DATE: 1791

DESCRIPTION: First ten amendments to the U.S. Constitution, guaranteeing individual rights, such as freedom of speech, freedom of the press, separation of church and state, the right to counsel, the right against self-incrimination, and due process.

SIGNIFICANCE: The Bill of Rights has posed an endless series of challenges for the Supreme Court to interpret the scope of personal liberties and the limits of government power.

When the Constitutional Convention adjourned in September, 1787, and submitted its new Constitution to a curious public, three of the remaining delegates refused to sign the new charter. One, George Mason of Virginia, declared that he would "sooner chop off this right hand than put it to a constitution without a Bill of Rights." Fearing that Mason and other Antifederalists might scuttle the ratification of the new Constitution, James Madison promised his fellow Virginians that if they supported the new charter (and elected him to the First Congress), he would sponsor a Bill of Rights. Each side kept its end of the bargain.

In December, 1791, the Bill of Rights was ratified, launching more than two hundred years of Supreme Court decisions interpreting, defining, and refining the nature of the relationship between the government and its citizens.

The Constitution was essentially a plan of government, establishing the legislative, executive, and federal branches and delineating their powers and responsibilities. Although the Constitution purported to grant only limited powers to Congress to pass laws in specified areas, it also provided that Congress had the authority to "make all Laws which shall be necessary and proper for carrying into Execution the foregoing Powers, and all other Powers vested by this Constitution in the Government of the United States, or in any Department or Officer thereof." This elastic catch-all clause worried those who feared that the Constitution would install an all-powerful national government, free to dominate the people and the states. It was the Bill of Rights that gave these critics some measure of solace that the new federal government would not become the same tyrannical seat of power that they had so recently fought to escape.

From the outset, the Supreme Court played a special role in giving meaning to the Bill of Rights. In March of 1789, Thomas Jefferson wrote to Madison that "the Bill of Rights is necessary because of the legal check which it puts into the hands of the judiciary." Jefferson was referring to a "legal check" on unwarranted government interference with the rights of the citizens.

The Bill of Rights touches on every realm of human affairs. It has fallen to the Supreme Court to interpret its elusive and elastic language. In every generation, the Court has been called on to grapple with the challenge of applying its 413 words, written in the late eighteenth century, to circumstances unknown to the authors, arising in the nineteenth, twentieth, and twenty-first centuries. The Bill of Rights protects both substantive and procedural rights. In contrast to the Constitution itself, which says what the government *can* do, the Bill of Rights says what the government *cannot* do.

FIRST AMENDMENT

The most powerful articulation of individual rights against government intrusion is found in the First Amendment, which is considered by many to be the most important of all the Amendments. The opening words speak volumes about the purpose and intent of the Bill of Rights: "Congress shall make no law. . . ." These five words set the tone for all that follows. However, the simplicity is deceiving and the Supreme Court has the responsibility of deciding which laws pass constitutional muster and which do not.

Specifically, under the First Amendment, Congress is prohibited from making laws "respecting an establishment of religion or prohib-

Currier and Ives print depicting the signing of the Declaration of Independence in 1776. (Library of Congress)

iting the free exercise thereof." In one phrase, the First Amendment simultaneously guarantees the right of individuals to follow the beliefs and practices of their chosen religious faiths, while at the same time, it prohibits the government from singling out any particular religious denomination as a state-sponsored church. The First Amendment built what Jefferson called a "wall of separation" between church and state.

The free exercise and establishment clauses generated great consternation for the Court on controversial issues. From prayer in school to religious symbols on public property, from religious invocations at high school graduations to vouchers using public funds to subsidize parochial schools, the Court struggled to ensure that government remains neutral, but not hostile, in matters of religion.

The First Amendment next prohibits Congress from "abridging the freedom of speech, or of the press, or the right of the people peaceably to assemble, and to petition the Government for a redress of grievances." No portion of the Bill of Rights has engaged the Court's attention with more intensity, drama, and public interest than its protection of freedom of expression and freedom of assembly. Volumes have been written about how and why the Court decided whether particular speech or gatherings are constitutionally protected.

No majority of Supreme Court justices ever treated the protections guaranteed by the First Amendment as absolute. Instead, the Court recognized exceptions for obscenity, libel, criminal solicitation, perjury, false advertising, and fighting words. Within and beyond these categories, the Court has shifted, especially in times of war or during external threats, from the protection of wide-open, robust debate to the punishment of controversial ideas.

SECOND AMENDMENT

The Second Amendment has been controversial; however, it was addressed by the Court only on rare occasions. It is popularly known for guaranteeing "the right of the people to keep and bear arms." However, in its most significant pronouncement, the Court unanimously held that this right is qualified by the opening phrase which reads: "A well regulated Militia, being necessary to the security of a free State. . . ." In the light of that limitation, most recently the Court declined to hear an appeal from a lower court ruling upholding a municipal ban on hand guns.

THIRD AMENDMENT

The Third Amendment, prohibiting the quartering of soldiers in private houses in times of peace without the consent of the owner, or in times of war, except as prescribed by law, while vitally important when it was written, is no longer the subject of serious Court review.

FOURTH AMENDMENT

The Fourth Amendment is a catalog of important personal rights that the Court has sought to interpret by balancing the right of privacy against the legitimate needs of law enforcement. It begins by declaring that the "right of the people to be secure in their persons, houses, papers, and effects, against unreasonable searches and seizures, shall not be violated." The very presence of the undefined term "unreasonable" has required the Court to delve into every manner of search and seizure, developing specific rules that police must follow in order to avoid the exclusion of evidence at trial. The Court has repeatedly articulated that the consequence for an illegal search or seizure is suppression of the evidence, thereby creating an incentive for police to scrupulously follow constitutional requirements.

The Fourth Amendment also guarantees that "no Warrants shall issue, but upon probable cause." Here again the Court developed rules to determine whether probable cause exists. In essence, the Court uses a standard of reasonableness based on all of the facts and circumstances surrounding a challenged search or arrest. The Court places itself in the position of the reasonable police officer, relying on particularized suspicion and past experience, but rejecting mere hunches or guesswork.

FIFTH AMENDMENT

The Fifth Amendment also protects the rights of persons charged with crimes. It prohibits double jeopardy ("subject for the same offence to be twice put in jeopardy of life or limb"), self-incrimination (being "compelled in any criminal case to be a witness against himself"), denial of due process (being "deprived of life, liberty, or property, without due process of law"), and a taking without compensation (having "private property . . . taken for public use without just compensation"). The Court takes these rights very seriously because they set critical boundaries on what government may do in prosecuting crime.

SIXTH AMENDMENT

The Sixth Amendment protects the rights of persons charged with criminal violations. Often mischaracterized as mere "technicalities" protecting the "guilty," Sixth Amendment rights were included in the Bill of Rights because the Founders had lived under a government that frequently arrested, jailed, convicted, and punished individuals without any semblance of fairness or justice.

Under the Sixth Amendment, the accused has a "right to a speedy and public trial." Both elements of this right are very important. The right to a trial is of little value if the accused is kept in jail for several months or years waiting to be tried. Generally speaking, unless the accused waives the time limit, he or she is entitled to go to trial within sixty days after arrest. Likewise, a "public" trial is vital to ensure that an overzealous prosecutor or corrupt judge does not trample on the rights of the accused. Exposing criminal trials to the bright light of public scrutiny allows the general public and the press to observe the proceedings and see for themselves whether the accused is getting a fair trial. The days of the notorious "Star Chamber," where Englishmen were tried in secret, are a thing of the past.

Anyone accused of a crime is also entitled to "an impartial jury" chosen from the geographical area where the crime was committed. The Sixth Amendment guarantees that no one may sit on a jury if he or she has a demonstrable bias or prejudice against the accused, either individually, or because of his or her gender, race, religion, ethnicity, or any other immutable characteristic. Generally, trial judges go to great lengths to question prospective jurors in order to ferret out those who cannot discharge their duties in an impartial manner.

Anyone accused of a crime has a right under the Sixth Amendment "to be informed of the nature and cause of the accusation." Obviously, in order to defend himself, the accused must know what he is being accused of so that he can establish an alibi or find witnesses who may assist in proving his innocence. Only by knowing the charges can the accused's attorney challenge the sufficiency of the indictment or the validity of the statute or regulation involved.

Closely allied to this right is the important right under the Sixth Amendment "to be confronted with the witnesses against him." An accused is entitled to know who will testify against him or her so that the accused and his or her lawyer can prepare adequate cross-examination. From experience, the Founders knew that it is more difficult to lie to another's face than to do so when the other person is not present.

Also, under the Sixth Amendment, an accused has the right "to have compulsory process for obtaining witnesses in his favor." In other words, the accused has the right to subpoena other persons and require them to come to court to testify and to bring papers and documents. Because the government already has this power, this right ensures a level playing field, where an accused can force reluctant witnesses to present evidence that may exonerate him or her or prove that a witness for the prosecution is lying. Without this right, an accused would be confined to presenting only testimony or documents from persons who voluntarily chose to take the time to come to court.

Finally, and perhaps most importantly, the Sixth Amendment

guarantees the accused the right "to have Assistance of Counsel for his defense." No person should face a criminal trial without competent legal counsel at his or her side. Only attorneys trained in the rules of evidence and trial procedures can adequately navigate through the complexities of a criminal trial. Indeed, so vital is the right to legal counsel that the law requires the state to provide a lawyer free of charge for the most serious crimes where the accused cannot afford one.

It is worth noting, before leaving the Sixth Amendment, that it contains no reference to the fundamental principle—considered the very foundation of Anglo-Saxon law—that one is innocent until proven guilty. Indeed, the presumption of innocence appears nowhere in the Bill of Rights or the Constitution. Yet this essential right has repeatedly been recognized by the courts and remains a vital guarantee of American justice.

SEVENTH AMENDMENT

The Seventh Amendment provides that in civil cases in federal courts at common law, where the value in controversy exceeds twenty dollars, "the right of trial by jury shall be preserved." Essentially, any civil case that entitled a litigant to a jury in 1791 still entitles the litigant to a jury today. Numerous rules (too extensive to be discussed here) have been developed by the courts to determine which civil claims must be tried before a jury and which may not.

The Seventh Amendment also guarantees that once a fact has been decided by a jury, it may not be otherwise reexamined in any federal court, except as provided by common law. Here again, because juries were viewed by the Founders as a protection against injustice and tyranny, it was important to ensure that once a jury had decided the facts in a case, a judge could not overturn that finding, except in limited circumstances provided in the common law.

EIGHTH AMENDMENT

Further protections for criminal defendants are found in the Eighth Amendment, beginning with the guarantee that "excessive bail shall not be required." Persons awaiting trial are entitled to be released from jail, provided they post reasonable bail, in cash or property, which will be returned as long as they appear in court where required. The prohibition against excessive bail ensures that an accused is not arbitrarily detained because a judge has set an unreasonably high bail.

Closely related is the Eighth Amendment's prohibition against "excessive fines." This provision ensures that once convicted, an individual will be fined in proportion to his or her crime or in keeping with guidelines for similar offenses under similar circumstances.

The most important provision of the Eighth Amendment states that "cruel and unusual punishment" shall not be inflicted. This prohibition limits the kinds of punishment that can be imposed on those convicted of crimes. It proscribes punishment grossly disproportionate to the severity of a crime, and it imposes substantive limits on what can be made criminal and punished as such. At its most basic level, the prohibition against cruel and unusual punishment was intended to eliminate torture and other barbaric methods of punishment, although as recently as 1963, twenty lashes as part of the sentence for robbery was found not to be in violation of the Eighth Amendment.

By far, the most serious—and controversial—application of the prohibition on cruel and unusual punishment came in 1972 when the Court used it to strike down the death penalty (which was then reinstated four years later). The Court found that to the extent the death penalty was administered in an arbitrary and capricious manner, amounting to little more than a lottery, it constituted cruel and unusual punishment in violation of the Eighth Amendment.

Generally, in determining whether a punishment is cruel and unusual, the courts consider a variety of factors, including the age of the defendant, the attitude of the defendant, the availability of less severe punishments, contemporary standards of decency, the frequency of imposition, the disparity in punishments for the same or lesser crimes, the proportionality to the offense, the inhuman shocking or barbarous nature of the punishment, and the totality of the circumstances.

NINTH AMENDMENT

One of the least known but most important provisions of the Bill of Rights is the Ninth Amendment, which in simple but meaningful terms states that the "enumeration in the Constitution, of certain rights, shall not be construed to deny or disparage others retained by the people." In many ways, these twenty-one words speak volumes about the very nature of the United States' constitutional democracy.

As set forth in the Declaration of Independence, people are born with certain inalienable rights. They are not granted their rights by a benevolent government; they are born with those rights and they establish governments in order to preserve and protect them. Thus, people speak of the Bill of Rights as "guaranteeing" constitutional rights, not "creating" them.

The Founders firmly believed in those principles. Indeed at first, the drafters of the Constitution did not include a Bill of Rights because they did not contemplate that the Constitution posed any threat to the inalienable rights of all citizens. However, as noted at the outset, many feared that a new and powerful national government would seize all the power it could, thereby jeopardizing personal rights and liberties.

However, when James Madison set about to draft the Bill of Rights during the First Congress in 1789, he faced a dilemma: How could he write a comprehensive list of *all* rights enjoyed by Americans without the risk of leaving some out? The solution was the Ninth Amendment. There, Madison, with utter simplicity, stated that the fact that "certain rights" were enumerated in the Constitution did not mean that "others retained by the people" were denied or disparaged. Consequently, any analysis of constitutional rights cannot stop by merely examining the specific rights: the "certain rights" spelled out in the first eight amendments. One must go further to determine whether there are "others retained by the people."

One of the most profound applications of the Ninth Amendment relates to the right of privacy. Few rights are more important to Americans than the right to be let alone, yet the right to privacy is nowhere mentioned in the Constitution or the Bill of Rights. To some extent, the entire Constitution and Bill of Rights express a right to privacy, that is, a set of limited and enumerated powers delegated to the government, with all other powers and rights held by the people. When the Supreme Court in the 1960's and 1970's began to address laws restricting contraception and abortion, it found that the right of privacy was rooted in several amendments, including the First, Fourth, Fifth, and Ninth, and what it called the "penumbras" emanating from all of the amendments.

Trivialized by certain judges and scholars as a mere "water blot" on the Constitution, the Ninth Amendment, on serious examination, may well reflect the true meaning of the Bill of Rights.

TENTH AMENDMENT

Parallel to the Ninth Amendment, the Tenth Amendment rounds out the Bill of Rights. It provides that the "powers not delegated to the United States by the Constitution, nor prohibited by it to the States, are reserved to the States respectively, or to the people." Thus, as all *rights* not expressed in the Constitution are retained by the people, all *powers* not delegated to the federal government are reserved to the individual States or to the people. The Tenth Amendment re-emphasizes the *limited* nature of the national government, underscoring the fact that the government possesses only the powers expressly delineated in the Constitution and no others.

The Tenth Amendment is rather obscure on the question of whether the reserved powers belong to the states or to the people. This was surely intentional. Having made his point that the national government was a creature of limited powers, Madison and his colleagues left it to others, including state legislatures, state courts, and the people themselves to sort out their respective relationships when it came to these reserved powers.

The Bill of Rights continues to serve the majestic purposes for which it was written more than two hundred years ago. Sometimes with intentional ambiguity, often with passionate eloquence and always with elusive simplicity, the Bill of Rights represents one of the most masterful declarations of individual rights and civil liberties in human history. Yet, as a charter written by people to last the test of time, the Bill of Rights demands continuous study and interpretation to meet the challenges of the next century.

Stephen F. Rohde

Further Reading

The Bill of Rights, edited by Thomas Tandy Lewis (2 vols. Pasadena, Calif.: Salem Press, 2002), provides comprehensive coverage of the Bill of Rights, with articles on each of the amendments, the Constitution, the incorporation doctrine, and many other topics, as well as 280 individual court cases. Christopher E. Smith's *Constitutional Rights: Myths and Realities* (Belmont, Calif.: Thompson Wadsworth, 2004) offers a thorough discussion of the rights included in the Bill of Rights that challenges conventional wisdom about the application of constitutional rights.

Don Nardo's *The Bill of Rights* (San Diego, Calif.: Greenhaven Press, 1998) provides an overview of the original debate over the need for a bill of rights and explores some of the later debates about rights. Books that examine the origins of the Bill of Rights include Akhil Reed Amar's *The Bill of Rights: Creation and Reconstruction* (New Haven, Conn.: Yale University Press, 1998), Leonard Levy's *Origins of the Bill of Rights* (New Haven, Conn.: Yale University Press, 1999), and *The Essential Bill of Rights: Original Arguments and Fundamental Documents* (Lanham, Md.: University Press of America, 1998), edited by Gordon Lloyd and Margie Lloyd.

Works that examine the legacy of the Bill of Rights include Ellen Alderman and Caroline Kennedy's *In Our Defense: The Bill of Rights in Action* (New York: Bard, 1998), *The Bill of Rights, the Courts and the Law: The Landmark Cases that Have Shaped American Society* (3d ed., Charlottesville, Va.: Virginia Foundation for the Humanities and Public Policy, 1999), by Lynda Butler et al., and Nat Hentoff's *Living the Bill of Rights: How to Be an Authentic American* (New York: HarperCollins, 1998). *1791-1991: The Bill of Rights and Beyond* by the Commission on the Bicentennial of the United States Constitution, edited by Herbert M. Atherton et al. (Washington, D.C.: Commission on the Bicentennial of the U.S. Constitution, 1990), provides an interesting look back at the Bill of Rights.

See also Bail; Double jeopardy; Eighth Amendment; Fifth Amendment; First Amendment; Fourth Amendment; Fundamental rights; Incorporation doctrine; Ninth Amendment; Second Amendment; Sixth Amendment; Tenth Amendment.

Birth Control and Contraception

DESCRIPTION: The temporary or permanent prevention of pregnancy by barrier devices, hormonal pills and implants, surgery, spermicides, intrauterine devices, or other means.

SIGNIFICANCE: The Supreme Court's landmark 1965 ruling struck down a law preventing the distribution of contraceptives to married couples and established an implied constitutional "right of marital privacy." This right to privacy was cited in the 1973 ruling that found state antiabortion laws unconstitutional.

In the 1800's some Christians viewed contraception as immoral, believing that its widespread use would lead to promiscuity, marital infidelity, divorce, child abandonment, and abortion. In the mid-nineteenth century several states passed statutes banning the dissemination and use of contraceptives. In 1873 Congress enacted a law forbidding the sending of contraceptives or information about them through the mail.

Early in the twentieth century, Margaret Sanger and others began campaigning for public acceptance of birth control and the repeal of laws against contraception. Some campaigners viewed contraception as an instrument of women's liberation, some sought the freedom to have sex without fear of pregnancy, and others were principally motivated by eugenic goals.

By the 1940's most states permitted physicians to prescribe contraceptives. Nonprescription distribution of contraceptives was still legally restricted although these laws were rarely enforced. Procontraception groups challenged these restrictions on contraceptives in federal courts. Their initial efforts were unsuccessful. In *Gardner v. Massachusetts* (1938), *Tileston v. Ullman* (1943), and *Poe v. Ullman* (1961), the Supreme Court supported legislation placing restrictions on contraceptive use and distribution.

In *Griswold v. Connecticut* (1965), however, the Court struck down a state law that forbade the distribution of contraceptives to and their use by married couples. Writing for the Court, justice William O. Douglas claimed that the statute violated a "right of marital privacy," which was found in "penumbras formed by emanations" from various specific Bill of Rights guarantees. In concurring opinions, several justices proposed alternative justifications for the holding. Most notably, Arthur J. Goldberg suggested treating marital contraception as an "unenumerated right" under the Ninth Amendment.

In dissent, Hugo L. Black and Potter Stewart argued that nothing in the text, logic, structure, or original understanding of the Constitution prevents a state from restricting contraception pursuant to its police power to protect public health, safety, and morals. They faulted the majority for substituting an allegedly enlightened judicial view of the requirements of public morality for the contrary judgment of the elected representatives of the people of Connecticut.

Griswold purported to protect the institution of marriage against legal interference with spousal decisions about birth control. In *Eisenstadt v. Baird* (1972), the Court ruled that this right to privacy extended to individuals, married or single, who wished to use contraceptives. A year later, the right of privacy was invoked in a ruling against state laws forbidding abortion in *Roe v. Wade* (1973).

Opponents of judicial activism criticized the Court's invalidation of laws against contraceptives as a step toward judges injecting their personal views about morality and public policy into the Constitution. Supporters of the right of privacy doctrine were sometimes disappointed by the Court's cautious approach in expanding the doctrine beyond decisions about child bearing to embrace other areas of intimate relationships. In *Bowers v. Hardwick* (1986), for example, the Court upheld laws criminalizing homosexual sodomy, although privacy-doctrine advocates were delighted when the Court overturned this decision and prohibited such laws in *Lawrence v. Texas* (2003).

Robert P. George
Updated by the Editor

FURTHER READING

Appleby, Brenda Margaret. *Responsible Parenthood: Decriminalizing Contraception in Canada.* Toronto: University of Toronto Press, 1999.

Critchlow, Donald T. *Intended Consequences: Birth Control, Abortion, and the Federal Government in Modern America.* New York: Oxford University Press, 1999.

Hilliard, Bryan. *The U.S. Supreme Court and Medical Ethics: From Contraception to Managed Health Care.* St. Paul, Minn.: Paragon House, 2004.

Mason, J. K. *Medico-legal Aspects of Reproduction and Parenthood.* Brookfield, Vt.: Dartmouth, 1990.

SEE ALSO Abortion; Black, Hugo L.; Douglas, William O.; Gender issues; Goldberg, Arthur J.; *Griswold v. Connecticut*; Judicial activism; *Lawrence v. Texas*; *Planned Parenthood of Southeastern Pennsylvania v. Casey*; Privacy, right to; *Roe v. Wade*; *Webster v. Reproductive Health Services*.

Hugo L. Black

IDENTIFICATION: Associate justice (August 19, 1937-September 17, 1971)

NOMINATED BY: Franklin D. Roosevelt

BORN: February 27, 1886, Harlan, Alabama

DIED: September 25, 1971, Bethesda, Maryland

SIGNIFICANCE: During his thirty-four years on the Court, Black led the drive to make the rights of the first eight amendments of the U.S. Constitution binding on the states, while working vigorously to expand constitutional rights, especially in the areas of free speech and civil rights.

The son of a poor storekeeper in rural Alabama, Hugo L. Black took a keen interest in both books and politics at a young age. Although a disciplinary incident prevented him from graduating from high school, he studied for a year in medical school and then transferred to the University of Alabama's law school. Immediately after earning his law degree at the age of twenty, he began to practice law in the city of Birmingham.

Orienting his practice toward working people and labor unions, Black became one of Alabama's most successful personal injury lawyers. His courtroom style combined fiery presentations and detailed knowledge of relevant facts. He joined many civic organizations, and despite his religious skepticism, he taught a popular adult class at a Baptist church. He also served as a part-time police court judge in 1910-1911.

POLITICAL CAREER

In 1914 Black was elected prosecutor of Alabama's Jefferson County. He effectively emptied a large docket, and he once prosecuted police officers for forcing confessions from African American defendants. He joined the Army during World War I and rose to the rank of captain but never left the United States. After returning to Birmingham, he married and had three children. Meanwhile, his law practice flourished.

Black was a member of the Ku Klux Klan from 1923 to 1925 and was elected to the U.S. Senate with Klan support in 1926. Like other

Hugo L. Black.
(Library of Congress)

southern populists of the time, he campaigned on the theme of promoting economic justice for the poor and the weak. Because the Republican Party controlled Congress during Black's first Senate term, he spent much of his time pursuing his interests in history and philosophy. However, the Democratic Party's electoral triumph in 1932 gave him the opportunity to exercise a leadership role in the Senate.

As Democratic Party whip in the Senate, Black played a crucial role in helping to pass President Franklin D. Roosevelt's New Deal legislation. He was also a leading force in congressional investigations of lobbying practices and misappropriation of government subsidies. Black sponsored the earliest minimum-wage and maximum-hours law. A longtime critic of the Supreme Court's economic conservatism, he bitterly resented the Court's striking down of New Deal legislation and enthusiastically supported Roosevelt's Court-packing plan.

APPOINTMENT TO THE COURT

On August 12, 1937, Roosevelt named Black to fill the first Supreme Court vacancy that opened during his presidency. A mere five days later, the Senate confirmed Black's nomination by a vote of sixty-three to sixteen. Black served on the Court until failing health forced his resignation on September 25, 1973. He died just eight days later.

As an associate justice, Black argued that framers of the Fourteenth Amendment (1868) had intended to incorporate all the rights guaranteed by the first eight amendments into their new amendment. For that reason, he argued, those rights should apply to the state governments, as they already did to the federal government. In his view, the Fourteenth Amendment's "liberty" and "privileges or immunities" meant the states should have the full protections of the Bill of Rights. Defending this position in his dissent in *Adamson v. California* (1947), he amassed an impressive amount of historical material, but critics observed that he ignored contradictory evidence. On this issue, he often came into conflict with Justice Felix Frankfurter, who argued that the Fourteenth Amendment applied selective guarantees based on their fundamental fairness. Black never persuaded a majority of his colleagues to accept his principle of total incorporation but succeed in launching the piecemeal incorporation of most of the specific rights of the first eight amendments. By the time he retired in 1971, the debate over incorporation had largely ended, and most provisions of the Bill of Rights had been applied to the states.

PARTICULAR RIGHTS

Believing that the First Amendment's guarantees of freedom of speech and press were at the heart of a free government, Black accepted the "preferred position" of these freedoms in the 1940's. He vigorously argued that all speech and writing was absolutely protected from governmental sanction. Like his close friend on the Court, William O. Douglas, he believed that this protection extended to all forms of obscenity, and he therefore refused to review adult movies to determine if they were obscene. At the same time, Black made a sharp distinction between conduct and verbal expression, and did not generally support the notion of "symbolic speech." In *Tinker v. Des Moines Independent Community School District* (1969), his bitter dissent insisted that the First Amendment did not protect any right of children to wear controversial political symbols in the public schools.

Black endorsed Thomas Jefferson's view that the First Amendment erected a wall separating church and state and that governmental funds must never support religious institutions. He wrote the majority opinion in *Everson v. Board of Education of Ewing Township* (1947), which theoretically applied this understanding of the establishment clause to the states, while permitting states to pay transportation costs to parochial schools. Many southerners were outraged when Black wrote *Engel v. Vitale* (1962), forbidding state-sponsored prayers in public schools.

In criminal trials, Black generally took an expansionist view on the Fifth and Sixth Amendments. One of his first majority opinions, *Johnson v. Zerbst* (1940), held that counsel must be provided for indigent defendants in federal prosecutions. In *Betts v. Brady* (1942), he registered a strong dissent when the majority refused to apply the principle to the states. Twenty years later, Black saw *Betts* overturned, and he had the honor of writing for a unanimous court in the famous case of *Gideon v. Wainwright* (1963). Black's views on the Fourth Amendment were more restrained. In *Katz v. United States* (1967), for example, he argued that personal conversations were not protected under the amendment.

EQUAL PROTECTION

Black consistently took a firm stand against Jim Crow racial discrimination. When the school segregation cases were first argued in the early 1950's, he was one of only four justices to vote to overturn *Plessy v. Ferguson* (1896). His opinion in *Griffin v. County School Board of Prince Edward County* (1964) firmly rejected attempts to avoid compliance with school desegregation and declared that the "time for mere 'deliberate speed' had run out." In cases such as *Shapiro v. Thompson* (1969), however, he opposed the application of the strict scrutiny test in equal protection claims not involving racial discrimination. In his later years, Black angered liberals when he argued in dissent that the Constitution did not provide any guarantee that citizens could engage in civil rights protests on private property.

Black has been especially criticized for his majority opinion in *Korematsu v. United States* (1944), which upheld the forced removal and internment of Japanese Americans living on the West Coast after the United States entered World War II. Although there was no real evidence that Japanese Americans had posed a threat to national security, Black continued to insist that the decision was justified by the exigencies of war. Ironically, Black's *Korematsu* opinion later had a liberal influence as the Court's first reference to race as a suspect classification that should be subjected to the "most rigid scrutiny."

CONSTITUTIONAL PHILOSOPHY

In his book, *A Constitutional Faith* (1968), Black expressed a quasireligious devotion to the text of the Constitution. A critic of judicial discretion, he argued that judges should base their decisions on a literal reading of the Constitution, while taking into account the intent of the Framers. Called a "judicial positivist," he opposed subjective interpretations in which justices found unenumerated rights in either natural law, substantive due process, or the Ninth Amendment. Believing that judges were fallible, he never placed a high value on judicial precedents. During his early career, he denounced the concept of a probusiness "liberty of contract," just as he later became a vociferous critic of an unenumerated "right to privacy." When the Court overturned a law prohibiting the sale of contraceptives in *Griswold v. Connecticut* (1965), Black wrote a strong dissent, accusing the majority of reviving the excesses of the early twentieth century *Lochner v. New York* (1905) era, when the Court intervened excessively in commerce laws.

Thomas Tandy Lewis

FURTHER READING

Steve Suitts's *Hugo Black of Alabama: How His Roots and Early Career Shaped the Great Champion of the Constitution* (Montgomery: NewSouth Books, 2005) is an impressively researched and beautifully written study of Black's entire life. Roger K. Newman's *Hugo Black: A Biography* (New York: Pantheon, 1994) is a scholarly and well-written study of Black's life and career. James Magee's *Mr. Justice Black: Absolutist on the Court* (Charlottesville: University Press of Virginia, 1980) presents a critical analysis of his judicial philosophy, with an emphasis on his absolutist views on free expression.

For an interesting comparative approach, see James Simon's *The Antagonists: Hugo Black, Felix Frankfurter and Civil Liberties in Modern America* (New York: Simon & Schuster, 1989). For a detailed study of his career until 1937, see Virginia Van der Veer Hamilton's *Hugo Black: The Alabama Years* (Baton Rouge: Louisiana State University Press, 1972). Hugo Black, Jr., presents a delightful look at the man in *My Father: A Remembrance* (New York: Random House, 1975). Irving Dilliard edited a collection of many of his Supreme Court opinions in *One Man's Stand for Freedom: Mr. Justice Black and the Bill of Rights* (New York: Alfred A. Knopf, 1963).

Other recommended works include Tony Freyer's *Hugo L. Black and the Dilemma of American Liberalism* (Glenview, Ill.: Scott, Foresman, 1990); Howard Ball's *Hugo L. Black: Cold Steel Warrior* (New York: Oxford University Press, 1998); Michael Parrish's *New Deal Justice* (New York: Random House, 1998); and Tinsley Yarbrough's *Mr. Justice Black and His Critics* (Durham, N.C.: Duke University Press, 1988).

SEE ALSO Constitutional interpretation; Court-packing plan; Due process, substantive; Frankfurter, Felix; *Gideon v. Wainwright*; Incorporation doctrine; New Deal; Race and discrimination; Religion, establishment of.

Harry A. Blackmun

IDENTIFICATION: Associate justice (June 9, 1970-June 30, 1994)
NOMINATED BY: Richard M. Nixon
BORN: November 12, 1908, Nashville, Illinois
DIED: March 4, 1999, Arlington, Virginia
SIGNIFICANCE: Blackmun wrote the 7-2 majority decision in the controversial abortion case, *Roe v. Wade* (1973). In twenty-four years on the Supreme Court, he left his mark on disparate constitutional disputes involving federalism, criminal law, commercial speech, and the rights of aliens.

Harry A. Blackmun was raised in St. Paul, Minnesota, leaving to take his undergraduate and law degrees at Harvard University in 1929 and 1932, respectively. He had a lifelong interest in medicine and was

Harry A. Blackmun
(Library of Congress)

general counsel to the Mayo Clinic in Minnesota from 1950 to 1959. In 1959 President Dwight D. Eisenhower appointed him to the U.S. Court of Appeals for the Eighth Circuit. He was President Richard M. Nixon's third choice for a position on the Supreme Court, winning confirmation as a justice after the unsuccessful nominations of Clement Haynsworth, Jr., and G. Harrold Carswell.

ON THE COURT

Many thought that Blackmun would reinforce Nixon's drive to move the Court in a more conservative direction than had characterized it since the 1950's. Initially this proved to be the case, with Blackmun generally voting to support governmental authority in criminal justice and free speech matters. He voted to support the death penalty in *Furman v. Georgia* (1972) and again in *Gregg v. Georgia* (1976) despite personal discomfort with the practice. His personal views did not crystallize into firm opposition to capital punishment until late in his career. He dissented in *New York Times Co. v. United States* (1971), siding with the Nixon administration in its efforts to prevent publication of the Pentagon Papers. He also dissented in *Cohen v. California* (1971), siding with the state in its effort to curb vulgar and offensive speech. However, in *Bates v. State Bar of Arizona* (1977), Blackmun wrote the majority decision striking down legal ethics guidelines that prevented lawyers from advertising their services. In addition to its First Amendment implications, the case in essence ended the claim of the U.S. legal profession to the relatively unrestricted power of self-regulation.

Despite his early sympathy with the general police power of the state, Blackmun's most renowned shift away from this view also came early in his Court career. In *Roe v. Wade* (1973), Blackmun relied on the putative right to privacy implied by the Fourteenth Amendment's due process clause to support a woman's right to abortion absent state interference (except in matters relating to maternal health) in the first trimester of pregnancy. Blackmun constructed his decision at least partially around research he had conducted at the Mayo Clinic in the summer of 1972. He later characterized the decision as a landmark in the drive to emancipate women.

Later in his career, Blackmun passionately dissented in the case of

Webster v. Reproductive Health Services (1989), in which, he claimed, the Court had allowed the government to intrude improperly on what he believed to be the freedom of women to control their bodies. In *Planned Parenthood of Southeastern Pennsylvania v. Casey* (1992), Blackmun, dissenting in part, openly lamented what he claimed to be the dangers to individual liberty that would follow his retirement if one more anti-*Roe* justice were appointed to a Court narrowly divided on the abortion issue. In *Bowers v. Hardwick* (1986), Blackmun wrote a stinging dissent from the Court's refusal to extend the right to privacy to homosexual sodomy. Blackmun claimed that the fundamental "right to be let alone" was under assault in the case and that the majority's understanding of privacy and other constitutional issues was cramped.

Blackmun's concern for individual rights also manifested itself early on in his majority opinion in *Graham v. Richardson* (1971), holding alienage to be a suspect classification under the Fourteenth Amendment. By so holding, the Court made any governmental classifications based on alienage subject to the highest level of judicial scrutiny. He generally supported the rights of aliens against state discrimination in subsequent alienage cases.

In *Regents of the University of California v. Bakke* (1978), Blackmun voted against the application of strict scrutiny to racial classifications that are not stigmatizing, thus in effect, casting a vote in favor of governmentally sponsored affirmative action.

In general, by the 1980's, Blackmun had firmly joined the Court's liberal camp, often voting with Justices William J. Brennan, Jr., and Thurgood Marshall. He opposed prayer in public schools on establishment clause grounds. In *Garcia v. San Antonio Metropolitan Transit Authority* (1985), Blackmun reinforced the Court's dominant interpretation of the commerce clause, writing the majority opinion that eliminated virtually all judicial limitations on Congress's power under this clause. The decision allowed federal economic regulation of areas in which state jurisdiction had traditionally been supreme. Many observers argued that this opinion—later effectively overturned by *United States v. Lopez* (1995)—rendered federalism largely inoperable.

CONSTITUTIONAL PHILOSOPHY

Blackmun's steady shift from moderate conservatism to judicial liberalism, conjoined with his largely pragmatic, nontheoretical approach to issues, makes it difficult to characterize his constitutional philosophy. Blackmun has been viewed as a centrist blessed with the virtue of moderation and a judicial activist bent on reinterpreting the Constitution to suit his own views. How he is characterized often varies with the constitutional philosophy of the person making the characterization.

Bradley C. S. Watson

FURTHER READING

Bader, William H., and Roy M. Mersky, eds. *The First One Hundred Eight Justices.* Buffalo, N.Y.: William S. Hein, 2004.

Brennan, William J., et al. "A Tribute to Justice Harry A. Blackmun." *Harvard Law Review* 108, no. 1 (November, 1994).

Greenhouse, Linda. *Becoming Justice Blackmun: Harry Blackmun's Supreme Court Journey.* New York: Henry Holt, 2005.

Hair, Penda D. "Justice Blackmun and Racial Justice." *Yale Law Journal* 104, no. 1 (October, 1994).

Reuben, Richard C. "Justice Defined." *ABA Journal* 80 (July, 1994).

Rosen, Jeffrey. "Sentimental Journey: The Emotional Jurisprudence of Harry Blackmun." *The New Republic* 210, no. 18 (May 2, 1994).

SEE ALSO Abortion; Breyer, Stephen G.; Burger, Warren E.; Capital punishment; Commerce, regulation of; Dissents; Due process, substantive; *Garcia v. San Antonio Metropolitan Transit Authority; Lopez, United States v.; Roe v. Wade; Webster v. Reproductive Health Services.*

John Blair, Jr.

IDENTIFICATION: Associate justice (February 2, 1790-October 25, 1795)
NOMINATED BY: George Washington
BORN: 1732, Williamsburg, Virginia
DIED: August 31, 1800, Williamsburg, Virginia
SIGNIFICANCE: One of the original members of the Supreme Court, Blair worked to strengthen the powers of the federal government over the individual states.

John Blair, Jr.
(Library of Congress)

John Blair, Jr., graduated in 1754 from the College of William and Mary. In 1755 and 1756 he studied law at the Middle Temple in London. He established a law practice in Williamsburg, Virginia, and in 1765 was elected to represent the College of William and Mary in Virginia's House of Burgesses.

As a burgess, Blair opposed Patrick Henry's 1765 Stamp Act as too radical a move. However, after the British Crown dissolved the burgesses in 1769 and 1770, Blair sided with fellow Virginians advocating independence. He helped create Virginia's new government as a delegate to the Virginia Convention in 1776 and was chosen as a general court judge. A series of court appointments followed. His most memorable decision came while sitting on the First Court of Appeals, when he and his fellow judges ruled in *Virginia v. Caton* (1782) that the court had the power to determine the constitutionality of legislative acts. This decision helped set the stage for a strong Supreme Court a few years later.

In 1787 Blair was a delegate to the Constitutional Convention and voted for the adoption of the Constitution. After the new government formed, President George Washington nominated Blair as one of the original five associate justices of the Supreme Court; Blair was confirmed by the Senate two days later.

Perhaps the most far-reaching decision of Blair's career was in *Chisholm v. Georgia* (1793), when he sided with the majority view that a citizen might bring suit against states in federal court. Blair's opinion demonstrated his belief in the Constitution as the supreme legal authority in the nation and strengthened the federal government's power over the states. The unfavorable reaction to this decision helped usher in the Eleventh Amendment, which restricted federal court power to hear suits against states brought by aliens or citizens of other states.

Early justices, in addition to their duties on the Supreme Court, presided over circuit courts. In Middle Circuit Court in 1792, Blair and fellow judges ruled in *Collet v. Collet* (1792) that if the U.S. government naturalized a citizen, states must accept that decision, once again strengthening the power of the central government over that of individual states.

Because of failing health and exhaustion brought on by riding the judicial circuit, Blair retired from the bench in 1796 to return to Williamsburg, where he died in 1800.

Carol G. Fox

FURTHER READING

Bader, William H., and Roy M. Mersky, eds. *The First One Hundred Eight Justices.* Buffalo, N.Y.: William S. Hein, 2004.

Friedman, Leon, and Fred L. Israel, eds. *The Justices of the United States Supreme Court: Their Lives and Major Opinions.* 5 vols. New York: Chelsea House, 1997.

Harrington, Matthew P. *Jay and Ellsworth, The First Courts: Justices, Rulings, and Legacy.* Santa Barbara, Calif.: ABC-Clio, 2007.

Marcus, Maeva, and James Perry, eds. *The Documentary History of the Supreme Court of the United States, 1789-1800.* New York: Columbia University Press, 1985.

SEE ALSO *Chisholm v. Georgia*; Circuit riding; Constitutional interpretation; Eleventh Amendment; Federalism; Jay, John.

Samuel Blatchford

IDENTIFICATION: Associate justice (April 3, 1882-July 7, 1893)

NOMINATED BY: Chester A. Arthur

BORN: March 9, 1820, New York, New York

DIED: July 7, 1893, Newport, Rhode Island

SIGNIFICANCE: Known as a workhorse, Blatchford wrote 430 opinions in his eleven years on the Supreme Court. In an 1892 decision, he extended the interpretation of the Fifth Amendment by emphasizing that it prevented a person from giving evidence in any criminal case.

Samuel Blatchford graduated as class valedictorian from Columbia College in 1837. He began studying law in his father's New York office, but soon was asked to serve as the private secretary of New York governor William Seward. In 1842 Blatchford was admitted to the New York bar and practiced in New York City with his father for the next three years. Subsequently, he became a law partner with Seward,

Samuel Blatchford.
(Library of Congress)

which contributed greatly to Blatchford's later success.

In 1852 Blatchford began compiling reports of federal court decisions and ultimately published twenty-four volumes of previously uncollected decisions of the U.S. Court of Appeals for the Second Circuit. He also published *Blatchford's and Howland's Reports* (1855) of admiralty cases decided between 1827 and 1837 in the district court for the southern district of New York, as well as *Blatchford's Prize Cases* (1865), which covered prize cases in circuit and district courts of New York from 1861 to 1865. Between 1867 and 1872, Blatchford served as a federal district judge for the southern district of New York. He was then elevated to the U.S. Court of Appeals for the Second Circuit.

After Roscoe Conkling and George F. Edmunds each declined invitations to fill a vacancy in the Supreme Court, President Chester A. Arthur nominated Blatchford on March 13, 1882. Blatchford was easily confirmed in the Senate two weeks later. Being a judicial moderate, Blatchford usually supported the majority opinions of the Court, writing only two dissents out of his 430 opinions. Known as one of the hardest-working and most productive justices ever to sit on the Court bench, he also became known for his encouragement of younger members of the legal profession and for his kind, patient, courteous manner.

In 1890 Blatchford was cast into the national spotlight when he wrote the pivotal opinion for *Chicago, Milwaukee, and St. Paul Railway Co. v. Minnesota*. Blatchford claimed that it was unconstitutional for a government-established commission to have the last word in whether railway rates were fair or not. He argued that it violated the railway's right to due process. However, less than two years later in *Budd v. New York* (1892), Blatchford ruled that the legislature could indeed set rates for businesses that affect the public interest. His contradictory decisions were highly criticized. However, he demonstrated his wisdom in *Counselman v. Hitchcock* (1892), when he broadly interpreted the Fifth Amendment's right against self-incrimination, giving individuals increased protection against federal authority.

Alvin K. Benson

SEE ALSO Circuit riding; Fifth Amendment; Opinions, writing of.

Boerne v. Flores

CITATION: 521 U.S. 507
DATE: June 25, 1997
ISSUES: Separation of powers; freedom of religion
SIGNIFICANCE: In striking down the Religious Freedom Restoration Act of 1993, the Supreme Court declared that congressional enforcement powers in the Fourteenth Amendment may not be used to override the Court's interpretations of the Constitution.

In *Sherbert v. Verner* (1963), the Supreme Court required a compelling state interest as justification for any indirect restraint on religion. In *Employment Division, Department of Human Resources v. Smith* the Court allowed the states more discretion when balancing claims of religious freedom against the states' interests in enacting and enforcing reasonable laws of general application. Congress responded to the controversial *Smith* decision with the Religious Freedom Restoration Act of 1993, which required states to apply the more demanding *Sherbert* standards. A Roman Catholic Church in Boerne, Texas, desired to replace its old and small church building, but the city had classified the structure as a historic landmark that must be preserved. The bishop sued in federal court, asserting that the 1993 act prevented the city from interfering with the church's decision to construct a new building.

By a 6-3 vote, the Court ruled that the 1993 act was unconstitutional. Justice Anthony M. Kennedy's opinion argued that section 5 of the Fourteenth Amendment gave Congress the power only to enforce the rights protected by the amendment, not to decree the substantive meaning of the amendment. The clear intent of the 1993 act was to veto a constitutional interpretation made by the Court. Kennedy insisted that such a challenge to the Court's proper authority is contrary to the U.S. tradition of separation of powers. Three justices dissented from the majority's continued support for the *Smith* decision.

Thomas Tandy Lewis

SEE ALSO *Employment Division, Department of Human Resources v. Smith*; Fourteenth Amendment; *Good News Club v. Milford Central School*; Judicial scrutiny; Religion, freedom of; Separation of powers; *Sherbert v. Verner.*

Bolling v. Sharpe

CITATION: 347 U.S. 479

DATE: May 17, 1954

ISSUES: Segregation; substantive due process

SIGNIFICANCE: The Supreme Court unanimously held that de jure segregation by the federal government violated the due process clause of the Fifth Amendment.

The *Bolling v. Sharpe* decision dealt with school segregation in Washington, D.C., and was announced the same day as *Brown v. Board of Education* (1954). The equal protection clause of the Fourteenth Amendment did not apply to acts of Congress, so the two cases had to be considered separately. Speaking for the Supreme Court, Chief Justice Earl Warren implicitly used a substantive due process interpretation of the Fifth Amendment. He stated that because segregation in education was not reasonably related to a proper governmental function, it imposed a burden on African American children that constituted "an arbitrary deprivation of their liberty." Ironically, Warren referred to the Japanese American relocation cases, in which the Court's opinions had recognized an "equal protection component" in the concept of due process. *Bolling* established that the federal government and the states are usually accountable to the same standards in equal protection cases.

Thomas Tandy Lewis

SEE ALSO *Brown v. Board of Education*; Due process, substantive; Fifth Amendment; Japanese American relocation; Race and discrimination; Warren, Earl.

Boy Scouts of America v. Dale

CITATION: 530 U.S. 640
DATE: June 28, 2000
ISSUES: Gay rights; equal protection; free association
SIGNIFICANCE: Emphasizing that private organizations have the rights of free expression and free association under the First Amendment, the Supreme Court held that government could not force the Boy Scouts to accept openly gay adults to work with the group.

After enactment of the Civil Rights Act of 1964, several state legislatures enacted antidiscrimination statutes that went further than federal law in two ways: first, they defined public accommodations more broadly, and second, they increasingly outlawed discrimination based on sexual orientation. In *Roberts v. United States Jaycees* (1984), the Supreme Court held that these state laws were binding on some private organizations, but it also acknowledged that organizations committed to particular points of view have freedoms of expression and association that trump antidiscrimination laws.

When officials of the Boy Scouts of New Jersey discovered that assistant scoutmaster James Dale was openly gay and a member of a gay rights organization, they revoked his membership. In 1992, Dale brought a lawsuit under a New Jersey law prohibiting discrimination against gays or lesbians in places of public accommodations. Although Dale lost in the trial court, the state appellate court agreed with his claim for two reasons. First, the court held that the public accommodations law applied to the organization because of its broad-based membership and its connection to public agencies. Second, it observed that the Boy Scouts' literature did not explicitly mention any antigay point of view, from which they concluded that Dale's inclusion would not significantly interfere with the organization's ability to carry out its mission. New Jersey's supreme court affirmed the ruling.

At the U.S. Supreme Court, however, the justices overturned the ruling by a margin of five to four. Speaking for the majority, Chief Justice William H. Rehnquist reaffirmed that civil rights laws may not de-

prive persons of their constitutional rights of "expressive association." To require the Scouts to accept a gay troop leader, in effect,
would force the organization to convey a message that "is inconsistent with the values it seeks to instill."

The ruling did not break any new ground but it clarified the circumstances in which antidiscrimination laws may be applied to private organizations. The decision was controversial, but opponents
usually directed their anger at the Boy Scouts rather than the Supreme Court.

Thomas Tandy Lewis

SEE ALSO Employment discrimination; Gay and lesbian rights; Gender issues; Rehnquist, William H.

Joseph P. Bradley

IDENTIFICATION: Associate justice (March 23, 1870-January 22, 1892)
NOMINATED BY: Ulysses S. Grant
BORN: March 14, 1813, Berne, New York
DIED: January 22, 1892, Washington, D.C.
SIGNIFICANCE: As a Supreme Court justice, Bradley often dissented
  when the Court favored states' rights over the power of the national
  government to regulate the economy. However, he voted with the
  majority to restrict the ability of Congress and the Constitution to
  protect women and African Americans from discrimination.

The eldest of twelve children born to a poor farming couple, Joseph P. Bradley inherited a lifelong love of learning from his parents.
By the time he was sixteen, he had read most of the books in the
town's library, taught himself algebra, and become a teacher in his local school. However, it was not until he was twenty years old that he
began college. Always a hardworking student with a broad range of
interests, he graduated from Rutgers College in three years. Originally intending to study theology, Bradley soon turned to the study
of law. After graduation, he apprenticed for the bar in the office of a
Newark, New Jersey, lawyer.

Soon after his admission to the bar in 1839, Bradley rose to prominence in the New Jersey legal community. He spent most of his legal career as counsel for a number of railroads, eventually becoming general counsel, secretary of the board, and a member of the Executive Committee of the Joint Companies of New Jersey (which included the Camden and Amboy Line). Although New Jersey was a predominantly Democratic state, Bradley joined the new Republican Party before the Civil War (1861-1865).

APPOINTMENT TO THE COURT

On February 7, 1870, President Ulysses S. Grant nominated Bradley and William Strong to the two vacancies on the Supreme Court created by the resignation of Justice Robert C. Grier and enactment of the Judiciary Act of 1869, which restored the Court to its pre-Civil War membership of nine. On March 21, the Senate confirmed Bradley's nomination by a vote of forty-six to nine. He was sworn in two days later and served on the Court until January 22, 1892.

The appointments of Bradley and Strong came at a time when the Court was grappling with the important constitutional question of Congress's power to enact the Legal Tender Act of 1862. The Act required creditors to receive paper money issued by the United States in payment of debt. Although there is no evidence that Grant appointed Bradley and Strong with this issue in mind, both of these new justices voted to uphold the constitutionality of the act.

FOURTEENTH AMENDMENT AND RECONSTRUCTION

During his twenty-one-year service on the Court, Bradley participated in many of the decisions that endured as bedrock principles of states' rights. Therefore, although Bradley initially voted against the Court's evisceration of the privileges or immunities clause of the Fourteenth Amendment, he later became a solid member of the majority, sometimes writing for the Court, in cases repudiating Reconstruction legislation designed to protect the rights of newly freed African Americans to equality under the law. He also was a chief architect of the modern doctrine that the states are immune from suit in federal courts.

During Bradley's service, the Court had the task of defining the scope of the Fourteenth Amendment. In the Court's first decision,

Joseph P. Bradley.
(Library of Congress)

the *Slaughterhouse Cases* (1873), a majority of the Court severely limited the reach of the privileges or immunities clause. In dissent, Bradley contended that the clause protected businesses from unreasonable state regulations. However, in *Bradwell v. Illinois* (1873), he voted with the majority to reject Myra Bradwell's Fourteenth Amendment challenge to an Illinois statute that barred women from practicing law. The case is as well known for Bradley's concurring opinion as it is for the result. Bradwell had no right to practice law, in Bradley's view, because "[t]he paramount destiny and mission of women are to fulfill the noble and benign offices of wife and mother. This was the law of the Creator."

Through a series of decisions, from 1870 to 1886, the Court contributed to the dismantling of Congress's Reconstruction plan and to the interweaving of racial segregation into the nation's social fabric. Bradley played a key role in these developments, generally by voting with the majority in cases such as *United States v. Cruikshank* (1876), which limited Congress's power to enforce the Fourteenth Amendment against the states, and *Baldwin v. Franks* (1876), which, along with *United States v. Harris* (1882), restricted Congress's authority to enact legislation protecting voting rights from state interference.

More specifically, Bradley helped make racial segregation immune from constitutional and congressional attack with his opinion in the *Civil Rights Cases* (1883), holding the Civil Rights Act of 1875 unconstitutional. Here, Bradley argued that neither the Thirteenth nor the Fourteenth Amendment gave Congress the power to enact the statute. Private discrimination, Bradley reasoned, was not a badge or incident of slavery that Congress could outlaw without "running the slavery argument into the ground." As to the Fourteenth Amendment, he argued, Congress could reach only discrimination carried on by the state itself, not the private acts of inns, theaters, and railroads. Bradley even suggested that the Civil Rights Act amounted to Congress treating African Americans as "the special favorite of the laws."

STATES AND SOVEREIGN IMMUNITY

The issue of civil rights of African Americans was not the only question to plague the Court in the aftermath of the Civil War. The Court also confronted the vexing question of whether the southern states could escape from their war debts in a number of cases between 1883 and 1890. Here, Bradley's influence was large; he wrote the majority opinion for the Court in the most important of these cases, *Hans v. Louisiana* (1890). *Hans*, which is the cornerstone of the Court's modern Eleventh Amendment jurisprudence, stands for the proposition that the Constitution protects a state's sovereign immunity from suit in federal court. The soundness of the history and logic Bradley employed to reach the decision in *Hans* was questioned by numerous constitutional scholars and even other justices of the Court.

Barbara Holden-Smith

FURTHER READING

Ely, James W., Jr. *The Fuller Court: Justices, Rulings, and Legacy.* Santa Barbara, Calif.: ABC-Clio, 2003.

Fairman, Charles. "Mr. Justice Bradley." In *Mr. Justice*, edited by Allison Dunham and Phillip B. Kurland. Chicago: University of Chicago Press, 1956.

————. *Reconstruction and Reunion, 1864-88, Part I.* New York: Macmillan, 1971.

Friedman, Leon. "Joseph Bradley." In *The Justices of the Supreme Court: Their Lives and Major Opinions*, edited by Leon Friedman and Fred L. Israel. 5 vols. New York: Chelsea House, 1997.

Lurie, Jonathan. *The Chase Court: Justices, Rulings, and Legacy.* Santa Barbara, Calif.: ABC-Clio, 2004.

Stephenson, Donald Grier, Jr. *The Waite Court: Justices, Rulings, and Legacy.* Santa Barbara, Calif.: ABC-Clio, 2003.

SEE ALSO *Bradwell v. Illinois*, *Civil Rights Cases*; *Cruikshank, United States v.*; Eleventh Amendment; Fourteenth Amendment; Gender issues; Grier, Robert C.; Race and discrimination, Reconstruction; Strong, William.

Bradwell v. Illinois

CITATION: 83 U.S. 130
DATE: April 15, 1873
ISSUE: Sex discrimination
SIGNIFICANCE: The Supreme Court upheld a state's denial of the right of women to enter a profession traditionally reserved for men.

Myra Bradwell studied law with her attorney husband, and she edited and published the *Chicago Legal News*, a leading publication of the Midwest. Although she had passed the bar exam, her application for a state license to practice law was rejected solely because of her sex. She argued that her rights under the privileges or immunities clause of the Fourteenth Amendment were violated. By an 8-1 vote, the Supreme Court rejected her claim. Speaking for the Court, Justice Samuel F. Miller applied the restrictive interpretation of the Fourteenth Amendment that he had announced the previous day in the *Slaughterhouse Cases*. The granting of licenses to practice law was entirely in the hands of the states and therefore not related to any question of national citizenship. In a concurring opinion, Joseph P. Bradley noted: "The natural and proper timidity and delicacy which belongs to the female sex evidently unfits it for many of the occupations of civil life."

Although the Illinois supreme court allowed Bradwell to practice law in 1890, it was not until *Reed v. Reed* (1971) that the Court applied the Fourteenth Amendment to overturn discriminatory laws based on sex.

Thomas Tandy Lewis

SEE ALSO Bradley, Joseph P.; Equal protection clause; Gender issues; Privileges and immunities; Reconstruction; *Reed v. Reed*; *Slaughterhouse Cases*.

Louis D. Brandeis

IDENTIFICATION: Associate justice (June 5, 1916-February 13, 1939)
NOMINATED BY: Woodrow Wilson
BORN: November 13, 1856, Louisville, Kentucky
DIED: October 5, 1941, Washington, D.C.
SIGNIFICANCE: Brandeis's focus on the facts of the case was part of a philosophy of sociological jurisprudence. His sympathy for the weak and poor and opposition to big corporate and government control helped shape the political response to both the excesses of corporate America and government incursions against personal liberties.

Except for three years spent in Central Europe, Louis D. Brandeis's formative years were not much different from those of other successful middle-class youth. He came from a very tightly knit, hard-working Bohemian German Jewish family and followed the American dream. He was an outstanding student at Harvard Law School and developed a commercial law practice in Boston.

The practice flourished, a testimony to Brandeis's skills as a lawyer: mastery of detail, logic of argument, clarity of communication, and focus on goals. His reputation spread and his wealth grew. Along the way, however, he became interested in protecting the rights of those who were disadvantaged and suffered from the damages caused by rapid industrialization and the immense power of the new corporate giants.

THE TWO PASSIONS

Much of Brandeis's work revolved around one central idea—the evil of bigness. He was convinced that excessive size and power were evil and incorrect. Bigness led to abuse of power and to corruption; moreover, it was inefficient, not just for the individual company but also for the society because it stifled competition.

For Brandeis, the issue was not simply economic—it was a moral crusade. Early on, in Boston, he started to fight big corporations: the railroad company that sought to monopolize the local railway, big banks, and utility companies. As his practice grew, Brandeis became more involved in public law, offering his service for free—a very uncommon practice then. His success in the courtroom led to wider contacts and to cases across the county, of sufficient repute that he was called the "people's lawyer." In one such case, *Muller v. Oregon* (1908), Brandeis prepared a very detailed, long legal brief explaining in much detail the impact on women of working long hours. This practice became known as a Brandeis Brief.

Brandeis's success in attacking big corporations and big government brought him into contact with leading Progressives. Although raised a progressive, antislavery Republican, he later switched to the increasingly liberal Democrats and became close to Woodrow Wilson. Brandeis consulted closely with the president and became one of the architects for Wilson's "New Freedom" program, basically regulation of business excesses, including the Clayton Act, a 1914 antitrust statute.

The second major passion was Zionism. Raised without formal religion and with little identification as a Jew, Brandeis became committed to Zionism as an adult. Over the course of his lifetime, he became the best-known leader of the American Zionist movement and a major activist on the world scene. His commitment to a Jewish state was built on his sympathy for the persecuted Jews of Eastern Europe and their need for a place of refuge.

ON THE COURT

Brandeis's reputation preceded him to the Supreme Court. He examined closely the facts of the cases and continued to be unsympathetic to large institutions. Nevertheless, he learned to use judicial restraint. He believed that the Court should not usurp the role of the legislature and that the national government should not suppress attempts by the state legislatures to regulate their economies. However, he also thought that no level of government should infringe on personal liberty.

Louis D. Brandeis.
(Library of Congress)

Brandeis challenged and eventually persuaded the Court to stop using the due process clause of the Fourteenth Amendment to strike down economic legislation, including regulation of child labor, as an infringement on the freedom of contract. He dissented in a number of cases that struck down New Deal legislation; again, the Court came around to his position. Ironically, Brandeis personally opposed much of this legislation because it created too strong a national government.

Brandeis also helped reverse the rule whereby federal courts could not ignore state law in favor of federal common law, in *Erie Railroad Co. v. Tompkins* (1938). This rule had allowed commercial litigants to move their cases to the federal courts where they could evade state commercial regulation.

In the area of civil liberties, however, Brandeis did believe that the Constitution set out strictures on the government that also applied to the states, especially in the matter of speech. It was not the government's business to regulate what the people heard; he believed that the people were eventually capable of making the right decisions.

Dissenting in *Gilbert v. Minnesota* (1920), Brandeis suggested that the liberty guaranteed by the Fourteenth Amendment extended beyond property rights to include personal freedoms such as those found in the Bill of Rights. Five years later, in *Gitlow v. New York* (1925), the Court accepted this idea, at least for freedom of speech. Later, many of the other provisions of the Bill of Rights were incorporated and applied to the states. Brandeis later wrote one of the most eloquent defenses of free expression in *Whitney v. California* (1927). Beyond free speech, Brandeis argued for the inclusion of privacy as one of the fundamental rights. Brandeis's powerful dissent in the wiretapping case *Olmstead v. United States* (1928) was used forty years later to protect privacy against a series of limitations set by the states, including the right to an abortion.

Brandeis's reputation and words long outlived him on the Court. Few justices had as strong an impact on the guidelines for preparing legal briefs and the acceptance of the relevance of sociological facts. Years later, his vision of personal liberty became accepted as the dominant constitutional standard.

Alan M. Fisher

119

FURTHER READING

Bader, William H., and Roy M. Mersky, eds. *The First One Hundred Eight Justices.* Buffalo, N.Y.: William S. Hein, 2004.

Dawson, Nelson L., ed. *Brandeis and America.* Lexington: University of Kentucky, 1989.

Mason, Alpheus T. *Brandeis: A Free Man's Life.* New York: Viking, 1946.

Paper, Lewis J. *Brandeis.* Englewood Cliffs, N.J.: Prentice-Hall, 1983.

Parrish, Michael E. *The Hughes Court: Justices, Rulings, and Legacy.* Santa Barbara, Calif.: ABC-Clio, 2002.

Renstrom, Peter G. *The Taft Court: Justices, Rulings, and Legacy.* Santa Barbara, Calif.: ABC-Clio, 2003.

Strum, Philippa. *Brandeis: Beyond Progressivism.* Lawrence: University of Kansas, 1993.

Urofsky, Melvin. *A Mind of One Piece: Brandeis and American Reform.* New York: Scribners, 1971.

Vile, John R., ed. *Great American Judges: An Encyclopedia.* Foreword by Kermit L. Hall. Santa Barbara, Calif.: ABC-Clio, 2003.

SEE ALSO Clarke, John H.; Common law; Dissents; First Amendment; Fourteenth Amendment; *Gitlow v. New York*; Incorporation doctrine; Privacy, right to; Progressivism; Taft, William H.; Takings clause.

Brandenburg v. Ohio

CITATION: 395 U.S. 444

DATE: February 27, 1969

ISSUE: Freedom of speech and assembly

SIGNIFICANCE: The Supreme Court overturned the conviction of a man under a criminal syndicalism statute, ruling that the advocacy of illegal action could be punished only if it was likely to produce imminent lawless action.

Clarence Brandenburg, a Ku Klux Klan member, was convicted of violating a criminal syndicalism statute for appearing in a television report brandishing a shotgun and advocating racial strife. The Supreme Court, in a unanimous unsigned *per curiam* decision, found it unconstitutional for a state to impose a criminal syndicalist statute punishing the mere advocacy of the overthrow of the U.S. government.

This ruling overturned *Whitney v. California* (1927), in which the Court had upheld a similar statute, and brought an end to fifty years of largely futile efforts to make the vague clear and present danger test of *Schenck v. United States* (1919) work in varying circumstances. At times, this test allowed the government to prosecute for speech that demonstrated a bad tendency or, as in *Dennis v. United States* (1951), for plans to publish unpopular views. By insisting that the government must demonstrate that the action was likely to incite imminent lawless action before prosecuting, the Court provided a much more concrete test that substantially strengthened free speech and validated the imminence test suggested in Justice Oliver Wendell Holmes's dissent in *Abrams v. United States* (1919).

Richard L. Wilson

SEE ALSO Bad tendency test; Censorship; First Amendment; *Gitlow v. New York*; *Schenck v. United States*; Seditious libel; Smith Act; Symbolic speech.

William J. Brennan, Jr.

IDENTIFICATION: Associate justice (October 16, 1956-July 20, 1990)
NOMINATED BY: Dwight D. Eisenhower
BORN: April 25, 1906, Newark, New Jersey
DIED: July 24, 1997, Arlington, Virginia
SIGNIFICANCE: Supreme Court justice Brennan created a legal philosophy designed to advance the dignity of all people. The goal of his jurisprudence of "libertarian dignity" was a highly egalitarian and pluralistic order that extended broad protection for freedom of expression and individual self-determination.

The son of an Irish Catholic, William J. Brennan, Jr., graduated from the University of Pennsylvania (1928) and Harvard Law School (1931). He drew inspiration from his father, who rose from laboring as a boiler attendant soon after arriving from Ireland in 1890 to become a city commissioner and director of public safety in Newark, New Jersey. After a tour of duty in World War II (1941-1945) and promotion to the rank of colonel in the U.S. Army, Brennan, a Democrat, soon found himself elevated to the New Jersey superior court in 1949 by Republican Governor Alfred Driscoll, then to the state supreme court in 1952.

Four years later, President Dwight D. Eisenhower, another Republican, announced that he had selected Brennan to fill Justice Sherman Minton's seat on the U.S. Supreme Court. The appointment of Brennan, a moderate Democrat, occurred during the height of the presidential campaign of 1956 and had definite political overtones. His selection was expected to be well received by Catholics in the Northeast and by Eisenhower Democrats. Brennan's emergence as a leader of the Court's liberal bloc by the early 1960's, however, led Eisenhower to regret his decision. By the time Brennan announced on July 20, 1990, that he was retiring from the Court for reasons of failing health, his authorship of trailblazing First and Fourteenth Amendment decisions had made him the leading liberal jurist of the last half of the twentieth century. From affirmative action to gender discrimination to general freedom of expression, Brennan's opinions chartered new ground for post-New Deal America. For his efforts, he received the Medal of Freedom, the nation's highest civilian award, from President Bill Clinton on November 30, 1993. In a tribute to Brennan, Associate Justice Byron R. White bluntly declared that his former colleague would be remembered "as among the greatest Justices who have ever sat on the Supreme Court."

ROLE OF THE JUDICIARY

The foundational pillars of Brennan's jurisprudence can be found in his thoughts on the power of the judiciary and on the oath of office taken by judicial officials. Brennan's judicial activism was a product of the conviction that it is not possible to accept the deficiencies of U.S. politics, some in the form of unchecked majoritarianism, and simultaneously be faithful to the Constitution. His willingness to cast judges as active participants in the process of adjusting the meaning of the Constitution to suit new challenges and new times is a hallmark of his jurisprudence. He defended an expansive interpretation of the federal habeas corpus power and of rules of justiciability such as standing requirements that affect when and how the courts may use their authority. His aim was to open up the judicial department to the largest number of possible claimants. His opinion for the Court in *Baker v. Carr*, a 1962 Tennessee malapportionment case, opened the door to judicial review of challenges to state electoral arrangements. In 1971 Brennan invited aggrieved parties to use the courts for redress in cases involving federal officials who historically had been shielded from suits by the sovereign immunity doctrine (*Bivens v. Six Unknown Named Narcotics Agents*, 1971).

Of particular concern to Brennan were threats posed by the modern administrative state. Writing in dissent in a 1976 disabilities case in which the claimant asserted a constitutional right to an oral hearing before the suspension of benefits under the Social Security program, Brennan rejected the government's appeal to costs and the sufficiency of post-termination procedures (*Mathews v. Eldridge*, 1976). Lurking behind his defense of judicial superintendence of the constitutional system was a belief that the judicial oath represented a sacred obligation to work for the achievement of a society based on the principle of libertarian dignity. He once declared that members of the legal profession should not rest until they have done everything within their power to ensure that the judicial system does not contribute to the denial of rights or perpetuate suffering due to unredressed injuries.

FIRST AMENDMENT

The process of freeing expression from significant restraints was initiated before Brennan joined the Court. What came of age with his assistance was a vigorous judicial defense of self-expression that challenged the constitutional bona fides of restraints historically associated with promoting respect for political institutions (flag desecration laws) or protecting the American way of life (libel and obscenity regulations). A relatively early articulation of Brennan's views on freedom of expression appears in his opinion in *New York Times Co. v. Sullivan* (1964), a civil rights-related case that challenged a judgment rendered against the *Times* under an Alabama libel law. Declaring that "debate on public issues should be uninhibited, robust and wide-open," Brennan set out the now famous "malice rule," which requires public officials to show that allegedly offensive statements are made with "'actual malice'—that is, with knowledge that [they are] false or with reckless disregard of whether [they are] false or not" in order to recover damages. The effect was to make it extremely difficult for public officials to win libel cases. With the chilling effect of these types of suits reduced, the visual and print media enjoyed a measure of freedom unparalleled in U.S. history. Brennan extended the effects of *Sullivan* in 1971 in *Rosenbloom v. Metromedia* with a ruling that applied the malice test to a civil libel action based on a radio broadcast about a person's involvement in an event of public interest. The "public interest" principle significantly expanded the malice rule beyond its original application to public officials.

Brennan reaffirmed his commitment to preserving a wide-open public forum two years after *Rosenbloom* in a dissent in *CBS v. Democratic National Committee* (1973) in which he asserted that the preservation of "an uninhibited marketplace of ideas" requires that people have access to "forums of communication" that will permit the widest possible dissemination of their views. In the Pentagon Papers case, *New York Times Co. v. United States* (1971), he argued that the Court should make it extremely difficult for the government to enjoin the publication of information even about secret military affairs. The defense of uninhibited expression led him to overturn state and national efforts to restrict flag burning as a form of expression in his final years on the Court. When the Court in 1978 permitted the Federal Communications Commission to place a warning in the file of a radio station that had aired a "Filthy Words" monologue by comedian George Carlin during daytime hours, Brennan characterized the ruling as "another in the dominant culture's inevitable efforts to force groups who do not share its mores to conform to its way of thinking, acting, and speaking." Five years earlier, he had dissented in two obscenity and pornography cases, *Miller v. California* and *Paris Adult Theatre v. Slaton*, on the grounds that the states should exercise little control over the entertainment habits of consenting adults. For Brennan, the republic of the First Amendment must not only permit but also really invite people to "flout majoritarian conventions." He believed that it was up to the people to decide whether they wished to engage in provocative communication or hear such expression from others. His frankly stated ideal was a "marketplace unsullied by the censor's hand."

FOURTEENTH AMENDMENT

Justice Brennan's role in articulating and defending expansive interpretations of due process and equal protection principles under the Fourteenth Amendment was similar to that he had played in interpreting First Amendment law. He skillfully used the due process and equal protection language of the Fourteenth Amendment to bring about an expansion in the sphere of individual rights and liberties. Brennan's major contribution in the Fourteenth Amendment due process area was not in first-time incorporation cases but in cases that went beyond questions having to do with whether specific Bill of Rights guarantees apply to state action. For example, Brennan defended pretermination hearings in welfare and disability benefits cases such as *Goldberg v. Kelly* (1970). In like fashion, he did not author separate opinions in groundbreaking substantive due process cases such as *Griswold v. Connecticut* (1965) and *Roe v. Wade* (1973), but he actively lobbied for extending the principles of these cases in *Cruzan v. Director, Missouri Department of Health* (1990) and *DeShaney v. Winnebago County Department of Social Services* (1989).

Notwithstanding the importance of Brennan's opinions in procedural and substantive due process cases, it is his authorship of major opinions dealing with the use of racial and gender classifications in equal protection clause cases that is principally responsible for the reputation he acquired in Fourteenth Amendment law. Brennan understood the potential of the equal protection principle for changing the United States. Especially noteworthy in this regard was his willingness to extend Congress almost unfettered power under section 5 of the Fourteenth Amendment to strike at discriminatory practices. He championed the so-called "benign" use of racial categories to remedy the lingering effects of historical discrimination in *Regents of the University of California v. Bakke* (1978) and *Metro Broadcasting v. Federal Communications Commission* (1990).

In *Katzenbach v. Morgan*, a 1966 voting rights act case, he combined

125

the power of the necessary and proper clause with the deference applied in commerce clause cases to enhance the power of the federal government to address equal protection claims. It was Brennan who led the way in urging the Court to treat gender distinctions as inherently suspect in *Frontiero v. Richardson* (1973). He was as impatient with delays in purging outdated gender distinctions from the law as he was with delays in making good on the promise to end racial segregation in *Green v. County School Board of New Kent County* (1968).

LIBERTARIAN DIGNITY

By addressing the difficulties associated with New Deal-style coalitional politics (such as perpetuation of discriminatory practices and malapportionment) and the modern bureaucratic state, Justice Brennan's jurisprudence can be viewed as an effort to complete the work of the political and judicial liberals who preceded him. His conviction that the United States could satisfy its historical destiny only when it was fully reconciled to being a "facilitative, pluralistic" society and not an "assimilative, homogeneous" one was matched by the belief that the country had reached a point in its development when practice might be expected to fulfill the high demands of theory. His opinions make clear that he believed the time had come to insist on government action that liberated the human will by removing or weakening constraints on the pursuit of preferred lifestyles while also compensating the victims of such constraints, for example, indigents or illegitimate children. Believing that government has a moral obligation *to do* whatever it *can do* to ensure comprehensive protection for all rights and redress for all grievances, Brennan had no difficulty in concluding that government officials can be guilty of sins of omission as well as of commission.

Although leading Founders such as George Washington and James Madison were careful to guard the capacity of the government to govern the people and defended institutions and practices that pointed the people in the direction of law-abidingness, Brennan shrank what government might do in the name of self-defense while inviting people to affirm their individual dignity through robust and uninhibited expression. It is not unreasonable to ask whether Brennan was demanding a better world than political life can offer. It is, however, the purity of Brennan's defense of the ideal of authentic individualism that warrants his identification as one of the major figures of American liberalism in the twentieth century.

David E. Marion

FURTHER READING

Brennan's Supreme Court career can be studied through three handy general reference works on the the three chief justices under whom he served: Melvin I. Urofsky's *The Warren Court: Justices, Rulings, and Legacy* (Santa Barbara, Calif.: ABC-Clio, 2001), Tinsley E. Yarbrough's *The Burger Court: Justices, Rulings, and Legacy* (Santa Barbara, Calif.: ABC-Clio, 2000), and Thomas R. Hensley's *The Rehnquist Court: Justices, Rulings, and Legacy* (Santa Barbara, Calif.: ABC-Clio, 2006). Peter Irons's *Brennan vs. Rehnquist* (New York: Alfred A. Knopf, 1994) uses the comparative method to accentuate the distinctive qualities of Brennan's jurisprudence and the role that he played as the dominant liberal justice during the last half of the twentieth century. *The Jurisprudence of Justice William J. Brennan, Jr.: The Law and Politics of "Libertarian Dignity"* by David E. Marion (Lanham, Md.: Rowman & Littlefield, 1997) presents a sober constitutionalist view of Brennan's opinions by offering frequent comparisons with the political and legal thinking of James Madison, John Marshall, Alexis de Tocqueville, and Abraham Lincoln.

For a careful review of the events surrounding Brennan's appointment to the Court, see Stephen Wermiel's "The Nomination of Justice Brennan: Eisenhower's Mistake? A Look at the Historical Record," *Constitutional Commentary* 11 (Winter, 1994-1995): 515-537. A useful account of Brennan's first decade on the Court appears in Stephen J. Friedman's "William Brennan," in *The Justices of the United States Supreme Court, 1789-1969: Their Lives and Major Opinions*, edited by Leon Friedman and Fred L. Israel (New York: Chelsea House, 1969). Brennan summarized his own thoughts on constitutional evolution and interpretation in "Reason, Passion, and 'the Progress of the Law,'" *Cardozo Law Review* 10 (1988): 3-23 and "Address to the Text and Teaching Symposium," in *The Great Debate: Interpreting Our Written Constitution* (Washington, D.C.: The Federalist Society, 1986).

SEE ALSO *Baker v. Carr;* Constitutional interpretation; Due process, procedural; Due process, substantive; First Amendment; Flag desecration; Fourteenth Amendment; Incorporation doctrine; Judicial activism; Minton, Sherman; *New York Times Co. v. Sullivan;* Obscenity and pornography; Race and discrimination; *Regents of the University of California v. Bakke.*

David J. Brewer

IDENTIFICATION: Associate justice (January 6, 1890-March 28, 1910)
NOMINATED BY: Benjamin Harrison
BORN: June 20, 1837, Smyrna, Asia Minor (later Izmir, Turkey)
DIED: March 28, 1910, Washington, D.C.
SIGNIFICANCE: In more than two decades on the Supreme Court, Brewer was the intellectual leader of an activist majority that regularly declared unconstitutional government-imposed labor and industrial regulations and interpreted the Constitution to protect private property and economic laissez-faire.

Although born in Asia to New England missionary parents, David J. Brewer returned to Connecticut in 1839, where he was reared in a climate of wealth and privilege. After graduating from Yale University at the age of eighteen, Brewer attended Albany Law School and was admitted to the bar in 1858. Shortly thereafter, he moved to Kansas to practice law in Leavenworth. Brewer served as commissioner of the federal circuit court, probate court judge, state district court judge, Kansas Supreme Court justice, and federal Eighth Circuit Court of Appeals judge.

In December, 1889, Brewer was nominated to the Supreme Court by President Benjamin Harrison. His nomination was approved in the Senate by a vote of fifty-two to eleven, and he took his seat on January 6, 1890. Brewer's record on the Court is a mixed one, although he is primarily remembered for his devotion to the protection of private property and his opposition to government regulation of the economy, labor unions, and laws protecting working people.

Writing the majority opinion for *In re Debs* (1895), Brewer upheld the

David J. Brewer.
(Library of Congress)

power of the government to stop labor strikes. In *Lochner v. New York* (1905), he joined the majority in declaring unconstitutional a state law that established the maximum number of hours per day that bakers could work. In *United States v. E. C. Knight Co.* (1895), he joined the majority in reading the Sherman Antitrust Act of 1890 so that many monopolies would remain untouched by it. However, it was Brewer who wrote the unanimous opinion in *Muller v. Oregon* (1908) upholding a maximum-hour workday law for women employed in laundries.

On race issues, Brewer's record was similarly mixed. Although he opposed slavery and favored the rights of Asian immigrants (*United States v. Wong Kim Ark*, 1898) and American Indians (*Brown v. Steele*, 1880), he also held in favor of segregated railway cars (*Louisville, New Orleans & Texas Railway Co. v. Mississippi*, 1890) and voted to uphold a state law prohibiting integrated classrooms in private schools and colleges (*Berea College v. Kentucky*, 1908). Likewise, he also voted to uphold a Virginia law prohibiting women from joining the bar (*In re Lockwood*, 1894).

Michael W. Bowers

129

FURTHER READING

Brodhead, Michael J. *David J. Brewer: The Life of a Supreme Court Justice, 1837-1910*. Carbondale: Southern Illinois University Press, 1994.

Ely, James W., Jr. *The Fuller Court: Justices, Rulings, and Legacy*. Santa Barbara, Calif.: ABC-Clio, 2003.

Gillman, Howard. *The Constitution Besieged: The Rise and Demise of Lochner Era Police Power Jurisprudence*. Durham, N.C.: Duke University Press, 1993.

SEE ALSO *Baker v. Carr*; Commerce, regulation of; *Debs, In re*; *Lochner v. New York*; Race and discrimination; Segregation, de jure.

Stephen G. Breyer

IDENTIFICATION: Associate justice (August 3, 1994-   )
NOMINATED BY: Bill Clinton
BORN: August 15, 1938, San Francisco, California
SIGNIFICANCE: A respected expert in the fields of administrative, antitrust, and environmental law, Breyer has been widely recognized to be a pragmatic and conciliatory justice, even as he has usually voted with the liberal wing of the Court.

Raised in a middle-class, politically active Jewish family in San Francisco, Stephen G. Breyer was an outstanding student and successful debater in high school. He earned bachelor's degrees from both Stanford and Oxford Universities. While attending Harvard Law School, he served as editor for its law review. After graduating magna cum laude 1964, he worked as a clerk for Supreme Court justice Arthur J. Goldberg. He then served as assistant to the attorney general for antitrust (1965-1967) and as assistant special prosecutor in the Watergate investigations of 1973. He taught law and public policy at Harvard University from 1967 to 1980.

In 1980, President Jimmy Carter named Breyer to the Court of Appeals for the First Circuit, where he gained a reputation for outstanding judicial work in a large variety of fields, including the jurisprudence of Puerto Rico. He also found time to write a balanced and highly regarded book, *Regulation and Its Reform* (1982), which analyzed agency accountability, cost-benefit analysis, and legislative oversight. In addition, he served as a leading member of the U.S. Sentencing Commission from 1985 to 1989, and he was elevated to the chief judgeship of the First Circuit in 1990. In 1994, President Bill Clinton chose him to replace retiring Harry A. Blackmun on the Supreme Court. The Senate easily confirmed the noncontroversial nomination with a vote of eighty-seven to nine.

JURISPRUDENCE AND DECISIONS

On the bench, Breyer's approach to constitutional issues has been pragmatic and moderately left of center. He explains his perspective in *Active Liberty: Interpreting Our Democratic Constitution* (2005), which in some ways is a refutation of Justice Antonin Scalia's approach of looking primarily to the original meaning of the text. Rather than this originalism, Breyer advocates that judges should attempt to help achieve the democratic intentions of the Constitution. He also suggests that an international consensus can help define American principles of human rights. Such views tended to associate Breyer with the more liberal members of the Court: Justices John Paul Stevens, Ruth Bader Ginsburg, and David H. Souter.

Breyer consistently has held that the due process clause protects broad "liberty interests," including "a woman's right to choose" to have an abortion. Writing the opinion for the 5-4 majority in *Stenberg v. Carhart* (2000), he argued that Nebraska's late-term abortion law was unconstitutional because it placed an "undue burden" on the woman's right and did not have an exception in cases of threatened health. Likewise, in the case of *Lawrence v. Texas* (2003), he joined the majority in ruling that the due process clause protected the liberty of consenting adults to engage in homosexual relationships in a private home. While agreeing in *Washington v. Glucksberg* (1997) that the Constitution protects no right to have assistance in committing suicide, Breyer wrote that the Court should recognize a right to die with dignity.

Breyer could also be counted on to join the liberal justices in cases involving equal protection and affirmative action. In *Adarand Constructors v. Peña* (1995), he opposed application of strict scrutiny when reviewing affirmative action programs. In *Grutter v. Bollinger* (2003), he firmly supported the use of racial preferences in university admissions policies. In *Boy Scouts v. Dale* (2000), he dissented from the majority's ruling that the organization's rights of association trumped the state's interest in outlawing discrimination based on sexual orientation.

Breyer has been highly critical of the more conservative justices' interpretations on the Tenth Amendment and Congress's powers to regulate commerce. When a five-member majority in *United States v. Lopez* (1995) ruled that the federal government could not regulate the possession of firearms in school zones, Breyer wrote a strong dissent, arguing that the majority had approved of government regulations of schools in matters such as illegal drugs and asbestos. Like-

Justice Stephen G. Breyer with his wife and granddaughter as he prepares to throw the ceremonial first pitch at a Boston Red Sox game in July, 2006. (AP/Wide World Photos)

wise, in *Printz v. United States* (1997), he joined the dissenters in arguing that the federal government under its commerce powers should be allowed to require local law-enforcement officers to make background checks of persons buying firearms.

The respective positions were reversed in the case of *Bush v. Gore* (2000), when the five more conservative justices made a unique application of the equal protection clause and ordered an end to the Florida vote recount, thereby assuring that George W. Bush would be the next president. In this instance, Breyer argued that no federal issue was involved and that Florida's government should have been allowed to decide which candidate had won the state's electoral votes. The legal profession tended to agree more with Breyer than with Rehnquist and his allies.

Breyer has shown a special interest in technical and arcane cases. Given his expertise in administrative law, it is surprising that he was chosen to write the opinion for the Court in *Dickinson v. Zurko* (1999), a patent case that focused on whether the "substantial evidence" standard that is used in reviewing a federal agency's finding was the same as the "clearly erroneous" standard that federal appeals courts used in reviewing district courts. He concluded that there was a "subtle" difference, but that it was of little consequence in actual practice. As the Court began examining more complex cases involving complex matters of science and technology, it was expected that Breyer would play a central role.

Although identified with the liberal wing of the Court, Breyer regularly advocated an examination of each case on its merits with an elimination of ideological bias to the extent possible. He has always avoided dogmatism and his language has never been caustic. He has enjoyed giving speeches and has frequently appeared in television interviews. Despite the workload of the Court, he has continued to find time to write articles and books for publication.

Thomas Tandy Lewis

FURTHER READING

Breyer, Stephen G. *Active Liberty: Interpreting Our Democratic Constitution.* New York: Knopf, 2005. Expresses his relatively liberal views on jurisprudence.

Deegan, Paul. *Stephen Breyer.* Minneapolis: Abdo, 1996.

Gottlieb, Stephen. *Morality Imposed: the Rehnquist Court and the State of Liberty in America.* New York: New York University Press, 2000.

Hensley, Thomas R. *The Rehnquist Court: Justices, Rulings, and Legacy.* Santa Barbara, Calif.: ABC-Clio, 2006.

Perry, Barbara. *The Supremes: Essays on the Current Justices of the Supreme Court.* New York: P. Lang, 2001.

SEE ALSO Affirmative action; Blackmun, Harry A.; *Boy Scouts of America v. Dale*; *Bush v. Gore*; Die, right to; Environmental law; Goldberg, Arthur J.; *Gratz v. Bollinger/ Grutter v. Bollinger*; Scalia, Antonin.

Briefs

DESCRIPTION: Written arguments submitted to the Supreme Court by the parties in the cases and other interested individuals or organizations. The documents are called briefs because the Court limits the scope and length of documents it permits to be filed.

SIGNIFICANCE: Briefs present the case to the Court in a clear and concise manner. As the first contact of the Court with the case, briefs have great influence on the justices.

Of the thousands of *certiorari* petitions filed each year, only about one hundred twenty cases are selected to be heard by the Supreme Court. Therefore, the importance of the briefs filed to the Court cannot be overstated. Although oral argument may provide a dramatic stage for presenting the case, the written briefs contain the advocate's best efforts in written persuasion, and the Court will have scrutinized the briefs before hearing oral argument.

CONTENT OF THE BRIEF

Various briefs are filed with the Court. Each is required to be bound with a particular binding: blue for petitioner, red for respondent, yellow for reply briefs, green for *amicus curiae* briefs, gray for the solicitor general's briefs, and tan for appendices briefs. Under the Court rules, the briefs are generally limited to fifty pages and must adhere to certain requirements of order, format, and content. The brief for the petitioner, for example, must include the following sections in the order stated: Questions Presented, List of Parties and Corporations, Tables of Contents and Authorities, Opinions Below, Jurisdiction, Statutes Involved, Statement of the Case, Summary of the Argument, Argument, and Conclusion. Although the Argument is the longest section in the brief, two sections in the preliminary parts of the brief are vitally important. In the Questions Presented section, counsel articulates the exact questions raised in the appeal, and in the Statement of the Case, counsel establishes the factual foundation on which the argument is based. Both these preliminary sections, although short, must provide the Court with a clear overview of the brief's position.

The Argument section of the brief thoroughly explains and promotes the party's position. An effective argument is written in clear, plain English and is well organized. Mere citation of cases never supplants the careful analysis and application of those cases to the issue before the Court. The analysis of a cited case involves demonstrating its relevance to the appeal, an analysis of the cited case's reasoning, and a demonstration of its application to the issue at hand, usually by analogizing the facts of the decided case to the facts of the issue now before the Court. The Argument will discuss not only favorable precedent but also that which opposes the proposition advanced. Because a decision by the Court usually has far-reaching policy implications, briefs must also contain persuasive policy arguments that illustrate the reasonableness of the argument promoted.

Some of the rhetorical devices used in the Argument section can be traced to classical antiquity where the term "rhetoric" was more closely attached to legal argument than it is today. Although these early arguments were indeed oral arguments, many of those rhetorical devices are seen in the Argument sections of effective briefs, including not only the discovery of available arguments but also their arrangement and rebuttal. Hence it is not unusual to identify various rhetorical devices being used by the skillful advocate.

ORDER AND PROCEDURE

The petitioner's brief is filed first, followed by the respondent's brief, which is followed in turn by the petitioner's reply brief. The petitioner's brief faces some special problems in that the petitioner's brief is written and filed without seeing the respondent's brief. Hence the petitioner must anticipate the arguments and the cases that the opposition may plan to use. The lawyer is also under an ethical obligation governed by the Code of Professional Responsibility, which requires that a lawyer disclose to the Court legal authority that is directly adverse to the client's position. Apart from the ethical obligation, it is effective advocacy to include hostile precedent because it provides the brief writer with an opportunity to present these cases in a light that still illuminates the strength of the position argued. Here the advocate must distinguish the unfavorable precedent from the present case on its facts, establish that the reasoning of the case is flawed, or show that to adopt the holding of the case would be bad policy. To overlook unfavorable precedent would play into the opposition's hands. The petitioner, by filing its brief first, has the advantage of defining the issues first so that the respondent must redirect the Court's attention rather than just argue the respondent's position. Well-written respondent's briefs are more than mere responses to the petitioner's brief; they are also able to weave their affirmative arguments into that response. Finally, the petitioner also has the right to a reply brief, a shorter brief, usually no more than twenty-five pages, that attempts to rebut arguments raised in the respondent's brief, somewhat similarly to the way the petitioner uses rebuttal on oral argument.

In a departure from tradition, in 1997 a brief in compact disk format was filed with the Court. This brief contained internal hypertext markup language (html) with electronic links to the record and cases cited in the brief.

Amicus curiae ("friend of the court") briefs are filed by individuals or organizations that, although not a party to the appeal, have an interest in the appeal. These briefs are filed only with the permission of both the party the brief favors and the Court. Controversial issues usually invite such briefs. Most *amicus* briefs are filed by the solicitor general on behalf of the federal government. In some years the Court may see as many as three thousand such briefs.

Paul Bateman

FURTHER READING

Aldisert, Ruggero J. *Winning on Appeal: Better Briefs and Oral Argument.* Notre Dame, Ind.: National Institute for Trial Advocacy, 1996.

Del Carmen, Rolando V., and Jeffrey T. Walker, eds. *Briefs of Leading Cases in Law Enforcement.* 5th ed. Cincinnati: Anderson, 2004.

Simpson, Reagan William. *The Amicus Brief: How to Be a Good Friend of the Court.* 2d ed. Chicago: ABA, Tort Trial and Insurance Practice Section, 2004.

Stern, Robert L., Eugene Gressman, and Stephen M. Shapiro. *Supreme Court Practice.* 6th ed. Washington, D.C.: Bureau of National Affairs, 1986.

United States Supreme Court. *Landmark Briefs and Arguments of the Supreme Court of the United States.* Washington, D.C.: University Publications of America, 1893-   .

Ward, Artemus, and David L. Weiden. *Sorcerers' Apprentices: One Hundred Years of Law Clerks at the United States Supreme Court.* New York: New York University Press, 2006.

SEE ALSO Conference of the justices; Oral argument; Review, process of; Rules of the Court; Solicitor general.

Henry B. Brown

IDENTIFICATION: Associate justice (January 5, 1891-May 28, 1906)
NOMINATED BY: Benjamin Harrison
BORN: March 2, 1836, South Lee, Massachusetts
DIED: September 4, 1913, Bronxville, New York
SIGNIFICANCE: Appointed to the Supreme Court largely for his expertise in admiralty law, Brown ultimately was remembered as the author of the 1896 opinion upholding the legality of "separate but equal" facilities for blacks and whites.

Born into a wealthy merchant family in South Lee, Massachusetts, Henry B. Brown graduated from Yale University in 1856. He moved to Detroit, Michigan, three years later and studied law at a private law office, subsequently completing his legal education by attending lec-

Henry B. Brown.
(Library of Congress)

tures at both Harvard and Yale. Admitted to the bar in 1860, Brown was appointed deputy U.S. marshal for Michigan one year later and in 1868 resigned his position to begin a lucrative private practice in Detroit.

Republican Brown made an unsuccessful bid for Congress before securing an appointment by President Ulysses S. Grant as U.S. District Court judge for eastern Michigan. Appointed in 1875, he acquired a nationwide reputation as an authority on admiralty law. The large number of admiralty cases arising out of shipping on the Great Lakes made *Brown's Admiralty Reports* universally accepted as the final word on that area of the law. He also became a regular lecturer on that topic at Michigan University.

Appointed to the Supreme Court by Benjamin Harrison in 1890, Brown took his seat on January 5, 1891. He acquired a reputation for impartiality, patience, courtesy, and a willingness to admit past errors during his fifteen years of service. Justice Brown was viewed as a moderate who favored property rights over civil rights. Concurring with the majority in *Lochner v. New York* (1905), he rejected New York's maximum-hour workday law as a violation of contractual freedom. Brown also joined the Court in its unanimous ruling destroying the power of the Sherman Antitrust Act of 1890 in *United States v. E. C. Knight Co.* (1895). He was the only northern justice to vote to uphold the legality of the income tax in *Pollock v. Farmers' Loan and Trust Co.* (1895) and authored opinions sanctioning the acquisition of Puerto Rico by the United States. However, Brown's most famous (or infamous) opinion was in the 1896 case of *Plessy v. Ferguson.* By upholding a Louisiana statute allowing for "separate but equal" facilities in that state's public transportation system, he in effect incorporated the concept of Jim Crow into the U.S. Constitution and thus initiated a constitutional crisis that was not to begin to correct itself until the *Brown v. Board of Education* decision of 1954.

Brown's abilities were severely impaired when a malady cost him his sight in his right eye in 1900 and rendered him unable to work without the assistance of others. The next year, Brown was further weakened by the death of his wife of thirty-seven years. Brown remarried in 1904 and retired from the bench two years later.

Harvey Gresham Hudspeth

FURTHER READING

Bader, William H., and Roy M. Mersky, eds. *The First One Hundred Eight Justices.* Buffalo, N.Y.: William S. Hein, 2004.

Ely, James W., Jr. *The Fuller Court: Justices, Rulings, and Legacy.* Santa Barbara, Calif.: ABC-Clio, 2003.

Glennon, Robert Jerome. *Justice Henry Billings Brown: Values in Tension.* Denver: University of Colorado Law Review, 1971.

SEE ALSO *Brown v. Board of Education*; Livingston, Brockholst; *Lochner v. New York*; *Plessy v. Ferguson.*

Brown v. Board of Education

CITATION: 347 U.S. 483
DATE: May 17, 1954
ISSUE: Desegregation
SIGNIFICANCE: The Supreme Court unanimously held that de jure (legally mandated) segregation of the public schools was prohibited by the equal protection clause of the Fourteenth Amendment.

Following the Civil War (1861-1865), racial segregation in public accommodations and education—through so-called "Jim Crow" laws—was one of the major tools of the southern states for maintaining a social system of white supremacy. In *Plessy v. Ferguson* (1896), the Supreme Court allowed state-mandated racial segregation based on the separate but equal doctrine. In *Cumming v. Richmond County Board of Education* (1899), the Court simply ignored the equal part of the doctrine when it allowed a community to maintain a public high school for white students without any similar institution for African Americans. In *Gong Lum v. Rice* (1927), the Court explicitly recognized the "right and power" of the states to require segregation in the public schools.

THE CHALLENGE BEGINS

In the 1930's the Legal Defense Fund of the National Association for the Advancement of Colored People (NAACP) began to mount a serious challenge to the constitutionality of Jim Crow laws in education. Rather than confronting *Plessy* directly, the NAACP first concentrated on equality of opportunity at publicly funded law schools. Decisions such as *Missouri ex rel. Gaines v. Canada* (1938) and *Sweatt v. Painter* (1950) indicated that the Court would insist on substantial equality of educational opportunity. In *McLaurin v. Oklahoma State Regents for Higher Education* (1950), the Court recognized that the policy of required separation was sometimes relevant to educational equality. With these victories, Thurgood Marshall and other NAACP lawyers decided that the time was ripe to question the constitutionality of segregation in elementary and secondary education.

Linda Carol Brown, an eight-year-old black girl, was not allowed to attend the all-white school in her neighborhood of Topeka, Kansas. Her parents did not want her to be bused to the all-black school, which was far from home, and they filed a suit charging a violation of the Fourteenth Amendment. When the case was appealed to the Supreme Court, it was consolidated with similar cases from South Carolina, Virginia, Delaware, and Washington, D.C. The cases were listed in alphabetical order, so that the name *Brown v. Board of Education* appeared first. The cases were first argued in December, 1952. Marshall and other NAACP lawyers emphasized the psychological and sociological evidence of negative effects from mandated segregation. In defense of segregation, the school districts invoked *Plessy* and claimed that their all-black schools either had or would soon have equal funding for facilities and teachers' salaries.

THE COURT'S RESPONSE

Because of the great opposition to school integration in the South, the justices recognized the desirability of presenting a united front in both the decision and the opinion. At least six of the justices agreed that *Plessy* should be reversed, but they strongly disagreed about how rapidly to proceed. One justice, Stanley F. Reed, argued on behalf of the continuation of *Plessy*, and another justice, Robert H. Jackson, wanted to move very cautiously and appeared determined to write a concurring opinion if the majority opinion were too critical of the Court's past approval of segregation. Deciding that it needed more information about the original intention of the Framers and ratifiers of the Fourteenth Amendment, the Court scheduled a second argumentation of the cases for December, 1953. That summer, Chief Justice Fred M. Vinson, a moderate who was hesitant to order massive desegregation, unexpectedly died, and he was quickly replaced by the popular governor of California, Earl Warren. After Brown was reargued, Warren persuaded his colleagues to defer the question of relief, and he skillfully consulted with the various justices in order to get a consensus. About a week before the decision was announced, Jackson decided not to issue a concurrence and Reed agreed not to dissent.

Warren's opinion for the Court, written in thirteen paragraphs of nontechnical language, declared that segregation in public education was "inherently unequal" and therefore unconstitutional. The public interpreted racial segregation of students "as denoting the inferiority of the Negro group," generating among African Americans "a feeling of inferiority as to their status in the community that may affect their hearts and minds in a way unlikely ever to be undone." Warren found that the historical evidence about the original intent of the Fourteenth Amendment was "inconclusive." Even if the Framers and ratifiers had not intended to prohibit segregation in education, they had wanted to provide equal rights for public services, and the experiences of the twentieth century demonstrated that segregated schools were incompatible with the goal of equality. Formal education in the twentieth century, moreover, was much more important for a person's life chances than it had been when the Fourteenth Amendment was written.

IMPLEMENTING DESEGREGATION

The following year, in a decision commonly called *Brown II*, the Court addressed the issue of implementing desegregation. The NAACP wanted to proceed rapidly with firm deadlines, and the states warned that rapid desegregation would lead to withdrawal from the public schools and acts of violence. The Court settled on a cautious and ambiguous formula, requiring that segregation end "with all deliberate speed." The implementation of *Brown II*, which left much discretion to federal district judges, proceeded somewhat slowly for the first ten years. In *Alexander v. Holmes County* (1969), the Court abandoned the deliberate speed formula and ordered an immediate end to all remaining de jure segregation.

Brown is probably the most momentous and influential civil rights case of the twentieth century. In effect, the decision meant the eventual elimination of all state-sanctioned segregation. When *Brown* was announced, its implications were unclear in regard to the constitutionality of freedom of choice plans and de facto segregated schools based on housing patterns. The Court began to move beyond the issue of de jure segregation in *Green v. County School Board of New Kent County* (1968), ruling that previously segregated school districts had an "affirmative duty" to take the steps necessary to promote racially integrated schools.

Thomas Tandy Lewis

FURTHER READING

Bell, Derrick. *Silent Covenants: "Brown v. Board of Education" and the Unfulfilled Hopes for Racial Reform.* New York: Oxford University Press, 2004.

Clotfelter, Charles T. *After Brown: The Rise and Retreat of School Desegregation.* Princeton, N.J.: Princeton University Press, 2004.

Friedman, Leon, ed. *Brown v. Board: The Landmark Oral Argument Before the Supreme Court.* New York: New Press, 2004.

Kluger, Richard. *Simple Justice: The History of "Brown v. Board of Education" and Black America's Struggle for Equality.* New York: Alfred A. Knopf, 1976.

Martin, Waldo. *"Brown v. Board of Education": A Brief History with Documents.* Boston: Bedford/St. Martin's, 1998.

Ogletree, Charles J., Jr. *All Deliberate Speed: Reflections on the First Half Century of "Brown v. Board of Education."* New York: W. W. Norton & Co., 2004.

Patterson, James T. *"Brown v. Board of Education": A Civil Rights Milestone and Its Troubled Legacy.* New York: Oxford University Press, 2002.

Sarat, Austin, ed. *Race, Law, and Culture: Reflections on "Brown v. Board of Education."* New York: Oxford University Press, 1997.

Webb, Clive, ed. *Massive Resistance: Southern Opposition to the Second Reconstruction.* New York: Oxford University Press, 2005.

Whitman, Mark. *Removing a Badge of Slavery: The Record of "Brown v. Board of Education."* Princeton, N.J.: Wiener, 1992.

SEE ALSO *Bolling v. Sharpe*; Fourteenth Amendment; *Plessy v. Ferguson*; Race and discrimination; *Schechter Poultry Corp. v. United States*; Segregation, de jure; Warren, Earl.

Brown v. Mississippi

CITATION: 297 U.S. 278
DATE: February 17, 1936
ISSUES: Coerced confessions; defendants' rights
SIGNIFICANCE: The Supreme Court held that the due process clause of the Fourteenth Amendment prohibited states from using criminal confessions obtained by means "revolting to the sense of justice."

In the early 1930's, three African American tenant farmers in Mississippi were convicted of murdering a white planter. The main evidence was their confessions. At trial, police officers admitted that they had employed brutal whippings and threats of death to obtain the confessions. The defendants, nevertheless, were convicted and sentenced to be hanged. The Mississippi Supreme Court upheld the constitutionality of their trials and convictions.

By a 9-0 vote, the Supreme Court reversed the state court's ruling. Chief Justice Charles Evans Hughes's opinion held that coerced confessions violated a principle "so rooted in the traditions and conscience of our people as to be ranked as fundamental." At the same time, however, the Court reaffirmed that the self-incrimination clause of the Fifth Amendment was not binding on the states. Despite its modest requirements, *Brown* was the first in a line of cases requiring fundamental fairness for the use of confessions in state trials.

Thomas Tandy Lewis

SEE ALSO Due process, substantive; Fifth Amendment; Hughes, Charles Evans; Incorporation doctrine; Miranda rights; Self-incrimination, immunity against.

Buck v. Bell

CITATION: 274 U.S. 200
DATE: May 2, 1927
ISSUE: Compulsory sterilization
SIGNIFICANCE: This case upheld the authority of states to require sterilization of any person deemed to be mentally defective.

In 1924 the Virginia legislature passed a statute that required the sexual sterilization of many "feebleminded" persons in state mental institutions. The law provided for procedural rights, including a hearing, appointment of a guardian, approval of an institution's board, and appeals to the courts. The superintendent of the Virginia State Colony for Epileptics and Feebleminded recommended sterilization for Carrie Buck, who was classified as feebleminded and a "moral delinquent." Because Buck's mother and daughter were also alleged to be mentally deficient, she was considered an ideal test case for the law. After state courts decided in favor of the state's position, the Supreme Court upheld the lower court decisions by an 8-1 vote.

Justice Oliver Wendell Holmes, writing the opinion for the majority, found that the law did not violate any principles of equal protection and that its procedural guarantees were more than adequate. Accepting the eugenics notions of the day, Holmes argued that if society could call on its "best citizens" to sacrifice their lives in war, it could call upon those who already sap the strength of the State for these lesser sacrifices." In this context, he made the notorious statement that "three generations of imbeciles are enough." Holmes had no way of knowing that Carrie Buck's child was the result of a rape and that she had actually done acceptable work in school until withdrawn by her guardians to do housework.

After the *Buck v. Bell* ruling, many states passed similar sterilization laws, and more than fifty thousand persons were sterilized nationwide. The practice of sterilization, however, was generally discontinued by the 1970's. Although *Buck* was never directly overturned, it was based on eugenics theories later considered invalid and appears inconsistent with several of the Court's decisions upholding reproductive freedom.

Thomas Tandy Lewis

SEE ALSO Birth control and contraception; Equal protection clause; Fundamental rights; Gender issues; Holmes, Oliver Wendell; Privacy, right to.

Warren E. Burger

IDENTIFICATION: Chief justice (June 23, 1969-September 26, 1986)
NOMINATED BY: Lyndon B. Johnson
BORN: September 17, 1907, St. Paul, Minnesota
DIED: June 25, 1995, Washington, D.C.
SIGNIFICANCE: Burger, who spent seventeen years on the Supreme Court, served the longest term as chief justice in the twentieth century, earning high praise for his achievement in judicial administration. As a jurist, Burger was most noted for his opinions on the separation of powers, desegregation, religion, obscenity, and procedure.

Warren E. Burger was the fourth of seven children born to Charles Joseph and Katharine (Schnittger) Burger. His father worked as a railroad cargo inspector and salesman. Burger described his mother as running an "old-fashioned German house," instilling "common sense" in her children. Burger always loved the U.S. Constitution and wanted to be a lawyer, even as a young boy. Suffering from polio at age eight, he was kept home from school for a year, and his teacher brought many biographies of great judges and lawyers for the boy to read.

In high school, Burger was president of the student council, editor of the school paper, and a letterman in hockey, football, track, and swimming. He earned a scholarship from Princeton University but turned it down to stay at home and help support his family. Attending night school at the University of Minnesota from 1925 to 1927, he was president of the student council. He attended night classes at the St. Paul College of Law (later the William Mitchell College of Law) and graduated with his LL.B. magna cum laude in 1931. He sold life insurance while attending evening classes in college and law school.

POLITICAL CAREER

Burger started working in a law firm in 1931, made partner in 1935, and taught law at his alma mater. During the course of his law work, he met Republican Harold E. Stassen. Burger organized Stassen's successful campaign for governor in 1938.

Warren E. Burger.
(Robert Oakes/
Collection of the
Supreme Court of
the United States)

In 1948 Burger went to the Republican Party National Convention, where he met Richard M. Nixon, another Stassen supporter. At the 1952 Republican convention, when Dwight D. Eisenhower emerged as the party's leading presidential hopeful, Burger was the key figure in a floor decision shifting Stassen support to ensure Eisenhower's nomination on the first ballot. Eisenhower was favorably impressed, and in 1953 Burger was appointed U.S. assistant attorney general.

On June 21, 1955, Eisenhower nominated Burger to a judgeship on the District of Columbia Circuit Court of Appeals. His confirmation was stalled when discrimination charges were made by employees whom Burger had fired for incompetence. Burger was finally sworn in on April 13, 1956. Burger developed an early interest in court administration and worked with the American Bar Association to create an efficient and competent federal judiciary. His critique of "moral neglect" by the Supreme Court in decisions on insanity and self-incrimination gained him national attention.

APPOINTMENT TO THE SUPREME COURT

On May 21, 1969, Burger was nominated as chief justice by President Nixon. Burger was to be the "law and order" appointee for whom Nixon had campaigned. He was confirmed by a Senate vote of seventy-four to three on June 9, 1969, with numerous endorsements from leaders of the American Bar Association and other bar groups. Departing chief justice Earl Warren swore him in on June 23, 1969.

Burger served seventeen court terms as chief justice, a tenure as chief justice exceeded only by John Marshall, Roger Brooke Taney, and Melville W. Fuller. On June 17, 1986, President Ronald Reagan announced Burger's resignation and the nomination of William H. Rehnquist to succeed Burger. On September 26, 1986, at age seventy-eight, Burger officially retired as chief justice.

BURGER AND JUDICIAL ADMINISTRATION

Even Burger's critics admit that he accomplished more in the area of judicial administration than anyone in U.S. legal history. Burger's greatest accomplishment was his innovation of improvements in judicial operations.

Burger contributed to judicial administration in at least six major areas. He added new administrative support to the Court with an administrative assistant to the chief justice, judicial fellows, public relations professionals, librarians, clerks, and vast improvements to the law library and technology of the Court. He continued his efforts with the American Bar Association in judicial education programs with the National Judicial College. He developed the Federal Judicial Center and National Center for State Courts to gather data on courts, research judicial reforms, and train and inform the judiciary. He convened lectures and colloquia to bring together key decision makers to discuss judicial administration. He urged training in actual legal skills and litigation practice in law schools, continuing education for lawyers, and programs such as the American Inns of Court. Burger is considered the father of alternative dispute resolution and court mediation, arbitration, and other alternatives to litigation.

Burger believed the greatest threat to the Court was its case docket overload, which had climbed from 4,202 cases and 88 signed opinions in the 1969 term to 5,158 cases and 161 signed opinions in the 1985 term. Burger was successful in lobbying Congress to limit the Court's mandatory jurisdiction docket, narrow federal three-judge court jurisdiction, place sanctions against attorneys for abuse of process, and create a special Court of Appeals for the Federal Circuit for expertise in patent, copyright, and trademark. He was not successful in such reforms as an Intercircuit Tribunal to take a burden off the Court for resolving conflicts between the federal circuits. Burger wanted a central judicial administrator similar to the Lord Chancellor of England, which did not come to fruition.

BURGER AS A JURIST

Burger proved to be difficult to categorize as a jurist. He was supposed to have been "Nixon's man" and lead the Court in a conservative revolution. Instead he rejected Nixon's arguments for executive privilege, limited congressional oversight of the bureaucracy, joined to establish abortion rights, upheld school busing, and defended freedom for religious minorities. Some analyses conclude that Burger was neither conservative nor liberal but pragmatic and concerned with street-level implementation and administrative aspects of decisions. He was more concerned with efficiency and democratic accountability than in preserving tradition or some other conservative impulse.

As chief justice, Burger wrote 265 opinions of the Court in addition to separate concurring and dissenting opinions. Although this was a high output, most of his opinions have not endured as landmark decisions. Greatly distracted by judicial administration matters, Burger tended to assign the landmark decisions to others, and he believed in a limited role of the judiciary in resolving public controversies. However, he was most noted for three opinions on the separation of powers in the federal government, as well as a few opinions on desegregation, religion, obscenity, and procedure.

SEPARATION OF POWERS

Burger's lifelong love for the Constitution is demonstrated by three landmark decisions on separation of powers. In *United States v. Nixon* (1974), a unanimous Court ruled against President Nixon and ordered him to comply with subpoenas of the special prosecutor investigating the Watergate Hotel burglary and other crimes. Burger rejected Nixon's argument of executive privilege to keep confidential the tape recordings of White House discussions. Separation of powers was preserved by the Court not only by affirming the special prosecutor's power of subpoena over the president but also in this "declaration of independence" of the Court by Burger and three other justices appointed by Nixon.

In *Immigration and Naturalization Service v. Chadha* (1983), Burger preserved separation of powers between Congress and the federal bureaucracy by striking down the legislative veto. The legislative veto allowed Congress to delegate duties to the Immigration and Naturalization Service to decide to deport individual aliens yet also revoke the specific immigration service decision to deport Mr. Chadha in a one-house legislative action. Although used by Congress in more than two hundred statutes since the 1930's, Burger reasoned that separation of powers did not allow Congress to take back agency decisions in this piecemeal fashion.

Bowsher v. Synar (1986) was Burger's last opinion for the Court. The Gramm-Rudman-Hollings Act of 1985 had created the office of comptroller general to identify spending reductions as mandated by the statute to balance the federal budget, an executive function. However, the comptroller general was removable from office by Congress. Burger concluded this crossover of function and removal powers was unconstitutional.

OTHER LANDMARK DECISIONS

Burger upheld the use of busing and other remedies to desegregate public schools in *Swann v. Charlotte-Mecklenburg Board of Education* (1971). He also developed a three-part constitutional test for public benefits to religion in *Lemon v. Kurtzman* (1971). Burger defended the freedom of religious minorities in *Wisconsin v. Yoder* (1972), refusing to require Amish parents to send their children to public high schools. His definition of obscenity in *Miller v. California*; *Paris Adult Theatre v. Slaton* (1973) allowed for local "contemporary community standards" rather than national definitions of obscenity. Other landmark decisions by Burger are not as popularly known to the general public but concern more technical court procedures, such as jurisdiction, and are in keeping with his intense interests in judicial administration.

CRITICS

Burger gathered many critics in his long tenure as chief justice. Scholars such as Vincent Blasi, in *The Burger Court: The Counter-Revolution That Wasn't* (1983), described him as a man of limited capacity with no discernible coherent philosophy. Burger's working-class background, night-school legal education, and pragmatic philosophy have all been subject to intense personal attack. Bob Woodward and Scott Armstrong in *The Brethren: Inside the Supreme Court* (1979) present a dismal portrait of Burger's leadership on the Court, alleging that even the old friendship between Harry A. Blackmun and Burger went sour. Justices Thurgood Marshall, John Paul Stevens, Potter Stewart, and Blackmun publicly aired their complaints about the Court's conflicts along with bitter personal criticisms of Burger.

However, Justice William J. Brennan, Jr., credited Burger with "boundless considerateness and compassion for the personal and family problems of every member of the Court" that kept relations cordial between justices of sharply divided philosophies. Justice Powell also claimed that good relations and comradeship existed between justices, and Justice Blackmun claimed to remain Burger's best friend to the end.

A MAN AND THE CONSTITUTION

Before resigning from the Court, Burger was appointed chairman of the Commission on the Bicentennial of the Constitution of the United States by President Reagan in 1985. After resigning as chief justice, he regularly worked double shifts on the commission through the bicentennial of the ratification of the Bill of Rights in 1991. Burger believed it was more than coincidence that the two-hundredth birthday of the Constitution on September 17, 1987, was also his eightieth birthday. He described the greatest decisions of the Court in a book, *It Is So Ordered: A Constitution Unfolds* (1995).

Bradley Stewart Chilton

FURTHER READING

Two comprehensive surveys of Burger's tenure as chief justice are Tinsley E. Yarbrough's *The Burger Court: Justices, Rulings, and Legacy* (Santa Barbara, Calif.: ABC-Clio, 2000) and Earl M. Maltz's *The Chief Justiceship of Warren Burger, 1969-1986* (Columbia: University of South Carolina Press, 2000). Burger's personal papers are at the William Mitchell School of Law in St. Paul, Minnesota, and library staff at the Loyola University School of Law prepared *Warren E. Burger: A Bibliography of Works Written by and About the Chief Justice* (New Orleans, La.: Loyola University School of Law, 1984). Burger's account of his time on the Supreme Court is *It Is So Ordered: A Constitution Unfolds* (New York: W. Morrow, 1995). The Philippine Bar Association released a tribute book of Burger's opinions: *Significant Supreme Court Opinions of the Honorable Warren E. Burger, Chief Justice of the United States* (Manila, Philippines: Philippine Bar Association, 1984).

In spite of Burger's importance on the Court, few scholarly biographies exist. Stanley H. Friedelbaum has a scholarly and well-written chapter on Burger's life on the Court in *The Burger Court: Political and Judicial Profiles*, edited by Charles Lamb and Steven Halpern (Urbana: University of Illinois Press, 1991). Carl Tobias surveyed Burger's many contributions to judicial administration in "Warren Burger and the Administration of Justice," *Villanova Law Review* 41 (December 15, 1996): 505-519. Phillip Craig Zane focused on Burger's concurring and dissenting opinions in his study, "An Interpretation of the Jurisprudence of Chief Justice Warren Burger," *Utah Law Review* 1995 (Fall, 1995): 975-1008. A symposium in *Oklahoma Law Review* 45 (Spring, 1992): 1-168, was entitled "The Jurisprudence of Chief Justice Warren E. Burger" and included scholarly analyses of Burger's opinions in several areas of law.

Other related books by scholars that examine the Burger Court include Arthur L. Galub's *The Burger Court, 1968-1984* (Millwood, N.Y.: Associated Faculty Press, 1986), Vincent Blasi, ed., *The Burger Court: The Counter-Revolution That Wasn't* (New Haven, Conn.: Yale University Press, 1983), and Francis Graham Lee, ed., *Neither Conservative nor Liberal: The Burger Court on Civil Rights and Liberties* (Malabar, Fla.: R. E. Krieger, 1983). Popular books tend to focus on criticism of the Burger Court but give some insights into Burger's life. They include Bob Woodward and Scott Armstrong's *The Brethren: Inside the Supreme Court* (New York: Avon Books, 1979), Herman Schwartz's *The Burger Years: Rights and Wrongs in the Supreme Court, 1969-1986* (New York: Viking Press, 1987), and Bernard Schwartz's *The Ascent of Pragmatism: The Burger Court in Action* (Reading, Mass.: Addison-Wesley, 1990). Bernard Schwartz has also edited *The Burger Court: Counter-Revolution or Confirmation?* (New York: Oxford University Press, 1998), which contains essays included by justices, journalists, feminists, and lawyers.

Many fine tributes and symposia have been assembled both surrounding Burger's retirement from the Court in 1986 and upon his death in 1995. The more complete of these tributes, such as *Texas Law Review* 74 (December, 1995): 207-236 and *William Mitchell Law Review* 22 (Fall, 1996): 1-65, feature writings by fellow justices, law clerks, judicial fellows, and close professional colleagues.

SEE ALSO Blackmun, Harry A.; Chief justice; *Lemon v. Kurtzman*, *Reed v. Reed*; Rehnquist, William H.; Separation of powers; *Swann v. Charlotte-Mecklenburg Board of Education*; *Wisconsin v. Yoder*.

Harold H. Burton

IDENTIFICATION: Associate justice (October 1, 1945-October 13, 1958)

NOMINATED BY: Harry S. Truman

BORN: June 22, 1888, Jamaica Plain, Massachusetts

DIED: October 28, 1964, Washington, D.C.

SIGNIFICANCE: Burton was the first Republican appointed as an associate justice on the Supreme Court by a Democratic president. Known for his thoroughness and for keeping tension among the justices to a minimum, Burton was a strong supporter of the Court's efforts in civil rights cases.

Associate Justice Harold H. Burton (right) with his family. (Library of Congress)

Harold H. Burton graduated from Bowdoin College in 1909 and from Harvard Law School in 1912. For the next two years, he engaged in a private legal practice in Cleveland, Ohio, and then worked as legal counsel for a series of public utilities in Utah and Idaho. During World War I he served in an infantry regiment of the U.S. Army, achieved the rank of captain, and was awarded the Purple Heart and the Belgian Croix de Guerre.

After the war Burton and his wife returned to Cleveland, where he again established a private practice. In 1928 Burton was elected to one term as a Republican in the Ohio House of Representatives. From 1929 to 1932 he also served as the director of law for Cleveland. After serving a term as acting mayor of Cleveland from 1931 to 1932, Burton was elected mayor in 1935 and was reelected twice. In 1940 he was elected to the U.S. Senate, serving for four years and becoming a close associate of fellow senator Harry S. Truman.

On September 19, 1945, Burton was nominated to the Supreme

Court by President Truman, a Democrat. Chief Justice Harlan Fiske Stone gave his advance approval of Burton, believing that his legislative experience would be helpful in establishing legislative intent in many cases. In his thirteen years on the Supreme Court, Burton wrote ninety-six majority, fifty dissenting, and fifteen concurring opinions. Wanting his opinions to be quickly and clearly understood, his writing style was direct and simple. His thoroughness required a vast amount of research by himself and his clerks.

Burton strongly supported the government in cases against subversion. He also strongly supported the Court's efforts in civil rights cases. For example, in *Henderson v. United States* (1950), he concluded that all people should be treated without discrimination in the operation of public transportation regulated by federal statutes. In labor cases, Burton typically upheld the rights of states to limit the picketing activities of unions. Burton and Justice Felix Frankfurter believed that picketing was not protected as a freedom of expression. In *Toolson v. New York Yankees* (1953), a case in which the Court reaffirmed the antitrust exemption of major league baseball, Burton dissented on the grounds that baseball should be treated as a big business. In addition to his duties on the Court, Burton wrote many articles about Court history, Chief Justice John Marshall, and the Supreme Court building.

Alvin K. Benson

SEE ALSO Antitrust law; *Brown v. Board of Education*; *Everson v. Board of Education of Ewing Township*; Frankfurter, Felix; Marshall, John.

Bush v. Gore

CITATION: 531 U.S. 98
DATE: December 12, 2000
ISSUES: Equal protection clause; presidential elections; federalism
SIGNIFICANCE: By ordering the end to all recounts of Florida's presidential ballots in the 2000 election, the Supreme Court in effect decided that George W. Bush, not Albert Gore, would be the next president.

155

After votes were counted on the evening of the presidential election of November, 2000, the outcome depended on whether George W. Bush or Albert Gore would be able to claim the electoral votes of Florida. Although it initially appeared that Bush had probably won the state's popular vote by a few hundred votes, the Gore campaign demanded manual recounts of ambiguous punch-out ballots in four heavily Democratic counties. They argued that perhaps 50,000 of the ballots had not been counted because the punch-out holes, or chads, had not been counted because they were not entirely removed, and that it would nevertheless be possible to discern the voters' intents in many instances. Bush's legal team, happy with the initial count, naturally tried to prevent all hand recounts.

The controversy produced a complex series of legal maneuvering. On November 21, the Florida Supreme Court ordered Florida's Secretary of State Katherine Harris to include the results of manual recounts as part of the final tally. After reviewing the order, the U.S. Supreme Court issued *Bush v. Palm Beach County*, asking unanimously for the Florida court to clarify whether its order was based on state or federal law. Informed observers understood that the Court's conservative wing was attempting to establish that the Florida court had based the order on federal law in violation of Section II of the Constitution, which left the manner of selecting electors to the state legislatures.

On December 8, before responding to the inquiry, the Florida Supreme Court pleased the Gore camp when it ordered hand recounts to begin in counties having significant numbers of "undercounted" ballots. In response, Bush's lawyers petitioned the U.S. Supreme Court for an emergency review. The next day, the Court issued a 5-4 emergency injunction which stopped the recount, Justice Antonin Scalia explaining that the recount threatened "irreparable harm" to the country and to Bush's reputation as the legitimately elected president. On December 12, the Court heard oral arguments, and the following day, it announced *Bush v. Gore*, which was a *per curiam* opinion containing two rulings.

The first ruling, based on a 7-2 vote, announced that Florida's recount order was inconsistent with the equal protection principle because it used different standards of counting in different areas without any clear directions on how the chads were to be assessed. The second ruling, based on a 5-4 vote, which reflected the conservative-liberal split on the Court, declared that there was insufficient time to carry out a recount, referring to Florida's legislature's presumed desire to take advantage of the federal "safe harbor" deadline, the date that would ensure that Florida's electoral vote would not be contested. The two justices agreeing with the first ruling but not with the second ruling argued that the case should be remanded to the state court to resolve the equal protection problem. Concurring with both majority rulings, Chief Justice William H. Rehnquist denounced the Florida Supreme Court for substituting its judgment for that of the state legislature.

Each of the four dissenters of the second ruling wrote separate opinions, arguing that the dispute should have been left up to Florida's court and legislature. Finding that no federal questions were involved, the four liberals suggested that the five-justice majority, who usually defended states' rights, had been motivated by an

Gore and Bush supporters awaiting the Court's ruling on Bush v. Gore *outside the Supreme Court on December 11, 2000.* (AP/Wide World Photos)

ideological bias. They noted, moreover, that the Constitution authorized Congress rather than the Court to resolve disputed presidential elections and other political controversies. Judge John Paul Stevens wrote that the legacy of the decision would be a decline in "the Nation's confidence in the judge as an impartial guardian of the rule of law." Many people in the country, especially those sympathetic to the Democratic Party, agreed with this statement.

Bush v. Gore is one of the most controversial rulings in Supreme Court history. Critics have noted that the majority's application of the equal protection clause to demand the same standard for deciding voters' intent was contrary to tradition. A particular weakness was the acknowledgment in the per curium opinion that the requirement for a uniform standard would apply only to the "present circumstances," and that in future elections different standards might be decided in different parts of a state. Despite the Court's disclaimer, it is nevertheless possible that the application of the equal protection principle might again be applied to the way that votes are counted.

Thomas Tandy Lewis

FURTHER READING

Dershowitz, Alan. *Supreme Injustice: How the High Court Hijacked Election 2000.* New York: Oxford University Press, 2002.

Dworkin, Ronald, ed. *A Badly Flawed Election: Debating "Bush v. Gore," the Supreme Court, and American Democracy.* New York: W. W. Norton, 2002.

Gilman, Howard. *The Votes that Counted: How the Courts Decided the 2000 Presidential Election.* Chicago: University of Chicago Press, 2001.

Hasen, Richard L. *The Supreme Court and Election Law Judging Equality from "Baker v. Carr" to "Bush v. Gore."* New York: New York University Press, 2003.

Ryden, David K. *The U.S. Supreme Court and the Electoral Process.* 2d ed. Washington, D.C.: Georgetown University Press, 2002.

Whitman, Mark, ed. *Florida 2000: A Sourcebook on the Contested Presidential Election.* Boulder, Colo.: Lynn Rienner, 2004.

SEE ALSO Equal protection clause; Fifteenth Amendment; Gerrymandering; *McConnell v. Federal Election Commission*; Political questions; Presidential powers; Representation, fairness of.

Pierce Butler

IDENTIFICATION: Associate justice (January 2, 1923-November 16, 1939)

NOMINATED BY: Warren G. Harding

BORN: March 17, 1866, Pine Bend, Minnesota

DIED: November 16, 1939, Washington, D.C.

SIGNIFICANCE: During seventeen years on the Supreme Court, Butler supported Court decisions that limited the authority of the states and the federal government to regulate private businesses. In the 1930's he was one of the Court's Four Horsemen, who consistently held New Deal legislation regulating economic affairs to be unconstitutional.

The son of Irish immigrants, Pierce Butler was raised on a farm in Dakota County, Minnesota. In 1887 he received a bachelor's degree from Carleton College. Admitted to the Minnesota Bar in 1888, Butler served from 1890 to 1896 as a prosecuting attorney for Ramsey County, Minnesota. He then entered private practice representing corporate clients and excelled as a courtroom attorney. In 1908 he was elected president of the Minnesota State Bar Association. He specialized in defending railroads in valuation cases that determined railroad rates and gained a national reputation when he defended the railroads before the Supreme Court in the *Minnesota Rate Cases* (1913).

On November 22, 1922, President Warren G. Harding named Butler to fill the vacancy created by Justice William R. Day's resignation. On December 21, 1922, Butler was confirmed by a Senate vote of sixty-one to eight. He took the oath on January 2, 1923, and served on the Court until his death on November 16, 1939.

During his Court tenure, Butler consistently supported laissez-faire legal doctrines that upheld the right of private businesses to operate without regulation by state and federal law. He voted against government regulation in every case involving freedom of contract that was decided by a divided Court. In rate and valuation cases involving railroads and utilities, Butler voted for the corporate position in all eighteen cases decided by a divided Court between 1924 and 1939. In 1935 and 1936 Butler and Justices George Sutherland, Willis Van Devanter, and James C. McReynolds were known as the Four Horsemen of the Court because they consistently voted together in Court decisions that held President Franklin D. Roosevelt's New Deal legislation regulating economic affairs to be unconstitutional.

The most significant Court opinion written by Butler was *Morehead v. New York ex rel. Tipaldo* (1936). His majority opinion in a 5-4 decision held that New York's law providing a minimum wage for

Pierce Butler.
(Library of Congress)

women workers and minors was unconstitutional because it violated the due process clause of the Fourteenth Amendment, imposing an unconstitutional state interference with the freedom of contract between an employee and an employer. This decision, coming soon after Court decisions that held federal economic legislation unconstitutional, meant that both federal and state governments had minimal constitutional authority to regulate economic affairs. These Court decisions led to President Roosevelt's attack on the Court after his landslide reelection in 1936. The outcome was the judicial revolution of 1937, when moderate justices joined economic liberals on the Court to overturn laissez-faire precedents in Court decisions. When Justice Butler died in 1939, Roosevelt chose an economic liberal, Frank Murphy, as his successor.

Jim D. Clark

FURTHER READING

Bader, William H., and Roy M. Mersky, eds. *The First One Hundred Eight Justices*. Buffalo, N.Y.: William S. Hein, 2004.

Brown, Francis Joseph. *The Social and Economic Philosophy of Pierce Butler.* Washington: Catholic University Press, 1945.

Friedman, Leon, and Fred L. Israel, eds. *The Justices of the United States Supreme Court: Their Lives and Major Opinions.* 5 vols. New York: Chelsea House, 1997.

Parrish, Michael E. *The Hughes Court: Justices, Rulings, and Legacy.* Santa Barbara, Calif.: ABC-Clio, 2002.

Renstrom, Peter G. *The Taft Court: Justices, Rulings, and Legacy.* Santa Barbara, Calif.: ABC-Clio, 2003.

SEE ALSO Commerce, regulation of; Contract, freedom of; Contracts clause; Court-packing plan; Day, William R.; Due process, substantive; New Deal.

James F. Byrnes

IDENTIFICATION: Associate justice (July 8, 1941-October 3, 1942)
NOMINATED BY: Franklin D. Roosevelt
BORN: May 2, 1879, Charleston, South Carolina
DIED: April 9, 1972, Columbia, South Carolina
SIGNIFICANCE: A judicial conservative who believed that the Supreme
Court's role was to interpret rather than make law, Byrnes served
on the Court for slightly more than a year although his career in
politics and public service lasted more than forty years.

James F. Byrnes's first job in a career in politics and public service
that spanned more than forty years was as a messenger boy in a law office. In 1900 he became the official court reporter in Aiken County,
South Carolina. In 1903 he was admitted to the bar; the same year, he
became editor and publisher of the *Aiken Journal and Review.* He was
first elected to the U.S. House of Representatives in 1910 by a fifty-
seven-vote margin. He served in this position until 1924, when he ran
for the U.S. Senate but was defeated. After practicing law for six years,
he again ran for the Senate and was elected. He served there for
nearly eleven years until President Franklin D. Roosevelt nominated
him for an associate justice seat on the Supreme Court. On June 12,
1941, the Senate unanimously confirmed his nomination.

During his tenure on the Court, Byrnes followed a philosophy of
judicial conservatism. As a strict constructionist, he believed that the
role of the Court was to interpret rather than to make law. He regarded the Court as the defender of the Constitution against actions
by the president or Congress that violated that document. However,
he believed that the activism of the Court had resulted in a situation
in which Congress and the president had to defend the Constitution
against the usurpation of legislative power by the Court itself. His
best-known decision while on the Court was *Edwards v. California*
(1941), in which he nullified a California statute that prohibited
indigents from entering the state.

Byrnes served on the Court for slightly more than a year. In October, 1942, he resigned to head the wartime Office of Economic
Stabilization. In May, 1943, he became director of war mobilization.

James F. Byrnes.
(Library of Congress)

President Roosevelt referred to Byrnes as his "assistant president"; however, Roosevelt did not select Byrnes as his running mate in 1944 because he was advised that a southern segregationist on the ticket would hurt his chances for reelection. Byrnes did, however, accompany Roosevelt to Yalta and Harry S. Truman to the Potsdam Conference. He also served as Truman's secretary of state from July, 1945, to January, 1947. In 1946 *Time* magazine named him its "Man of the Year"—an honor it gave to persons having the greatest impact on the year's news. From 1951 to 1955 Byrnes served as governor of South Carolina. In 1953 he was appointed by President Dwight D. Eisenhower as a delegate to a session of the United Nations.

As governor of South Carolina, Byrnes concentrated on equalizing school funding for black and white schools in order to meet the Court's doctrine of separate but equal. When the Court declared the policy unconstitutional in *Brown v. Board of Education* (1954), Byrnes criticized the Court for reversing the long-standing doctrine.

William V. Moore

163

FURTHER READING

Bader, William H., and Roy M. Mersky, eds. *The First One Hundred Eight Justices*. Buffalo, N.Y.: William S. Hein, 2004.

Brown, Walter J. *James F. Byrnes of South Carolina: A Remembrance*. Macon, Ga.: Mercer University Press, 1990.

Byrnes, James F. *All in One Lifetime*. New York: Harper, 1958.

Parrish, Michael E. *The Hughes Court: Justices, Rulings, and Legacy*. Santa Barbara, Calif.: ABC-Clio, 2002.

Renstrom, Peter G. *The Stone Court: Justices, Rulings, and Legacy*. Santa Barbara, Calif.: ABC-Clio, 2001.

Robertson, David. *Sly and Able: A Political Bibliography of James F. Byrnes*. New York: W. W. Norton, 1994.

SEE ALSO *Brown v. Board of Education*; Constitutional interpretation; Executive privilege; Judicial activism.

Calder v. Bull

CITATION: 3 U.S. 368
DATE: August 8, 1798
ISSUES: Ex post facto laws; judicial review; natural law
SIGNIFICANCE: While ruling that the ex post facto limitation did not apply to civil laws, the Supreme Court justices debated the concepts of judicial review and natural law.

The Connecticut legislature passed a resolution that granted a new hearing in a probate trial. The disappointed litigants, Calder and his wife, contended that the resolution was an ex post facto law, which was prohibited to the states by the U.S. Constitution. By a 4-0 vote, the Supreme Court concluded that the term "ex post facto" applied only to retroactive criminal laws and not to laws dealing with civil matters. After much controversy, the Court reaffirmed this definition in *Collins v. Youngblood* (1990).

In *Calder*, the justices wrote seriatim opinions, discussing possible ways to decide the case. Justice Samuel Chase denied the "omnipotence" of the legislatures and asserted that "the very nature of our free Republican governments" will override and invalidate laws contrary to fundamental principles of "reason and justice." Justice James Iredell answered that judges did not have any right to invalidate a statute simply because they might consider it "contrary to the principles of natural justice," but he explicitly recognized the duty of the Court to strike down legislative acts that violate the Constitution. Beginning in the 1820's, the Court has assumed the validity of Iredell's theoretical perspective, but the natural law approach has sometimes reappeared, most often in the form of substantive due process.

Thomas Tandy Lewis

SEE ALSO Bill of attainder; Chase, Samuel; Iredell, James; Judicial review; Natural law; Nominations to the Court.

John A. Campbell

IDENTIFICATION: Associate justice (April 11, 1853-April 30, 1861)
NOMINATED BY: Franklin Pierce
BORN: June 24, 1811, Washington, Georgia
DIED: March 12, 1889, Baltimore, Maryland
SIGNIFICANCE: Campbell's opinion in the 1857 case involving slave Dred Scott cast him as a proslavery Southerner. As a lawyer before the Supreme Court in 1873, he argued that the Fourteenth Amendment should be used to limit state police powers in cases involving slaughterhouses.

A native of Georgia and graduate of the University of Georgia, John A. Campbell moved to Alabama in 1830. A Democrat, he served in the state's legislature and practiced law, earning a reputation for sound arguments and superior writing. He began to argue cases before the Supreme Court in 1850, gaining favorable national attention.

Although Campbell defended states' rights and opposed abolitionism, he opposed Southern nationalists and only mildly endorsed slavery. His moderation made him attractive to Northern Democrats, and his Southern birth garnered support from Southern Democrats. Therefore, President Franklin Pierce nominated him to fill a seat on the Court that had been open for nearly a year. The sectional politics that marked his appointment colored his career on the bench.

As a justice, Campbell voted with the majority in *Scott v. Sandford* in 1857, which declared that Dred Scott remained a slave although he had resided in a free state. Campbell's vote in this case made him staunchly proslavery in many people's minds, but what he actually wrote in his opinion reveals a somewhat more moderate stance. He consistently argued that Congress could enact only laws pursuant to the powers enumerated in the Constitution. Although its Article IV gave Congress power to "make all needful Rules and Regulations" for territories under its jurisdiction, this power did not extend to interfering with the "relations of the master and slave." However repugnant in result, Campbell's opinion was not different in reasoning

John A. Campbell. (Handy Studios/ Collection of the Supreme Court of the United States)

from his dissent in *Dodge v. Woolsey* (1856), in which he chided the Court for extending regulatory authority over state-chartered corporations without strict constitutional warrant.

Campbell used his office to back the national government to its fullest. In 1858 he convened a grand jury in Mobile to stop the filibustering expedition by William Walker, because filibustering violated the neutrality laws of the United States. The following year, he joined the other members of the Court in overturning the interposition of the Wisconsin Supreme Court in a matter involving the Fugitive Slave Act of 1850 because that act rested upon a specific constitutional authority and, under the Constitution, was the supreme law of the land.

Campbell resigned in 1861, the first year of the Civil War, and served for a time as assistant secretary of war for the Confederate States of America. In private practice after the war, Campbell represented butchers in New Orleans who ran afoul of a state law to regulate their trade. In the *Slaughterhouse Cases* (1873), Campbell held that the Louisiana regulation overextended police powers and interfered with the right to earn a living, making it an unreasonable law that wrongfully harmed an insular segment of the population. Campbell's novel use of the Fourteenth Amendment was rejected in this case but within two decades was embraced by the Court.

Edward R. Crowther

FURTHER READING

Bader, William H., and Roy M. Mersky, eds. *The First One Hundred Eight Justices*. Buffalo, N.Y.: William S. Hein, 2004.

Huebner, Timothy S. *The Taney Court: Justices, Rulings, and Legacy*. Santa Barbara, Calif.: ABC-Clio, 2003.

Saunders, Robert, Jr. *John Archibald Campbell: Southern Moderate, 1811-1889*. Tuscaloosa: University of Alabama Press, 1997.

Siegel, Martin. *The Taney Court, 1836-1864*. New York: Associated Faculty Press, 1987.

SEE ALSO Civil War; Fourteenth Amendment; Ninth Amendment; *Scott v. Sandford*; *Slaughterhouse Cases*; Taney, Roger Brooke.

Capital Punishment

DESCRIPTION: The killing of a convict by the state for purposes of punishment or to reduce future crime.

SIGNIFICANCE: The death penalty, although infrequently applied, has symbolic importance and has sharply polarized public opinion. The Supreme Court entered this fray only briefly, first to restrict executions, then to permit capital punishment, increasingly free of federal court supervision.

During the colonial period and the founding of the United States, the execution of convicts was not only routine but also a public spectacle. The hangman's noose, a humane alternative to beheading, was employed with a liberality that would disturb modern sensibility. In eighteenth century England, for example, it is estimated that approximately 240 crimes were punishable by death, with the sentence commonly carried out in the town squares. In contrast to millennia of practice, the nineteenth and twentieth centuries have seen a gradual civilization of punishment. Incarceration replaced execution for most crimes. Hangings were removed from public view and placed instead behind prison walls. The abolition of physical torture as a legitimate part of punishment followed, eventually culminating in efforts to also circumscribe the infliction of psychological pain. Thus, the noose was replaced by electrocution, followed by the gas chamber, and more recently by lethal injection, all in a search for a humane method of depriving the convict of life, as the ultimate punishment. In the eyes of many ethicists, legal scholars, and moral leaders, the fulfillment of this historical trend would be the abolition of capital punishment altogether. In the United States, one of the last democratic nations retaining the death penalty, this debate has often acquired a constitutional dimension.

THE DEATH PENALTY AND THE CONSTITUTION

It is clear from the text of the Constitution that the Framers envisioned executions as a part of their legal regime. The Fifth Amendment provides that "no person shall be held to answer for a capital or otherwise infamous crime" absent an indictment by a grand jury. It

168

further provides that no person shall "be subject for the same offense to be twice put in jeopardy of life and limb" nor be "deprived of life, liberty, or property without due process of law." The Fourteenth Amendment, adopted after the Civil War, similarly commands that no state shall deny any person "life, liberty, or property, without due process of law." Proponents of a contractual constitution, interpreted according to the historical intent of its Framers, are on apparently solid ground when they contend that the Constitution, in principle, sanctions capital punishment.

Opponents of the death penalty point to the same pair of due process clauses, promises of legal fairness, to condemn the application of the death penalty as arbitrary, capricious, even, in the words of Justice Potter Stewart, "freakishly imposed." They also point to the Fourteenth Amendment's requirement that states accord all persons the "equal protection of the laws" and raise questions concerning possible racial bias in the meting out of death sentences. Finally, and most tellingly, the Eighth Amendment's proscription of "cruel and unusual punishments" might provide a flat ban on capital punishment. The latter seems to have been adopted to end corporal punishments or the infliction of torture. However, in *Weems v. United States* (1910), the Supreme Court held that a constitutional principle "to be vital must be capable of wider application than the mischief which gave it birth." Abolitionists contend that these clauses create evolutionary constitutional rules, progressively driven by contemporary moral theory, that now proscribe the death penalty, regardless of accepted practice at the time of their adoption.

Judicial appeals to contemporary morality are always risky, especially regarding an emotionally contentious subject such as capital punishment. However, it is difficult to reconcile the death penalty, as practiced in the United States, with any of the common theoretical justifications for punishment. The death penalty is obviously not intended to accomplish the rehabilitation of the offender. There is little evidence in support of any general deterrence produced by the death penalty beyond that already achieved by incarceration and considerable evidence against the claim. Incapacitation of dangerous or repeat offenders can also be accomplished by means short of execution. Retribution, the theory that crime is a moral offense that must be redressed by the infliction of proportional pain to expiate the original offense, might justify capital punishment for heinous crimes, especially first-degree murder. The biblical injunction of "an eye for an eye and a tooth for a tooth" is a concise summary of retributive punishment. The problem is that retribution, if consistently followed, is a nondiscretionary punishment—a sentence proportional to the crime *must* be carried out, with no room for mercy or selection. Proponents of capital punishment who appeal to retribution would have to countenance the execution of all defendants convicted of crimes for which capital punishment is authorized. The result would be a rate of executions unprecedented in U.S. history. Public opinion overwhelmingly supports capital punishment. However, polls and jury behavior also show that Americans want the death sentence to be employed sparingly.

The modern Court's initial foray into death penalty law was not encouraging to abolitionists. In *Louisiana ex rel. Francis v. Resweber* (1947), the Court rejected the contention that a second attempt at executing a prisoner, the electric chair having malfunctioned the first time, was either double jeopardy or cruel and unusual punishment. Despite the Court's permissive attitude, the number of executions in the United States was already in decline. National statistics on executions date only from 1930, with 1935 the largest single year, with 199 executions. By the 1960's this number had declined to a trickle. Since the early 1980's, however, the number of annual executions in the United States has again been rising, especially in southern states. Sixty-eight executions were carried out in 1998.

THE DEATH PENALTY MORATORIUM

Encouraged by the Court's activism in civil rights and defendants' rights cases, death penalty opponents in the 1960's began a campaign to enlist the Court in the cause of abolition. The Legal Defense Fund (LDF) of the National Association for the Advancement of Colored People, later joined by the American Civil Liberties Union, orchestrated a threefold attack on capital punishment. First, the routine exclusion of "scrupled" jurors, those opposed to the death penalty on principle, was said to result in nonrepresentative juries skewed toward conviction and execution. Second, the determination of guilt and passing of sentence in a single trial procedure put defendants in an untenable position of having to offer evidence in mitigation of a crime they also contended they did not commit. Finally, the nearly complete discretion accorded juries in deciding when to impose death (the only sentencing question juries are called on to decide) resulted in an unpredictable, arbitrary, and discriminatory application of the death penalty.

In *Witherspoon v. Illinois* (1968), the Court banned the blanket exclusion of all scrupled jurors merely by virtue of their voicing objections to capital punishment. The state could still exclude those who would automatically or invariably vote against a death sentence, but not those expressing only "general objections" to capital punishment. The practical result of *Witherspoon* was to require commutation or resentencing of nearly all death sentences for prisoners then on death row. Until further litigation sorted out all potential *Witherspoon* claims, a de facto moratorium on capital punishment had been achieved. From 1967 until 1977, no executions were carried out in the United States.

Further LDF challenges to capital punishment were in the works. In *Furman v. Georgia* (1972), a fragmented Court adopted the third LDF critique of the death penalty as then practiced in all the states authorizing capital punishment, that unguided jury discretion produced arbitrary results. Only Justices William J. Brennan, Jr., and Thurgood Marshall held capital punishment to be cruel and unusual punishment per se in contravention of the Eighth Amendment. Dissenters William H. Rehnquist, Warren E. Burger, Lewis F. Powell, Jr., and Harry A. Blackmun found no constitutional prohibition to unbridled jury discretion to mete out death and would have deferred on the issue to state legislative politics (although Blackmun eloquently expressed personal misgivings concerning capital punishment). This left Justices William O. Douglas, Potter Stewart, and Byron R. White to cast limited but decisive votes against Georgia's capital punishment statute. Douglas expressed concerns that the death penalty was applied disproportionately to poor and socially disadvantaged defendants, in effect reading into the Eighth Amendment an equality requirement. Stewart held that the rare imposition of death made capital punishment cruel and unusual in the minority of cases in which it was imposed. White agreed, arguing that its infrequency deprived the death penalty of any deterrent effect or ability to meet the test of retribution. For the first time, the Court had struck down a death sentence as cruel and unusual punishment. However, the long-term impact of *Furman* depended on the continued support of either Justice White or Justice Stewart, both centrists whose opposition to capital punishment seemed weak.

Public reception of *Furman* was immediate and hostile. Within a few years, thirty-five states had reenacted death penalty statutes purporting to meet the Court's objections. Three possibilities seemed available in the wake of *Furman*. States could enact mandatory death penalty statutes, imposing death in all cases where the death penalty was available, without discretion. This seemed to meet the objections of the Douglas, Stewart, and White bloc but would also have resulted in a large number of executions. A second option was to forgo death as a punishment altogether, but this seemed politically unlikely given the climate of public opinion. The third option was to enact guided discretion statutes, supplying juries with a host of aggravating and mitigating circumstances that would be considered in a separate sentencing phase of the trial, following a previous determination of guilt. This procedure met the LDF's second challenge to capital punishment, that the combined procedures for determining guilt and sentence imposed untenable choices on the defense. It also seemed to meet the issue of jury discretion head on, with neither the unpopular abolition of capital punishment nor the volume of executions that might follow adoption of mandatory capital punishment laws.

These laws came under the Court's scrutiny in *Gregg v. Georgia* (1976). Actually a compendium of five cases testing mandatory death penalty statutes in North Carolina and Louisiana and guided discretion statutes in Georgia, Texas, and Florida, *Gregg* also resulted in a badly fragmented Court. Justices Brennan and Marshall continued their per se opposition to the death penalty. Chief Justice Burger, along with Rehnquist, Blackmun, and White, voted to uphold all five death penalty regimes. As with *Furman*, the Court's decision rested on the centrists, now Justices Stewart, Powell, and John Paul Stevens. They approved of Georgia's death penalty regime, requiring a bifurcated procedure that separated the determination of guilt from the passing of sentence. In addition, before death could be imposed, a jury had to find beyond a reasonable doubt that at least one of ten aggravating circumstances had been met. Mitigating circumstances were also to be considered, and all death sentences were subject to mandatory appeal. Thus, a death penalty regime based on guided jury discretion now passed constitutional muster. The decision for a companion case, *Woodson v. North Carolina* (1976), specifically banned mandatory death sentences.

It is not at all clear that the death penalty regime approved in *Gregg* is able to meet the objections of jury discretion and arbitrary application of capital punishment that underlie *Furman*. Although

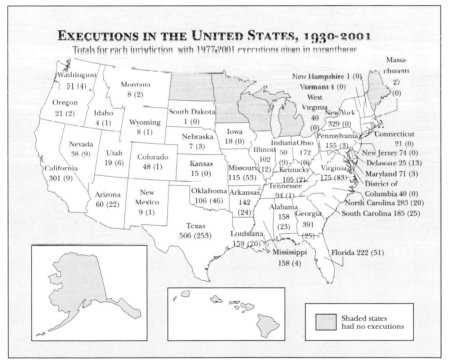

EXECUTIONS IN THE UNITED STATES, 1930-2001
Totals for each jurisdiction, with 1977-2001 executions given in parentheses

Note: There were 4,291 total executions, 1930-1997, including 33 prisoners executed in the federal system. The total for 1977-1997 of 432 prisoners executed includes no federal executions.

Source: U.S. Department of Justice, Bureau of Justice Statistics, *Capital Punishment 1997* (December, 1998); *Understanding Constitutional Issues: Selections from the CQ Researcher* (Washington, D.C.: CQ Press, 2004).

subsequent litigation struck down jury guidelines that were deemed too vague, juries were still called on to consider unique circumstances pertaining to each case. Further inconsistency was introduced into the application of the death penalty through such practices as prosecutorial charging discretion, plea bargaining, and executive clemency. It thus appeared that *Gregg* marked a changed political sentiment on the part of the Court, perhaps even, as a practical matter, overruling *Furman*. With the decision in *Gregg*, the Court signaled a green light to executions. The death penalty moratorium came to an end in January of 1977, when the state of Utah executed Gary Gilmore by firing squad.

RACE AND THE DEATH PENALTY

The interest of the LDF in capital punishment should have surprised no one. It was long known that the death penalty was applied most frequently to society's outcast groups, especially the poor and members of minority groups. Over half of the convicts executed for all capital crimes between 1930 and 1995 were African Americans, far exceeding their proportion of the nation's population. Even more striking, of the 450 executions for rape between 1930 and 1965, more than 90 percent involved African American convicts. Criminologist Marvin Wolfgang, in a 1966 study, found that of 119 convicted rapists executed in twelve southern states between 1945 and 1965, 110 were black. The question remained as to whether these discrepancies could be explained by nonracial factors, such as a propensity to commit more heinous crimes.

A research team led by David Baldus studied more than 2,400 criminal homicide cases in Georgia, from 1973 to 1980, tried under the death penalty regime approved in *Gregg*. Taking account of more than 230 separate characteristics of each case, they employed sophisticated statistical analysis to weigh the effect of each in producing death sentences. Their results found that, when adjusted for legitimate nonracial factors, the race of the *defendant* did not result in a strikingly disproportionate application of the death penalty. However, a strong correlation was uncovered between the race of the *victim* and the passing of a capital sentence.

In raw numbers, white or black killers of white victims were eleven times more likely to receive the death penalty than were killers of African American victims. Even when nonracial variables were factored in, killers of white victims were executed 4.3 times as often as were killers of blacks. The discrepancy was inexplicable, except by the inference that race prejudice continued to affect the death penalty regime, even after *Gregg*. In fact, the race of the victim proved to be a stronger predictor of a capital sentence than such factors as the defendant's prior history of violence, that the victim was a police officer, or that the killing occurred during an armed robbery. The supposition drawn from these results was that prosecutors, when faced with the killer of an African American victim, were less likely to seek the death penalty or more likely to accept a plea bargain eliminating death. Alternatively, juries, even guided statutorily by nonracial aggravating and mitigating circumstances, were less likely to impose death for the killing of a black victim, perhaps valuing the life of a black person less highly than that of a white victim.

These data formed the basis for the LDF's next challenge to capital punishment, in *McCleskey v. Kemp* (1987), as violating both the Eighth Amendment and the equal protection clause of the Fourteenth Amendment. Such a disparate racial impact would seem to call into question the effectiveness of *Gregg* in eliminating the arbitrary or discriminatory factors in applying the death penalty that had informed *Furman*. However, writing for the Court, Justice Powell held that to make an equal protection claim, McCleskey had to demonstrate that either the Georgia legislature or the jury in his particular case was motivated by racial animus or a discriminatory purpose. The social background data revealed in the Baldus study were insufficient to make even a prima facie case that McCleskey had personally suffered from racial discrimination and, in any event, were more appropriately considered in a legislative forum. Similarly the discrepancy revealed in the Baldus study was insufficient to demonstrate a violation of the Eighth Amendment because it did not offend society's evolving standards of decency. Justices Brennan, Marshall, Stevens, and Blackmun dissented.

In *Furman* and *Gregg*, the Court had sought to remove arbitrary and capricious factors, presumably including racial prejudice, from the application of the death penalty in the United States. However, with *McCleskey*, the Court appeared to be turning its back on that promise by foreclosing the last avenue for arguing for the per se unconstitutionality of capital punishment. It did find in the Eighth Amendment limits to the kinds of crimes that could be deemed capital offenses. In *Coker v. Georgia* (1977), the Court found a capital sentence disproportionate to the crime of rape and therefore barred by the Eighth Amendment. Similarly, *Enmund v. Florida* (1982) barred the death penalty for a felony murder in which the defendant did not commit, nor intend or contemplate, the killing. However, this ruling was modified in *Tison v. Arizona* (1987) to permit sentencing to death of a codefendant in a felony murder in which there was major participation in the felony combined with reckless indifference to human life. These rulings indicate that the Court views the Eighth Amendment as imposing substantive limits on the death penalty, at least concerning the issue of proportionality.

CONTINUING CONTROVERSY

During the early years of the twenty-first century, thirty-eight states authorized capital punishment for first-degree murder. The federal government also had capital statutes for certain homicides, as well as for espionage, treason, and running large-scale drug enterprises. From 1976, the year of *Gregg*, until 2003, a total of 882 persons were executed in the United States. More than three-quarters of these executions were carried out in southern states. At the end of the year 2004, thirty-six states and the federal prison system held 3,314 prisoners on death row. Of these, 1,850 prisoners were classified as white, 1,390 as black, 32 as of Asian descent, 28 as Native Americans, and 14 as of unspecified race. Only 52 women were under sentences of death. In 2005, 60 persons (including one woman) in sixteen states were executed, one more than in 2004.

Death row inmates are overwhelmingly poor and uneducated and disproportionately African American and from the South. Many inmates under sentences of death, moreover, have experienced the misfortune of having inadequate assistance of counsel at trial. Recognizing this problem in *Strickland v. Washington* (1984), the Supreme Court held that the Sixth Amendment requires an effective assistance of counsel, but in order to overturn a conviction, the Court required a "reasonable probability" that the outcome would have been different with an efficient counsel. The number of executions increased significantly during the 1990's. Supporting this development, the Court required petitioners to show reasons for second or third habeas corpus petitions in federal courts in *McCleskey v. Zant* (1991). In its controversial *Herrera v. Collins* ruling in 1993, the Court rejected habeas corpus relief for a defendant who claimed to have new evidence proving his innocence. The goal of the Court's conservative majority in this case was apparently to reduce the numbers of appeals and allow the states to apply post-*Gregg* death penalty law with only minimal supervision by the federal courts. When Congress passed the 1996 Anti-Terrorism and Effective Death Penalty Act, which trimmed back the conditions for federal habeas corpus relief, the Court quickly approved the legislation in *Felker v. Turpin* (1996).

In several subsequent rulings, however, the majority of the justices signaled their interest in renewing the Court's controls over capital punishment cases within the states. For example, in the cases of *Wiggins v. Smith* (2003) and *Rompilla v. Beard* (2005), the Court overturned two death sentences because defense attorneys failed to look for mitigating circumstances during the sentencing phases of their trials. The Court's majority has also continued to subscribe to the theory that the meaning of the Eighth Amendment should be drawn from the evolving standards of decency within the general population. The decisions, moreover, have continued to increase the categories of persons whose executions are judged to be inherently cruel and unusual, regardless of the seriousness of the crimes committed. Among these categories are the insane (*Ford v. Wainwright*, 1986), those with mental disabilities (*Atkins v. Virginia*, 2002), and persons under the age of eighteen at the time of their offenses (*Roper v. Simmons*, 2005).

John C. Hughes

FURTHER READING

Bohm, Robert M. *Deathquest: An Introduction to the Theory and Practice of Capital Punishment in the United States.* Cincinnati: Anderson Publishing, 2003.

Carter, Linda E., and Ellen Krietzberg. *Understanding Capital Punishment Law.* Newark, N.J.: LexisNexis, 2004.

Cole, David. *No Equal Justice: Race and Class in the American Criminal Justice System.* New York: New Press, 1998.

Constanzo, Mark. *Just Revenge: Costs and Consequences of the Death Penalty.* New York: St. Martin's Press, 1997.

Foley, Michael A. *Arbitrary and Capricious: The Supreme Court, the Constitution, and the Death Penalty.* New York: Praeger, 2003.

Haines, Herbert H. *Against Capital Punishment: The Anti-Death Penalty Movement in America, 1972-1994.* New York: Oxford University Press, 1999.

Kronenwetter, Michael. *Capital Punishment: A Reference Handbook.* 2d ed. Santa Barbara, Calif.: ABC-Clio, 2001.

Latzer, Barry, ed. *Death Penalty Cases: Leading Supreme Court Cases on Capital Punishment.* 2d ed. Burlington, Mass.: Butterworth Heineman, 2002.

Mello, Michael A. *Dead Wrong: A Death Row Lawyer Speaks Out Against Capital Punishment.* Madison: University of Wisconsin Press, 1997.

Protess, David. *A Promise of Justice: The Eighteen-Year Fight to Save Four Innocent Men.* New York: Hyperion, 1998.

Sarat, Austin. *When the State Kills: Capital Punishment and the American Condition.* Princeton, N.J.: Princeton University Press, 2001.

Williams, Mary E., ed. *Capital Punishment.* Farmington Hills, Mich.: Greenhaven, 2005.

SEE ALSO Constitutional interpretation; Double jeopardy; Due process, procedural; Eighth Amendment; Fourteenth Amendment; *Furman v. Georgia*; *Gregg v. Georgia*; Habeas corpus; *McCleskey v. Kemp*; *Payne v. Tennessee*; Plea bargaining; Race and discrimination; *Rompilla v. Beard*; *Roper v. Simmons*; Stewart, Potter.

Capitalism

DESCRIPTION: Economic system based on private property, competition, and the production of goods for profit, with the market rather than a central government making decisions about production and distribution.

SIGNIFICANCE: The Supreme Court's responsibility is to weigh the constitutional limits of governmental interference against the market's free operation. The Court defines the rules governing the market's operation, adjusts market mechanisms that are not functioning properly, and considers the claims of the many groups involved.

In a basically free-market economic system, the Supreme Court has been obligated to set restrictions on the power of the states and the federal government to intervene in the market's growth and direction. In the nineteenth century, the Court frequently cited substantive due process in rebuffing state proposals to regulate wages or free trade. It upheld freedom of contract, encouraged corporations, and regulated competition.

The Court tried to minimize political interference with capitalism by restricting state authority to the state's own borders and by limiting federal powers to the area of interstate commerce. *Swift v. Tyson* (1842) allowed federal judges to bypass state law in cases between citizens of different states, a decision extended in *Watson v. Tarpley* (1855) to cover not only common-law rules but also state statutes. In *Chicago, Milwaukee, and St. Paul Railway Co. v. Minnesota* (1890), a state regulatory agency was forbidden to set railroad rates. A change of philosophy occurred during the administration of President Franklin D. Roosevelt, when *Swift* was overturned by *Erie Railroad Co. v. Tompkins* (1938) and a general turn toward acceptance of regulation took place on the Court.

FREEDOM OF CONTRACT

In the nineteenth century, the Court's preference for an unregulated market contributed to several important decisions involving freedom of contract. The contracts clause (Article I, section 10, clause 1, of the Constitution, 1789) says that "No State shall . . . pass any Law impairing the Obligation of Contracts," and its interpretation featured in several early Court decisions opposing actions by states. The private branch of contracts clause jurisprudence dealt mostly with state attempts to weaken contracts between private parties, usually to effect debtor relief. In *Sturges v. Crowninshield* (1819), the Court allowed creditors to attach a debtor's wages, and in *Bronson v. Kinzie* (1843), the Court denied mortgagors additional redemption rights on foreclosed property, a ruling nullified by *Home Building and Loan Association v. Blaisdell* (1934), in which contracts were made subject to reasonable policing by states. In *Gelpcke v. Dubuque* (1864), the Court ruled against the claim that final authority in interpreting the state's laws lay with the state judges, overturning the Iowa Supreme Court's decision that Dubuque could invalidate its own municipal bonds.

The public branch of contracts clause jurisprudence forced the states to uphold their contracts faithfully. In *Fletcher v. Peck* (1810), the Court, led by Chief Justice John Marshall, forbade the state of Georgia from rescinding a land grant even though the transaction had been shot through with bribery. When the New Hampshire legislature moved to revise the Dartmouth College charter, the Court held in *Dartmouth College v. Woodward* (1819) that Dartmouth's contract was a charter and that the college was a private corporation not subject to state interference. In *Charles River Bridge v. Warren Bridge* (1837), the proprietors of the Charles River Bridge sought to halt construction of an adjacent bridge, arguing that the contracts clause protected them from a new bridge that would lessen their toll income. Chief Justice Roger Brooke Taney's opinion for the 4-3 majority stated that the rights and needs of the community overrode the rights of private property. The bridge case illustrates well how the principle of contract often clashed with the vision of those like Taney who realized how regressive it could be, and from then on, the states were allowed greater freedom in regulating their corporations. Part of this change resulted from the dilemma confronting early jurists who were caught between their devotion to contracts and their contempt for the many privileges the states had conferred on corporations in the early nineteenth century.

SUBSTANTIVE DUE PROCESS

Whereas procedural due process ensures fair procedures, the doctrine of substantive due process derived from the Fourteenth Amendment and enabled the Court to judge the substance of legislation. It evolved from American reverence for a free market and assumed tremendous importance in the late nineteenth century. Justice Stephen J. Field's dissent in the *Slaughterhouse Cases* (1873) and his concurrence in *Butchers' Union Co. v. Crescent City Co.* (1884) stressed the "liberty of the individual to pursue a lawful trade or employment." With this new doctrine, the Court was able to judge all state regulatory statutes. In *Allgeyer v. Louisiana* (1897), the Court struck down a Louisiana law forcing corporations trading with Louisiana residents to pay fees to the state. In *Lochner v. New York* (1905), a statute governing maximum work hours for bakers was found unconstitutional. In *Coppage v. Kansas* (1915), a state law forbidding yellow dog contracts (contracts in which employees agreed not to join a union) was overturned, and in *Adkins v. Children's Hospital* (1923), the Court invalidated the District of Columbia's employment commission's minimum-wage-setting authority.

Even in its period of strongest support of substantive due process, however, the Court took a generally broad view of issues. State regulation of railroad rates, for example, was accepted with the understanding that investors must be allowed reasonable competitive profits. In *Muller v. Oregon* (1908), a ten-hour workday law like that in *Lochner* was upheld because it applied only to women, who were thought to have special needs. In *Euclid v. Ambler Realty Co.* (1926), the Court demonstrated a sensitivity to community welfare by upholding broad land-use and zoning statutes. Probusiness regulatory legislation suffered the same disfavor accorded wage and hour legislation, as shown by the Court's decision in *Liggett v. Baldridge* (1928), in which a statute calling for licensing of pharmacists was struck down as an attempt to discourage competition. In *New State Ice Co. v. Liebmann* (1932), ice makers lost their bid to force potential competitors to demonstrate a need for more ice manufacturers.

Criticism by Progressives combined with the New Deal to end the dominance of substantive due process in economic affairs. In *Nebbia v. New York* (1934), the Court accepted the formation of a New York commission to regulate milk prices on the grounds of health concerns. In *West Coast Hotel Co. v. Parrish* (1937), a divided Court approved a Washington state minimum-wage law for women. In a reversal of Justice Field's earlier argument for free labor, Chief Justice Charles Evans Hughes stated in *West Coast Hotel* that the due process clause entailed "the protection of law against the evils which menace the health, safety, morals, and welfare of the people." After these rulings, substantive due process has shifted in emphasis from economics to social issues regarding various manifestations of discrimination.

CORPORATIONS

The Court handed down several important decisions in the nineteenth century establishing corporations as individuals. The old view that shareholders had to be named separately in any suit was overthrown in *Bank of the United States v. Dandridge* (1827). In *Bank of the United States v. Deveaux* (1809), the Court ruled that corporations were collections of individual shareholders and that in any suit each shareholder had to come from a different state than its disputants, making federal jurisdiction difficult to claim. However, *Deveaux* was invalidated by *Louisville, Cincinnati, and Charleston Railroad Co. v. Letson* (1844), which held that corporations were citizens of their incorporating states, thus enabling federal court jurisdiction over suits between corporations and out-of-state parties. In *Santa Clara County v. Southern Pacific Railroad Co.* (1886), the Court defined a corporation as a "person" under the Constitution, with the effect that only the corporation, not its individual shareholders, could make constitutional claims on behalf of the corporation.

In *Welton v. Missouri* (1876), the Court abandoned the traditional understanding that corporations could not do business directly outside their own states. Welton held that a corporation could not build a plant outside its own state but that its products could not be barred from sale in other states. However, in *Western Union Telegraph Co. v. Kansas* (1910), the Court held that as a person, a corporation could not be prevented from doing any legal business in a given state. In another important case, *Sawyer v. Hoag* (1873), the Court established the trust fund doctrine to safeguard against watered stock by demanding that shareholders had to make up any difference between what they had actually paid in and what the corporation claimed. The Court in these years frequently ruled that a corporate action was *ultra vires*, or beyond the limits of the corporate charter, holding, for example, in *Thomas v. West Jersey Railroad* (1979), that for one railroad to lease its track to another would create a de facto merger. Ironically, a corporate merger with a competitor, despite its potential dampening of competition, was safe because it did not result in business beyond the corporate charter; however, the relatively innocuous conglomerate merger could be forbidden as *ultra vires*. The practice of invoking actions as *ultra vires* soon waned, however, as the Court ruled in *Jacksonville, Mayport, Pablo Railway and Navigation Co. v. Hooper* (1896) that a railroad could purchase a hotel for its passengers. This kind of integration aided corporate growth. In *Briggs v. Spaulding* (1891), the Court relaxed its restraints even further, allowing corporate directors broad authority to make decisions without a threat of stockholders filing liability suits.

Beginning with the New Deal in the 1930's, the Court allowed more state and federal regulation of corporations, as in *Federal Trade Commission v. F. R. Keppel and Bros.* (1934), which gave the Federal Trade Commission increased oversight of business practices. Several later decisions gave more freedom to the market. In *Chiarella v. United States* (1980) and *Basic v. Levinson* (1988), the market for corporate securities was judged efficient enough to relieve corporate managers of the responsibility to provide information about their corporation's securities to buyers and sellers. In *Dirks v. Securities and Exchange Commission* (1983), the Court allowed buying and selling corporate stock on the basis of secret information about corporate wrongdoing as a practice that encouraged market efficiency.

REGULATION OF COMPETITION

Before the passage of the Sherman Antitrust Act in 1890, the Court relied on the common law of trade restraint in making decisions, but a series of rulings after the act's passage disallowed price fixing and anticompetitive mergers. In *United States v. Trans-Missouri Freight Association* (1897), the Court rejected the argument that railroads were a unique industry that needed an industrywide plan for rate scheduling. In *Loewe v. Lawlor* (1908), agreements by workers on the wage they could demand were outlawed, although laborers were to receive expanded bargaining rights in *National Labor Relations Board v. Jones and Laughlin Steel Corp.* (1937). In *Northern Securities Co. v. United States* (1904), the Court forbade an anticompetitive merger between two transcontinental railroads, and the Court has commonly applied the rule of reason to judge the effects of mergers. The rule of reason remains controversial, largely because one person's reason can be another's prejudice.

Frank Day

FURTHER READING

Paul Bowles's *Capitalism* (New York: Pearson/Longman, 2006) is a general consideration of the subject. Two books that focus on capitalism and the law are Herbert Hovencamp's *Enterprise and American Law, 1836-1937* (Cambridge, Mass.: Harvard University Press, 1991) and Arthur Selwyn Miller's *The Supreme Court and American Capitalism* (Westport, Conn.: Greenwood Press, 1968). An excellent study is Kermit L. Hall's *The Magic Mirror: Law in American History* (New York: Oxford University Press, 1989).

Among the topics that Hall treats in his bibliographical essay on "Law and the Economy" is the controversy prompted by Morton J. Horwitz in *The Transformation of American Law, 1780-1860* (New York: Oxford University Press, 1977), in which Horwitz argued that the body of common law developed in the nineteenth century worked for entrepreneurs against laborers and farmers.

James Willard Hurst is the author of several important books, including *The Legitimacy of the Business Corporation in the Law of the United States, 1780-1970* (Charlottesville: University Press of Virginia, 1970) and *Law and Markets in United States History: Different Modes of Bargaining Among Interests* (Madison: University of Wisconsin Press, 1982). Lawrence M. Friedman's *A History of American Law* (3d ed., New York: Simon & Schuster, 2005) has important chapters on law and the economy: 1776-1850, corporation law, and commerce, labor, and taxation. Charles R. Geisst's *Wall Street: A History* (New York: Oxford University Press, 1997) details the struggles between financial institutions and the Court. For a comprehensive history of the stock market, see Charles R. Geisst's *Wall Street: A History—From Its Beginnings to the Fall of Enron* (Rev. ed. New York: Oxford University Press, 2004).

SEE ALSO Bankruptcy law; Commerce, regulation of; Contract, freedom of; Contracts clause; Due process, substantive; Field, Stephen J.; *Lochner v. New York*; *Slaughterhouse Cases*; Zoning.

Benjamin N. Cardozo

IDENTIFICATION: Associate justice (March 14, 1932-July 9, 1938)
NOMINATED BY: Herbert Hoover
BORN: May 24, 1870, New York, New York
DIED: July 9, 1938, Port Chester, New York
SIGNIFICANCE: As Supreme Court justice, Cardozo advocated a philosophy of law based on life experience and a theory of justice that needs to account for a changing social, economic, and technological reality.

Benjamin N. Cardozo's father, Albert Cardozo, was a successful lawyer elected to the New York State Supreme Court. However, he was forced to resign in response to charges of undue favors toward Tammany Hall cohorts. The younger Cardozo lived much of his judicial and personal life attempting to whitewash that family stain. His was a life of extreme probity and personal puritanism. For example, Cardozo conscientiously avoided owning stock shares in any company for fear that it might bias him in some case, even indirectly. Cardozo entered Columbia College at age fifteen, then attended Columbia University Law School.

JUDICIAL CAREER

For twenty-two years, Cardozo practiced business law, becoming a highly successful trial lawyer who specialized in appellate litigation. Although not involved in partisan politics, he was a progressive Democrat who was nominated by an anti-Tammany Fusion coalition, winning election to the New York Supreme Court in 1913. Almost immediately afterward, he was shifted to the court of appeals, to which he was elected in 1917.

In 1927 Cardozo was elected chief judge of the court of appeals, with strong bipartisan support. Because New York state was the commercial hub and the court was staffed with generally outstanding jurists, the court of appeals was widely recognized as the most distinguished common-law tribunal in the nation. Cardozo was one of the founders and an active member of the prestigious American Law Institute. He lectured and published extensively.

Cardozo was so well regarded that in 1932 he was recommended to President Herbert Hoover for appointment to the Supreme Court. Politically, his selection was highly unusual in that the Court already had two New Yorkers and one Jew; and on top of that, Hoover was a Republican. However, based on his outstanding reputation, Cardozo won unanimous approval.

JUDICIAL PHILOSOPHY AND IMPACT

In both style and process, Cardozo was like his personal hero, Oliver Wendell Holmes, whom he replaced on the bench. Although politically he was the darling of the Progressives—for challenging the imperialistic

Benjamin N. Cardozo. (Harris and Ewing/ Collection of the Supreme Court of the United States)

power of the big corporations—judicially Cardozo was a pragmatist. He was skeptical of broad abstract principles and law as simply logical deduction from previous cases; rather, he thought that each case had to be judged in light of the particular circumstances. Cardozo argued that judges should look at the realities of the world—economic, political, and social—and not impose their own abstract ideas of justice. In general, Cardozo attempted to make the law adapt to what reasonable people would expect from a contract, thus making the law fit human needs and not imposing alien concepts.

Substantively, he is most noted for his decisions in the area of torts—specifically, liability, negligence, and contracts. Generally, he expanded the sphere of liability and made the process easier for injured parties. In contract law, he helped instill fairness into ambiguous contracts. Cardozo generally believed in allowing the legislature discretion in economic regulation. He was a mainstay in supporting the constitutionality of New Deal legislation. He wrote the majority opinion in the seminal Social Security decisions that turned the Court around, *Helvering v. Davis* (1937) and *Steward Machine Co. v. Davis* (1937). In civil liberties, especially their applicability to states, Cardozo believed in selective incorporation. Those rights that were fundamental, such as free speech, were imposed on the states. In *Palko v. Connecticut* (1937), he ruled that a second trial in the state, free of errors, did not deny due process.

Cardozo wrote five books, two of which became standards. The most enduring, *The Nature of the Judicial Process* (1921), was the first and arguably still the best book written on how judges actually make decisions. The respect and admiration for Cardozo—both personal and intellectual—helped translate his ideas, including the emphasis on case studies rather than abstract textbook concepts, into dominant trends. Sixty years after his death, Cardozo was still one of the most frequently cited justices, his decisions regularly used in law texts, especially in torts.

Alan M. Fisher

FURTHER READING
Bader, William H., and Roy M. Mersky, eds. *The First One Hundred Eight Justices.* Buffalo, N.Y.: William S. Hein, 2004.

Cardozo, Benjamin N. *The Nature of the Judicial Process.* New Haven, Conn.: Yale University Press, 1921.

Hellman, George S. *Benjamin N. Cardozo: American Judge.* New York: Russell & Russell, 1940.

Kaufman, Andrew L. *Cardozo.* Cambridge, Mass.: Harvard University Press, 1998.

Parrish, Michael E. *The Hughes Court: Justices, Rulings, and Legacy.* Santa Barbara, Calif.: ABC-Clio, 2002.

Polenberg, Richard. *The World of Benjamin Cardozo: Personal Values and the Judicial Process.* Cambridge, Mass.: Harvard University Press, 1997.

Posner, Richard A. *Cardozo: A Study in Reputation.* Chicago: University of Chicago Press, 1990.

SEE ALSO Contracts clause; Holmes, Oliver Wendell; Hughes, Charles Evans; Incorporation doctrine; New Deal; *Palko v. Connecticut.*

United States v. Carolene Products Co.

CITATION: 304 U.S. 144
DATE: April 25, 1938
ISSUES: Levels of judicial scrutiny; discrimination; fundamental rights
SIGNIFICANCE: The fourth footnote in the Court opinion in this case proposes the use of strict judicial scrutiny when considering explicit constitutional guarantees and discrimination against minorities. Called "the most famous footnote in American constitutional history," it later provided a theoretical foundation for judicial activism in defense of minorities and fundamental rights.

While upholding a relatively minor congressional regulation of commerce in this case, the Court employed a presumption of legislative constitutionality, just as it had done in earlier cases dealing with economic regulations of business. Because the Court had not utilized this presumption of constitutionality when examining a restriction on the freedom of the press in *Near v. Minnesota* (1931), Justice

Harlan Fiske Stone, encouraged by Chief Justice Charles Evans Hughes, included a three-paragraph footnote written to justify the use of different presumptions for different legal issues. Although Stone spoke for a 5-2 majority in the major ruling of the case, he actually only spoke for himself and two other justices in the most crucial passage of the footnote.

In essence, the footnote explained why it was appropriate for the Court to apply different standards of judicial scrutiny for different kinds of legislation. The first paragraph asserts that the presumption of constitutionality might be of "narrower scope" when the challenged legislation appeared to contradict a specific prohibition explicitly written in the Constitution, as in the Bill of Rights. The second paragraph suggests that courts might need to use heightened scrutiny when reviewing legislation restricting those political processes that usually make it possible to bring about the repeal of undesirable legislation. The third paragraph suggests that a "more searching judicial inquiry" might be necessary in order to preserve the constitutional rights of racial or religious minorities, because such minorities commonly possess limited political influence.

After World War II, the majority of the Supreme Court justices would endorse a modified version of the *Caroline Products* footnote, requiring application of strict judicial scrutiny when dealing with two issues: racial classifications and restrictions on fundamental rights.

Thomas Tandy Lewis

SEE ALSO Bill of Rights; Due process, procedural; Due process, substantive; Equal protection clause; Federalism; Incorporation doctrine; Judicial scrutiny; Judicial self-restraint; Stone, Harlan Fiske.

John Catron

IDENTIFICATION: Associate justice (May 1, 1837-May 30, 1865)
NOMINATED BY: Andrew Jackson
BORN: c. 1786, probably in Pennsylvania
DIED: May 30, 1865, Nashville, Tennessee
SIGNIFICANCE: While on the Supreme Court, Catron guarded the rights of states and opposed the accumulation of wealth and power within institutions and corporations. During the Civil War, he worked to preserve the union at great cost to himself.

Though little is known of John Catron's early years, his background probably was marked by poverty. After serving under General Andrew Jackson in the War of 1812, he was admitted to the bar in 1815 in Tennessee. While practicing and serving as a prosecuting attorney in a regional circuit court, he became knowledgeable in issues of land litigation. Because of his reputation, he was appointed to the Tennessee Supreme Court (then called the Supreme Court of Errors and Appeals) in 1818. He became its chief justice in 1831, a post he retained until the abolition of the court in 1834.

After he returned to private practice, Catron became more active on the political front, emerging as one of the leading supporters of Jackson's campaign for president. Like Jackson, Catron denounced many practices of the Bank of the United States, especially its loan practices and alleged usury. During the 1836 presidential election, he successfully managed Martin Van Buren's campaign in Tennessee. In recognition of his party loyalty, Jackson nominated him to the Supreme Court on March 3, 1837, the last day of his administration.

Catron's advocacy of states' rights influenced many of his Court decisions. In *License Cases* (1847), for example, he ruled that the provision for federal supervision of interstate commerce in the Constitution did not exclude a state's right to enforce state regulations. In *Cooley v. Board of Wardens of the Port of Philadelphia* (1852), he argued that states could legislate even if regulations were incidentally applied to foreign or interstate commerce. Corporate power was another area important to Catron. In *Marshall v. Baltimore and Ohio Railroad Co.* (1853), for example, he rejected the notion that all stockholders of a corporation could be regarded as a collective citizen and, instead, held that its officers should be responsible for the acts of a corporation.

Catron was also involved in judicial issues arising from the apprehension of fugitive slaves. In *Scott v. Sandford* (1857), Catron held that Dred Scott was a slave when he filed the suit and a slave when the case was decided. In the crucial period preceding secession, Catron believed that the maintenance of federal judicial power in the disaffected states was of historic importance. In St. Louis, he denounced secessionists as rebels and, as a result of his strong Unionist stand, was forced to leave his home in Nashville and his property was confiscated. He died shortly after the Confederate surrender assured the preservation of the Union to which he was devoted.

Christine R. Catron

John Catron. (Handy Studios/Collection of the Supreme Court of the United States)

191

FURTHER READING

Bader, William H., and Roy M. Mersky, eds. *The First One Hundred Eight Justices.* Buffalo, N.Y.: William S. Hein, 2004.

Cushman, Clare, ed. *The Supreme Court Justices: Illustrated Biographies, 1789-1995.* 2d ed. Washington, D.C.: Congressional Quarterly, 1995.

Friedman, Leon, and Fred L. Israel, eds. *The Justices of the United States Supreme Court: Their Lives and Major Opinions.* 5 vols. New York: Chelsea House, 1997.

Huebner, Timothy S. *The Taney Court: Justices, Rulings, and Legacy.* Santa Barbara, Calif.: ABC-Clio, 2003.

Lurie, Jonathan. *The Chase Court: Justices, Rulings, and Legacy.* Santa Barbara, Calif.: ABC-Clio, 2004.

SEE ALSO Civil War; *Scott v. Sandford*; States' rights and state sovereignty; Taney, Roger Brooke.

Censorship

DESCRIPTION: Narrowly defined, censorship is a governmental system for controlling which publications and expressions are permitted to circulate in the population. Broadly defined, the word refers to all restrictions—particularly those of governments—on speech, publications, and performances.

SIGNIFICANCE: Recognizing that freedom of expression can never be absolute, the Supreme Court has always allowed some forms of restrictions on oral and written communication. Since 1931, however, the Court has held that almost all prior restraints of expression violate the First Amendment, allowing exceptions only when necessary to protect some compelling governmental interest, such as the need for secrecy in an imminent military operation. Since the second half of the twentieth century, moreover, the Court has significantly limited the extent to which government may prohibit or restrict expressions based on objectionable content.

The eighteenth century framers of the First Amendment to the U.S. Constitution intended to prohibit most government prior restraints on publications, especially the practice of requiring licenses for the publication of books and periodicals. The framers were influenced by the noted jurist, William Blackstone, who had written that "liberty of the press . . . consists in laying no previous restraints upon publications, and not in freedom from censure for criminal matter when published." Blackstone thus endorsed the government's right to punish people who publish material that "is improper, mischievous, or illegal." Following the great controversy over the federal Sedition Act of 1798, however, the meaning of censorship gradually changed in the United States. By the early nineteenth century many American jurists were arguing that the First Amendment prohibited the federal government from punishing a person for expressing political or religious ideas.

For more than a century, the First Amendment's restrictions on censorship applied only to the federal government. State and local governments were not bound by any First Amendment provisions, and many states enacted censorship statutes, often in the form of sedition acts. In 1925, in *Gitlow v. New York*, the Supreme Court held that the prohibitions of the First Amendment were applicable to state and local governments through the incorporation of the Fourteenth Amendment, thus opening the door to challenges to state censorship statutes. However, the Court rejected Gitlow's claim that his freedom of speech rights had been violated and upheld his conviction under a New York criminal anarchy statute for the distribution of pamphlets advocating the establishment of socialism.

PRIOR RESTRAINT

The landmark case for censorship was *Near v. Minnesota* (1931). The state of Minnesota had passed a public nuisance statute that allowed public officials to obtain injunctions to stop publication of "malicious, scandalous and defamatory" newspapers or periodicals. The county attorney in Minneapolis used the statute against Jay Near's anti-Semitic periodical sheet that was accusing many public leaders of improprieties, frequently in offensive terms. By a 5-4 vote, the U.S. Supreme Court overturned the injunction and also struck down the underlying statute as a "gag law" that constituted the "essence" of censorship. In the opinion for the majority, Chief Justice

Charles Evans Hughes interpreted the First Amendment primarily from the perspective of Blackstone's condemnation of prior restraint. *Near v. Minnesota* was for many years the measure of whether state and local legislation constituted impermissible restriction on freedom of speech and press.

Following *Near,* the Court took the position that prior restraint, or any attempt to prevent the circulation of material or suppress part of its content before it reaches the public, is presumptively unconstitutional, a violation of the First Amendment. The Court insisted on determining whether materials are possibly seditious or obscene through criminal prosecution *after* publication or broadcast. In addition to not violating the no-prior restraint principle, the postexpression prosecutions ensured jury trials, with the input of "community standards" and requiring conviction beyond a reasonable doubt.

The Court's most famous prior restraint case was *New York Times Co. v. United States* (1971), which dealt with the Pentagon Papers, the top-secret Vietnam War documents that were leaked to *The New York Times* by a government employee, Daniel Ellsberg, who opposed the war. Following the newspaper's publication of some of the documents, the U.S. District Court in New York issued a temporary restraining order preventing the *Times* from further publication pending a decision on the government's application for an injunction. The case went to trial in the district court under Judge Murray R. Gurfein. Although Gurfein was initially disposed to favor the government's position, he changed his view during the course of this first trial and denied the government's application for an injunction but kept the restraining order in place long enough for the government to appeal. In his decision, Gurfein said that while "prior restraint" might be possible in this case, the evidence adduced in the trial by the government did not support it, and hence the presumption against prior restraint prevailed.

Meanwhile, the *Washington Post* had also acquired a copy of the Pentagon Papers, though it is not clear if the *Post*'s copy was identical to that received by *The New York Times*. The *Post*, eager to establish its reputation as a national newspaper, decided to publish an article based on the papers, despite requests from the government to refrain. Accordingly, the government also applied for a restraining order, preliminary to an injunction, against the *Post*. However, when the *Post* case went to trial before District Judge Gerhard Gesell, he, too, denied the government's application, though he also permitted further temporary restraint to give the government time to appeal. On the appeals level, the courts divided. The federal Appeals Court in the Second District (New York) reversed Judge Gurfein, while the Appeals Court in the District of Columbia upheld Judge Gesell.

The lower courts were aware that their decisions were preliminary to an appeal to the Supreme Court, though haste was necessary as the Court was about to adjourn for the summer. The Court agreed to hear the case on an expedited basis. On June 30, 1971, the Court issued a *per curiam* judgment stating that the government had not met its burden of demonstrating that publication of the Pentagon Papers would endanger lives and harm the national interest. Only three justices wanted to declare that prior restraint would never be justified under the First Amendment. The majority acknowledged that prior restraint might be permitted in extraordinary circumstances, but not in this particular instance. Chief Justice Warren Burger wrote that the newspapers could be criminally prosecuted for illegally publishing classified information, but only after publication had occurred.

The Pentagon Papers decision did not affect the federal government's prerogative of providing criminal punishment for persons who illegally reveal classified information about national security. In fact, Daniel Ellsberg was indicted and tried for leaking the Pentagon Papers. However, the result in his case was a mistrial because of the Nixon administration's misdeeds.

In subsequent cases, the Court has reaffirmed the constitutional right of newspapers not to be limited by prepublication restrictions. In *Nebraska Press Association v. Stuart* (1976), for example, the Court held that trial judges may not use gag orders to prevent newspapers from publishing information that is potentially prejudicial to a criminal defendant when such information is obtained in open court. The Court unanimously refused to erode an established First Amendment right because of a speculative danger that the publication of material might harm a defendant's right to a fair trial.

However, the Court has not disapproved all licensing systems that involve some prior restraints of speech. In the cases of *Marchetti v.*

United States (1968) and *Snepp v. United States* (1980), it approved the Central Intelligence Agency's rules requiring former employees to submit proposed writings for review before publication. When reviewing local ordinances requiring licenses for parades, as in *Cox v. New Hampshire* (1941), the Court has recognized the validity of time, place, and manner restrictions so long as they are reasonable and not based on the speech content of the parade. Elementary and secondary schools were granted the right to censor student publications in *Hazelwood School District v. Kuhlmeier* (1988). In *Walker v. City of Birmingham* (1967), the Supreme Court recognized that judges may punish persons who disobey court orders restraining speech, even if the restriction might later be found unconstitutional.

A government postal inspector, Anthony Comstock conducted a personal crusade against what he regarded as immorality. In 1873, when the U.S. Congress passed a law making it illegal to mail "obscene, lewd, and/ or lascivious" materials, the act became known as the "Comstock Law." (Library of Congress)

OBSCENITY

In 1865, the U.S. Congress enacted the Postal Act, making it a crime to use the mails to send any "publication of a vulgar or indecent character." Anthony Comstock led a crusade to make the postal regulations even more restrictive. In 1873, Congress responded with a statute that created special agents to seize "lewd or lascivious" materials and provided criminal penalties of up to five years for a first offense. Often courts applied what was known as the Hicklin rule, which went back to the British case *Regina v. Hicklin* (1868). That rule allowed materials to be prosecuted on the basis of isolated passages that had bad effects on susceptible persons. Even serious books, such as Theodore Dreiser's *Sister Carrie* (1900) were sometimes proscribed. Few jurists argued that the Comstock laws violated the First Amendment. In the *Near v. Minnesota* decision of 1931, Chief Justice Charles Evans Hughes thought it obvious that "the primary requirements of decency may be enforced against obscene publications." Until 1957, the Court upheld the Comstock laws in numerous rulings.

As American culture became more liberal, however, restrictions on the publication and circulation of what many people considered obscenity presented problems for the Court. Two of the most liberal justices appointed by President Franklin D. Roosevelt, William O. Douglas and Hugo L. Black, took the position that *any* restriction on freedom of speech or of the press was unconstitutional, but they never won over a majority of their colleagues. Consequently, during the second half of the twentieth century, the Court was engaged in the difficult task of balancing the rights of free expression against the rights of people who do not wish to be exposed to materials they find offensive and against the need to protect children from the negative effects of pornographic materials.

In *Roth v. United States* (1957), the Court upheld the conviction of a bookseller under the Comstock statute for selling obscene materials. In upholding the conviction, Justice William J. Brennan, Jr., wrote that obscenity was not protected by the First Amendment, but he defined the term obscenity narrowly. Rejecting the old Hicklin rule, Brennan insisted that courts must examine works as a whole, rather than isolated portions of them. He further defined obscenity as sexual material appealing to a prurient interest, as understood by the average person in the community. Although he reaffirmed that obscenity has no constitutional protection, the *Roth* ruling was particularly important for establishing that obscenity must be narrowly defined on the basis of the First Amendment rather than on the common law. Soon after the *Roth* ruling, literary works such as D. H. Lawrence's *Lady Chatterley's Lover* (1928) appeared in bookstores and on newsstands.

The *Roth* standard of obscenity was rather unclear. From 1967 to 1973, the Court decided obscenity cases largely on a case-by-case basis, changing the guidelines every few years. In 1973, in *Miller v. California* and its companion case, *Paris Adult Theatre v. Slaton*, the majority of the justices finally agreed on a definition of obscenity. An obscene work, they ruled, "taken as a whole, appeals to the prurient interest," depicts sexual acts in a "patently offensive way," and lacks "serious literary, artistic, political, or scientific value." The Court also decided that local community standards, not national ones, were to be used in determining obscenity. In *New York v. Ferber* (1982) the Court approved prosecution of pornographic materials—whether obscene or indecent—that portray children involved in sexual acts. In cases involving child pornography, the Court even allowed criminal prosecutions for the mere possession of such materials in the privacy of one's home.

FILM AND BROADCASTING

The emergence of new communication technologies has also raised numerous issues of censorship. Films were uniquely susceptible to prior restraint forms of censorship, and several states established agencies empowered to decide which films would be allowed in the state. In *Mutual Film Corporation v. Ohio* (1915) the Supreme Court held that films were a "business pure and simple," not having any protection from censorship under the First Amendment. However, in *Burstyn v. Wilson* (1952), the Court overturned its 1915 ruling and held for the time that films were a medium for expressing ideas, therefore deserving of some degree of protection under the First and Fourteenth Amendments. In this case, moreover, the court unanimously found that New York censors had acted unconstitutionally in prohibiting the showing of *The Miracle*, a film opposed by the Roman Catholic Church. Writing for the Court, Justice Tom C. Clark wrote that pre-exhibition censorship would be justified only in exceptional cases, and that standards must not permit unfettered discretion by censors. In *Freedman v. Maryland* (1965), the Court continued to allow some censorship of films, but prohibited viewpoint censorship and required procedures for prompt judicial review.

After 1973, a few films were prosecuted as indecent under the *Miller* standards. In *Jenkins v. Georgia* (1973), the Court found that the movie *Carnal Knowledge* was not obscene, even though many communities and lower courts had found otherwise. The Court clearly stated in *Sable Communications v. Federal Communications Commission* (1989) that "sexual expression that is indecent but not obscene is protected by the First Amendment." By the turn of the twenty-first century, as American society became increasingly permissive toward sexuality, it became almost impossible for prosecutors to convince either juries or appellate courts that a film was obscene. However, the public tended to support the notion of using zoning ordinances to restrict the locations of adult entertainment establishments. The Court, as in *City of Renton v. Playtime Theatres* (1986), has usually been receptive to such restrictions.

When examining the policies of the Federal Communications Commission when censoring radio and television broadcasts, the Court has shown a great deal of deference. In *Federal Communications Commission v. Pacifica Foundation* (1978), the justices voted five to four to uphold a Federal Communications Commission (FCC) rule that limited the times of the day for broadcasting nonobscene "indecent material." Justice John Paul Stevens wrote that "of all forms of communications," broadcasting has the most limited First Amendment protection because of its direct intrusion into private homes where it was uniquely accessible to children.

THE INTERNET

The Internet, which is often available to children, has created special problems. In 1996, Congress attempted to protect children with the Communications Decency Act (CDA), making it a criminal offense "knowingly" to transmit "obscene or indecent" material to anyone under the age of eighteen. In *Reno v. American Civil Liberties Union* (1997), the Court struck down the CDA because of its excessive abridgment of adults' rights to gain access to nonobscene sexually oriented materials that are constitutionally protected. The government, concluded Justice Stevens, had not met its burden of showing why a more narrowly tailored law would not protect children.

After the CDA was declared unconstitutional, Congress responded with the passage of another law, the Children's Online Protection Act of 1998 (COPA), which required online providers to prevent children from accessing sexual materials deemed to be harmful. A district court, supported by the Third Circuit Court of Appeals, prohibited implementation of the law in anticipation that the statute would likely fail the "strict scrutiny" test, because it was not narrowly tailored and failed to use the least restrictive means available to achieve its objective. When the Supreme Court reviewed the injunction in *American Civil Liberties Union v. Ashcroft* (2004), the justices agreed with the lower court by a 5-4 margin. Writing for the majority, Justice Anthony Kennedy argued that the injunction was not an abuse of judicial discretion because the record indicated the availability of "less restrictive alternatives to the statute," such as home filters.

The Supreme Court was more sympathetic to the Children's Internet Protection Act of 2000 (CIPA), which was designed to prevent minors from accessing obscene materials at Internet terminals in public libraries. In order to receive federal funding, the CIPA required that libraries install software to block out indecent images. In *United States v. American Library Association* (2003), the justices decided by a 6-3 margin to uphold the constitutionality of the statute. Writing for the majority, Chief Justice Rehnquist argued that government may set reasonable standards for the programs it sponsors, that Internet access in a library is not a public forum, and that adults could ask librarians for permission to access proscribed Web sites.

Nancy M. Gordon
Revised and updated by the Editor

FURTHER READING

A standard work on the subject of media law and censorship is Don R. Pember and Clay Calvert's *Mass Media Law* (14th ed. New York: McGraw-Hill, 2004), which is known for its well-organized case studies. Each new edition keeps up with current issues. The early history of federal censorship is detailed in James C. N. Paul and Murray L. Schwartz's *Federal Censorship: Obscenity in the Mail* (New York: Free Press of Glencoe, 1961). Morris L. Ernst and Alan U. Schwartz also provide much useful information on censorship issues in *Censorship: The Search for the Obscene* (London: Collier-Macmillan, 1964). Recent issues are included in Herbert Foerstel's *Free Expression and Censorship in America* (Westport, Conn.: Greenwood Press, 1997), which also includes a table of cases.

Cass R. Sunstein's *One Case at a Time: Judicial Minimalism on the Supreme Court* (Cambridge, Mass.: Harvard University Press, 1999) argues that in the 1990's the Court has tried to avoid sweeping judgments. David Rudenstine's *The Day the Presses Stopped: A History of the Pentagon Papers Case* (Berkeley: University of California Press, 1996) is a comprehensive account of the case. *Anatomy of Censorship: Why the Censors Have It Wrong*, by Harry White (Lanham, Md.: University Press of America, 1997), is a polemic but provides some useful information.

SEE ALSO *Ashcroft v. Free Speech Coalition*; *Brandenburg v. Ohio*; Cold War; First Amendment; *Gitlow v. New York*; *Near v. Minnesota*; *New York Times Co. v. United States*; Obscenity and pornography; *Roth v. United States/Alberts v. California*; Sedition Act of 1798; Speech and press, freedom of.

Writ of *Certiorari*

DESCRIPTION. Written order issued by the Supreme Court exercising discretionary power to direct a state supreme court or court of appeals to deliver the record in a case for review. If the Court grants a writ to a petitioner, the case comes before the Court.

SIGNIFICANCE: The Court determines which cases it will hear—and thus what legal issues it will review—through the issuance of writs of *certiorari*.

The U.S. Constitution and Congress determine the Supreme Court's jurisdiction to review cases. Article III of the Constitution and various congressional statutes grant the Court two main areas of jurisdiction:

original and appellate. To relieve the Court of its rapidly growing caseload burden, Congress established the federal circuit court of appeals with the Judiciary Act of 1891. The act also authorized the Court to review final decisions in certain categories of cases through the issuance of writs of *certiorari*.

Although the Constitution does not expressly grant the Court *certiorari* jurisdiction in the state courts, the Court may grant *certiorari* for those state court decisions that implicate federal law. Statutes limit *certiorari* jurisdiction to federal questions that have been decided in final judgments of the states' highest courts. The Court may review final judgments or decrees of the states' highest court if the validity of a treaty or statute of the United States is questioned. It may also review a state court decision if a state statute is viewed as violating the Constitution, treaties, or laws of the United States. The Court may not review a case involving federal law if the state court's decision can be upheld purely on state law.

The Court reviews the majority of its cases through appellate jurisdiction. Within its appellate jurisdiction, the power to grant or deny *certiorari* gives the Court discretion in determining which cases it will review. The passage of the Judiciary Act of 1925 greatly expanded the Court's *certiorari* jurisdiction in an effort to reduce its overwhelming docket of cases. The act also enhanced the Court's status and power by largely allowing it to set its own agenda. Since the act's passage, the number of *certiorari* petitions greatly expanded, and by the 1970's, writs of *certiorari* were responsible for 90 percent of the Court's caseload.

The Court reviews petitions for writs of *certiorari* solely at its discretion. If the Court grants *certiorari*, it agrees to review the judgments in question in that case. It will generally simply issue its decision to either grant or deny *certiorari* without giving any explanations for the decision. *Certiorari* is essential to the Court's functioning because of the high number of cases brought to it each year. In the late twentieth century, the Court granted full review to about 160, or 6 percent, of the nearly 5,000 cases submitted through petitions for writs of *certiorari* each year. If the Court decides not to hear a particular case by denying the petition for a writ of *certiorari*, there are almost no other avenues that the petitioner can pursue to have the lower court's judgment reviewed.

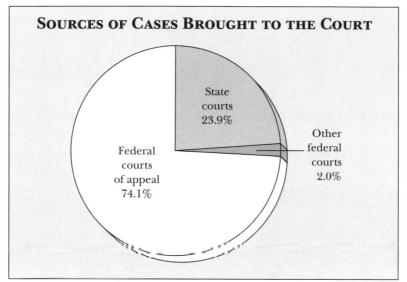

SOURCES OF CASES BROUGHT TO THE COURT

State courts
23.9%

Other federal courts
2.0%

Federal courts of appeal
74.1%

Note: Figures, which do not include original jurisdiction cases, apply to cases in which the Court granted or denied hearings in October, 1996.
Source: Lawrence Baum, *The Supreme Court* (6th ed. Washington, D.C.: Congressional Quarterly, 1998), p. 13.

The Court grants writs of *certiorari* only for compelling reasons. It pays special attention to resolving conflicts among the federal courts of appeals, the federal district courts, and the state courts on important legal principles or issues of law.

PETITIONS

A party to any civil or criminal case in which a judgment was entered by a state court of last resort or a U.S. court of appeals may petition for a writ of *certiorari* requesting the Supreme Court to review the lower court's judgment. A party may also petition the Court for a writ of *certiorari* in a case in which a judgment was entered by a lower state court if the state court of last resort has issued an order denying its discretionary review. Parties involved in the same judgment may file a petition jointly or separately. The person petitioning the Court for a writ of *certiorari* is known as the "petitioner" and the opposing party as the "respondent."

The petition must be accurate, brief, and clear in its presentation of the information necessary for the Court to review the case. The petition contains the questions the petitioner wishes the Court to review, when and how these questions were raised, and the names of the parties involved in the proceeding of the court that rendered the judgment in question. It also includes citations of the courts' and administrative agencies' opinions and orders issued in the case, the basis for the Court's jurisdiction, and the constitutional provisions, treaties, statutes, ordinances, and regulations involved in the case. All this information is necessary for the justices to review the petition and make a sound judgment on whether the Court should review the case.

REVIEW OF PETITIONS

The Court may review cases on appeal, by certification, by an extraordinary writ, or by *certiorari*. The Court must review cases on appeal, meaning that Congress has mandated review of that type of case, whereas the Court may grant or deny *certiorari* at its discretion. Because Congress eliminated most categories of appeals in 1988 and original jurisdiction represents only one or two cases a year, the majority of the cases the Court hears are those granted *certiorari*.

Each justice handles the petitions for *certiorari* sent to the Court differently; however, justices generally either depend on memos written by their own law clerks or those prepared by clerks in the *certiorari* pool. Some justices have one of their law clerks read the petition and prepare a memo for them recommending what action the Court should take. Other justices use the *certiorari* pool that began in 1972 at the behest of several justices. In the pool, the petitions are divided randomly among the clerks, and the clerks read each petition assigned to them and prepare a single memo for all the justices. The justices' individual clerks then receive the memos and may mark them for their particular justice. These memos contain a brief summary of the case, the relevant facts, the lower court's decision, the parties' contentions, an evaluation of the petition, a recommendation for action, and any additional information necessary to an understanding of the case.

Cases the justice feels are worthy of review are added to the Court's list of petitions to be voted on by all the justices. The justices then discuss these cases at their twice-weekly conferences. The Court also schedules several daylong conferences in September to discuss those petitions that have accumulated over the Court's summer recess. About 70 percent of the petitions for *certiorari* do not make the discussion list and are automatically denied *certiorari*. The chief justice announces those cases that the justices will discuss, and the justices then vote in order of seniority on whether to grant or deny *certiorari*. The justices may speak on an individual case if they feel it merits discussion rather than simply a vote. The Court will grant *certiorari* if four of the nine justices are in favor of the petition. The justices developed this informal rule of four after the 1891 Judiciary Act broadened the Court's discretionary jurisdiction. The rule became public knowledge in 1924. Clerks, secretaries, and visitors may not be present at these conferences, and the Court does not release its votes on *certiorari* petitions to the public. Justices who dissent from the decision to either grant or deny *certiorari* rarely publish their dissent or their reasons for dissenting.

If the Court grants the petition for a writ of *certiorari*, the Court clerk will prepare, sign, and enter the order and notify the council of record and the court whose judgment is in question. The clerk will also schedule the case for briefing and oral argument before the Court. A formal writ of *certiorari* will not be issued unless specially directed. If the Court denies *certiorari*, the clerk will prepare, sign, and enter the order and notify the counsel of record and the court whose judgment was in question. A denial of *certiorari* simply means that the Court will not review the case. It does not mean that the Court agrees with the lower court's ruling although that ruling will stand. The denial of *certiorari* does not constitute a ruling on any legal issues raised by the case although some scholars would argue that it is an informal indication of the Court's position.

David Trevino

FURTHER READING
Robert G. McCloskey's *The American Supreme Court* (4th ed. Chicago: University of Chicago Press, 2005) offers a good general introduction to the Supreme Court and its jurisdiction. Doris Marie Provine's *Case Selection in the United States Supreme Court* (Chicago: University of Chicago Press, 1980) and Lee Epstein and Jack Knight's *The Choices Jus-*

tices Make (Washington, D.C.: Congressional Quarterly, 1998) both offer an overview of the Court's vital process of deciding which cases it will review. Peter Linzer offers a view on whether the Court's denial to review cases informally constitutes a decision on the merits of the case in his article "The Meaning of *Certiorari* Denials" in the *Columbia Law Review* 79, no. 7 (November, 1979): 1227-1305.

SEE ALSO Appellate jurisdiction; Briefs; Clerks of the justices; Conference of the justices; Review, process of; Rules of the Court; Solicitor general; Workload.

Salmon P. Chase

IDENTIFICATION: Chief justice (December 15, 1864-May 7, 1873)
NOMINATED BY: Abraham Lincoln
BORN: January 13, 1808, Cornish, New Hampshire
DIED: May 7, 1873, New York, New York
SIGNIFICANCE: Presiding over the first impeachment trial of a U.S. president, Chief Justice Chase exercised judicial restraint in a highly partisan atmosphere. As an influential national figure, he brought political wisdom and moderation to the constitutional issues raised by the Reconstruction of the South after the Civil War.

Salmon P. Chase was the eighth child of a Cornish, New Hampshire, couple. His father was a farmer, but several of his uncles were well-educated professionals. One uncle supervised his early education, and an aunt assisted the hard-pressed family by financing further study at Dartmouth College. Young Chase studied law under U.S. attorney general William Wirt, passed his bar examination in 1829, and began practicing law the next year in Cincinnati, Ohio, where interest in the plight of fugitive slaves ran high.

In an early indication of a compelling interest, Chase defended in 1837 a black woman employed by abolitionist James G. Birney but arrested under provisions of the Fugitive Slave Act of 1793. Chase lost the case but impressed observers by his argument that the United States and state governments were mutually independent entities, neither of which could regulate the other. An intensely ambitious man, Chase led the Liberty Party in Ohio in the 1840's and, as a United States senator from 1849 to 1855, spearheaded opposition to the extension of slavery into the territories.

After contributing to the formation of the Republican Party and serving as the first Republican governor of Ohio (1855-1859), he failed in 1856 and 1860 to gain his party's nomination for president but served ably as Abraham Lincoln's secretary of the treasury from 1861 to 1864. Lincoln saw in Chase a person whose antislavery reputation would appease radicals but who could be expected to promote moderation in the difficult post-Civil War Reconstruction. On December 6, 1864, a month after Lincoln won reelection with support from Chase, the Senate confirmed Lincoln's appointment of Chase as chief justice. After taking the oath of office nine days later, Chase twice swore in presidents: Lincoln, on March 4, 1865, and, six weeks afterwards, Andrew Johnson, following Lincoln's assassination.

RECONSTRUCTION

Chase's reputation as a leader added greatly to the Court's prestige, then at low ebb. He regarded universal male suffrage as the key to Reconstruction, but he hoped that the states would take the lead in granting the vote to African American men. Quietly he deflected efforts to try Jefferson Davis, the president of the Confederacy, as a war criminal, for several reasons, one of them constitutional. Article III, he pointed out, provides that trials for crimes other than impeachment take place in the state where the crimes were committed. Not only did he consider such a determination impossible to make, he doubted that an impartial jury of Davis's peers could be found in any state. Chase prudently discouraged such action until postwar tempers had cooled, and Davis was never tried.

Reconstruction challenged the Court with a series of thorny jurisdictional problems. In *Ex parte Milligan* (1866), the justices heard the case of a man charged with organizing a rebellion in Indiana for attempting to free Confederate prisoners in the Midwest and subsequently condemned to death by one of the military courts then operating in some Northern as well as Southern states. The Court ruled that the military commission had no jurisdiction. In another conflict of this type, counsel for a southern newspaper editor arrested by military authorities for libel petitioned unsuccessfully in a district court for a writ of habeas corpus. In 1868 when it appeared to Chase that a Court ruling for the defendant upon appeal might well jeopardize the Reconstruction Act (1867), Chase persuaded his colleagues to postpone a decision. He was much criticized for his seeming to bow to congressional pressure in the earlier phase of Reconstruction, but when political pressure had eased in 1869, the Court, in *Ex parte McCardle*, again ruled this action of a military court to be unconstitutional.

Late in Chase's term as chief justice, *Collector v. Day* (1871) attested his continuing interest in preserving the boundaries between federal and state power. Associate Justice Samuel Nelson, in delivering the majority opinion that the federal government exceeded its authority in levying an income tax on the salary of a state judge, drew heavily upon arguments Chase had previously employed in conflicts between state and federal authority.

Salmon P. Chase.
(Library of Congress)

IMPEACHMENT TRIAL

Chase presided at the first impeachment trial of a U.S. president in the Senate chamber, a venue otherwise outside the authority of a Supreme Court justice. President Andrew Johnson had been charged with several offenses, the most significant being violation of the recently enacted Tenure of Office Act (1867) by removing Secretary of War Edwin M. Stanton without congressional approval. Without precedents to go by but equipped with a keen awareness of the extent to which partisan opposition to Johnson was operating in the charges against the president, Chase managed to inject elements of judicial procedure into a trial that he knew would eventually be governed mainly by Senate rules. He also forced the Senate to grant him a vote to decide the matter in the case of a tie. As it turned out, however, the effort to remove Johnson lost by one vote. Both in this trial and in Chase's more usual judicial duties, his commanding presence and keen understanding of the art of politics, rather than pure legal scholarship, were his distinguishing assets.

Robert P. Ellis

FURTHER READING

Bader, William H., and Roy M. Mersky, eds. *The First One Hundred Eight Justices.* Buffalo, N.Y.: William S. Hein, 2004.

Blue, Frederick. *Salmon P. Chase: A Life in Politics.* Kent, Ohio: Kent State University Press, 1987.

Fairman, Charles. *Reconstruction and Reunion, 1864-1888.* New York: Macmillan, 1971.

Kutler, Stanley I. *Judicial Power and Reconstruction Politics.* Chicago: University of Chicago Press, 1968.

Lurie, Jonathan. *The Chase Court: Justices, Rulings, and Legacy.* Santa Barbara, Calif.: ABC-Clio, 2004.

Niven, John. *Salmon P. Chase: A Biography.* New York: Oxford University Press, 1995.

SEE ALSO Habeas corpus; *Milligan, Ex parte;* Nelson, Samuel; Reconstruction; Salaries of justices; *Slaughterhouse Cases.*

Samuel Chase

IDENTIFICATION: Associate justice (February 4, 1796-June 19, 1811)
NOMINATED BY: George Washington
BORN: April 17, 1741, Somerset County, Maryland
DIED: June 19, 1811, Baltimore, Maryland
SIGNIFICANCE: Chase was the only Supreme Court justice impeached for misconduct on the bench. During the Court's early years, he was an influential justice whose opinions established enduring constitutional interpretations.

Samuel Chase was admitted to the bar in 1761. From 1764 to 1788 he was a member of the Maryland assembly and a vigorous supporter of U.S. rights. In 1774 the assembly sent him to the Continental Congress in Philadelphia where he became a prominent member, serving on thirty different committees. When Maryland instructed its delegates to vote against independence in 1776, Chase returned home and conducted a vigorous campaign that led the state to reverse its position. He returned to Philadelphia on July 1, cast the state's vote for independence, and signed the Declaration of Independence. In 1778 Chase left Congress after Alexander Hamilton denounced him for using secret information to speculate on the price of flour.

Chase vigorously criticized the new Constitution during the Maryland ratifying convention in 1787 and voted against its adoption. In 1788 he had become chief judge of the Baltimore city court and in 1791 chief judge of Maryland's general court. By 1795 he had become a Federalist, supporting a strong central government. That year Chase resigned his Maryland position, accepting President George Washington's nomination to the Supreme Court.

INTERPRETING THE CONSTITUTION

During the 1790's each justice read his opinion in turn, with the most recent appointee, in this case Chase, speaking first. In several precedent-setting cases, Chase's powerfully written opinions were so persuasive that the justices who followed did little more than agree with his views. The newest justice on the bench thus became the formulator of significant constitutional doctrine.

Chase's opinion in *Hylton v. United States* (1796) ruled that a federal tax on carriages was an excise tax, not a direct tax subject to constitutional limitations. Chase defined federal direct taxes as either poll or land taxes, a definition that held as constitutional law until overturned in an 1895 income tax ruling. In *Ware v. Hylton* (1796), Chase vigorously asserted the supremacy of national treaties over state laws, setting an enduring principle of constitutional law.

In *Calder v. Bull* (1798), Chase ruled that the ex post facto clause of the Constitution applied to criminal, not civil, cases. Chase also asserted that natural law principles, even if not spelled out in the Constitution, limited legislative actions. Commentators have viewed Chase's opinion as establishing the basis for interpreting the Fifth and Fourteenth Amendments as guaranteeing extensive civil rights not mentioned in the Constitution. Although Chase's opinion in *Calder* supports a "loose construction" of the Constitution, a circuit court opinion by Chase points toward a "strict constructionist" view. In *United States v. Worrall* (1798), Chase (dissenting from the opinion

Samuel Chase. (H. B. Hall/Collection of the Supreme Court of the United States)

held by other federal judges) asserted that the federal courts did not have jurisdiction over common-law crimes but could act only when Congress passed specific legislation. The Supreme Court adopted his view in 1812.

IMPEACHMENT

In the early nineteenth century, Supreme Court justices were required to regularly "ride the circuit" and join lower court judges in conducting trials. A passionate supporter of the Federalist Party, Chase's domineering and highly partisan behavior when conducting politically significant trials infuriated Jeffersonian Republicans, who tried to remove him from office.

When presiding over the treason trial of John Fries in 1800, Chase prevented Fries's lawyers from using their planned defense. Fries had led a mob that freed a group of Pennsylvanians held by a federal marshal. His attorneys wanted to argue that the action of the mob did not meet the constitutional definition of treason—levying war against the United States. When Chase prevented them from raising this issue, the lawyers withdrew. The jury convicted Fries, and Chase sentenced him to death, but President John Quincy Adams pardoned him.

Chase's conduct was even more aggressive and partisan in the May, 1800, trial of James Callender for violating the Sedition Act of 1798 by his abusive criticisms of President Adams. Chase refused to excuse a juror who said he had already decided that Callender was guilty. Chase required the defense attorneys to submit in writing the questions they intended to ask their main witness, then refused to let the witness testify. At Chase's Senate trial, Chief Justice John Marshall, who had been in the audience during the Callender trial, admitted that he had never known another judge to act in this manner. Chase proceeded to interrupt and insult defense counsel until they withdrew from the case.

The immediate occasion of Chase's impeachment was his charge to a Baltimore grand jury on May 2, 1803, attacking the leading ideas of the Jeffersonian Republicans. He criticized the recent adoption of universal manhood suffrage in Maryland as preparing the way for a mobocracy and asserted that the idea that "all men in a state of society are entitled to equal liberty and equal rights . . . will rapidly progress until peace and order, freedom and property, will be destroyed."

On March 12, 1804, the House of Representatives impeached Chase. His attorneys argued that only indictable offenses met the constitutional standard of "high crimes and misdemeanors," insisting that Chase had not violated any laws. All nine Federalist senators voted to acquit Chase. When six Republican senators agreed with the Federalists, the vote to convict fell four votes short of the required two-thirds majority. Most commentators view the failure to remove Chase as affirming the independence of the judiciary against partisan attack. Others disagree, arguing the lesson learned was that judges should avoid partisan behavior on the bench.

After the acquittal, Chase played only a minor role on the Court, writing few opinions and deferring to Chief Justice Marshall, until his death in 1811. His decisions during the 1790's, however, established Chase as the most influential justice of the early Court.

Milton Berman

FURTHER READING

Bader, William H., and Roy M. Mersky, eds. *The First One Hundred Eight Justices.* Buffalo, N.Y.: William S. Hein, 2004.

Clinton, Robert, Christopher Budzisz, and Peter Renstrom, eds. *The Marshall Court: Justices, Rulings, and Legacy.* Santa Barbara, ABC-Clio, 2007.

Ellis, Richard E. *The Jeffersonian Crisis: Courts and Politics in the Young Republic.* New York: Oxford University Press, 1971.

Harrington, Matthew P. *Jay and Ellsworth, The First Courts: Justices, Rulings, and Legacy.* Santa Barbara, Calif.: ABC-Clio, 2007.

Haw, James A., Francis F. Beirne, Rosamond R. Beirne, and R. Samuel Jett. *Stormy Patriot: The Life of Samuel Chase.* Baltimore: Maryland Historical Society, 1980.

Rehnquist, William H. *Grand Inquests: The Historic Impeachments of Justice Samuel Chase and President Andrew Johnson.* New York: William Morrow, 1992.

SEE ALSO *Calder v. Bull;* Marshall, John; Sedition Act of 1798.

Chicago, Burlington, and Quincy Railroad Co. v. Chicago

CITATION: 166 U.S. 226

DATE: March 1, 1897

ISSUES: Incorporation doctrine; takings clause; substantive due process

SIGNIFICANCE: By combining the common law with the approach of substantive due process, the Supreme Court, for the first time in history, held that one of the provisions of the Bill of Rights is binding on the states under the due process clause of the Fourteenth Amendment.

Justice John Marshall Harlan II wrote the 7-1 majority opinion with Justice David J. Brewer dissenting in part and Justice Melville W. Fuller not participating. The Supreme Court unanimously held that the Fourteenth Amendment's due process clause required the states to grant just compensation when it took private property for a public purpose. The ruling was unanimous because Justice Brewer concurred on this point even though he dissented on other issues.

The Illinois Supreme Court had upheld a jury verdict of one dollar awarded to the Chicago, Burlington, and Quincy Railroad for loss of its money-making ability when the city of Chicago created a street across its railroad track. *Chicago, Burlington, and Quincy Railroad Co.* was one of the earliest attempts to use the right of substantive due process to control a state's attempt to regulate economic behavior. Although this latter purpose has been set aside by other decisions, this case remains valid law for the proposition that the Fourteenth Amendment due process clause incorporates specific guarantees for the Bill of Rights. In this case, the Fifth Amendment's guarantee of just compensation when private property is taken for public purpose was incorporated and applied to the states. Although not explicitly affirmed in Justice Harlan's opinion, the ruling had the effect of partially overturning *Barron v. Baltimore* (1833).

Richard L. Wilson

See also Bill of Rights; Brewer, David J.; Due process, procedural; Due process, substantive; Employment discrimination; Fifth Amendment; Fourteenth Amendment; Incorporation doctrine; Takings clause.

Chief Justice

DESCRIPTION: Justice designated as administrator of the Supreme Court. Duties include distributing the workload among the other justices, assigning the writing of opinions, and often writing opinions.

SIGNIFICANCE: The chief justice leads the eight other justices, assigning the writing of opinions and often casting the deciding vote in split decisions.

Before the Supreme Court was instituted in 1789, Congress decreed that the Court would have five associate justices and a chief justice. The six justices were viewed as being essentially equal, although the chief justice had certain specific, additional duties. Accordingly, the chief justice was paid more than the associate justices, but the salary disparity was never substantial. In 1988 the chief justice received $115,000, just $5,000 more than the associate justices.

The first person President George Washington appointed to the Court was John Jay of New York, who served from 1789 to 1795 as chief justice. The early court, which first met officially in 1790, dealt with an average of five cases a year during its first five years. This caseload was light and manageable compared with the more than two hundred cases a year handled by the Court in the twentieth century. Five associate justices and the chief justice were able to handle such a caseload easily.

QUALIFICATIONS

The Constitution does not specify qualifications for the position of Supreme Court justice. Although justices articulate the most significant legal decisions made in the country, they need not be lawyers, although most of them are. The only requirement for a person to

CHIEF JUSTICES OF THE UNITED STATES, 1789 TO 2006

Name	Term	Appointed by
John Jay	1789-1795	George Washington
John Rutledge[1]	1795	George Washington
William Cushing[2]	1796	George Washington
Oliver Ellsworth	1796-1800	George Washington
John Marshall	1801-1835	John Adams
Roger B. Taney	1836-1864	Andrew Jackson
Salmon P. Chase	1864-1873	Abraham Lincoln
Morrison R. Waite	1874-1888	Ulysses S. Grant
Melville W. Fuller	1888-1910	Grover Cleveland
Edward D. White	1910-1921	William H. Taft
William H. Taft	1921-1930	Warren G. Harding
Charles E. Hughes	1930-1941	Herbert Hoover
Harlan F. Stone	1941-1946	Franklin D. Roosevelt
Frederick M. Vinson	1946-1953	Harry S. Truman
Earl Warren	1953-1969	Dwight D. Eisenhower
Warren E. Burger	1969-1986	Richard M. Nixon
William H. Rehnquist	1986-2005	Ronald W. Reagan
John Roberts	2005-	George W. Bush

1. Rutledge was not confirmed by Congress.
2. Cushing sat as chief justice for one week in January, 1796, and then declined the appointment and returned to serving as associate justice.

become a chief justice is that he or she be a citizen nominated by the president of the United States. This nomination must be confirmed by the Senate. Chief justices need not have served as associate justices, although usually they have.

Some chief justices have been consummate legal scholars, but experience has proved that the best legal scholars do not necessarily make the best chief justices and the best chief justices are often not the best legal scholars. Justices, including the chief justice, are served by cadres of well-trained law clerks, many of whom have more specific knowledge of the law than the people for whom they work. The law clerks often research and write the first drafts of the justice's opinions.

Most Important Characteristics

The greatest responsibility of chief justices is leadership. They call the other justices into conference to discuss cases and are the first to speak. In doing so, they become the person best able to direct the course of the court's actions, although each justice acts independently and is not beholden to the chief justice.

The individual justices must work autonomously. Disagreement over the interpretation of the Constitution and over individual decisions does not evoke charges of disloyalty and, ideally at least, does not invite retaliation. People appointed chief justice are generally selected because they can remain dispassionate and disinterested in matters before the Court. To function effectively, chief justices must deal with the other justices and their clerks diplomatically, in nonconfrontational ways. Their major functions are to clarify and persuade rather than to direct and confront.

Ironically, although legal scholars often make excellent associate justices because they become deeply involved in the details of law and of the Constitution, those who have become the most effective chief justices are noted more for their administrative skills than for their legal scholarship. The office of chief justice has, through the years, been affected most significantly by the personalities of the justices themselves.

Specific Duties

Aside from writing opinions, which is one of their major functions, chief justices have substantial power because they preside over the Court in oral arguments and in conference. In conference, a chief justice can channel discussions into important areas and can suggest alternatives.

Chief justices also create the discuss list, or the list of cases to be considered for adjudication. They cannot act unilaterally to exclude petitions for hearings, but they substantially influence the decisions of their colleagues. The chief justices, with the assistance of legal clerks, draw up the discuss list, which gives them the greatest role in determining which cases come before the Court.

The chief justice is also responsible for assigning to the associate justices the cases for which they will write opinions. Some chief justices have themselves written a huge number of opinions, and others delegate a great deal of this important work. The opinions chief justices and associates are required to write involve the legal analysis of extremely complex issues that, in recent times, have become increasingly technological in nature. The written opinions must be buttressed by a full discussion of legal precedents and by references to past cases and to legal protocol.

Usually draft opinions are prepared by bright young assistants, usually newly graduated from law school and recently admitted to the bar. Many of them were editors of their universities' law reviews. They research legal documents extensively to write opinions that they then pass on for revision, emendation, and review by the justices, including the chief justice. In the final analysis, however, the justices rewrite the opinions, putting them into their final form, which is the official form that enters the Court's records.

The chief justice is also specifically designated as the person who will preside over impeachment hearings brought against a president of the United States. William H. Rehnquist served in this capacity during the impeachment hearings of President Bill Clinton early in 1999.

The chief justice has various Court management duties, which include tasks such as administration of the Court's bureaucracy and preparation of budget estimates. He or she also chairs the Judicial Conference of the United States, composed of lower federal court judges. This conference meets and makes recommendations to Congress.

JOHN MARSHALL'S MODEL

Among the most important decisions of the early Court was *Marbury v. Madison* (1803), which, under the leadership of Chief Justice John Marshall, who served as chief justice for thirty-four years, scored a double victory and set important precedents. Outgoing President John Quincy Adams, under the Judiciary Act of 1801, attempted to pack the courts with Federalist jurists, among them William Marbury, who was to serve as a justice of the peace for the District of Columbia. Adams's term ended at midnight on March 3, 1801. Thomas Jefferson was inaugurated the next day, but the appointment papers for Marbury and several others were still on

Adams's desk. James Madison, Jefferson's secretary of state, refused to receive these papers. When Marbury's promised appointment was held up, he took his case to the Court. President Adams had appointed Marshall to the Court as chief justice only weeks before. It was expected that Marshall would support Adams's efforts to pack the courts with "midnight judges," as these last-minute appointments were called. If Marshall supported Marbury in this case, the judiciary would remain in the hands of the Federalists.

In the end, however, newly elected Democratic-Republicans, who now controlled Congress, repealed the Judiciary Act of 1801 under which the judgeships Adams sought to fill in his last hours as president were created. With this repeal, Congress forbid the Court to convene for fourteen months, which meant that the legislative branch sought to control the judicial branch, clearly in violation of the separation of powers that the founding fathers envisioned.

The Court did not meet during 1802, acceding to the congressional mandate. When it met in February, 1803, however, the case of *Marbury v. Madison* was on the docket. For this complicated case, Chief Justice Marshall wrote the opinion in two parts. In the first part, he found that Marbury had every right to the position he had been promised. He added, however, that the Court had no power to force Madison to deliver it. The Judiciary Act of 1789 gave that power to the Court, but in doing so, Marshall found, it was giving a power that, under the Constitution, it could not bestow. Congress had over-

JURISTS WHO SERVED AS BOTH ASSOCIATE AND CHIEF JUSTICES

Justice	Associate tenure	Chief justice tenure	Years on Court
John Rutledge	Feb., 1790-Mar. 1791	Aug.-Dec. 1795	1
William Cushing	Feb., 1790-Sept., 1810	Jan., 1796[1]	20
Edward D. White	Mar., 1894-Dec., 1910	Dec., 1910-May, 1922[2]	27
Charles Evans Hughes	Oct., 1910-June, 1916	Feb., 1930-July, 1941	17
Harlan F. Stone	Mar., 1925-July, 1941	July, 1941-Apr., 1946[2]	21
William H. Rehnquist	Jan., 1972-Sept., 1986	Sept., 1986-Sept., 2005[2]	33

1. Cushing served as chief justice for one week.
2. Died in office.

stepped its authority, thereby failing to follow the mandates of the Constitution.

It was the force of Marshall's leadership that resulted in bringing about a landmark decision that assured the separation of powers that has been a cornerstone of the political strength of the United States. *Marbury v. Madison* established for all time the concept of judicial review, which was perhaps the greatest single contribution of the Marshall Court.

During Marshall's long tenure as chief justice, the size of the Court changed, being reduced in 1801 from six to five, then, in 1807, being increased to seven. (In 1869 it grew to nine justices.) Having an odd number of people on the court prevents split votes. With an odd number of justices, it is usually the chief justice who casts the deciding vote. Marshall, more than any other chief justice, imposed his beliefs on the other justices. A staunch Federalist, he nearly always found in favor of the national government in cases that involved actions against it. Late twentieth century chief justices have found it much more difficult to impose their wills on their colleagues, who accord them little deference.

THE IMPORTANCE OF OPINION ASSIGNMENT

Customarily, chief justices have assigned the writing of the Court's opinions at times when they are in the majority on the initial vote in conference, which is most of the time. In instances where this is not the case, the senior justice in the majority makes the assignment.

The selection of the writer of an opinion will often determine whether the initial majority is retained and how large it will be. Chief justices who know their associate justices well will assign the writing of opinions to those who are most likely to achieve the ends they have in mind. Chief justices can also exercise their power by assigning the writing of opinions to themselves. Most chief justices assign the writing of opinions to those in their own ideological camps.

R. Baird Shuman

FURTHER READING

A major resource for the study of chief justices is the ABC-Clio series on the courts of individual justices. Its coverage ranges from the first chief justice, John Jay (scheduled for 2007), through William H. Rehnquist. Titles include *The Warren Court: Justices, Rulings, and Legacy*, by Melvin I. Urofsky (Santa Barbara, Calif.: ABC-Clio, 2001); *The Burger Court: Justices, Rulings, and Legacy*, by Tinsley E. Yarbrough (Santa Barbara, Calif.: ABC-Clio, 2000); and *The Rehnquist Court: Justices, Rulings, and Legacy*, by Thomas R. Hensley (Santa Barbara, Calif.: ABC-Clio, 2006). *The First One Hundred Eight Justices*, edited by William H. Bader and Roy M. Mersky (Buffalo, N.Y.: William S. Hein, 2004), offers brief profiles of all the justices to serve on the Court up to 2004.

Bernard Schwartz's *A History of the Supreme Court* (New York: Oxford University Press, 1993) presents a comprehensive history of the Court and its justices. Briefer, but also useful, is Lawrence Baum's *The Supreme Court* (8th ed., Washington, D.C.: Congressional Quarterly, 2004), whose chapters on decision making and on policy outputs are fresh and incisive. Henry J. Abraham, in *Justices and Presidents: A Political History of the Supreme Court* (3d ed., New York: Oxford University Press, 1992), examines the political implications of appointments to the Court, including those involving chief justices. This book is significant and is well presented.

Juvenile readers will find Ann E. Weiss's *The Supreme Court* (Hillside, N.J.: Enslow, 1987), Catherine Reef's *The Supreme Court* (New York: Dillon Press, 1994), and Barbara Aria's *The Supreme Court* (New York: Franklin Watts, 1994) useful.

SEE ALSO Burger, Warren E.; Chase, Salmon P.; Conference of the justices; Ellsworth, Oliver; Fuller, Melville W.; Housing of the Court; Hughes, Charles Evans; Jay, John; Judiciary Act of 1789; *Marbury v. Madison*; Marshall, John; Opinions, writing of; Rehnquist, William H.; Roberts, John; Rutledge, John; Salaries of justices; Stone, Harlan Fiske; Taft, William H.; Taney, Roger Brooke; Vinson, Fred M.; Waite, Morrison R.; Warren, Earl; White, Edward D.

Chimel v. California

CITATION: 395 U.S. 752

DATE: June 23, 1969

ISSUE: Search and seizure

SIGNIFICANCE: The Supreme Court held that when a valid arrest is made, the Fourth Amendment permits the police to search the arrested person and the area "within his immediate control," but not any additional area.

Using an arrest warrant, the police arrested Ted Chimel at his home on burglary charges. Ignoring Chimel's objections, the police then conducted a search of the entire house and discovered stolen property that provided the basis for Chimel's conviction. Rejecting Chimel's appeal, the California courts noted that the Supreme Court had upheld a similar warrantless search incident to an arrest in *United States v. Rabinowitz* (1950).

By a 6-2 vote, the Court ruled Chimel's trial unconstitutional and overruled *Rabinowitz*. Speaking for the majority, Justice Potter Stewart recognized that it was reasonable for the police to search the person arrested in order to remove any concealed weapons and to prevent the concealment or destruction of evidence. Likewise, the police had a legitimate reason to search the area into which an arrestee might reach for a weapon.

The Court applied the *Chimel* rationale to allow more extensive searches during arrests when justified by exigent circumstances. In *Maryland v. Buie* (1990), for example, the Court approved of a protective sweep of a home believed to harbor an individual posing a danger to the arrest scene.

Thomas Tandy Lewis

SEE ALSO Automobile searches; Exclusionary rule; *Ferguson v. City of Charleston*; Fourth Amendment; *Hudson v. Michigan*; Privacy, right to; Search warrant requirement; *Terry v. Ohio*.

Chinese Exclusion Cases

Chew Heong v. United States; United States v. Jung Ah Lung; Chae Chan Ping v. United States; Fong Yue Ting v. United States; Wong Quan v. United States; and Lee Joe v. United States

CITATIONS: 112 U.S. 536; 124 U.S. 621; 130 U.S. 581; 149 U.S. 698 (three cases)

DATES: December 8, 1884; February 13, 1888; May 13, 1889; May 15, 1893 (three cases)

ISSUE: Immigration

SIGNIFICANCE: Using the Fourteenth Amendment, the Supreme Court first ruled in favor of challenges to laws excluding the Chinese from immigrating and becoming U.S. citizens, then succumbed to popular sentiment and upheld exclusionary statutes.

In 1882 Congress enacted the first Chinese Exclusion Act, prohibiting Chinese laborers and miners from entering the United States. An 1884 amendment required resident Chinese laborers to have reentry certificates if they traveled outside the United States and planned to return. The 1888 Scott Act prohibited Chinese laborers temporarily abroad from returning, thereby stranding thousands of Chinese. Merchants and teachers were exempted from the Scott Act if they had "proper papers," thereby beginning the practice of using "paper names" to create new identities so that Chinese could return. The 1892 Geary Act banned all future Chinese laborers from entry and denied bail to Chinese in judicial proceedings. All Chinese faced deportation if they did not carry identification papers. The 1893 McCreary Act further extended the definition of laborers to include fishermen, miners, laundry owners, and merchants. The 1902 Chinese Exclusion Act permanently banned all Chinese immigration.

The Supreme Court initially attempted to defend Chinese rights under the Fourteenth Amendment; however, as anti-Chinese sentiment grew more pronounced, it withdrew even its limited protections from Chinese immigrants. The Court defended the right of Chinese to reenter the United States in *Chew Heong* and *Jung Ah Lung*. In *Chae Chan Ping*, it found the Scott Act unconstitutional. However,

One of the most blatantly discriminatory pieces of immigration legislation in U.S. history was the aptly named Chinese Exclusion Act of 1882. This early twentieth century illustration from Puck *suggests five ways in which a would-be Chinese immigrant ("John") might enter the United States in violation of the act: as an anarchist, as an Irishman, as an English wife-hunter, as a yacht racer, or as a Sicilian. The joke underlying the cartoon was the fact that all five alternative immigrant types were unpopular among native-born Americans.* (Library of Congress)

in the three 1893 cases, it upheld a law retroactively requiring that Chinese laborers have certificates of residence or be deported.

Richard L. Wilson

SEE ALSO Bail; Bill of Rights; Citizenship; Due process, procedural; Due process, substantive; Fourteenth Amendment; Immigration law; Incorporation doctrine; Japanese American relocation.

Chisholm v. Georgia

CITATION: 2 U.S. 419
DATE: February 18, 1793
ISSUE: State sovereignty
SIGNIFICANCE: In its first major decision, the Supreme Court held that the U.S. Constitution allowed a citizen of one state to sue another state in federal court.

Article III of the U.S. Constitution granted federal jurisdiction over "controversies between a state and citizens of another state." During ratification of the Constitution, Federalists asserted that this provision would not override the doctrine of sovereign immunity, which meant that the government may be sued only with its consent. Two South Carolina citizens, executors of an estate of a British decedent, attempted to recover property that Georgia had confiscated during the American Revolution. Georgia refused to appear, claiming immunity as a sovereign state.

By a 4-1 vote, the Supreme Court ruled against the state and endorsed the authority of the federal judiciary over the states. In seriatim opinions, Justices John Jay and James Wilson emphasized strong nationalistic views. They declared that the people of the United States had acted "as sovereigns" in establishing the Constitution and that the states, by virtue of membership in a "national compact," could be sued by citizens throughout the nation. In dissent, Justice James Iredell, a southerner who had participated in a ratifying convention, argued that the English common-law doctrine of sovereign immunity had not been superseded by constitutional provision or by statute.

The *Chisholm* decision was bitterly denounced by partisans of states' rights. The controversy resulted in the drafting and ratification of the Eleventh Amendment, the first of four amendments to directly overrule a decision of the Court.

Thomas Tandy Lewis

SEE ALSO Blair, John, Jr.; Cushing, William; Eleventh Amendment; Federalism; Iredell, James; Jay, John; Seriatim opinions; States' rights and state sovereignty; Wilson, James.

Church of Lukumi Babalu Aye v. Hialeah

CITATION: 508 U.S. 520

DATE: June 11, 1993

ISSUE: Freedom of religion

SIGNIFICANCE: Overturning a local ban on animal sacrifices, the Supreme Court announced that it would use the strict scrutiny test in examining any law targeting religious conduct for special restrictions.

Believers in the Santería religion, which combines African and Roman Catholic traditions, practice animal sacrifices in order to appeal to spirits to heal the sick and promote good fortune. Many other people in the United States, however, find such ceremonies to be highly offensive. In 1987 a Santería congregation announced plans to establish a house of worship in the city of Hialeah, Florida. Responding to a public outcry, the Hialeah city council passed several ordinances that made it illegal to kill animals in religious ceremonies, while still allowing the killing of animals for human consumption.

After federal district and appellate courts upheld the ordinances, the justices of the Supreme Court ruled they were unconstitutional. Speaking for a unanimous Court, Justice Anthony M. Kennedy explained that when a law is plainly directed at restricting a religious practice, it must satisfy two tests: The restriction must be justified by a compelling state interest, and the restriction must be narrowly tailored to advance that interest. General and neutral laws may proscribe cruelty to animals or require the safe disposal of animal wastes; however, a community may not place a direct burden on an unpopular religious practice without a strong secular justification.

Justice Kennedy's opinion did not entirely please libertarians because it did not overturn *Employment Division, Department of Human Resources v. Smith* (1990), which allowed for the more lenient test of rationality in examining laws putting an incidental burden on a religious practice. Three justices—David H. Souter, Harry A. Blackmun, and Sandra Day O'Connor—concurred with the ruling but expressed disagreement with the *Smith* precedent.

Thomas Tandy Lewis

SEE ALSO *Employment Division, Department of Human Resources v. Smith*; Judicial scrutiny; Kennedy, Anthony M.; Religion, freedom of; *Sherbert v. Verner.*

Circuit Riding

DESCRIPTION: Supreme Court justices traveled hundreds, even thousands, of miles as members of a circuit court designed to bring the federal judiciary system to the people.

SIGNIFICANCE: Direct involvement in jurisdictions outside the nation's capital enabled Supreme Court justices to stay attuned to local law as they contributed to the formation of national law.

The Judiciary Act of 1789 divided the states into three circuits, the eastern, the middle, and the southern, with a circuit court consisting of two Supreme Court justices and one federal district judge meeting twice a year in each region. In 1793, Congress reduced the number of justices on any circuit court bench from two to one.

DISTANCES RIDDEN BY JUSTICES ON CIRCUIT IN 1839

Justice	Miles
Roger B. Tancy	458
Henry Baldwin	2,000
James M. Wayne	2,370
Philip P. Barbour	1,498
Joseph Story	1,896
Smith Thompson	2,590
John McLean	2,500
John Catron	3,464
John McKinley	1,000
Total	17,776

Source: Bernard Schwartz, *A History of the Supreme Court* (New York: Oxford University Press, 1993), page 153.

Both original and appellate jurisdiction were in the hands of the justices, creating a controversial dual role. In response to potential conflicts of interest for justices and the rigors of circuit travel, circuit riding was eliminated by a section in the Judiciary Act of 1801. However, the Judiciary Act of 1802 repealed the 1801 act, assigning each justice a specific circuit without rotation.

To meet the needs of territorial expansion, the Judiciary Act of 1837 added new circuits and new justices until there were nine of each. In 1869 Congress approved a measure authorizing the appointment of nine new circuit judges, reducing the justices' circuit duties to one term every two years. The Judiciary Act of 1891 lightened the court docket of the justices by creating U.S. circuit courts of appeals and assigning all appellate work to them. However, the original circuit courts were not abolished until 1911.

Kevin Eyster

SEE ALSO Appellate jurisdiction; Blair, John, Jr.; Judiciary Act of 1789; Sedition Act of 1798.

Citizenship

DESCRIPTION: Legal membership in a country, attained at birth or through naturalization, that conveys certain rights and requires certain responsibilities.

SIGNIFICANCE: In numerous cases, the Supreme Court generally supported Congress's authority to determine who is eligible to be a U.S. citizen. It also interpreted the rights and responsibilities inherent within citizenship.

Article I, section 8, of the U.S. Constitution gives Congress the right to make laws outlining who is eligible to become a naturalized citizen of the United States and detailing how that eligibility can be established. In January, 1790, President George Washington, in his annual message, expressed his concern over citizenship and naturalization issues, urging Congress to develop naturalization laws. In response to Washington's concerns, Congress passed a law later that year providing for naturalization of free white aliens who had resided in the United States for at least two years and who made application for citizenship. Over the years, Congress adjusted the residency requirement several times, but it was not until 1866, when the Fourteenth Amendment was ratified, that people of color were accepted as citizens of the United States.

CONGRESS'S POWER TO DEFINE CITIZENSHIP

In various decisions, the Supreme Court supported the right of Congress to define citizenship and to control immigration and naturalization. In *Chy Lung v. Freeman* (1875), the Court held that legislation passed by states to control immigration was illegal, stating that only Congress had the right to pass laws concerning the admission and entry into the United States of foreign nationals.

In 1885 in the *Head Money Cases*, the Court placed Congress's right to control immigration within the commerce clause of the Constitution. Although this right was challenged many times in subsequent years in cases involving the Chinese Exclusion Acts (1882-1902), the Court continued to uphold congressional responsibility for control of issues relating to immigration and naturalization. However, in deciding these cases, the Court did not always base its decisions on the commerce clause.

In the *Chinese Exclusion Cases* (1884-1893), the Court stated that Congress might exclude aliens even if they came from a country at peace with the United States. It said Congress was free to exclude any group that it believed could not assimilate into American culture and, therefore, might affect American peace and security.

In *United States v. Ju Toy* (1904), the Court indicated that Congress had the right to exclude anyone from the United States, even citizens. Ju Toy, returning to the United States from China, claimed that he was a naturalized citizen. However, the secretary of labor and commerce agreed with a lower court that Toy was not eligible for entry to the United States under the Chinese Exclusion Act. The Court decision supported the secretary's actions. However, naturalized citizens' rights were somewhat protected in *Quon Quon Poy v. Johnson* (1926), in which the Court stated that, when citizenship was challenged, the person claiming citizenship had the right to a fair and thorough administrative hearing. The 1933 decision in *Volpe v. Smith* confirmed Congress's right to control immigration and naturalization, stating that its right to determine who could enter the United States was "no longer open to question."

In *Trop v. Dulles* (1958), the Court affirmed that only Congress had the authority to decide citizenship matters. Trop, who had been stripped of his citizenship rights by a military court, sued to regain those rights. The Court ruled that only Congress, and not the military courts, could deprive citizens of their citizenship rights. However, in 1967, in *Afroyim v. Rusk*, it was held that not even Congress could strip a citizen of the right to citizenship. Citizenship was held to be a constitutionally protected right that could not be taken away without the assent of the citizen.

ELIGIBILITY FOR CITIZENSHIP

In answering the question of who is eligible for citizenship, the Court made interpretations based on the 1790 law. One of the Court's most famous statements on eligibility for citizenship was made in *Scott v. Sandford* (1857), also known as the *Dred Scott Case*. Dred Scott, a slave who had been taken into the free states of Illinois and Wisconsin, sued for his freedom. Justice Roger Brooke Taney, speaking for the court majority, said that the suit would have to be dismissed because no black person, free or slave, could ever be a citizen and, therefore, was not eligible to bring suit in court. The decision was based on the 1790 act in which Congress gave the right to naturalization to free, white aliens.

The Dred Scott decision was not the only one in which race or color was held as an appropriate test for citizenship. In *Elk v. Wilkins* (1884), the Court ruled that Elk, who had left his Native American tribe to live among white people in Omaha, Nebraska, could not be considered a citizen because Native Americans were dependents of the state, in a ward-guardian relationship with the federal government. Native Americans were granted citizenship by Congress in 1924. This right to citizenship was affirmed by the Nationality Code of 1940.

The case of *Toyota v. the United States* (1924) also illustrated the Court's adherence to the principles of the 1790 law. Toyota had served in the U.S. Coast Guard and had even fought for the United States during World War I. When a 1918 act of Congress gave alien veterans permission to apply for citizenship, Toyota took advantage of the law and applied for and received a certificate of naturalization. However, the Court revoked his certificate, indicating that the 1918 law did not eliminate the 1790 requirement that naturalized citizens be free whites.

In the 1922 *Ozawa v. United States* decision, the Court ruled that people who were born in Japan could never become citizens of the United States because they were not free, white aliens. In this case the Court defined white as "Caucasian." In *Morrison v. California* (1934), the Court again ruled that a person born in Japan could not become a U.S. citizen. Before the *Ozawa* case, a number of Chinese and Japanese people had become naturalized U.S. citizens. In the *United States v. Thind* (1922), a native of India who had been granted citizenship by an Oregon court was deemed ineligible for citizenship because he did not meet the definition of white. In this case white was defined not as "Caucasian" but as being of European stock.

In 1943 an act of Congress expressly granted Chinese the right to naturalization. In 1945 people from India and the Philippines became eligible for U.S. citizenship. In 1952 the Immigration and Naturalization Act lifted all racial bars to naturalization.

Although in the 1800's and early 1900's the Court often ruled that foreign nationals of color could not become naturalized citizens, it was willing to accept the citizenship of people of African or Asian heritage who were born in the United States. The 1898 decision in *United States v. Wong Kim Ark* established the citizenship of a child born in the United States of Chinese parents. The Court held that this child's citizenship was guaranteed under the provisions of the Fourteenth Amendment.

However, in 1998, when a petitioner attempted to use *Wong Kim Ark* to establish her citizenship in *Miller v. Albright*, the petitioner's right to citizenship was denied. The petitioner was born in the Philippines to an American father and a Filipino mother. Although the father acknowledged paternity, he did not know of his daughter's existence until she was twenty-one years old. The Court ruled that if a child wishes to claim U.S. citizenship, paternity must be established or acknowledged by the time the child is eighteen years old.

CITIZENSHIP RIGHTS

The Court ruled on the nature of citizens' rights and responsibilities as well as on the nature of citizenship itself. In ruling on cases involving who can be naturalized, the Court often helped all citizens understand what it means to be a U.S. citizen.

In the *Slaughterhouse Cases* (1873), the Court ruled that all citizens have both national citizenship and state citizenship. The bulk of citizens' rights are regulated by the states; national citizenship rights are outlined by the Constitution. For example, in *Edwards v. California* (1941), the Court ruled that a citizen's right to move from state to state is a national right that is protected by the Constitution.

The Court examined various requirements of U.S. citizenship in cases involving naturalized citizens. In *Girouard v. United States* (1946), the Court ruled that Girouard, who had refused to swear to defend the country, could become a naturalized citizen. In the opinion, Justice William O. Douglas wrote that taking up arms to defend the country is not a specific requirement of U.S. citizenship. In *Schneiderman v. United States* (1939), the Court refused to revoke Schneiderman's certificate of naturalization because he was a member of the Communist Party when he took the oath of citizenship. The Court said citizens should not be subjected to the idea of guilt by association. The Court also refused to revoke the citizenship of pro-Nazi Baumgartner in *Baumgartner v. United States* (1944), ruling that naturalized citizens had as much right to association as citizens born in the United States. This was a very important statement for the rights of naturalized citizens.

In *Mandoli v. Acheson* (1952), the Court ruled that a native-born citizen cannot lose citizenship for not returning to the United States during adulthood. Similarly, in *Schneider v. Rusk* (1964), the Court ruled that a naturalized citizen can retain U.S. citizenship even if that citizen is out of the country for a long time. A native-born citizen would not lose citizenship for an extended stay outside the country, and a naturalized citizen has the same rights as a citizen born in the United States. Also, in *Perkins v. Elg* (1939), the Court ruled that a child who acquires U.S. citizenship at birth does not automatically lose that citizenship if her parents take her abroad to live in another country.

JAPANESE AMERICANS AND WORLD WAR II

During the administration of President George H. W. Bush, the U.S. government apologized to Japanese Americans for its treatment of them during World War II. Part of this treatment consisted of rulings made by the Court. In *Hirabayashi v. United States* (1943), the Court declared that the March 21, 1942, act of Congress placing a curfew on people of Japanese ancestry was legal even though many of the people who were subjected to the curfew were U.S. citizens. In *Korematsu v. United States* (1944), the Court held that the internment of Japanese Americans was legal and necessary for national security. This decision was reached in spite of the fact that many of those interned were native-born citizens.

Annita Marie Ward

FURTHER READING

Good starting points for studying this subject are Thomas Alexander Aleinikoff's *Semblances of Sovereignty: The Constitution, the State, and American Citizenship* (Cambridge, Mass.: Harvard University Press, 2002) and Ronald B. Flowers's *To Defend the Constitution: Religion, Conscientious Objection, Naturalization, and the Supreme Court* (Lanham, Md.: Scarecrow Press, 2002), both of which examine the role of the Supreme Court in the definition and application of American citizenship. D. J. Herda thoroughly examines *Scott v. Sandford* in *The Dred Scott Case: Slavery and Citizenship* (Springfield, N.J.: Enslow, 1994). Thomas Janoski's *Citizenship and Society: A Framework of Rights and Obligations in Liberal, Traditional, and Social Democratic Regimes* (London: Cambridge University Press, 1998) introduces and explains the concept of citizenship, discusses the balance between citizenship rights and obligations, and traces changes in citizenship rights over several centuries.

Early historical developments related to U.S. citizenship are examined by J. H. Kettner in *The Development of American Citizenship, 1608-1870* (Chapel Hill: University of North Carolina Press, 1978). Issues that historically affected the Asian immigrant's ability to become naturalized are explored by M. R. Konvitz in *The Alien and the Asiatic in American Law* (Ithaca, N.Y.: Cornell University Press, 1946). Richard Sinopoli discusses the values associated with U.S. citizenship in *The*

Foundations of American Citizenship: Liberalism, the Constitution, and Civic Virtue (New York: Oxford University Press, 1992).

Eve P. Steinberg's *How to Become a U.S. Citizen* (New York: Macmillan General References, 1998) explains what steps an immigrant must take to become a naturalized citizen. Aliza Becker, Laurie Edwards, and the Travelers and Immigrants Aid of Chicago also describe the steps in the naturalization process in *Citizenship Now: A Guide for Naturalization* (Lincolnwood, Ill.: NTC, 1990).

SEE ALSO *Chinese Exclusion Cases*; Comity clause; *Cruikshank, United States v.*; Immigration law; Japanese American relocation; *Korematsu v. United States*; *Scott v. Sandford*; Waite, Morrison R.

Civil Law

DESCRIPTION: Body of law that deals primarily with relationships among individuals; it is distinct from criminal law, which deals with offenses against the state.

SIGNIFICANCE: As the federal government began to play a larger role in commercial and environmental regulation, the Supreme Court had to rule on many new civil issues and the complex jurisdictional issues resulting from commercial and property litigation in a federal system.

The term "civil law" originally referred to the system of Roman jurisprudence and was used to distinguish it from natural and international law. In the United States, the term distinguishes between the legal relationships of individuals—normally property relationships—and crimes, which are established by either federal or state penal statutes. Civil law covers nearly every important human relationship: property ownership, torts, land titles, making and enforcing contracts, buying and selling, employment of labor, business regulation, environmental and workplace safety, marriage and divorce, responsibility for children, and inheritance.

The common-law tradition, which was brought to North America by English settlers, established a complex system of judge-made rules to regulate individual relationships. So complicated had the rules of practice as well as the substance of the law become that a movement to simplify and "codify" the law sprang up in the middle of the nineteenth century. David D. Field, brother to Supreme Court Justice Stephen J. Field, drafted such a code and campaigned vigorously for its adoption in New York state. In 1846 the Field Code was enacted by the New York legislature. It became the prototype for civil codes in all states within the United States except Louisiana. It is also the historical root of the modern Uniform Commercial Code and the rules of civil procedure that exist all over the country.

The Supreme Court's involvement with civil law is primarily in two areas: procedures and content or substance. In 1934, Congress passed the Rules Enabling Act, which authorized the Court to establish rules for lower federal courts. In 1938 the Court promulgated the Federal Rules of Civil Procedure for the first time. These were widely acclaimed for their simplicity and clarity. Most states have adopted some or all of these rules.

Regarding the content or substance of civil law, there are two major issues: the federal government's diversity jurisdiction and the content of civil laws. The diversity referred to is diversity of state citizenship. When litigants are from different states, they have the choice of having their case heard in state or federal courts. However, most commercial and property rules in the United States are state law rather than federal law, so the question arises of what law should be applied. In *Erie Railroad Co. v. Tompkins* (1938), the Court held that unless federal law or the constitution directly applies to a case, the federal courts must apply state case law, usually that of the state of the defendant in the suit. These issues may be particularly complex when there are multiple plaintiffs and defendants, for example in a case that might involve airline negligence. Because of the proliferation of diversity cases, Congress in 1958 established ten thousand dollars as the minimum amount being litigated before a federal court may take jurisdiction. The amount was raised to eighty thousand dollars in 1988. Even with that increase, the principal effect of diversity jurisdiction is to allow large corporations that are sued in state courts to get their cases into federal courts. Such cases now make up one-quarter of the workload of the federal courts.

The Court's role in the content of civil law results from the increased regulatory activity of the federal government. After 1933, primarily using the power to regulate interstate commerce, Congress immensely expanded the scope of federal law. National laws touch on business issues, the environment, product safety, medicine, civil rights, taxation, and workplace safety. These all raise civil law issues. When questions arise, whether of constitutional or statutory interpretation, the Court is the final arbiter. Most of the Court's workload is made up of civil rather than criminal or constitutional cases.

Robert Jacobs

FURTHER READING

Abadinsky, Howard. *Law and Justice: An Introduction to the American Legal System.* 5th ed. Chicago: Nelson-Hall, 2003.

Carter, Lief, Austin Sarat, Mark Silverstein, and William Weaver. *New Perspectives on American Law: An Introduction to Private Law in Politics and Society.* Durham, N.C.: Carolina Academic Press, 1997.

Field, David Dudley. "The Index of Civilization." In *The Golden Age of American Law,* edited by Charles Haar. New York: George Braziller, 1965.

Friedman, Lawrence M. *A History of American Law.* 3d ed. New York: Simon & Schuster, 2005.

Hall, Timothy L., ed. *The U.S. Legal System.* 2 vols. Pasadena, Calif.: Salem Press, 2004.

Holmes, Oliver Wendell, Jr. *The Common Law.* Boston: Little, Brown, 1964.

Johns, Margaret, and Rex R. Perschbacher. *The United States Legal System: An Introduction.* Durham, N.C.: Carolina Academic Press, 2002.

Llewellyn, Karl. *The Common Law Tradition.* Boston: Little, Brown, 1960.

Pound, Roscoe. *Jurisprudence.* St. Paul, Minn.: West Publishing, 1959.

Scheb, John M., and John M. Scheb II. *Introduction to the American Legal System.* Albany, N.Y.: Delmar Learning, 2001.

Schubert, Frank A. *Introduction to Law and the Legal System.* 8th ed. Boston: Houghton Mifflin, 2004. General college textbook with cases and explanations of evidentiary issues.

SEE ALSO *Calder v. Bull;* Commerce, regulation of; Common law; Diversity jurisdiction; Environmental law; Federalism; Field, Stephen J.; Natural law; Police powers.

Civil Rights Cases

CITATION: 109 U.S. 3
DATE: October 15, 1883
ISSUES: Race discrimination; state action
SIGNIFICANCE: Ruling that key provisions in a federal civil rights law were unconstitutional, the Supreme Court held that the Fourteenth Amendment applied to state action only and that Congress lacked authority to prohibit discrimination by private individuals.

The Civil Rights Act of 1875 outlawed racial discrimination in public accommodations, or privately owned businesses such as hotels, places of entertainment, and railroad cars. Five cases arising under the act were consolidated for argument before the Supreme Court. Speaking for an 8-1 majority, Justice Joseph P. Bradley narrowly interpreted the Fourteenth Amendment to mean that Congress could forbid only abridgment of civil rights by state government officials. Individual citizens, therefore, must look to state governments for protection against discrimination by privately owned businesses. Looking at the Thirteenth Amendment, Bradley conceded that Congress had the power to obliterate the badges and incidents of slavery, but he argued that elimination of these badges and incidents did not guarantee access to private businesses. Free blacks in the North had often faced private acts of discrimination, but they were still free citizens.

In a vigorous dissent, Justice John Marshall Harlan wrote that the majority was using a "narrow and artificial" interpretation of the Constitution. He emphasized that inequality in civil rights was one of the badges and incidents of slavery that Congress might forbid under the Thirteenth Amendment. Seventy-nine years later, the Court reversed the majority's decision in *Heart of Atlanta Motel v. United States* (1964), relying on congressional authority to regulate interstate commerce.

The Court accepted much of Harlan's broad interpretation of the Thirteenth Amendment in *Jones v. Alfred H. Mayer Co.* (1968).

Thomas Tandy Lewis

SEE ALSO Equal protection clause; *Heart of Atlanta Motel v. United States*; Race and discrimination; State action; Thirteenth Amendment.

Civil Rights Movement

DATE: 1950's-1970's

DESCRIPTION: Demonstrations, debates, boycotts, legislation, and litigation that attempted to secure the political, social, and economic rights of African Americans and all other U.S. citizens.

SIGNIFICANCE: The efforts of African Americans to secure their civil rights led to numerous challenges before the Supreme Court. The movement's ideologies and styles were adopted by other ethnic communities and minorities, including women and homosexuals, in their struggles to obtain their rights.

In the 1960's and early 1970's, the Civil Rights movement led by African Americans was most effective in altering the politics, culture, and mores of American society. The movement is often regarded as beginning with *Brown v. Board of Education* (1954), a Supreme Court decision that struck down racially segregated education; however, its roots can be traced back to the post-Civil War era.

The Civil War (1861-1865) resulted in the preservation of the union of states and in the freeing of the bulk of the black labor force in the South's cotton economy. It did not, however, provide the freed slaves with the rights of citizenship. The Republican Congress passed the Fourteenth and Fifteenth Amendments to the Constitution (ratified 1868 and 1870, respectively) to provide equal citizenship for the former slaves. However, after the end of Reconstruction, most southern states passed black codes that effectively kept African Americans from voting, segregated them by law in many areas of public life, and maintained their subservience. By the early 1900's, social historian W. E. B. Du Bois had written in his classic book *The Souls of Black Folk*

(1903) that African Americans felt a sense of "twoness": They were Americans but also blacks who were not fully allowed the civil rights all Americans were guaranteed. Early civil rights efforts were initially quite successful, but when poised against entrenched racist institutions, these successes were often reversed.

A MODERN CHALLENGE

The Civil Rights movement that began in the mid-1950's differed from earlier civil rights efforts in that its successes had far more lasting consequences. Its approach to the problem of a lack of rights was multifaceted, including legal challenges, economic boycotts, political empowerment, and even efforts to influence the arts and media. The National Association for the Advancement of Colored People (NAACP), through its Legal Defense Fund, offered up numerous legal challenges against segregation, voting restrictions, and other civil rights violations, many of which reached the Supreme Court.

Three events between the years 1954 and 1960 shaped the Civil Rights movement. The first was the historical Supreme Court decision in *Brown v. Board of Education* in which Chief Justice Earl Warren, in his opinion for the Court, ruled that the separate but equal doctrine had no place in the field of public education. This decision, a major victory for the NAACP, had the profound consequence of placing the federal government officially on the side of desegregation. The implication was that the U.S. government would support the demise of segregation in more than education—that is, that separate but equal facilities generally might not be lawful. This single legal decision by the Court emboldened blacks to challenge segregation and encouraged whites who supported them to participate in this growing movement.

The second critical event was the Montgomery, Alabama, bus boycott. In 1955 Rosa Parks, an African American bus rider, refused to relinquish her seat to a white man as required by the bus company. Black clergy united in support of Parks and organized a boycott of the bus company. The Reverend Martin Luther King, Jr., became the group's primary spokesperson. A previous incident in Baton Rouge, Louisiana, was as successful as the Montgomery boycott but was not well publicized. In both instances, African Americans gained the right to equal access and could sit where they chose on public transportation.

The third event was a series of demonstrations that began in Greensboro, North Carolina, in 1960, when black students from a local historically black university participated in a sit-in demonstration in which they occupied seats at a local segregated lunch counter and refused to leave until they were served. The sit-in was successful, and similar demonstrations were held in many other areas in the South. Some demonstrators were arrested for disturbing the peace or trespassing, and these cases were appealed to the Supreme Court. In *Garner v. Louisiana* (1961), the Court overturned the convictions of sixteen African Americans who had participated in a lunch counter sit-in, and in *Peterson v. City of Greenville* (1963), it reversed additional

Sit-in demonstration at a civil rights protest in Washington, D.C., in 1965. (Library of Congress)

sit-in cases, applying the state action doctrine to rule that the refusal to serve African Americans was not simply private discrimination.

The Court continued to expand its definition of state action to include what had been thought of as private conduct through most of the 1960's. For example, in *Burton v. Wilmington Parking Authority* (1961), the Court ruled against a restaurant that had refused to serve an African American because it was located in a parking garage owned by a government agency and the leasing arrangement allowed the agency to profit from the restaurant. The Court also supported the efforts of the Legal Defense Fund of the NAACP. In *National Association for the Advancement of Colored People v. Button* (1963), it blocked the Virginia legislature's attempt to stop the Legal Defense Fund by claiming its efforts were a solicitation of legal business, then prohibited by law.

INTERNAL CONFLICT

By the mid-1960's, groups within the Civil Rights movement, including the Student Nonviolent Coordinating Committee (SNCC) and the Congress of Racial Equality (CORE), began to question the fundamental strategies of more traditional groups, including the NAACP's emphasis on litigation and nonviolence. The passage of the Civil Rights Act of 1964 and the Voting Rights Act of 1965 also changed the movement's focus. SNCC, CORE, and other groups debated the value of nonviolence as a tactic, argued about whether blacks and whites should be working together in the Civil Rights movement, and asked whether the movement should be attempting reform or revolution. In the second half of the 1960's, some African American civil rights leaders began talking about "black power," the achievement of rights for blacks by blacks within the American sociopolitical system.

By the mid-1970's, the Civil Rights movement had largely ended, although many African Americans continued to work to improve their status and safeguard their civil rights. The focus and emphasis of these efforts changed, however. The first African American mayor of Atlanta claimed that politics was the substitute for civil rights activism. The Reverend Jesse Jackson, by contrast, claimed that ownership and managerial power in the economy was the substitute. The Civil

Rights movement was successful in gaining political and economic rights for African Americans, opening public facilities to them, and influencing American culture through the arts and the media. After it ended, however, an increasing gap emerged between those African Americans who had succeeded in the economy and those who remained part of an underclass. The movement, although it ended legal segregation and overt discrimination, could not eliminate all prejudice and discrimination, nor could it address all the social and economic needs of African Americans.

William Osborne
Dean Wagstaffe

FURTHER READING

Belfrage, Sally. *Freedom Summer.* New York: New York University Press, 1965.

Boxill, Bernard. *Blacks and Social Justice.* Totowa, N.J.: Rowman & Allanheld, 1984.

Broderick, Francis L. *W. E. B. Du Bois: Negro Leader in a Time of Crisis.* Reprint. Stanford, Calif.: Stanford University Press, 1966.

Carnoy, Martin. *Faded Dreams: The Politics and Economics of Race in America.* Cambridge, England: Cambridge University Press, 1994.

Cashman, Sean Dennis. *African Americans and the Quest for Civil Rights, 1900-1990.* New York: New York University Press, 1991.

Feagin, Joe R., and Melvin P. Sikes. *Living with Racism: The Black Middle-Class Experience.* Boston: Beacon Press, 1991.

Friedman, Leon, ed. *Brown v. Board: The Landmark Oral Argument Before the Supreme Court.* New York: New Press, 2004.

Horwitz, Morton J. *The Warren Court and the Pursuit of Justice.* New York: Hill and Wang, 1998.

Klarman, Michael J. *From Jim Crow to Civil Rights: The Supreme Court and the Struggle for Racial Equality.* New York: Oxford University Press, 2006.

Patterson, James T. *"Brown v. Board of Education": A Civil Rights Milestone and Its Troubled Legacy.* New York: Oxford University Press, 2002.

SEE ALSO Affirmative action; *Brown v. Board of Education*; *National Association for the Advancement of Colored People v. Alabama*; Race and discrimination; School integration and busing; State action.

Civil War

DATE: 1861-1865

DESCRIPTION: Also known as the War Between the States, the U.S. Civil War pitted eleven Southern states—which seceded to form the Confederate States of America—against the rest of the Union.

SIGNIFICANCE: The Civil War was a profound threat to the stability of the U.S. constitutional order. The Supreme Court played a role in the war's inception, the response by President Abraham Lincoln and Congress, and the war's conclusion and aftermath. Except for a few important and controversial decisions, however, the Court had limited significance during the Civil War.

The Civil War raised questions of fundamental importance to the U.S. constitutional order. Among these were questions about whether a state could secede from the Union, the distribution of the war-making powers between the president and Congress, and the authority of the Supreme Court to review those powers. What was undoubtedly a crisis for the country was no less a crisis for the Court. In the end, these fundamental constitutional issues were decided and resolved, not through appeals to the law or to the Supreme Court, but through political force.

THE ROAD TO WAR

A number of factors led to the war. Prominent among them was the issue of slavery, left unresolved at the nation's founding. Congress formally prohibited the slave trade in 1808 and tried to end the debate with the Missouri Compromise of 1820, but the problems slavery raised for the Union did not dissipate. The Court took up the issue in the case of *Scott v. Sandford* (1857). Dred Scott, a slave, claimed that he had become a free man because he had resided in areas where slavery was illegal under the Missouri Compromise. Writing for the Court, Chief Justice Roger Brooke Taney held that persons of African American descent, whether slaves or emancipated, were not citizens of the United States. For "more than a century," Taney wrote, African Americans had "been regarded as beings of an inferior order, and altogether unfit to associate with the white race . . . and so far inferior, that they had no rights which the white man was bound to respect."

The chief justice also ruled that the Missouri Compromise was unconstitutional because Congress had no constitutional authority to regulate slavery in the territories. Some critics of the Court complain that it should not have tried to resolve a divisive political issue through a legal decision. On the other hand, the Court had not come to the issue uninvited. President James Buchanan, for example, had encouraged the Court to rule on the issue, stating in his inaugural speech that slavery "was a judicial question, which legitimately belongs to the Supreme Court, before whom it is now pending and will . . . be speedily settled." The Court's controversial ruling, far from settling the matter, galvanized forces on both sides of the slavery question. Just four years later, the country was at war with itself.

SECESSION AND THE CONSTITUTION

In late 1860 South Carolina and several other states sought to secede from the Union. Such claims were not novel, at least as a matter of constitutional theory. The nullification controversy of 1832-1833 had involved similar claims. During that controversy, South Carolina had argued "that each state of the Union has the right, whenever it may deem such a course necessary . . . to secede peaceably from the Union, and that there is no constitutional power in the general government . . . to retain by force such stake in the Union." President Buchanan thought secession illegal, but he agreed that the federal government lacked the authority to prevent states from leaving. In *Kentucky v. Dennison* (1861), the Court sanctioned this understanding of the limits of federal power. The case involved a fugitive who had helped a slave escape from Kentucky. The fugitive ran to Ohio, and the Ohio governor refused to return him to Kentucky. Ruling for the Court, Chief Justice Taney refused to order the governor to turn over the fugitive, stating that the criminal extradition clause of the Constitution depended on the states for its enforcement. There is, he argued, "no power delegated to the General Government . . . to use any coercive means" to force a governor to act. Implicit in this opinion is the clear sense that President Abraham Lincoln lacked any constitutional authority to keep the states in the Union.

In his inaugural address, President Lincoln argued instead that "the Union of these States is perpetual. Perpetuity is implied, if not expressed, in the fundamental law of all national governments." Lincoln thus concluded that the Union, older than the Constitution, authorized him to prevent states from dissolving the bonds of the Union. One of his first actions was to resupply the Union troops at Fort Sumter. Forces in Charleston fired upon the fort, and the constitutional nature of the Union was left to be decided by military force and not by the Supreme Court.

PRESIDENTIAL AUTHORITY TO MAKE WAR

When he assumed office, President Lincoln was faced with the prospect of war. In his first inaugural address, he responded directly to the Court's decision in *Scott*.

> I do not forget the position assumed by some, that constitutional questions are to be decided by the Supreme Court. . . . At the same time the candid citizen must confess that if the policy of the government, upon vital questions affecting the whole people, is to be irrevocably fixed by decisions of the Supreme Court. . . . [T]he people will have ceased to be their own rulers. . . .

Lincoln's insistence upon his own authority to interpret the Constitution foreshadowed his interaction with the Court throughout the Civil War.

The first significant issue concerned the president's authority to conduct war without prior congressional approval. The issue was raised when Lincoln, responding to the South's declaration of independence from the Union, ordered a naval blockade of Southern ports in April, 1961. Acting pursuant to Lincoln's order, Union warships seized a number of Southern and foreign ships and put them and their cargoes up for sale. In the *Prize Cases* (1863), the owners of four such ships argued that the president had no constitutional authority to order the blockade, for the power "to declare war [and] make rules concerning captures on land and water" was given by the Constitution to Congress, not the president. Congress did not ratify the president's decision until July, 1861.

In a 5-4 decision, the Court ruled for Lincoln. Writing for the majority, Justice Robert C. Grier admitted that the Constitution gave to Congress alone the power to declare a national or foreign war. He noted also that the Constitution entrusts the position of commander in chief to the presidency. "If a war be made by invasion of a foreign nation," Grier continued, "the President is not only authorized but bound to resist by force." In this case, "the President was bound to meet [the war] in the shape it presented itself, without waiting for Congress to baptize it with a name." The Court further underscored the president's autonomy by declaring that "whether the President, in fulfilling his duties, as Commander-in-Chief, in suppressing an insurrection, has met with such armed resistance, and a civil war of such alarming proportions as will compel him to accord to them the character of belligerents, is a question to be decided *by him*, and this Court must be governed by the decisions and acts of the political department of the Government to which this power was entrusted."

In dissent, Justice Samuel Nelson agreed that "in one sense, no doubt this is war, but it is a statement simply of its existence in a material sense, and has no relevancy or weight when the question is what constitutes war in a legal sense . . . and of the Constitution of the United States." The Court's deference to the president's decision about when the war began was mirrored at war's end by its decision in *Freeborn v. the "Protector"* (1872), which held that the war was formally concluded when the president said so. Together, these cases have provided strong support for presidential decisions to initiate military actions without first seeking congressional authorization.

THE COURT AND CIVIL LIBERTIES

President Lincoln's decision to impose a naval blockade on Southern ports was just one part of a larger war effort. In addition to the blockade, Lincoln undertook a series of actions that amounted to the imposition of martial law. Among these were orders directing military authorities to search homes without warrants, imprisonment without charge or trial in civilian or in military courts, and suspension of the writ of habeas corpus. The most expansive order suspending the writ was issued in September, 1862; Lincoln did not seek congressional authorization for this order, and Congress did not finally authorize the president to suspend habeas corpus until the following March. Thousands of citizens were detained by the military and held without charge and without trial in either a civilian or a military court.

The constitutionality of Lincoln's decision to suspend the writ was first tested in a federal circuit court in Baltimore, Maryland, in 1861. The military had arrested John Merryman for his participation in an attack on Union forces. Merryman petitioned the court for a writ of habeas corpus. Chief Justice Taney, riding circuit, granted the writ and had it sent to the general in command of the fort where Merryman was detained. Sending an aide in his place, the general replied that he would not obey the writ because Lincoln had suspended its operation. In response, Chief Justice Taney found the general in contempt of court, an action with little practical effect, and issued an opinion that directly addressed the constitutionality of Lincoln's decision. Taney held that Lincoln had no authority to suspend the writ because Article I of the Constitution entrusted that authority to Congress "in language too clear to be misunderstood by anyone." Taney ordered a copy of the opinion sent to Lincoln. Lincoln failed to respond directly, instead stating in a later special session of Congress: "Now it is insisted that Congress, and not the Executive, is vested with [the power]. But the Constitution itself, is silent as to which, or who, is to exercise the power." In the same speech, Lincoln offered a more fundamental objection: "Are all the laws, *but one*, to go unexecuted, and the government itself go to pieces, lest that one be violated?"

The Supreme Court was presented with another claim concerning habeas corpus just two years later, in the case of *Ex parte Vallandigham* (1864). Vallandigham was arrested and tried by the military. He sought a writ of habeas corpus, but the Court dismissed his case, claiming that it had no authority over a military court. The Court's reluctance to entertain the case was symbolic of its silent posture on military interferences with civil liberties throughout the Civil War. Moreover, the Court would not again consider the constitutionality of Lincoln's wartime suspensions until well after the war was over, in the case of *Ex parte Milligan* (1866).

RECONSTRUCTION

The end of the Civil War left the Union with difficult questions about how to bring the Southern states back into the fold. Congressional representatives from the Northern states had denied that the

Southern states could validly leave the Union, but a return to the status quo that had existed before the hostilities was unlikely. Some congressional representatives and President Andrew Johnson, Lincoln's successor, favored a policy of accelerated reconstruction that included provisional state governments. However, so-called Radical Republicans in Congress insisted that the Southern states could be readmitted only on whatever terms Congress imposed. What followed was the imposition of military rule, which included trials in military courts and the use of federal troops to maintain order. The result was a great contest between the president and Congress, a contest that revolved around the question of how the South should be "reconstructed" and about which branch of government would be responsible for the process. The Supreme Court played a small, but nonetheless significant, part in this contest.

Initially the Court cast some doubt on the constitutionality of various Reconstruction measures. In the *Test Oath Cases* (1867, *Cummings v. Missouri* and *Ex parte Garland*), for example, the Court found the loyalty oaths required of voters, attorneys, and others in the Southern states a violation of the ex post facto clause. In the well-known *Milligan* case, the Court seemed to cast further doubt on the constitutionality of congressional reconstruction by holding that military courts could not try civilians in those areas in which the civilian courts were functioning. In this case, the military had arrested Milligan, and he was convicted and sentenced to be hanged by a military commission. He sought a writ of habeas corpus. Notwithstanding its earlier decision in *Vallandigham*, the Court ruled for Milligan. In his opinion for the Court, Justice David Davis wrote

> The Constitution of the United States is a law for rulers and for people, equally in war and in peace, and covers with the shield of its protection all classes of men, at all times, and under all circumstances. No doctrine, involving more pernicious consequences, was ever invented by the wit of man than that any of its provisions can be suspended during any of the great exigencies of government.

The Court did agree, though, "that there are occasions when martial law can be properly applied." If civilian courts are "actually closed" and it is "impossible to administer criminal justice according to law," then the military may supply a substitute for civilian authority. In Milligan's case, the courts had been open and functioning; consequently, Milligan's arrest by military authorities had been unconstitutional.

Although the Court did not fervently protect civil liberties until the war was over—in stark contrast to its behavior during the war—many congressional leaders saw in the case a more general threat to Reconstruction policy, which included military governments and tribunals. Thaddeus Stevens, for example, complained that the decision "although in terms not as infamous as the Dred Scott decision, is yet far more dangerous in its operation." Several bills were introduced in Congress to curb the Court, including one by Representative John Bingham of Ohio, who warned ominously of a constitutional amendment that could result "in the abolition of the tribunal itself."

OPPOSITION TO RECONSTRUCTION

Many congressional leaders believed that a case then working its way through the federal courts would give the Court a chance to declare much of the Reconstruction effort unconstitutional. The case, *Ex parte McCardle* (1869), concerned a newspaper editor in Mississippi who had been arrested and tried by a military commission. McCardle petitioned for a writ of habeas corpus, arguing that the Reconstruction statute that had authorized his trial was unconstitutional. An appellate court denied the writ, whereupon McCardle appealed to the Supreme Court under an 1867 statute that governed such appeals. The Court accepted the appeal and heard arguments on the case. Fearful of the ruling, Congress reacted by passing a new law repealing the 1867 statute. This led the Court to reschedule oral argument, this time focusing on the question of whether Congress could withdraw jurisdiction from the Court in a pending case. A unanimous Court concluded that the statute withdrawing its jurisdiction in *McCardle* was constitutionally permissible. No longer having jurisdiction, the Court dismissed McCardle's appeal.

Milligan aside, the Court generally refrained from inquiring into the constitutionality of Reconstruction. Thus, in *Mississippi v. Johnson*

(1867), the Court ruled that a president is immune from an injunction by a court to restrain enforcement of Reconstruction legislation. Mississippi had asked the Court to enjoin President Johnson from executing the Reconstruction acts because they were, according to Mississippi, unconstitutional. The Court declined to intervene, finding that such interference would be "an absurd and excessive extravagance." One year later, in a similar case (*Georgia v. Stanton*, 1868), the Court again indicated that it was unwilling to inquire into the details of Reconstruction policy by refusing to enjoin enforcement of the Reconstruction acts by the secretary of war.

In 1869 the Court put its imprimatur on Reconstruction—and on Lincoln's insistence that the Union was perpetual—in *Texas v. White*. The Court ruled, first, that Texas's decision to leave the Union was invalid because Texas "became one of the United States, she entered into an indissoluble relation. . . . There was no place for reconsideration, or revocation." Therefore, Texas had remained a "state" in the Union throughout the war. In some ways, the Court simply reaffirmed the result of the war, but the opinion is also an important statement of constitutional principle, for it held that the Union was not a mere "compact of states."

The case is also important for a second reason: The Court conceded that the initial responsibility for Reconstruction rested with the president in his capacity as commander in chief; however, that authority "must be considered as provisional" to the greater authority of Congress to "guarantee to every state in the Union a republican form of government."

John E. Finn

FURTHER READING

General works on the Civil War are voluminous; the works discussed here deal with both the war and the Supreme Court. A good starting place is Timothy S. Huebner's *The Taney Court: Justices, Rulings, and Legacy* (Santa Barbara, Calif.: ABC-Clio, 2003), which is a comprehensive reference work on the Court of the chief justice who directed the Court through most of the war. Jonathan Lurie's *The Chase Court: Justices, Rulings, and Legacy* (Santa Barbara, Calif.: ABC-Clio, 2004) is a similar work on Taney's successor.

Michael A. Ross's *Justice of Shattered Dreams: Samuel Freeman Miller and the Supreme Court During the Civil War Era* (Baton Rouge: Louisiana State University Press, 2003) examines the career of the associate justice whom Abraham Lincoln appointed to the Court in 1862 to bolster the Court's support of the war. For a broader study of Lincoln and the Civil War, see Herman Belz's *Abraham Lincoln, Constitutionalism, and Equal Rights in the Civil War Era* (New York: Fordham University Press, 1998). Still useful is James G. Randall's earlier study, *Constitutional Problems Under Lincoln* (Urbana: University of Illinois Press, 1964).

Charles Fairman's *History of the Supreme Court of the United States: Reconstruction and Reunion, 1864-88* (2 vols., New York: Macmillan, 1971) is a comprehensive account of the Court during the Reconstruction era. Harold Hyman's *A More Perfect Union: The Impact of the Civil War and Reconstruction upon the Constitution* (New York: Alfred A. Knopf, 1973) is still among the best treatments of the Civil War and the Constitution. Stanley Kutler, *Judicial Power and Reconstruction Politics* (Chicago: University of Chicago Press, 1968) examines Reconstruction's effect on the judiciary. For a later study of *Texas v. White* and Justice Salmon P. Chase, see Harold Hyman's *The Reconstruction Justice of Salmon P. Chase: "In Re Turner" and "Texas v. White"* (Lawrence: University Press of Kansas, 1997).

SEE ALSO Davis, David; Grier, Robert C.; Habeas corpus; Loyalty oaths; *Milligan, Ex parte;* Presidential powers; Reconstruction; States' rights and state sovereignty; War and civil liberties; War powers; Wayne, James M.

Tom C. Clark

IDENTIFICATION: Associate justice (August 24, 1949-June 12, 1967)
NOMINATED BY: Harry S. Truman
BORN: September 23, 1899, Dallas, Texas
DIED: June 13, 1977, New York, New York
SIGNIFICANCE: As attorney general, Clark designed and defended much of President Harry S. Truman's domestic anticommunism program. As a Supreme Court justice, he supported these and similar state-level loyalty programs and, in the Warren Court, opposed efforts to curb those programs.

Born into a family of Texas lawyers, Tom C. Clark served in World War I and received a bachelor's degree in 1921 from the University of Texas at Austin and a law degree from the same school in 1922. He practiced law in his father's Dallas firm, served as the civil district attorney for Dallas County, and gained the respect and friendship of leading Texas Democratic politicians including Senator Tom Connally and Congressman Sam Rayburn.

The election of Franklin D. Roosevelt in 1936 brought young Clark the opportunity to work for the Department of Justice in Washington, D.C. While at the department, Clark worked on wartime claims and the evacuation of Japanese Americans from the West Coast. In 1943 he was promoted to assistant attorney general to head the antitrust division and later the criminal division.

Clark's service in the Justice Department laid the groundwork for his later career. Then Missouri senator Harry S. Truman led an investigation of wartime fraud. Findings were submitted to Clark, who ably prosecuted those accused. Clark worked to secure the 1944 Democratic vice presidential nomination for Truman. When Truman assumed the presidency at Roosevelt's death, Clark's appointment as attorney general was one of Truman's important early appointments. As attorney general, Clark spoke for the Truman administration before congressional committees and personally argued several cases before the Supreme Court. However, Attorney General Clark was best known as one of the main designers of Truman's domestic anticommunism program, including the preparation of the first at-

Tom C. Clark
(Harris and Ewing,
Collection of the
Supreme Court of
the United States)

torney general's list of dangerous political organizations.

Preparing for the 1948 presidential election, Clark successfully and accurately refuted claims that the Truman administration was "soft on communism." His reward came one year after Truman's 1948 victory when Truman nominated him to the Supreme Court. Clark served Truman well as attorney general, and many believed the nominee would likely support then Chief Justice Fred M. Vinson's strong anticommunist views. Texas Democratic Party leaders and bar associations supported Clark's nomination. The Senate confirmed the nomination by a vote of seventy-three to eight.

Associate Justice Clark supported the anticommunist views of the chief justice, usually voting to uphold anticommunist and loyalty programs, including those established by state and local governments. However, he wrote for a unanimous court in *Wieman v. Updegraff* (1952) that mere membership of the accused in an organization on the attorney general's list did not prove disloyalty. As a judge, Clark ruled that prosecutors misused the list he drew up years before as attorney general.

In 1953 President Dwight D. Eisenhower's selection of Earl Warren to succeed Vinson as chief justice changed Clark's role on the Court. During the early years of the Warren Court, Clark wrote a series of noncontroversial antitrust majority opinions and was moved by Warren to join a unanimous Court seeking to end racially segregated public schooling and other early Warren Court civil rights decisions.

The appointment of William J. Brennan, Jr., in 1956 signaled the start of liberal dominance of the Court, led by Warren, Hugo L. Black, and William O. Douglas. Clark's long-held anticommunist views and his willingness to support police and prosecutorial powers of the state contrasted with the views of more liberal Court members. Clark dissented again and again as the Court moved to expand the rights of the accused. Regarding loyalty-security decisions, he was usually in the minority, upholding government power while the majority supported the claims of individuals alleging governmental abuses.

With the arrival of the 1960's, Clark turned to other matters. He led the Court in deciding *Mapp v. Ohio* (1961), which required police and prosecutors not to use illegally obtained evidence to get a conviction. He also concurred in a historic decision, *Baker v. Carr* (1962), which effectively required state legislatures to redraw electoral district boundaries to accommodate population shifts. Also, in *Abington School District v. Schempp* (1963), Clark held that state and local governments violated the First Amendment establishment clause when they required schoolchildren to open the school day by saying officially prescribed prayers or reading from the Bible. Even as the Court's concerns turned away from loyalty tests and related matters, Clark continued to resist challenges to state and local loyalty programs.

Family loyalty motivated Clark's retirement from the Court. In February, 1967, President Lyndon B. Johnson announced the appointment of Clark's son, Ramsey, as attorney general of the United States. Knowing that his son would be presenting cases to the Court, Tom Clark retired in June, 1967, completing eighteen years of service on the Court.

Gayle R. Avant

FURTHER READING

Bader, William H., and Roy M. Mersky, eds. *The First One Hundred Eight Justices*. Buffalo, N.Y.: William S. Hein, 2004.

Belknap, Michal R. *The Vinson Court: Justices, Rulings, and Legacy*. Santa Barbara, Calif.: ABC-Clio, 2004.

Commission on the Bicentennial of the United States. *The Supreme Court of the United States: Its Beginnings and Its Justices, 1790-1991*. Washington, D.C.: Author, 1992.

Kirkendall, Richard. "Tom C. Clark." In *The Justices of the United States Supreme Court: Their Lives and Major Opinions*, edited by Leon Friedman and Fred L. Israel. New York: Chelsea House, 1997.

Urofsky, Melvin I. *The Warren Court: Justices, Rulings, and Legacy*. Santa Barbara, Calif.: ABC-Clio, 2001.

SEE ALSO *Abington School District v. Schempp; Baker v. Carr; Brown v. Board of Education;* Cold War; Loyalty oaths; New Deal; Vinson, Fred M.; Warren, Earl.

John H. Clarke

IDENTIFICATION: Associate justice (August 1, 1916-September 18, 1922)

NOMINATED BY: Woodrow Wilson

BORN: September 18, 1857, New Lisbon, Ohio

DIED: March 22, 1945, San Diego, California

SIGNIFICANCE: During his short tenure on the Supreme Court, Clarke opposed the Court's nullification of social and economic regulatory legislation.

The son of a prominent Ohio attorney, John H. Clarke graduated from Western Reserve College in 1877 and was admitted to the Ohio bar in 1878 after studying law at Western Reserve and with his father. Clarke practiced law for nearly twenty years in Youngstown, where he was part owner of the *Youngstown Vindicator* and was active in state Democratic politics. Clarke moved to Cleveland in 1897, where he served as counsel for railroads. Meanwhile, Clarke became an outspoken advocate of such progressive measures as the initiative and referendum, the recall of public officials other than judges, regulations of the hours and conditions of labor, woman suffrage, and civil service reform. Clarke made unsuccessful bids for the U.S. Senate in 1904 and 1914.

Clarke's Progressive leanings, his Democratic loyalties and connections, his widely recognized legal abilities, and his dedication to vigorous prosecution of companies under the federal antitrust laws led to his appointment by President Woodrow Wilson in 1914 as a judge of the U.S. District Court for the northern district of Ohio. The same considerations resulted in Wilson's appointment of Clarke to the Supreme Court in 1916 after the resignation of Charles Evans Hughes.

Clarke's record on the Court was consistent with Wilson's expecta-

John H. Clarke.
(Harris and Ewing/
Collection of the
Supreme Court of
the United States)

tions. During his six years on the Court, Clarke regularly voted with the Court's Progressive bloc to sustain the constitutionality of social and economic regulatory legislation and to support vigorous enforcement of the antitrust laws. In some cases, Clarke cast the swing vote to sustain regulatory legislation. Clarke dissented in various cases in which the Court struck down such laws. In *Hammer v. Dagenhart* (1918), Clarke joined Justices Joseph McKenna, Louis D. Brandeis, and Oliver Wendell Holmes in dissenting from the Court's decision that a federal child labor law exceeded Congress's power to regulate interstate commerce. In *Bailey v. Drexel Furniture Co.* (1922), Clarke entered a sole dissent, without opinion, from the Court's decision that a reenacted child labor law that taxed goods produced by children was not within the congressional power to levy taxes.

In cases involving free speech, Clarke espoused the same broad view of state power that he expressed in cases involving social and economic regulations. Most notably, Clarke broke with Holmes and Brandeis to write the majority opinion in *Abrams v. United States* (1919), upholding the espionage convictions of political dissidents whose primary offense was to distribute written criticisms of the government's military policies.

Increasingly bored by what he perceived as the triviality of much of the Court's work and frustrated by what he perceived as his inability to promote his progressive philosophy on an increasingly conservative Court, Clarke resigned from the Court after only six years in order to work for world peace. After retiring from the Court, Clarke spoke and wrote widely on behalf of U.S. entry into the League of Nations and served as a trustee of the World Peace Foundation. He also became an outspoken critic of judicial activism by the Supreme Court and publicly supported Franklin D. Roosevelt's Court-packing plan in 1937.

William G. Ross

FURTHER READING

Bader, William H., and Roy M. Mersky, eds. *The First One Hundred Eight Justices.* Buffalo, N.Y.: William S. Hein, 2004.

Renstrom, Peter G. *The Taft Court: Justices, Rulings, and Legacy.* Santa Barbara, Calif.: ABC-Clio, 2003.

Shoemaker, Rebecca S. *The White Court: Justices, Rulings, and Legacy.* Santa Barbara, Calif.: ABC-Clio, 2004.

Warner, Hoyt Landon. *The Life of Mr. Justice Clarke: A Testament to the Power of Liberal Dissent in America.* Cleveland, Ohio: Western Reserve University Press, 1959.

SEE ALSO Court-packing plan; *Hammer v. Dagenhart*; Progressivism; Resignation and retirement.

Clerks of the Justices

DESCRIPTION: Employees of the Supreme Court who assist the justices in research, selecting the petitions for *certiorari* worthy of review and writing the opinions at the decision-on-the-merits stage.

SIGNIFICANCE: Although controversy continues surrounding the extent of influence that clerks wield in the Supreme Court's decision-making and opinion-writing processes, there is little debate regarding the role they play in screening the more than eight thousand petitions for writs of *certiorari* filed each October term.

Associate Justice Horace Gray was the first justice to employ a full-time clerk in 1882. His clerk's responsibilities included acting as his personal barber and fulfilling basic secretarial duties. In 1886 Congress permitted each justice to hire a stenographic clerk. Four of the justices of the Supreme Court hired personal clerks, whose responsibilities ranged from running personal errands to conducting basic legal research. During the 1946 to 1969 October terms, most of the associate justices employed two law clerks. In 1970 most of the justices hired three clerks and, in 1980, Congress authorized all the justices to employ as many as four clerks. Scholars found that as the numbers of clerks increased, so did the number of words in decisions, footnotes, and citations to other cases.

Although most law clerks serve only one term on the Court, some have stayed longer. Some clerks have worked for more than one justice, and others have become virtually permanent fixtures in the Court. A clerk for associate justice Pierce Butler, for example, served sixteen terms. It is also common for clerks to stay on a few weeks after the term has expired to train their replacements.

CRITERIA FOR SELECTION

The individual justices have complete discretion in choosing their clerks, although most of those selected have graduated near the top of their law school class and have served in an editorial position on their school's law journal. Researcher David M. O'Brien found that four basic factors appear to be central in the law clerk selection process: particular law schools, particular geographic regions, prior clerking experience on particular lower courts for certain judges, and personal compatibility. Although justices traditionally select law clerks from Ivy League law schools such as Yale and Harvard, they also draw from other schools, including their alma maters. Justices Sandra Day O'Connor and William II. Rehnquist, for example, are well known for choosing law clerks from their alma mater, Stanford Law School. Geographic region is also a prominent factor in the justices' law clerk selection process. For example, justice Hugo L. Black, an Alabaman, preferred clerks who grew up and attended law school in his home state.

Several justices regularly selected individuals who clerked in the chambers of certain lower court judges. For example, District of Columbia circuit court judge Skelley Wright's chambers often served as a breeding ground for future Supreme Court law clerks. Personal compatibility, moreover, is valued by the justices when searching for law clerks. Given the intimate working relations that a justice has with his or her clerks, the personal habits of an individual can be instrumental in his or her effectiveness. Personal compatibility can be related to similarities or differences in the ideological proclivities between the law clerk and the justice. Although some justices want clerks with similar policy preferences, others choose individuals with different views to get an insider's view of the adversary's position.

FUNCTIONS OF CLERKS

The practice of clerks reviewing petitions for *certiorari* (discretionary appeals filed by the losing party in lower court to the Supreme Court) began during Chief Justice Charles Evans Hughes's tenure on the Court. Hughes used his clerks to review the *in forma pauperis* petitions (petitions to allow an indigent person to bypass the costs of filing a discretionary appeal to the Court) that should be granted or denied by the Court. From the Hughes Court (1930-1941) to the Warren Court (1953-1968), the chief justices' clerks were responsible for reviewing *in forma pauperis* petitions and preparing short memorandums.

A cert pool was created in 1972. The cert pool process begins when an administrator in the chief justice's chambers divides the petitions for *certiorari* among the eight justices in the pool. A law clerk writes a memorandum (often called a pool memo) to the other justices regarding the lower court and the judges participating in the decision. The facts and contentions of all the parties are presented along with an analysis of the case, such as conflicts among lower court decisions on the issue before the Court. Section 5 of the memo includes a recommendation on the disposition of the case and other relevant information, including the name of the clerk writing the memo. When a pool memo arrives in the justices' chambers, each justice has one of his or her own law clerks review it. In most cases, the law clerk reviewing the memo echoes the initial recommendation, but in some situations, the clerk will do additional research and write an additional memo. All the petitions for *certiorari* are reviewed by the single justice who does not belong to the pool.

Although the role that law clerks play in reviewing petitions for *certiorari* is well established, their influence in the Court's decision making and opinion writing is less certain. Certain law clerks have claimed to author most of the justices' written decisions. Conversely, other law clerks claim that they were responsible only for the footnotes or citation checking in the justices' decisions. In all likelihood, the clerks' responsibilities fall somewhere in between these extremes and vary with each individual justice. Nonetheless, the power that law clerks have over the Court's decision making has sparked a contentious debate among the scholarly community. Given that law clerks are not presidential appointees, many scholars argue that they should not play such a principal part in the Court's decision-making and opinion-writing process.

FORMER CLERKS AS FUTURE LITIGATORS

Law clerks' experience reviewing petitions for *certiorari* and assisting the justices in writing their final decisions offers them an invaluable opportunity to see at first hand the internal decision-making dynamics of the Court. Researchers found that more than 51 percent of individuals who clerked between the 1958 and 1985 October terms later participated as direct or third parties before the Court. This percentage was much higher for law clerks than for those individuals with similar educational backgrounds who did not serve as law clerks. One of the reasons for this high participation rate is that the solicitor general's office, the body that represents the United States before the Supreme Court, actively hires former law clerks. In 1992 for example, approximately half of the lawyers in the office were former law clerks.

Because former law clerks have a potential advantage as litigators before the justices, Court rules stipulate that former law clerks cannot appear as counsel for two years after they leave. Law firms also recognize this unique experience, offering former law clerks as much as a $35,000 bonus in addition to their salaries.

John R. Hermann

FURTHER READING

Sorcerers' Apprentices: One Hundred Years of Law Clerks at the United States Supreme Court, by Artemus Ward and David L. Weiden (New York: New York University Press, 2006), is the most thorough and up-to-date examination of the role of clerks on the Supreme Court. Another comprehensive treatment of the subject with a historical perspective is Bradley J. Best's *Law Clerks, Support Personnel, and the Decline of Consensual Norms on the United States Supreme Court, 1935-1995* (New York: LFB Scholarly Publications, 2002).

Two works that provide excellent summaries of the functions of law clerks of the justices are David M. O'Brien's *Storm Center: The Supreme Court in American Politics* (7th ed., New York: W. W. Norton, 2005) and William H. Rehnquist's *The Supreme Court: How It Was, How It Is* (New York: William Morrow, 1983). For a historical perspective on law clerks, see Chester A. Newland's "Personal Assistants to Supreme Court Justices: The Law Clerks," *Oregon Law Review* 40 (1961):

299-317. For the debate regarding how much justices rely on their law clerks and its ramifications on the democratic process, see David Crump's "Law Clerks: Their Roles and Relationships with Their Judges," *Judicature* (December/January, 1986): 236-240; John P. Frank's "The Supreme Court: The Muckrakers Return," *American Bar Association Journal* (February, 1980): 160-164; Richard A. Posner's *The Federal Courts: Crisis and Reform* (Cambridge, Mass.: Harvard University Press, 1985); and Joseph Vining's "Justice, Bureaucracy, and Legal Method," *Michigan Law* 80 (1981): 252-270.

The frequent presence of former law clerks turned litigators before the Supreme Court is the subject of Kevin T. McGuire's *Supreme Court Practice: Legal Elites in the Washington Community* (Charlottesville: University Press of Virginia, 1993) and Karen O'Connor and John R. Hermann's "The Clerk Connection: Appearances Before the Supreme Court by Former Law Clerks," *Judicature* (March/April, 1995): 247-249.

SEE ALSO Black, Hugo L.; Butler, Pierce; *Certiorari*, writ of; Chief justice; Conference of the justices; Gray, Horace; Hughes, Charles Evans; Rehnquist, William H.; Workload.

Nathan Clifford

IDENTIFICATION: Associate justice (January 21, 1858-July 25, 1881)
NOMINATED BY: James Buchanan
BORN: August 18, 1803, Rumney, New Hampshire
DIED: July 25, 1881, Cornish, Maine
SIGNIFICANCE: Clifford spoke for the Supreme Court in nearly four hundred cases and presided over the commission that decided the disputed 1876 presidential election. He consistently dissented from Court opinions upholding federal power to confiscate property during wartime.

Nathan Clifford studied law under Josiah Quincy and was admitted to the New Hampshire bar in 1827. He served three terms in the Maine legislature and two terms in the U.S. House of Representatives. In 1846 he was appointed attorney general by President James K. Polk, and

Nathan Clifford.
(Library of Congress)

while serving as special commissioner to Mexico, he arranged the Treaty of Guadalupe Hidalgo that ended the Mexican War in 1848. After being nominated by President James Buchanan, Clifford took his seat on the Supreme Court in 1858.

Clifford concurred in the first of the *Legal Tender Cases, Hepburn v. Griswold* (1870) but dissented in *Knox v. Lee* (1871), declaring Congress's issuing of treasury notes to pay earlier debts to be constitutional. In *Loan Association v. Topeka* (1874), Clifford stated that state legislative power was almost absolute, subject only to specific state and federal constitutional provisions. Despite his proslavery views, he generally supported the government during the Civil War. Clifford argued in nearly four hundred Court cases, with most involving maritime and commercial law and laws affecting Mexican land grants.

Alvin K. Benson

SEE ALSO Civil War; Dissents; Resignation and retirement; *Slaughterhouse Cases*; War powers.

Clinton v. City of New York

CITATION: 524 U.S. 417

DATE: June 25, 1998

ISSUES: Presidential powers; separation of powers

SIGNIFICANCE: The Supreme Court ruled the line-item veto was unconstitutional because it allowed the president to amend legislation passed by Congress.

The Line-Item Veto Act of 1996 authorized the president to veto fiscal portions of a bill, with the goal of putting a limit on federal spending. In *Raines v. Byrd* (1997), the Supreme Court ruled that members of Congress had no standing to oppose the law in court. After President Bill Clinton vetoed several spending measures, however, the city of New York and other plaintiffs were adversely affected by the vetoes and were granted standing.

By a 6-3 vote, the Court struck down the veto law. In his opinion for the Court, Justice John Paul Stevens wrote that the Constitution did not authorize the president to enact, to amend, or to repeal statutes. Beginning with George Washington, presidents had recognized that the Constitution required them to "approve all the parts of a bill, or reject it in toto." To make such a change in the legislative process would require a constitutional amendment. The three dissenters believed that the line-item veto violated neither a textual constitutional command nor any implicit principle of the separation of powers doctrine.

Thomas Tandy Lewis

SEE ALSO Presidential powers; Separation of powers; Standing; Stevens, John Paul.

Clinton v. Jones

CITATION: 520 U.S. 681
DATE: May 27, 1997
ISSUE: Executive immunity
SIGNIFICANCE: The Supreme Court unanimously rejected President
Bill Clinton's claim of immunity from a civil suit while in office.

In 1994 Paula Jones brought a sexual harassment suit against President Bill Clinton. She alleged that an incident had taken place in 1991, when he was governor of Arkansas and she a state employee. President Clinton asserted that the suit should be postponed until after his term of office expired. He argued that the separation of powers doctrine places limits on the authority of the judiciary over the executive branch, and he also referred to *Nixon v. Fitzgerald* (1982), which provided presidents with absolute immunity from suits arising from their official duties of office.

Writing for the Supreme Court, Justice John Paul Stevens reasoned that a president was not totally immune from the jurisdiction of the federal courts and that it was appropriate for the courts to determine the legality of a president's conduct, both official and unofficial. Stevens suggested that the suit should not be especially "onerous" in time and efforts. A delay in the trial, he argued, would be unfair to Jones because it would increase the danger of prejudice from lost evidence.

Thomas Tandy Lewis

SEE ALSO Presidential powers; Separation of powers; Stevens, John Paul.

Cold War

DATE: Mid-1940's to late 1980's

DESCRIPTION: Nonviolent conflict between the United States and other Western nations and the Soviet Bloc. The efforts of the United States to combat communist ideology raised a number of constitutional issues that were addressed by the Supreme Court.

SIGNIFICANCE: Legal challenges to the laws and policies enacted to fight the Cold War reaching the Supreme Court involved fundamental civil rights, including freedom of speech and freedom of association, and the apportionment of war powers between Congress and the president.

Shortly after the end of World War II (1941-1945), the United States and the Soviet Union became engaged in a military, economic, and ideological rivalry known as the Cold War. For more than four decades, the United States carried out a foreign policy aimed at halting the spread of Soviet influence abroad. This "containment" strategy had a domestic counterpart: preventing the infiltration of Soviet agents and the spread of communist ideology in the United States.

After World War II, successive presidential administrations and congressional leaders were concerned that Soviet agents and communist sympathizers were attempting to convert American public opinion toward their cause. Many leaders worried that the Soviets had already infiltrated some media outlets, the film industry, various universities, and even certain departments of the U.S. government. In response, the U.S. government enacted laws, executive orders, and policies to reduce or eliminate these threats. The enactment of these laws and policies brought up various constitutional issues— most of which were addressed in some way by the Supreme Court. Among these issues were freedom of speech, freedom of association, and freedom of assembly.

LOYALTY OATHS AND BOARDS

In 1947 President Harry S. Truman issued Executive Order 9835, which established loyalty boards in each state department to adjudicate cases of alleged disloyalty to the state. Suspect federal employees would be removed from their positions if "reasonable grounds" were found to exist for a "belief" of disloyalty. President Dwight D. Eisenhower issued his own version of that policy in 1951, requiring only "reasonable doubt as to the loyalty" of a federal employee in order to trigger removal. Various states, school districts, and other government entities began to require loyalty oaths as a requirement for employment.

Loyalty oaths survived various legal challenges for most of the 1950's. However, in *Kent v. Dulles* (1958), the Court ruled that the State Department's requirement that a traveler sign a "noncommunist affidavit" to receive permission to travel violated the due process clause of the Fifth Amendment. Then, in a landmark decision, the Court ruled in *Keyishian v. Board of Regents* (1967) that a law requiring public school teachers in New York to sign a loyalty oath violated the First Amendment.

CENSORSHIP

Many domestic efforts during the Cold War sought to censor publications and speech that were deemed dangerous for various reasons. Some censorship laws, such as the Smith Act of 1940, targeted advocacy of violence against the government. Other efforts centered on sensitive military data and other information that could harm American security if released. In general, the Court upheld such efforts when it could be demonstrated that particular forms of speech posed a distinct and immediate danger to the state.

In other cases, however, the Court rejected efforts to censor putatively dangerous publications and speech. In *Lamont v. Postmaster General* (1965), for example, the Court ruled unanimously against a law requiring the Postmaster General to seize and destroy all unsealed mail from abroad deemed to be "communist political propaganda" because such an act violated the First Amendment.

GUILT BY ASSOCIATION

Some laws enacted during the Cold War attempted to eradicate communist "cells," which allegedly existed in a secret network directed by Moscow and intended to overthrow the U.S. government. The McCarran Act of 1950 and the Communist Control Act of 1954, for example, placed restrictions on communist organizations by requiring registration, excluding their members from certain posts, and even providing for the internment of communists during a national emergency.

Though these acts represent the height of anticommunist fervor in the United States, the Court did not rule on their constitutionality for a number of years. Eventually, though, major provisions of the acts were deemed to be unconstitutional.

THE VIETNAM WAR

The Vietnam War brought a host of occasions for the Court to rule on constitutional issues. In *United States v. Seeger* (1965), for example, the Court effectively extended the military exclusion for "conscientious objectors" to those who oppose war on the basis of sincere moral beliefs that are not part of a particular religious doctrine. In *Bond v. Floyd* (1966), the Court ruled against the Georgia legislature's refusal to seat a duly elected legislator, Julian Bond, because he had supported opponents of the draft. In *Tinker v. Des Moines Independent Community School District* (1969), the Court ruled against a public school that suspended students for wearing black armbands to protest the Vietnam War. The Court thus upheld the protection of "symbolic speech" under the First Amendment, even in schools.

The Court reined in the government's use of the national security argument for censoring factual military information in *New York Times Co. v. United States* (1971). In this case, a former official of the Department of Defense had leaked the Pentagon Papers (a study of the Vietnam War produced by the department) to *The New York Times*. The federal government attempted to halt the publication, but the Court held this case of prior restraint to be unconstitutional.

WAR POWERS

In addition to matters of civil rights and liberties, the Cold War raises constitutional questions about the apportionment of war powers between the president and Congress. The Vietnam War especially focused attention on this question, particularly as public sentiment turned against the war in the late 1960's. Congress had effectively delegated its power to declare war in the Tonkin Gulf Resolution of 1964 but attempted to regain those powers through the War Powers Act of 1973. Though the Court did not rule directly on the War Powers Act, other decisions by the Court, such as *Immigration and Naturalization Service v. Chadha* (1983), suggest that provisions of the act amount to an unconstitutional legislative veto.

The continuous sense of threat to the United States that existed during the Cold War, due in large part to the two superpowers' nuclear arsenals, spawned the idea that the president should have enormous discretion in military deployments and war making, although this ability was not consistent with the Constitution. In retrospect, the Cold War was an almost surreal period in which the Court faced the difficult task of preserving the ideals of the Constitution in a global environment that threatened the country, its ideological values, and its population.

Steve D. Boilard

FURTHER READING

Hogan, Michael J. *A Cross of Iron: Harry S. Truman and the Origins of the National Security State, 1945-1954.* New York: Cambridge University Press, 1998.

Neville, John F. *The Press, the Rosenbergs, and the Cold War.* Westport, Conn.: Praeger, 1995.

Theoharis, Athan. *Chasing Spies: How the FBI Failed in Counterintelligence but Promoted the Politics of McCarthyism in the Cold War Years.* Chicago: Ivan R. Dee, 2002. A skeptical account of FBI activities reveals the difficulty of securing convictions in espionage cases.

Urofsky, Melvin I. *Division and Discord: The Supreme Court Under Stone and Vinson, 1941-1953.* Columbia: University of South Carolina Press, 1997.

Zeinert, Karen. *McCarthy and the Fear of Communism in American History.* Springfield, N.J.: Enslow, 1998.

SEE ALSO Censorship; Espionage acts; Loyalty oaths; National security; Reed, Stanley F.; Seditious libel; Smith Act; Vietnam War; Vinson, Fred M.; War and civil liberties; War powers; World War II.

Comity Clause

DATE: 1789

DESCRIPTION: Article IV of the U.S. Constitution, providing a foundation for a state to give the courtesy of enforcing the laws of another state. This courtesy is afforded out of respect and friendship and not out of obligation.

SIGNIFICANCE: Comity clause cases that come before the Supreme Court often involve the extent to which one state court's judgment is enforceable in another state or the unequal treatment of residents and nonresidents.

The Articles of Confederation specifically mentioned interstate relations premised on the concept of comity. Article IV, sections 1 and 2, of the U.S. Constitution provide for comity and facilitate interstate relations through the full faith and credit, rendition, and privileges and immunities provisions. The full faith and credit provision requires that each state recognize and enforce the "public acts, records, and judicial proceedings of every other state." Congress first enacted implementation legislation for the full faith and credit provision, which has become a significant component of the U.S. legal system. The most significant issue arising under this provision entails the extent to which a valid final judgment of one state's court is enforceable in another state. In *Estin v. Estin* (1948), the Supreme Court determined that one state must honor the validity of a divorce decree granted by another state; however, it is not bound by the other state's court decision regarding alimony, child custody, and division of liabilities and assets.

The full faith and credit provision is inapplicable to criminal jurisprudence. The rendition provision, also known as the fugitive from justice clause and extradition, calls on one state to surrender to another state a fugitive from justice. In 1793 Congress enacted implementation legislation. In *Kentucky v. Dennison* (1861), the governor of Ohio refused to comply with Kentucky's demand to surrender a defendant charged in Kentucky with aiding the escape of a slave. The Court held that Ohio's governor had a moral, but unenforceable, duty to comply with Kentucky's extradition demand. In *Puerto Rico v.*

Branstad (1987), the Court overruled a portion of *Dennison* and held that federal courts have the authority to require a governor to perform his ministerial duty by delivering a fugitive upon a proper demand from another state.

The privileges and immunities provision, also known as the comity clause, provides that the "citizens of each state shall be entitled to all of the privileges and immunities of citizens in the several states." The Court in the *Slaughterhouse Cases* (1873) ruled that Article IV privileges and immunities addressed state citizenship; however, the Fourteenth Amendment protected only national citizenship. The Court has upheld the differential treatment of out-of-state citizens when a state has enacted a state citizenship or state residency classification. State laws differentiating between residents and nonresidents have been upheld by the Court regarding commercial fishing licenses, recreational fishing licenses, recreational hunting licenses, business licenses, the right to practice a profession, the privilege of voting in state elections, and running for state office. Presently the Court relies more heavily upon the equal protection and commerce clauses in order to facilitate interstate comity than the Article IV privileges and immunities provision.

Robert P. Morin

FURTHER READING

Chase, Harold W., and Craig R. Ducat. *Edward S. Corwin's The Constitution and What It Means Today.* 14th ed. Princeton, N.J.: Princeton University Press, 1978.

Ducat, Craig R. *Constitutional Interpretation.* 8th ed. Belmont, Calif.: Thomson/West, 2004.

Fried, Charles. *Saying What the Law Is: The Constitution in the Supreme Court.* Cambridge, Mass.: Harvard University Press, 2004.

Wiecek, William M. *The Birth of the Modern Constitution: The United States Supreme Court, 1941-1953.* New York: Cambridge University Press, 2006.

SEE ALSO Full faith and credit; Political questions; Privileges and immunities; *Slaughterhouse Cases.*

Regulation of Commerce

DESCRIPTION: Control, through laws, licenses, and other means, of the buying and selling of goods and services of all kinds, the related transportation of goods, and business and employment practices.

SIGNIFICANCE: The commerce clause, Article I, section 8, of the Constitution gives Congress plenary power to regulate commerce with foreign nations, among the states, and with the Indian tribes. The Supreme Court, in defining the boundaries of authority between the national and state governments, authorized Congress to regulate almost every aspect of business and the economy and to enact laws protecting the civil rights of citizens.

In the early 1800's New York granted a monopoly to a steamboat operating in New York waters, which conflicted with a congressional coastal license given to another person operating in waters between New York and New Jersey. In *Gibbons v. Ogden* (1824), Chief Justice John Marshall, writing the majority opinion for the Supreme Court, enunciated the fundamental principles of the power of Congress to regulate commerce in the face of contrary state action. He held that commerce is intercourse between nations and parts of nations in all its branches and that Congress has plenary power to prescribe rules to carry out that intercourse. Navigation is part of commerce, and the power of Congress to regulate such activity cannot stop at the state boundaries because the power to regulate "among the states" means intermingled with traffic in the interior of states. Nonetheless, Marshall ruled that commerce that is completely within a state is reserved for state regulation.

ABSENCE OF FEDERAL REGULATION

In *Cooley v. Board of Wardens of the Port of Philadelphia* (1852), the Court held that if Congress manifests a clear intent to leave the matter of commerce regulation to the states, it may do so. In subsequent decisions, the Court found that states might regulate commerce in the absence of congressional regulation if the regulation is wholly local and does not create uniform national standards. The rule in

Cooley was supplemented with a balancing of interests test designed to ascertain whether litigated state regulation creates an undue burden on interstate commerce. Therefore, for example, in *South Carolina State Highway Department v. Barnwell* (1938), the Court found that a width and weight limitation on trucks driving through South Carolina was a reasonable safety limitation when balanced against the national interest in the free flow of interstate commerce. Interest balancing, however, does not automatically result in upholding the state regulation, as was the case for Arizona's attempt to limit the length of freight trains traveling through that state in *Southern Pacific Co. v. Arizona* (1945).

The Court's decision in *Philadelphia v. New Jersey* (1978) illustrates how the Court adjudicates a classic federalism issue caused by a modern problem. To protect the quality of the state environment, the New Jersey state legislature enacted a law prohibiting the importation of most solid or liquid wastes that originated or were collected outside the state. Though waste by definition seems valueless, the Court ruled that it is, nonetheless, commerce. It then determined that New Jersey was trying to burden out-of-state companies by slowing the filling of its landfills. The basic principle of federalism is that one state in its dealings with another may not place itself in a position of economic isolation. Earlier the Court had occasion in *Edwards v. California* (1941) to emphatically assert this same principle when California attempted to keep poor residents of other states from migrating to that state.

PENETRATION OF FEDERAL REGULATION

The question of how far within the confines of state boundaries federal legislation may penetrate to regulate commerce is answered by two Court decisions during the first quarter of the twentieth century. In the first instance, the Interstate Commerce Commission responded to the discriminatory practices of a railway company in charging lower rates for intrastate shipments among east Texas locations than for interstate shipments over similar distances. The Court, in the *Shreveport Rate Cases* (1914), held that although the rate fixing was completely intrastate, Congress may regulate intrastate carriers in all matters that have a "close and substantial relation" to interstate

President Lyndon B. Johnson signing the Civil Rights Act of 1964, whose constitutional basis lay in the Constitution's commerce clause. (NARA)

commerce. In *Stafford v. Wallace* (1922), the Court decided that Congress could authorize the secretary of agriculture to regulate the business conducted in stockyards although cattle in stockyards are not in transit. Chief Justice William H. Taft concluded that "the stockyards are but a throat through which the current flows, and the transactions which occur therein are only incident to this current from the West to the East, and from one state to another."

Although matters affecting transportation were found to be firmly within the regulatory power of Congress, the Court limited the power of Congress under the commerce clause by creating a sharp distinction between commerce and manufacturing. Chief Justice Melville W. Fuller, writing for an 8-1 majority in *United States v. E. C. Knight Co.* (1895), held that the Sherman Antitrust Act (1890) is not applicable to monopolies in manufacturing or production because they have only an incidental or indirect relationship to commerce. Consequently, as applied in this case, the Sherman Antitrust Act represents an intrusion into the reserve power of the states under the Tenth

274

Amendment. The Court used similar reasoning to strike down congressional attempts to regulate child labor (*Hammer v. Dagenhart*, 1918), codes of fair competition (*Schechter Poultry Corp. v. United States*, 1935), wages and hours of workers in mining (*Carter v. Carter Coal Co.*, 1936), and even agricultural subsidies, although not as a violation of the commerce clause (*United States v. Butler*, 1936). These and other Court decisions represented a serious threat to President Franklin D. Roosevelt's New Deal. Consequently, the Court was subjected to considerable pressure that no doubt led to the alteration in the Court's commerce clause interpretation.

By 1937 the Court changed its antifederal government interpretations. The transition to a cooperative view of federalism as opposed to the dualistic and antagonist view of federal state relations occurs with the 5-4 decision in *National Labor Relations Board v. Jones and Laughlin Steel Corp.* (1937). The Court found the act establishing the right of organized labor to bargain collectively was a valid regulation of commerce. Although labor-management relations are intrastate in character when they are considered separately, these relationships have a "close and substantial relation" to interstate commerce as part of the "stream of commerce." Therefore, the Court discarded its previous direct-indirect decision rule. In subsequent decisions pertaining to maximum-hour and minimum-wage laws (*United States v. Darby Lumber Co.*, 1941) and the regulation of farm acreage allotments (*Wickard v. Filburn*, 1942), the Court upheld the power of Congress to regulate commerce. Virtually any amount of economic activity in one place affects activity elsewhere, and consequently there seemed no limit to the power of the national government.

CIVIL RIGHTS AND COMMERCE

The Court opted to base its interpretation of the 1964 Civil Rights Act on the commerce clause alone and not on the more obvious equal protection clause and its enforcement provision found in the Fourteenth Amendment. The Court found an interstate commerce link in cases involving hotels because of their role in interstate travel (*Heart of Atlanta Motel v. United States*, 1964), service at restaurants because foodstuffs are shipped via interstate carriers (*Katzenbach v. McClung*, 1964), and a resort located many miles from an interstate highway because the private park leased equipment from an out-of-state supplier (*Daniel v. Paul*, 1969). Conceding that when Congress enacted the 1964 Civil Rights Act it may have been addressing a moral wrong, Justice Tom C. Clark in *Heart of Atlanta* concluded that the act is nonetheless constitutional. The congressional power extends to local activity in the states of both origin and destination when the activity in question has a substantial and harmful effect upon commerce. The only restriction of congressional power is that it must be "reasonably adapted to the end permitted by the Constitution."

STATES' RIGHTS REACTION

Although a temporary setback for national power, Justice William H. Rehnquist's majority opinion in *National League of Cities v. Usery* (1976) represented a stunning victory for state power. He held when dealing with their own employees, cities need not abide by the minimum-wage and maximum-hour provisions of federal law. Rehnquist argued that the law impaired the integrity and ability of the states to perform their traditional government functions, thereby invading the Tenth Amendment power reserved to the states. Rehnquist effectively reversed the logic of a long line of cases beginning with *Gibbons* that held that if a federal law is within the congressional commerce power, then by definition there can be no violation of the Tenth Amendment. Ten years later, however, the Court specifically overruled its earlier 6-3 decision with a 5-4 majority in *Garcia v. San Antonio Metropolitan Transit Authority* (1985). Writing for the majority, Harry A. Blackmun expressed frustration with the Court's inability to draw a workable line defining what is and what is not a traditional governmental function. He found that wage and working conditions have an impact on interstate commerce and therefore may be regulated by Congress.

In *United States v. Lopez* (1995), the conservative majority of the Rehnquist Court concluded that the Gun-Free School Zones Act of 1990 violated the reserved power of the states because the statute was a criminal statute that had little to do with "commerce" or any type of economic activity. In his opinion, Rehnquist wrote that Congress may regulate the channels of interstate commerce; regulate and protect the instrumentalities of interstate commerce, even though the threat may come only from intrastate activities; and regulate those activities that substantially affect interstate commerce. He found that the law in question did not involve the channels or instrumentalities of interstate commerce and that the activity involved did not substantially affect interstate commerce. He rejected the view of the Justice Department and the four-member Court minority that a violent atmosphere in schools adversely affects the learning environment, which in turn ultimately substantially affects the economy. If the federal law against the carrying of weapons near and on school grounds was constitutionally permissible, then, Rehnquist stated, the Court could find no reason why Congress could not, for example, enact laws prescribing curriculum for local elementary and secondary schools.

At the beginning of the twenty-first century, the majority of the justices often held that state sovereignty trumped Congress's power to regulate interstate commerce. For example, in *United States v. Morrison* (2000), the Court held, by a 5-4 vote, that the commerce clause did not empower Congress to enforce the Violence Against Women Act. In *Raich v. Gonzales* (2005), on the other hand, the Court decided that the federal government had the authority to prosecute anyone who provided or consumed marijuana contrary to the Controlled Substances Act, even in states that legalized the drug for some medical reasons. In contrast to their action in *Morrison*, the majority of the justices found that the use of controlled substances involved economic activities that had a significant impact on interstate commerce. In *Gonzales v. Oregon* (2006), the justices voted six to three to uphold Oregon's physician-assisted suicide law. Although Congress would have the power to pass a law clearly outlawing prescriptions that are made with the purpose of producing death, the majority of justices concluded that the existing drug laws did not authorize the federal government to decide when prescription drugs were being used for a "legitimate medical purpose."

PREEMPTION, INDIANS, AND FOREIGN COMMERCE

Much of contemporary commerce clause litigation involves the federal preemption doctrine. If a state law conflicts with a federal law, the national law supersedes it. The Court must determine whether Congress intended, either explicitly or implicitly, by its extensive regulation to take over a field such as nuclear power (*Pacific Gas and Electric Co. v. State Energy Resources Conservation and Development Commission*, 1983). The commerce clause is also the primary constitutional tool that Congress possesses when legislating in the field of Indian affairs. This is especially the case after 1871, when Congress declared that there would be no more treaties with Native Americans. Finally, the Court consistently held that the congressional right to regulate commerce with foreign nations is quite extensive (especially in the light of state attempts to tax foreign products) because it is important for the nation to speak with one voice. However, that voice is Congress and not the president (*Barclays Bank v. Franchise Tax Board of California*, 1994).

Albert P. Melone
Updated by the Editor

FURTHER READING

For an up-to-date and comprehensive account of the topic, consult Dan T. Coenen's *Constitutional Law: The Commerce Clause* (New York: Foundation Press, 2004). Maurice G. Baxter's *The Steamboat Monopoly: "Gibbons v. Ogden," 1824* (New York: Alfred A. Knopf, 1972) is a good case study of Marshall's seminal opinion and a useful history of the commerce clause in the pre-Civil War years. Another work on this subject is Felix Frankfurter's *The Commerce Power Under Marshall, Taney, and Waite* (Chapel Hill: University of North Carolina, 1937). Edward S. Corwin's *The Commerce Power Versus States Rights* (London: Oxford University Press, 1936) treats competing Court interpretations of the commerce clause that preceded the conflict with the New Deal. Because the case in question is essential to understanding the history of the commerce clause, Richard C. Cortner's *The "Jones and Laughlin" Case* (New York: Alfred A. Knopf, 1970) is essential reading. Paul R. Benson, Jr.'s *The Supreme Court and the Commerce Clause, 1937-70* (New York: Dunellen, 1970) also provides a good historical account for the period covered. For a modern conservative and restrictive view of the commerce clause see Thomas W. Merrill's "Toward a Principled Interpretation of the Commerce Clause," *Harvard Journal of Law and Public Policy* 22 (1998): 31-43. A searching analysis of the modern conservative agenda with respect to federalism is found in

Peter A. Lauricella's "The Real 'Contract with America': The Original Intent of the Tenth Amendment and the Commerce Clause," *Albany Law Review* 60 (1997): 1377-1408.

SEE ALSO Capitalism; Constitutional interpretation; Environmental law; Federalism; *Gibbons v. Ogden*; *Heart of Atlanta Motel v. United States*; *Lopez, United States v.*; Race and discrimination; *Raich v. Gonzales*; States' rights and state sovereignty; Travel, right to.

Common Law

DESCRIPTION: Law generated from court cases and judicial decisions.
SIGNIFICANCE: The Supreme Court is a common-law court in that it generally follows earlier decisions made by judges.

Common law, or judge-made law, is generated from a succession of judicial decisions or precedents. In common-law systems, courts are bound by the rule called *stare decisis*, or "let the precedent stand." In the United States, common law is distinguished from equity law, which is based on reasoning about what is fair or equitable. It also differs from law based on statutes enacted by legislatures.

Common-law systems are contrasted with civil-law systems found on the continent of Europe and elsewhere, which are based on legal codes. Some of these systems are based on the Code Civil ("civil law") drafted in Napoleonic France, derived partially from Roman law. By contrast, the common-law system was developed in England and brought to the American colonies. By 1776 the colonial courts used common law as a matter of course. After the American Revolution, decisions made in U.S. courts added to the body of common law.

The Supreme Court is a common-law court. Its decisions are the basis of constitutional law and it generally adheres, except when changing circumstances warrant creation of new rules, to *stare decisis*. When government under the Constitution began in 1789, questions arose as to whether federal courts had jurisdiction over common-law cases. The question also arose as to whether federal cases would themselves become a kind of common law in civil or criminal cases. The Court's decisions regarding these questions had far-reaching consequences.

In *United States v. Hudson and Goodwin* (1812), the Court ruled that no federal court could exercise common-law jurisdiction in criminal cases. It therefore denied the existence of a federal common law of crimes. Whether a federal common law of civil cases exists, however, was another matter. In 1842 in *Swift v. Tyson*, the Court ruled that there is federal common law in commercial cases. This ruling prevailed for nearly a century; then the Court, departing from *stare decisis*, reversed itself, ruling in *Erie Railroad Co. v. Tompkins* (1938) that one of its own decisions—*Swift*—was unconstitutional. Speaking for the majority, Justice Louis D. Brandeis wrote: "There is no federal common law." Nevertheless, this ruling did not completely eliminate the idea of federal common law, though today it is limited to specialized subjects.

The common-law process of following precedent in making decisions has allowed the federal judiciary to assume the position it holds in the U.S. constitutional plan. When Chief Justice John Marshall rendered the key decision in *Marbury v. Madison* (1803) that established the federal courts' power to declare laws void, he was following the common-law obligation to apply all relevant law. Because of the force of precedent in common-law procedure, the Court's action in *Marbury* has reverberated through two centuries of legal tradition, helping to shape the theory and practice of U.S. government.

Charles F. Bahmueller

FURTHER READING

Farnsworth, E. Allan. *An Introduction to the Legal System of the United States.* 3d ed. Dobbs Ferry, N.Y.: Oceana Publications, 1996.

Friedman, Lawrence M. *A History of American Law.* 3d ed. New York: Simon & Schuster, 2005.

Hale, M., and C. Gray. *The History of the Common Law in England.* Chicago: University of Chicago, 2002.

Plucknett, Theodore Frank Thomas. *A Concise History of the Common Law.* 5th ed. Union, N.J.: Lawbook Exchange, 2001.

Schweber, Howard. *The Creation of American Common Law, 1850-1880: Technology, Politics, and the Construction of Citizenship.* New York: Cambridge University Press, 2004.

SEE ALSO Civil law; Constitutional law; Gray, Horace; Holmes, Oliver Wendell; Judicial review; *Marbury v. Madison*; Sedition Act of 1798; Statutory interpretation.

Conference of the Justices

DESCRIPTION: Formal meeting of the justices to conduct Supreme Court business, including the selection of cases to hear, votes on cases already argued, and the issuance of miscellaneous orders.

SIGNIFICANCE: The opportunity for face-to-face deliberation is an important component in the promotion of collegiality, enabling the justices to speak in a unified institutional voice. In the contemporary period, however, the conference is of declining significance.

The nature of the conference of the justices has evolved over time, reflecting the changing environment and developing role of the Supreme Court. During its first decade, the Court followed the English practice of issuing seriatim opinions, each justice writing a separate opinion for each case. Among the innovations of Chief Justice John Marshall, in 1801, was the adoption of the opinion of the Court. This permitted the Court to speak in a singular, unified voice, thus enhancing its prestige and promoting greater clarity in its legal pronouncements. Achieving this unity required the justices to negotiate a compromise among their individual opinions. Marshall's practice, followed through much of the nineteenth century, was to conduct conferences during the evening to deliberate cases argued each day. This was facilitated by the fact that Court sessions were then of short duration, the justices having circuit duties during the rest of the year. Residing in a common boardinghouse, the justices dined together and had ample time to reach a common result and a common rationale for the Court's decision. Dissents were relatively few, and concurring opinions were rare.

For much of the early twentieth century, conferences were held on Saturday during the Court's term. Chief Justice Earl Warren moved the conference to Friday in 1955. The justices usually spend the morning voting on writs of *certiorari* to choose the cases the Court will later hear from among those petitions on the discuss list. Typically, some attention is also given to routine orders, such as stays to delay action by the parties of a suit until the Court can resolve their dispute. The remainder of the conference is devoted to deciding the twelve cases argued the previous week. During the 1970's and 1980's an additional conference was introduced on Wednesday afternoon, to discuss the four cases argued the previous Monday, leaving the eight cases argued on Tuesday and Wednesday for the Friday conference.

A reduction in the number of cases heard by the Court eliminated the need for this supplementary conference, and cases were thereafter discussed on Fridays. However, during May and June, when the Court is not hearing oral arguments, the conference is moved to Thursday. In late September, the justices meet in special daylong conferences to discuss the *certiorari* petitions that have arrived over the summer. Additional conferences might be called to meet special needs.

CONFERENCE PROCEDURE

All conferences are held in the conference room, adjacent to the chief justice's chambers. After a ceremonial handshake among all the justices, the chief justice presides over the conference from the head of a long conference table. The senior associate justice sits at the opposite end, and the remaining justices sit around the table, usually in order of seniority. Absolute confidentiality is observed, and no outsider—not even the justice's clerks—may enter the room while the justices are meeting. If messages or items must be delivered to the conference room, a knock on the door will be answered by the most junior justice. Because of this secrecy, the conference is difficult to study. Knowledge of the proceeding comes from docket books and assorted notes by individual justices that have been saved and have become available to the public, often years after the justice's death. Occasional published reflections by justices also shed light on the subject. No doubt the tenor of the conference varies according to the personalities of the justices, the skills of the chief justice, the ideological divisions on the Court, and the contentiousness of the issues under discussion.

Conference discussion tends to be candid, even blunt, but brief.

The chief justice speaks first, outlining the issues of the case and stating his or her views. Other justices speak in order of seniority and may disagree with the chief justice's understanding of the case or its proper resolution. Previously, after every justice spoke, the justices voted in ascending order of seniority, but this practice has been discontinued. The position of each justice is implicit in his or her comments and an apparent majority can usually be discerned without an actual vote. Discussion will then move on to another matter. The assignment of opinion writing occurs soon after the conference. If in the majority, the chief justice assigns the opinion; if not, that task falls to the most senior member of the majority.

In the latter part of the twentieth century, the opportunity for face-to-face deliberation became a scarce luxury, sacrificed to burgeoning caseloads. No longer an instrument for building consensus, the modern conference is mainly an occasion for the justices to state their individual views, make a tentative vote, and gain a sense of the majority. Discussion on each case is perfunctory, with little attempt made to persuade or to negotiate a consensus. A justice might occasionally change his or her opinion on some matter as a result of conference discussion, but this appears to be the exception, not the rule. After many years of working together, the justices rarely surprise their colleagues, and time for extended discussion simply does not exist. The deliberative process continues, but the negotiation of common ground in support of the Court's pronouncements now occurs primarily through the process of drafting and circulating opinions. The pressure of the workload, the growth of the role of clerks, and modern office technology have isolated the justices from one another, as captured in Justice Lewis F. Powell, Jr.'s description of the modern Court as "nine small, independent law firms." Collegiality remains only to the degree that these separate firms come together to criticize each other's work. With this decline in collegiality, the Court has seen a rise in the number of concurrences and dissents filed. The result is that the Court now speaks in a less clear voice.

John C. Hughes

FURTHER READING

Dickson, Del, ed. *The Supreme Court in Conference, 1940-1985: The Private Discussions Behind Nearly Three Hundred Supreme Court Decisions.* New York: Oxford University Press, 2001.

Epstein, Lee, and Jack Knight. *The Choices Justices Make.* Washington, D.C.: Congressional Quarterly, 1998.

Johnson, Timothy Russell. *Oral Arguments and Decision Making on the United States Supreme Court.* Albany: State University of New York Press, 2004.

Lazarus, Edward. *Closed Chambers: The Rise, Fall, and Future of the Modern Supreme Court.* New York: Penguin Books, 1999.

O'Brien, David. *Storm Center.* 7th ed. New York: W. W. Norton, 2005.

Perry, H. W. *Deciding to Decide: Agenda Setting in the United States Supreme Court.* Cambridge, Mass.: Harvard University Press, 1991.

Rehnquist, William H. *The Supreme Court: How It Was, How It Is.* New York: Oxford University Press, 1987.

Schwartz, Bernard. *A History of the Supreme Court.* New York: Oxford University Press, 1993.

SEE ALSO Briefs; *Certiorari,* writ of; Chief justice; Clerks of the justices; Opinions, writing of; Seriatim opinions.

Constitutional Interpretation

DESCRIPTION: Process by which general principles of a constitution are applied by officials to individual laws or actions.

SIGNIFICANCE: The Supreme Court has traditionally had the last word on constitutional interpretation, which can change the powers of government and alter the degree of protection that individuals have from government action. In turn, the permissible scope of interpretation has been determined by what the Court did as it decided cases through its existence.

Chief Justice John Marshall noted, in *Marbury v. Madison* (1803), that the U.S. Constitution requires extensive interpretation. Although it was written and put into effect in the eighteenth century, its creators expected it to last for a long time and assumed that the three branches of the federal government it established would do different things at different times. Although the Constitution purports to control government action, the limits it creates are phrased in broad, general terms and are often vague. Therefore, questions about what each branch is constitutionally allowed to do and the rights of individuals are constantly recurring.

THE NEED FOR FINALITY

Of necessity, all three branches of the federal government, as well as state governments, must sometimes interpret the Constitution. A tacit part of the creation of any law is the assertion that the legislature has the power to pass it. Before the Civil War (1861-1865), when government exercised only traditional and well-explored functions, these interpretations were rarely controversial. After the war, however, because of national expansion and the Industrial Revolution, governments began to legislate in new areas, to impose new taxes, and in general to be more energetic. These new actions often raised questions over whether legislatures or the president had the constitutional power to make them. In the twentieth century, large businesses, political pressure groups, and litigious cranks often have incentives (and money) to file lawsuits to challenge interpretations with which they disagree.

If there is a question over what the Constitution means and it is properly raised in a federal lawsuit, usually the Supreme Court's interpretation prevails. As part of its power, the Court can declare that an action of another branch of government violates some limit on the power of that branch and is therefore void, or unconstitutional. This power of judicial review is the most important of the Court's powers. The Court thus serves as the "umpire" of the political game, telling the various elected "players"—Congress, the president, and the states—what they can and cannot do. Through the late 1990's, the Court declared more than two hundred acts of Congress unconstitutional and invalidated a much larger number of state laws. It is also the guarantor of individual rights, determining how much protection Americans enjoy from government action.

The Constitution does not explicitly grant the Court this interpretive finality, and it is by no means clear why the Court should have it. Marshall himself argued that if interpretation is needed, courts are best suited to the task because they have extensive experience interpreting written documents and because they are sworn to give the Constitution priority over ordinary legislation. Scholars have argued that because federal judges have lifetime appointments and are insulated from political pressure, they can interpret the Constitution relatively free of ambition and political bias. Further, because judges are trained in the law, they are more likely to base their interpretations on legal or moral principles than Congress or the president (who are more likely to be swayed by transitory political concerns). Finally, because courts are weaker than Congress or the president, they pose less danger of becoming tyrannical. If nothing else, a final arbiter is needed in a government with a separation of powers, and public opinion seems comfortable with the Court serving as that arbiter.

JUDICIAL RESTRAINT

However, the actions of elected presidents and legislators—who presumably try to do what the public wants in order to be reelected—can be set aside by the undemocratic decisions of nonelected judges. For this reason, most Court justices believe that they must restrain themselves to avoid coming into conflict with the elected branches too often. Justice Felix Frankfurter argued for this philosophy of judicial self-restraint in numerous texts between 1939 and 1962. He pointed out that courts have no financial or military power and depend on broad support from the public to persuade the other branches to enforce court decisions. If they set aside the democratic decisions of legislatures or presidents too often, this public support will evaporate. Moreover, judges typically have less education in the details of policy and taxation than legislators do.

Justices who follow the philosophy of restraint try to avoid or at least delay interpreting the Constitution. They raise procedural obstacles to prevent lawsuits from being brought or decide cases on non-constitutional grounds. If interpretation cannot be avoided, they try to make their interpretations as narrow and case-bound as possible. Above all, they presume that the actions of other branches are valid and do not declare them unconstitutional unless absolutely necessary.

JUDICIAL ACTIVISM

Justices who follow the philosophy of judicial activism have strong political preferences and believe that they should use constitutional interpretation to write these preferences into law, even if the elected branches disagree. Consequently, they are much more willing to invalidate actions of the other branches.

Activists who supported the economic ideology of laissez-faire controlled the Court between 1895 and 1936. Because they believed that business should be allowed to operate as free of government regula tion as possible, they interpreted the commerce clause and other parts of the Constitution very narrowly. They struck down many laws designed to protect worker health and safety or to otherwise limit how businesses were allowed to operate. By 1936, neither the states nor the federal government had much economic regulatory power left; consequently, neither was able to deal with the Great Depression. Public opinion turned against the Court, and the activist position was discredited. Judicial restraint justices, who became a majority after 1936, overturned many of the activist economic rulings, leaving it to legislatures to determine how extensively they could regulate the economy.

After 1936, most justices have been suspicious of activism. However, that stance enjoyed a resurgence between 1954 and 1969, when activist justices struck down state laws mandating racially segregated public schools and created new court procedures designed to protect the constitutional rights of people accused of crimes. Professor John Hart Ely argued that although elected branches usually can be trusted to operate constitutionally when they deal with economic issues, they can sometimes be perverted by improper election procedures or other structural flaws. If legislatures are malapportioned or voting registration procedures are corrupted so that some people cannot register to vote, the public may not be able to make its wishes known at elections. Majority rule and democracy will not occur. Ely argued that judicial activism is needed to correct these structural flaws when legislatures are unable or unwilling to do so. Following *Baker v. Carr* (1962), the Court ordered legislative reapportionment in many states to ensure that each person's vote counted equally in choosing legislators.

Some justices take compromise positions between activism and restraint. Justice Harlan Fiske Stone argued that courts can defer to legislatures when economics is involved but need to be especially vigilant when legislatures act to limit freedom of speech, press, or religion because these rights are fragile and easily lost. The Court must, in his words, give these political rights a preferred position. In the 1970's the Court used Stone's view as the basis for the strict scrutiny principle: Unlike economic legislation, laws that limit basic rights or that operate to harm politically weak minorities are presumed to be invalid unless they are indispensable to achieving some extremely important government goal. Through the 1990's, the Court continued to construe legislative power very narrowly in such cases.

INTERPRETIVISM

The dispute between judicial activists and restraintists is largely a dispute about when, or how often, the Court should interpret the Constitution. Justices are also divided over how the job should be done. Supreme Court justices have always assumed that they should function as a court of law, by applying principles of interpretation to individual cases in an objective and disinterested way and by treating like cases alike.

However, the Constitution does not contain principles for its own interpretation. These have to be discovered elsewhere, and justices and scholars disagree over the method. Interpretivists, sometimes called originalists, believe that the Constitution should be interpreted as intended by the people who wrote and ratified the Constitution—the Founders. Interpretivists typically believe that there are eternal political principles, such as the belief that power corrupts, which must be controlled if government is to operate fairly. The wise Founders knew these principles, embodied them in the Constitution, and expected these principles to control all constitutional interpretation. Thus, interpretivists claim that they are following the path marked out by the Founders.

In addition, as Justice Clarence Thomas and many others argued, the legitimacy of the Constitution depends on its having been accepted by the people in the ratification procedure in 1789. In that "constitution-making moment," a contract was created between the rulers and the ruled. The Constitution, which is the written part of that contract, secured the consent of the governed for the limited government it set up. However, the people accepted the Constitution as the Founders expected it to be interpreted. The interpretations of the Founders, the unwritten part of the agreement, are thus equally binding. If the Court interprets the Constitution in some other way, governments may come to exercise more powers than the people granted.

When controversies arise about what the Constitution means, interpretivists try to determine what the Founders intended. Most try to learn about the values of the Founders by studying their records and papers. Others seek principles in the records of American and British common law courts because courts discuss and apply the

The U.S. Constitution was first printed in The Pennsylvania Packet, *a daily newspaper, on September 19, 1787.* (Library of Congress)

political values of their times. Still others study traditions and customs. For example, the practice of beginning each session of Congress with a prayer, which has existed since the first Congress wrote the First Amendment in 1790, has been cited as proof that the Founders did not intend that Amendment to forbid all ceremonial prayer in government proceedings. Finally, others, called textualists, try to discover principles embedded in the language of the Constitution by studying how its words and phrases were used in the eighteenth century.

Sometimes the interpretive intent of the Founders can easily be discovered. For example, it is clear that the Founders did not intend the prohibition on cruel and unusual punishments to forbid the death penalty as such because they continued to use it. However, many parts of the Constitution remain stubbornly unclear. Sometimes the intent of the Founders cannot be discovered, and sometimes, they disagreed with one another. In more troubling cases, some values of the Founders, including their toleration of slavery, have become outdated or offensive. Professor Ronald Dworkin, for example, has observed that although the Founders overwhelmingly accepted racially segregated schools and many other governmental inequities, any constitutional interpretation that permitted these inequities to exist today would be overwhelmingly rejected by most Americans.

NONINTERPRETIVISM

For these reasons, noninterpretivists argue that the intent of the Founders should be given little weight in contemporary constitutional interpretation. Most noninterpretivists either deny that there are political principles of eternal validity or else believe that the few such principles that do exist are of such generality that they offer little guidance to dealing with concrete problems. As Chief Justice Earl Warren observed, the rule to "treat people equally except in exceptional cases" does not help a justice trying to decide whether segregated schools should constitute such an exception.

Nor, as Justice William J. Brennan, Jr., has noted, does the Constitution depend for its binding effect on the consent of people in 1789. Instead, he argues, the people must constantly accept the Constitution as it exists today. They do so tacitly, by obeying its requirements. They will continue to do so as long as the Constitution meets their expectations about what it should be like. If there is any conflict between what the law says the Constitution is and what the people want it to be at any moment, then the job of the Court is to sit as a "permanent constitutional convention" and, by interpretation, to revise the Constitution to fit the public expectations.

This is what the Court did in *Brown v. Board of Education* (1954), when it struck down the segregated schools that had long been legally accepted. Significantly, in *Brown*, the Court ignored the history urged on it by interpretivists, saying only that it could not "turn back the clock" to the Civil War or the colonial period. Instead, Chief Justice Warren emphasized sociology, stressing the importance of contemporary education to the ability of individuals to achieve their goals and function as citizens.

As compared with interpretivists, noninterpretivists assume that change is more rapid and cuts deeper into political values and beliefs. Though they insist that the values of contemporary citizens should be given priority, they offer little guidance on how to discover these values. Nor do they explain how to tell the difference between basic principles and values, which should govern views on many political issues over time, and short-term political principles specific to an issue. Finally, noninterpretivists do not explain the source of the power they claim to continually revise the Constitution. Though that document contains procedures for formal amendment, it nowhere gives the Court the right to serve as a "permanent amending convention."

OTHER VIEWS

In an influential 1959 article, Professor Herbert Wechsler argued that any constitutional interpretation, to be fair, must be made on the basis of a neutral principle, a rule capable of being applied uniformly to all similar cases without creating an advantage for any particular political force. Neutral principles may be those of the Founders or may be discovered later. His examples are derived from moral principles and relate to controversies of the period: A state cannot escape limits on public action by transferring some government function (such as holding primary elections) to private control, and racial segregation (a denial of equality per se) may constitute a denial of freedom of association. Presumably, the neutrality of such principles can be tested by philosophers who study critical cases.

Neutrality has long been an important consideration in constitutional law. Therefore, the holding that the First Amendment guarantees the right to hold peaceable public parades cannot be considered fair unless it is applied impartially to Republicans and Democrats and civil rights activists and members of the Ku Klux Klan. Professor Wechsler suggests that interpretive principles can be similarly neutral and should not be used by the Court unless they are.

The neutral principles approach seems intuitively fair. In legal proceedings, neutrality seems achievable. Thus, courts insist that laws be knowable in advance, for example, and that lawyers for both sides in a lawsuit have adequate time to prepare their cases. However, it may not be possible to find nontrivial principles that are truly neutral. Wechsler suggests that equality may be such a principle, but others have disagreed.

Most of the individual rights guaranteed by the Constitution are not meant to be absolute. The public is protected, for example, against only unreasonable searches and seizures; the privilege of habeas corpus must not be suspended "unless the public safety requires." However, some parts of the Constitution are phrased to suggest that they allow no exceptions. For these, absolutists argue that the Constitution should always be interpreted to forbid government action. For example, absolutists interpret the First Amendment statement that Congress shall make no law abridging freedom of speech as meaning that Congress cannot regulate sedition, the utterance of threats, or the publishing of obscene literature.

Absolutists make it unnecessary to draw precise legal lines between things that may be vague and subjective. If they prevailed, it would be unnecessary, for example, for justices to distinguish between obscene material, which legislatures could ban, and non-obscene pornography, which is protected under the First Amendment. However, this would require the acceptance of extremes of behavior offensive to both Founders and contemporary Americans. In practice, absolutists tend to allow exceptions by casuistry. Uttering a threat, for example, is said to be a form of action, not speech. The publication of obscene material is seen as an incitement of violence against women, rather than as freedom of the press.

Finally, in cases in which rights conflict, the Court has created legal rules, or doctrines, for handling the conflict. Sometimes rights are placed in a hierarchy. Those rights of criminally accused persons that are necessary for courts to hold fair criminal trials, for example, have been preferred to individual rights to speak or publish. The latter, in turn, have been preferred to the rights of political leaders and bureaucrats to act with "administrative efficiency."

In other cases, rights have been balanced against one another. In *United States v. Nixon* (1974), for example, in which the president unsuccessfully sought to keep secret audiotapes that had been requested by former aides who needed them to defend themselves against criminal charges, the Court balanced the need of the president to keep information confidential against the constitutional rights of the defendants in a criminal court.

Paul Lermack

FURTHER READING

For a good starting point for exploring how the Court influences constitutional change, see Westel Woodbury Willoughby's *The Supreme Court of the United States: Its History and Influence in Our Constitutional System* (Union, N.J.: Lawbook Exchange, 2001). *Creating Constitutional Change: Clashes Over Power and Liberty in the Supreme Court*, edited by Gregg Ivers and Kevin T. McGuire (Charlottesville: University of Virginia Press, 2004), offers a concise analysis of the process through which the justices go in making decisions that effect changes in the Constitution.

Maxwell L. Stearns's *Constitutional Process: A Social Choice Analysis of Supreme Court Decision Making* (Ann Arbor: University of Michigan Press, 2000) and Timothy Russell Johnson's *Oral Arguments and Decision Making on the United States Supreme Court* (Albany: State University of New York Press, 2004) both closely examine how the Court makes its decisions. Lee Epstein and Jack Knight have also described how the Court goes about its work in *The Choices Justices Make* (Washington, D.C.: Congressional Quarterly, 1998). The most comprehensive presentation of the various approaches to interpretation is Craig

Ducat's *Constitutional Interpretation* (8th ed. Belmont, Calif.: Thomson/West, 2004).

Activism and restraint are examined in *Supreme Court Activism and Restraint* (Lexington, Mass.: Lexington Books, 1982), edited by Stephen C. Halpern and Charles M. Lamb, and Christopher Wolfe's *Judicial Activism: Bulwark of Liberty or Precarious Security?* (Rev. ed. Lanham, Md.: Rowman & Littlefield, 1997). Leif Carter has written an accessible introduction to the problem of original intent, *Contemporary Constitutional Lawmaking* (New York: Pergamon, 1986). Judge Robert H. Bork argues for one form of interpretivism in *The Tempting of America* (New York: Simon & Schuster, 1990), and scholar Michael Perry examines noninterpretivism in *The Constitution, the Courts, and Human Rights* (New Haven, Conn.: Yale University Press, 1982) and interpretivism in *The Constitution in the Courts: Law or Politics?* (New York: Oxford University Press, 1994).

Herbert Wechsler's views are best described in his own article, "Toward Neutral Principles of Constitutional Law," *Harvard Law Review* 73 (1959). Mark Tushnet demonstrates the difficulty of applying such an approach in practice in "Following the Rules Laid Down: A Critique of Interpretivism and Neutral Principles," *Harvard Law Review* 96 (1983): 781. Finally, the Court's traditional control of interpretation has not gone unchallenged. Tushnet takes a critical perspective in *Taking the Constitution Away from the Courts* (Princeton, N.J.: Princeton University Press, 1999).

SEE ALSO *Baker v. Carr*; *Brown v. Board of Education*; Constitutional law; Judicial activism; Judicial review; Judicial self-restraint; *Marbury v. Madison*.

Constitutional Law

DESCRIPTION: Dynamic body of law that defines and limits the powers of government and sets out its organizational structure.

SIGNIFICANCE: As the fundamental law contained in the U.S. Constitution and in Supreme Court decisions interpreting that document, constitutional law blends legal decisions with elements of politics and political theory, history, economics, public policy, philosophy, and ethics.

A resilient document, the U.S. Constitution has endured with only twenty-seven amendments since its formulation in 1787. Its sweeping language and generalities allow change and interpretation in the face of altered circumstances, from the changing human condition to the changing composition of the Supreme Court. The Constitution contains few rules and is not self-explanatory. That lack of specificity was intentional. The Framers outlined their general intent to create the fundamentals of a national government, prescribing how it should operate and limiting its scope of power. The ongoing interpretative process allows the provisions of the Constitution to change and adapt over time. The Court refers to the original Constitution because by doing so, it can bring resolution of the new and often divisive issues of each generation. The genius of constitutionalism, therefore, lies in the opportunities provided in the document for change and continuity, the method of judicial interpretation, and the overall skill and sensitivity of the justices. The fact that the justices are lifetime appointees frees them from concerns about approval by political leaders and voters and permits concentration on the issues.

CONSTITUTIONAL DECISION MAKING

Virtually all cases before the Court involve seeking review of a decision by a federal court of appeals or a state supreme court. As the final authority on federal matters and questions dealing with the Constitution and treaties, the Court exercises appellate jurisdiction (appeals) and functions as a trial court (original jurisdiction) only in certain limited situations involving ambassadors or where a state is a party. Most of the cases reach the Court for review by means of a writ of *certiorari*, or through the exercise of the Court's discretion. This means that the Court has almost complete control of its docket. Of the 7,000 petitions for review annually, only 2 percent are granted. The Court issues an average of 110 opinions per year, permitting a selected group of policy issues to be addressed.

The Court is shrouded in secrecy, assuming some of the awe and mystery of the document it interprets. Some have criticized the Court for remaining in an "ivory tower" far removed from "we the people" set out in the preamble to the Constitution. Decisions to grant or deny review are made in secret conferences attended only by the nine justices with no support staff. A traditional unwritten rule specifies that a case is accepted for review if four justices feel that it merits the Court's attention (rule of four) and that it would serve the interests of justice. The Court does not have to explain its refusal.

When the Court decides to hear a case, the clerk schedules oral argument during which the justices may interrupt and ask questions of the attorneys to clarify, debate, or explain the written briefs. Cases are discussed in secret conferences following oral argument. It takes a majority vote to decide a case.

Following the conference and ensuing discussion, an opinion or reasoned argument explaining the legal issues in the case and the precedents on which the opinion is based must be drafted. The manner in which a majority opinion is written can have a great impact on Americans. That impact depends in part on who writes the opinion and how it is written, and also on the extent of support or dissent by the remaining justices. A 5-4 plurality opinion does not demonstrate the firm conviction of the Court that is present in a unanimous or 8-1 decision.

Any justice can write a separate opinion. If justices agree with the majority's decision but disagree with its reasoning, they may write a concurring opinion. If they disagree with both the result and reasoning contained in the majority opinion, they may write a dissenting opinion or simply go on the record as dissenting without an opinion. More than one justice can join in a concurring or dissenting opinion.

Decision making or opinion writing is a painstaking and laborious process. The time involved varies from one justice to another depending on the complexity of the issues in the case. The actual reporting of decisions has changed from the days in which members of the Court read long opinions aloud, sometimes taking days to do so. When Charles Evans Hughes became chief justice in 1930, he encouraged the delivery of summaries of opinions. That practice has continued, and the justice writing the majority opinion delivers the summary. Dissenting justices deliver their own opinions. Computerization and Lexis and Westlaw legal databases have made newly decided opinions accessible to all within hours of their release.

THE HIGHEST COURT

Decisions of the Court are final because there is no higher court to which to appeal. Its interpretation of statutes can be reversed only by congressional legislation, and its constitutional rulings overturned only by constitutional amendment. Absent these remedies, all courts are obliged to follow the Supreme Court in matters of federal law. In its decisions, the Court attempts to adhere to precedent, or *stare decisis*, and in that capacity serves as final authority in constitutional matters, thereby providing a uniform interpretation of the law, historical continuity, stability, and predictability. Just as the Court sets its own agenda and controls what it hears, accepting or rejecting cases according to individual and collective goals such as avoiding troublesome issues, resolving legal conflicts, and establishing policies favored by the justices, Court decisions are group products shaped by the law, the Court and the country's environment, and the personal value systems of and interactions among the justices.

The power to define the Constitution makes the Court unique among government institutions. Through the exercise of its constitutional role together with the rule of law, the Court has wielded far-reaching power. The proper functioning of federalism and the scope of the rights of the individual depend on the actions of the Court, whose words mark the boundaries of the branches and departments of government.

The justices function as "nine little law firms," autonomous but working as a collegial body to decide a case. In important cases, the opinions issued by the Court are often negotiated among the members, the result of a cooperative collaboration in which the end product is the joint work of all rather than the product of the named author alone.

SELF-IMPOSED LIMITATIONS

The Court imposes certain limitations or barriers before accepting a case for review. It poses certain threshold questions to deal with tactical issues that must be resolved before the Court reaches the substance of the controversy. Referred to as "judicial restraint," if these elements are not overcome, the Court will not exercise jurisdiction over a case. Article III, section 2, of the Constitution requires that there exist an ongoing "case or controversy" at all stages of the proceedings, including appeal. As interpreted by the Court, these words limit the power of federal courts to resolving disputes between adversaries whose rights are truly in collision. Often called "justiciability," the requirement provides concreteness when a question is precisely framed. The case, therefore, must present a live dispute.

Precluded are advisory opinions, or giving advice on abstract or hypothetical situations, as the Court ruled in *Muskrat v. United States* (1911), and moot cases, or those that have already been resolved, settled, or feigned, or those in which circumstances or time have removed the dispute or conflict because there is nothing for a court to decide, as it ruled in *DeFunis v. Odegaard* (1974). Several narrow exceptions to the mootness rule exist where conduct is of short duration but capable of repetition such as election disputes or abortion cases such as *Roe v. Wade* and its companion case *Doe v. Bolton* (1973). In *Baker v. Carr* (1962), the Court determined that political questions or those matters more properly applicable to another branch of government will not be accepted, nor will friendly or collusive suits and test cases. Standing to sue requires that the litigants have a personal stake in the outcome of the case, having suffered an actual injury, in order to assure concrete adverseness. Ripeness requires the issues in the case to be clearly delineated and sharply outlined, not premature, in flux, or abstract. Moreover, the Court will not engage in speculation, contingencies, or predictions or issue extrajudicial advice.

JUDICIAL REVIEW

Courts participate in the development of constitutional law through judicial review. In the landmark case *Marbury v. Madison* (1803), considered to be the point at which constitutional law begins, the Court held that Article III empowers courts to review government actions and invalidate those found to be repugnant to the Constitution by declaring them unconstitutional. The supremacy clause of Article IV states that no provision of state law and no legislative enactment may conflict with the national Constitution, which is the supreme law of the land.

The Framers of the Constitution decentralized control through federalism, considered one of the most important contributions to government. Federalism is a dual system in which powers are divided between national and state authorities.

BILL OF RIGHTS

Protecting the fundamental rights of individuals was considered of the utmost importance. The Framers believed that explicit enumeration of those rights would make the rights more secure. In order to achieve ratification of the main body of the Constitution, therefore, in 1791 the Framers appended to it a Bill of Rights, consisting of the first ten amendments of the present document. While the body of the main Constitution concerns government, the Bill of Rights represents the popular perception of constitutional guarantees.

Basic to American identity is the First Amendment and its central guarantees of freedom of speech, press, religion, assembly, and right to petition for redress of grievances. Despite language to the contrary, the rights contained in the Bill of Rights are not absolute. In the speech area, for example, certain categories of expression can be regulated; others are not protected at all. "Pure" speech that creates no danger to the public is protected. However, if speech advocates an imminent lawless action that presents a "clear and present danger," the speech loses its protection, as the Court ruled in *Schenck v. United States* (1919). In *Texas v. Johnson* (1989), the Court found that symbolic speech or use of actions as a substitute for words is generally protected, such as flag burning as a controversial but valid expression of political views. Obscenity or pornography, defamatory communications (libel and slander), and "fighting words" that provoke an immediate breach of the peace do not receive First Amendment protection.

Some rights that Americans consider basic to their fundamental freedoms are not mentioned specifically in the Constitution. Among these are the right of personal privacy, which protects the individual from state interference. The Court struggled with the constitutional foundation of the right, suggesting various sources: the due process guarantee of the Fourteenth Amendment and the penumbras or emanations from the interests protected by the First, Third, Fourth, Fifth, and Ninth Amendments (*Griswold v. Connecticut*, 1965).

Marcia J. Weiss

FURTHER READING

Maxwell L. Stearns's *Constitutional Process: A Social Choice Analysis of Supreme Court Decision Making* (Ann Arbor: University of Michigan Press, 2000) and Timothy Russell Johnson's *Oral Arguments and Decision Making on the United States Supreme Court* (Albany: State University of New York Press, 2004) are useful explorations of how the Supreme Court makes its decisions. For a broad overview of how Supreme Court decisions influence constitutional change, see Westel Woodbury Willoughby's *The Supreme Court of the United States: Its History and Influence in Our Constitutional System* (Union, N.J.: Lawbook Exchange, 2001).

Creating Constitutional Change: Clashes Over Power and Liberty in the Supreme Court, edited by Gregg Ivers and Kevin T. McGuire (Charlottesville: University of Virginia Press, 2004), offers a concise analysis of the process through which the justices go in making decisions that effect changes in the Constitution. Two well-written works containing detailed treatment with case references and quotations are Joan Biskupic and Elder Witt's *The Supreme Court and the Powers of the American Government* (Washington, D.C.: Congressional Quarterly, 1997) and *The Supreme Court at Work* (2d ed. Washington, D.C.: Congressional Quarterly, 1997), with biographical sketches of the justices and illustrations.

Lawrence Baum's *The Supreme Court* (8th ed. Washington, D.C.: Congressional Quarterly, 2004) examines the role of the Court, the justices, the decision-making process, factors that influence the Court, activism in policy making, and the Court's significance. Organized by case themes, *Decision: How the Supreme Court Decides Cases* (New York: Oxford University Press, 1996) by Bernard Schwartz offers a behind-the-scenes look at how the Court decides cases. Archibald Cox's *The Court and the Constitution* (Boston: Houghton

Mifflin, 1987) is a readable yet scholarly account of how the Court shaped constitutional law.

Peter G. Renstrom's *Constitutional Law and Young Adults* (Santa Barbara, Calif.: ABC-Clio, 1992) is a guide to the Constitution, the court system, and key provisions of the Bill of Rights and Fourteenth Amendment with case references. It is comprehensive in scope and comprehensible to the general reader. David P. Currie's *The Constitution of the United States: A Primer for the People* (Chicago: University of Chicago Press, 1988) contains an overview of the document and the major concepts contained in it in language intended for the general reader.

SEE ALSO Bill of Rights; Constitutional interpretation; Federalism; Fourteenth Amendment; Incorporation doctrine; Judicial activism; Judicial self-restraint; *Marbury v. Madison*; Separation of powers.

Freedom of Contract

DESCRIPTION: Also known as "liberty of contract," the doctrine that individual persons and business firms should be free to enter into contracts without undue interference from government.

SIGNIFICANCE: From 1897 to 1937, a probusiness Supreme Court used the freedom of contract doctrine to overturn numerous economic regulations designed to protect the interests of workers and the general public.

The Supreme Court recognized that the Fifth Amendment's due process clause protected some substantive rights to property and liberty as early as *Scott v. Sandford* (1857). The drafters of the Fourteenth Amendment, among other goals, wanted to protect the liberty and equality of African Americans to enter into legally binding contracts involving property and employment. With the growth of state regulations in the late nineteenth century, therefore, it was not surprising that proponents of laissez-faire capitalism seized on the Fourteenth Amendment's due process clause as a means of promoting substantive liberties in matters of business and economics. Justice Stephen J.

Field and jurist Thomas M. Cooley were among the most influential proponents of this substantive due process approach, which was soon accepted by several state courts.

After debating the concept on numerous occasions, a majority of the Court finally accepted the idea that the Fourteenth Amendment protected a substantive freedom of contract in *Allgeyer v. Louisiana* (1897). In this case, the Court invalidated a Louisiana law that made it illegal for residents of the state to enter into insurance contracts by mail with out-of-state companies. Writing for the majority, Justice Rufus W. Peckham declared that U.S. citizens enjoyed the freedom to make contracts relevant to the pursuit of their economic interests.

THE LOCHNER ERA

Through the four decades following *Allgeyer*, the Court looked on freedom of contract as a normative ideal and required states to assume a high burden for proving that any restraint on the liberty was justified on the basis of accepted police powers, such as protecting the public's safety, health, or morality. The most prominent cases usually involved legislation regulating terms of employment, such as maximum working hours and minimum wages. In *Lochner v. New York* (1905), for example, a five-member majority overturned a labor law limiting the number of hours that bakers could work each week, and the majority insisted that employees should have the freedom to work as many hours as they wished. In *Adair v. United States* (1908) and *Coppage v. Kansas* (1915), the Court struck down federal and state laws that outlawed yellow dog contracts (employment contracts in which workers agree not to join unions). The majority of the Court was not impressed with the inequality in bargaining positions between employers and workers. Justice Oliver Wendell Holmes wrote vigorous dissents in such cases.

Nevertheless, the freedom of contract doctrine was used in ways that would later be considered progressive. In *Buchanan v. Warley* (1917), for example, the concept was a major reason for the Court's overturning of a St. Louis segregation ordinance that prohibited whites from selling residential housing to African Americans.

The Court often accepted the constitutionality of restraints on the freedom of contract, but only when a majority concluded that a restraint was a reasonable means for enforcing legitimate police powers. For example, the Court in *Holden v. Hardy* (1898) upheld a Utah law that made it illegal for miners to work more than eight hours a day because of the manifest dangers of underground mining. Likewise, in *Muller v. Oregon* (1908), the Court determined that the special health needs of women provided justification for limiting their industrial workday to ten hours. Yet, in *Adkins v. Children's Hospital* (1923), a bare majority overturned the District of Columbia's law of minimum wage for women. The obvious inconsistency between *Muller* and *Children's Hospital* reflected the inherent subjectivity in all decisions grounded in substantive due process.

JUDICIAL REVOLUTION OF 1937

The Court began to moderate its position on freedom of contract after Charles Evans Hughes became chief justice in 1930. During President Franklin D. Roosevelt's first term, nevertheless, four conservative justices—dubbed the Four Horsemen—remained firmly committed to the *Lochner/Adair* line of thinking. In *Morehead v. New York ex rel. Tipaldo* (1936), Owen J. Roberts joined the four to overturn New York's minimum-wage law. During the 1936 election, *Morehead* was widely denounced and was one of several cases that led to Roosevelt's Court-packing plan. For several reasons, Roberts abandoned the Four Horsemen in *West Coast Hotel Co. v. Parrish* (1937), which upheld Washington state's minimum-wage law. Speaking for a majority of five, Hughes acknowledged that the Constitution protected liberty, but he defined liberty as the absence of arbitrary restraints. Two weeks later, the Court abandoned its *Adair* precedent in *National Labor Relations Board v. Jones and Laughlin Steel Corp.*, upholding the National Labor Relations (Wagner) Act's protections of labor's right to organize and join unions.

After the Court reversed itself in 1937, it never again struck down a public policy based on the freedom of contract doctrine. In effect, it almost entirely abandoned any judicial supervision based on the doctrine—a development that is part of its movement toward exercising only minimal scrutiny of all economic regulations. Since then, the Court has upheld economic regulations only when they have appeared to be rationally related to legitimate governmental interests.

303

The Court might resurrect the freedom of contract doctrine if it were to find some governmental regulation of contracts totally unreasonable or arbitrary. Although the Court lost interest in freedom of contract after 1937, it did not entirely stop reading substantive due process guarantees into the Fifth and Fourteenth Amendments.

Thomas Tandy Lewis

FURTHER READING

Cefrey, Holly. *The Sherman Antitrust Act: Getting Big Business Under Control.* New York: Rosen Publishing Group, 2004.

Corwin, Edward. *Liberty Against Government: The Rise, Flowering, and Decline of a Famous Judicial Concept.* Reprint. Westport, Conn.: Greenwood Press, 1978.

Ely, James, Jr. *The Guardian of Every Other Right: A Constitutional History of Property Rights.* New York: Oxford University Press, 1992.

Price, Polly J. *Property Rights: Rights and Liberties Under the Law.* Santa Barbara, Calif.: ABC-Clio, 2003.

Seigan, Bernard. *Economic Liberties and the Constitution.* Chicago: University of Chicago Press, 1980.

SEE ALSO *Allgeyer v. Louisiana*; Bankruptcy law; Capitalism; Commerce, regulation of; Contracts clause; Due process, substantive; Judicial scrutiny; *Lochner v. New York*; Police powers; Privacy, right to.

Contracts Clause

DATE: 1789

DESCRIPTION: Article I, section 10, of the U.S. Constitution prohibits states from impairing contractual obligations. Through Supreme Court interpretation, the prohibition extends to state impairment of contracts not only among private parties but also between private parties and the states themselves.

SIGNIFICANCE: During the nineteenth century, the contracts clause became a primary constitutional weapon to defend private business from state regulation, but it fell into relative disuse in the 1930's. The Court under Warren E. Burger revived the contracts clause in the late 1970's, although it did not regain its earlier status.

The Framers drafted the contracts clause because they were concerned with various attacks of the debtor class on property interests. In a variety of ways, state legislatures enacted laws that effectively relieved debtors of their contractual obligations. However, the first important Supreme Court interpretations of the contracts clause involved a legislative grant of land and the terms of a corporate charter, not a state impairment of contractual relations between private parties.

PROTECTION FROM THE STATES

In *Fletcher v. Peck* (1810), Chief Justice John Marshall found that public grants by a sovereign state are subject to the same limitations as are contracts among private parties. Once a contract is granted, the grantors imply they will not reassert their original rights, and therefore, a state does not possess the authority to revoke its own grants. Marshall applied this same absolutist mode of constitutional interpretation to *Dartmouth College v. Woodward* (1819). He held that a charter granted to the trustees of Dartmouth College in 1769 by the British crown could not be amended after the Revolutionary War by the New Hampshire legislature. In *Sturges v. Crowninshield* (1819), the Court held that in the absence of congressional legislation, states may enact bankruptcy laws. If a state bankruptcy law exists at the time when a contract is consummated, the Court held in *Ogden v. Saunders* (1827) that the state bankruptcy provisions are implied, and therefore, the contract is not impaired by the state law. Despite this particular setback for the doctrine of vested property rights, Marshall presided over a Court that created the judicial precedents protecting individual creditors and business organizations from the states' regulatory power.

The Court led by Chief Justice Roger Brooke Taney continued to apply the contracts clause to a wide array of disputes, including debtor-creditor relations, state legislation regulating and taxing banks, and even an agreement between the federal government and the states. The most noteworthy decision of the Taney Court is *Charles River Bridge v. Warren Bridge* (1837). Although the ruling in the case permits the exercise of state power, Taney's decision stands for the proposition that only those rights explicitly spelled out in corporate charters are protected by the contracts clause.

STRONGER STATES

After the Civil War (1861-1865) to the 1880's the Court continued to render decisions generally favorable to propertied interests. For example, during this period municipalities attempted to repudiate their bonded indebtedness. The Court ruled against them in all but a few of the two hundred cases that came before it. However, late in this period the Court began to recognize the legitimate use of state police powers as a limitation on private power in the economic market-place. It permitted states to change the terms of bond issues and to regulate the rates railroads charged their customers. The Court also refused to apply the contracts clause to the federal government. The most celebrated pronouncement of this period is found in Chief Justice Morrison R. Waite's opinion in *Stone v. Mississippi* (1880): "No legislature can bargain away the public health or the public morals. The people themselves cannot do it, much less their servants."

Chief Justice Charles Evans Hughes's majority opinion in *Home Building and Loan Association v. Blaisdell* (1934) marks the start of a rapid decline in the Court's willingness to strike down state laws in the name of the contracts clause. Minnesota sought to slow farm and home foreclosures by temporarily delaying the period of loan repayments. Hughes established criteria for when a state may interfere with the obligation of contracts among private parties. Because the state law did not alter the basic integrity of the contractual obligation and because the alteration was designed to apply in a temporary fashion, the Court's 4-3 majority was able to distinguish this case from the abuses that took place before the 1787 Constitutional Convention.

By the mid-1960's, the Court completed the process of rejecting constitutional absolutism in favor of a balancing-of-interests approach to contract clause interpretation. For example, Texas amended in 1941 a 1910 public land sale law. The original law allowed purchasers who had missed their payments to reinstate their claims at any time upon payment of the missed interest but before a third party obtained title to the land in question. The 1941 amendment limited the repayment option to five years. Upholding the unilateral change, Justice Byron R. White in *El Paso v. Simmons* (1965) explicitly rejects the absolutism of the past with the observation that not every modification of a contractual promise impairs the obligation of contract.

THE RESURGENCE

In a pair of cases, the Burger Court created the necessary precedents for a resurgence of the contracts clause. In *United States Trust Co. v. New Jersey* (1977) and *Allied Structural Steel Co. v. Spannaus* (1978), a majority of justices employed a balancing-of-interests approach in a way that favored the interests of private litigants over states' interests. After the contractual impairment in question was demonstrated to be significant and not minor, the Court carefully scrutinized whether the impairment was both necessary and reasonable. Using this version of the balancing test, the Burger Court found in both cases against the state and in favor of private property.

Subsequently, the Court was asked to extend its reasoning to eminent domain and equal protection matters, but it consistently refused to do so. The contracts clause does not appear to be destined to a resurgence reminiscent of the days of John Marshall. However, because the balancing-of-interests test by its nature is highly subjective, a sufficiently property-minded Court may employ it at any time.

Albert P. Melone

FURTHER READING

Ely, James, Jr. *The Guardian of Every Other Right: A Constitutional History of Property Rights*. New York: Oxford University Press, 1992.

Fried, Charles. *Saying What the Law Is: The Constitution in the Supreme Court*. Cambridge, Mass.: Harvard University Press, 2004.

Magrath, C. Peter. *Yazoo: The Case of "Fletcher v. Peck."* New York: W. W. Norton, 1966.

Melone, Albert P. "The Contract Clause and Supreme Court Decisionmaking: A Bicentennial Retrospective." *Midsouth Political Science Journal* 9 (1988): 41-63.

_____. "*Mendelson v. Wright*: Understanding the Contract Clause." *Western Political Quarterly* 41 (1988): 791-799.

Price, Polly J. *Property Rights: Rights and Liberties Under the Law*. Santa Barbara, Calif.: ABC-Clio, 2003.

Wright, Benjamin F., Jr. *The Contract Clause of the Constitution*. Cambridge, Mass.: Harvard University Press, 1938.

SEE ALSO Bankruptcy law; Capitalism; Commerce, regulation of; Contract, freedom of; Due process, substantive; Police powers; Privacy, right to.

Right to Counsel

DESCRIPTION: The opportunity for defendants in federal criminal proceedings to be represented by lawyers, as guaranteed by the Sixth Amendment to the U.S. Constitution.

SIGNIFICANCE: The right to legal counsel gives people accused of crimes access to expert help in defending themselves in the complex arena of a criminal trial. In 1963 the Supreme Court interpreted the Fourteenth Amendment as extending this element of due process to defendants in state trials.

Although the Sixth Amendment of the U.S. Constitution appeared to contain the right to legal counsel, the exact meaning of that provision was unclear until interpreted by Congress and the Supreme Court. In 1790, while the Sixth Amendment was still being ratified, Congress passed the Federal Crimes Act, which required that defendants in federal capital cases be provided with legal representation. The Court extended this same protection to all federal criminal cases, regardless of whether they involved the death penalty, in *Johnson v. Zerbst* (1938).

SPECIAL CIRCUMSTANCES DOCTRINE

Although some states required the appointment of lawyers even before the Sixth Amendment was ratified, there was no national code of due process that obligated the states to provide legal help for people accused of crimes. It was not until 1932 that the Court imposed even a limited requirement on state courts to provide legal counsel, and as late as 1963, some states still refused to pay for lawyers for indigent defendants.

In *Powell v. Alabama* (1932), the first Scottsboro case, the Court, by a 7-2 majority, overturned Alabama's convictions of nine African American youths for raping two white women. The young men had been given a *pro forma* trial and sentenced to death. Although they had received court-appointed lawyers, the attorneys provided a weak defense. The trial judge behaved in an overtly biased fashion toward the defendants, and evidence that might have cast doubt on Alabama's case was never presented by the young men's lawyers. In his majority opinion, Justice George Sutherland did not extend the right to counsel to all state criminal cases, but he did establish the "special circumstances" doctrine. The Court ruled that in state capital cases where there were special circumstances, such as the illiteracy of the defendant, state trial judges were obligated to appoint competent lawyers to represent the accused.

For more than thirty years, the special circumstances doctrine would be the law of the land, requiring state courts to appoint legal counsel in only the most obvious and serious situations of defendant need.

A RECONSIDERATION

Although the Court had the opportunity to apply the right to counsel to all state criminal cases in *Betts v. Brady* (1942), it declined to do so, sticking to the case-by-case scheme it had prescribed in the *Powell* case. It was not until the 1963 case of *Gideon v. Wainwright* that the Court finally retired the special circumstances doctrine. Clarence Gideon was a drifter with a history of committing petty crimes. He was accused of breaking into a pool hall and stealing some money and liquor. Although Gideon asked the trial judge to appoint to him a lawyer, the judge, relying on *Betts*, refused to do so. After a failed attempt at defending himself, Gideon was sentenced to a long term in prison. Gideon appealed his conviction on Sixth and Fourteenth Amendment grounds to the Supreme Court.

The Court had been looking for just the right case to overrule what most of them considered a flawed decision in *Betts v. Brady*. To reverse *Betts*, the Court needed a case in which an intelligent person, denied a lawyer, had been unable to successfully defend himself. Because Gideon was an intelligent man, there could be no question that the trial judge might have improperly denied him special circumstances status. Likewise, because Gideon was white, there could be no question of possible racial discrimination to muddy the waters. The charges against Gideon were not complicated. Gideon was an intelligent man, with a sympathetic, even helpful trial judge, who failed miserably to defend himself against noncomplex charges. This made *Gideon* the perfect case to overrule the special circumstances doctrine, and on March 18, 1963, a unanimous Supreme Court, speaking through Justice Hugo L. Black, applied the right to counsel to all state criminal proceedings.

In *Argersinger v. Hamlin* (1972) and *Scott v. Illinois* (1979), the Court extended the right to counsel to misdemeanor trials that resulted in jail sentences but not to those that resulted in fines or lesser punishment.

THE PRETRIAL PERIOD

Gideon left many important questions unanswered, including at what point in the criminal investigation a suspect who requested a lawyer had to be provided with one. In *Escobedo v. Illinois* (1964), the Court ruled that a suspect asking for counsel during a police interrogation had to be granted representation.

In *Miranda v. Arizona* (1966), the Court went a step further, requiring the police to advise suspects of their right to a lawyer even if they did not ask to speak with an attorney. According to the Court, a person suspected of committing a crime should be provided with a lawyer at the moment that individual ceases being one of several possible suspects and becomes the principal focus of the criminal investigation. The decisions in these two cases showed that, in the Court's collective mind, the Sixth Amendment right to counsel was firmly connected to the Fifth Amendment's protection from compulsory self-incrimination.

Marshall R. King

FURTHER READING

Garcia, Alfredo. *The Sixth Amendment in Modern American Jurisprudence.* Westport, Conn.: Greenwood, 1992.

Horne, Gerald. *"Powell v. Alabama": The Scottsboro Boys and American Justice.* New York: Franklin Watts, 1997.

Lewis, Anthony. *Gideon's Trumpet.* 1964. New York: Vintage, 1989.

Stephen, John, and Earl Sweeney. *Officer's Interrogation Handbook.* New York: LexisNexis, 2004.

Taylor, John B. *Right to Counsel and Privilege Against Self-Incrimination: Rights and Liberties Under the Law.* Santa Barbara, Calif.: ABC-Clio, 2004.

Tomkovicz, James J. *The Right to the Assistance of Counsel: A Reference Guide to the United States Constitution.* Westport, Conn.: Greenwood Press, 2002.

Wice, Paul B. *"Miranda v. Arizona": "You Have the Right to Remain Silent. . . . "* New York: Franklin Watts, 1996.

SEE ALSO Bill of Rights; Exclusionary rule; Fortas, Abe; Fourteenth Amendment; *Gideon v. Wainwright*; Incorporation doctrine; Miranda rights; *Rompilla v. Beard*; Self-incrimination, immunity against; Sixth Amendment.

Court-Packing Plan

DATE: 1937

DESCRIPTION: President Franklin D. Roosevelt's proposal to enlarge the federal judiciary in order to liberalize the Supreme Court and protect New Deal legislation.

SIGNIFICANCE: In the proposal's wake, the Court accepted the New Deal's expansion of government power, but Roosevelt lost congressional support and later New Deal social reform was derailed.

Franklin D. Roosevelt inherited a Republican-dominated federal judiciary when he became president in 1933 and had no opportunity to appoint a new justice during his first term. The Supreme Court then consisted of three liberal justices, two moderates, and four conservatives, with six of these justices over seventy years of age. The nation's economy was still suffering the effects of the Great Depression, and Roosevelt developed a set of New Deal programs designed to boost the economy through legislation and government regulation of business and industry.

In 1935 the Court began to reject New Deal legislation as giving unconstitutional powers to the federal government. These decisions were frequently divided, with moderate Justice Owen J. Roberts creating a majority by voting with the conservatives. In January of 1935, the Court rejected provisions of the National Industrial Recovery Act (NIRA) by an 8-1 vote. In May, the Court ruled five to four that the Railway Retirement Act of 1934 was unconstitutional. On May 27, a day known as Black Monday, the Court unanimously invalidated the code-making and price-fixing powers of Title I of the NIRA in *Schechter Poultry Corp. v. United States*, struck down the Frazier-Lemke Farm Bankruptcy Act of 1934 in *Louisville Joint Stock Land Bank v. Radford*, and voided presidential removal of regulatory commission members in *Humphrey's Executor v. United States*. The Court's 6-3 decision in *United States v. Butler* (1936) revoked the processing tax set up by the Agricultural Adjustment Act of 1933. During the spring of 1936, a divided Court announced its decision in *Carter v. Carter Coal Co.*, declaring the Guffey Coal Act of 1935 unconstitutional, and its decision in *Morehead v. New York ex rel. Tipaldo*, invalidating New York State's minimum-wage law. These rulings appeared to threaten the existence of Social Security, the National Labor Relations Act of 1935 (Wagner Act), and many other New Deal innovations.

ROOSEVELT'S RESPONSE

Roosevelt had been considering how to deal with the Court's resistance since January, 1935, when, in the *Gold Clause Cases*, it appeared as if the Court might overturn Congress's voiding of bond clauses pledging redemption in gold, which had provided the basis for devaluation and currency regulation. Immediate response became unnecessary when the Court ruled favorably on February 18, but the idea of restraining the Court took root. After *Schechter*, Roosevelt said, "We have been relegated to the horse-and-buggy definition of interstate commerce," causing a public uproar. He began to consider a constitutional amendment that would either give Congress new powers or limit the Court's power. Attorney General Homer Cummings, however, insisted that the problem lay with the Court's current composition. He suggested an increase in the number of justices to create a favorable majority or an amendment requiring retirement at age seventy. In early 1936, Roosevelt came to agree that an amendment would be too difficult to frame, too slow and difficult to pass, and too open to interpretation by the Court. He also was unwilling to propose a remedy during a presidential election year.

This editorial cartoon in the March 24, 1937, San Francisco Chronicle *ridiculed President Franklin D. Roosevelt's effort to put into effect his New Deal programs* (FDR Library)

THE PLAN

After his 1936 electoral landslide, Roosevelt was ready to act. Cummings developed a plan linking the number of justices over age seventy with new appointments to the Court, thus establishing a principle to legitimize Court packing. On February 5, 1937, Roosevelt submitted a judicial reform bill; at its heart was a proposal to give his office power to appoint a new federal judge or justice for every one with ten years' service who did not retire within six months after his seventieth birthday. Up to six new Court positions could be established and forty-four on the lower federal tribunals. Roosevelt justified this measure by arguing that aging judges could not keep up with the workload and that additional appointees would help clear out overcrowded federal court dockets, decreasing delays and expense to litigants. However, his intention to create a pro-New Deal Court majority was obvious. In March, he began instead to emphasize the necessity of bringing in younger justices who understood modern facts and circumstances and who would not undertake to override legislative policy.

CHANGING NUMBERS OF SEATS ON THE SUPREME COURT		
Year	Authorized	Actual
1789	6	6
1801	5	6
1802	6	6
1807	7	7
1837	9	9
1863	10	10
1866	7	10
1869	9	9

Note: Discrepancies between authorized and actual seats on the Court arose because Congress was not empowered to remove sitting justices.

The proposal was not unconstitutional; Congress had changed the Court's size several times during the nineteenth century. However, Roosevelt's open grab for power provided an opportunity for closet conservatives, previously afraid to attack the New Deal, to criticize him, charging him with attempting to move toward absolute power. Although moderates and liberals disagreed, many feared the precedent would allow later abuse by a reactionary president. Republicans let the Democrats lead the public opposition, hoping to profit from the split within the president's party.

Despite opposition, the proposal seemed headed for adoption until a series of surprising Court actions. On March 29, in *West Coast Hotel Co. v. Parrish* (1937), the Court announced a 5-4 decision upholding a Washington state minimum-wage law similar to that struck down in *Tipaldo,* Justice Roberts voting with the majority. This decision had been completed before the Court-packing proposal, so Roberts's "switch in time that saved nine" was not a response to the president's threat but an acknowledgment of the election results. The Court upheld the Wagner Act in a series of 5-4 decisions on April 12, including *National Labor Relations Board v. Jones and Laughlin Steel Corp.* (1937). On May 18, conservative Justice Willis Van Devanter announced his intention to retire. The

Court's decisions on May 24 in *Helvering v. Davis* (1937) and *Steward Machine Co. v. Davis* (1937) upheld Social Security.

THE END AND AFTERMATH

Given the Court's ideological repositioning, many politicians believed the Court-packing proposal was now unnecessary. Roosevelt, however, argued that it was still essential, despite the Senate Judiciary Committee's adverse report on the bill and bitter Senate debate. The bill was revised to authorize the appointment of one additional justice each year for each justice who remained on the Court after age seventy-five. The efforts of majority leader Joseph Robinson, expected to be Roosevelt's first Court appointee, made it appear possible in late June that the bill would pass. However, after Robinson died on July 14, the Senate voted seventy to twenty to send the bill back to the Judiciary Committee for further review. It never reemerged.

The Court-packing issue exacted a huge toll. It weakened the New Deal coalition and helped create a conservative coalition of Republicans and southern Democrats that blocked most liberal legislation from 1937 onward. However, Roosevelt (who ultimately appointed eight new justices) had permanently altered the constitutional interpretation of the Court, which from that time accepted a vast expansion of the power of government in American life.

Bethany Andreasen

FURTHER READING

Hall, Kermit L. *The Least Dangerous Branch: Separation of Powers and Court-Packing*. New York: Garland, 2000.

Kyvig, David. "The Road Not Taken: FDR, the Supreme Court, and Constitutional Amendment." *Political Science Quarterly* 104 (Fall, 1989): 463-481.

Leuchtenburg, William E. *The Supreme Court Reborn: The Constitutional Revolution in the Age of Roosevelt*. New York: Oxford University Press, 1995.

McDowell, Gary L. *Curbing the Courts: The Constitution and the Limits of Judicial Power*. Baton Rouge: Louisiana State University Press, 1988.

McKenna, Marian C. *Franklin Roosevelt and the Great Constitutional War: The Court-Packing Crisis of 1937*. New York: Fordham University Press, 2002.

Nelson, Michael. "The President and the Court: Reinterpreting the Court-Packing Episode of 1937." *Political Science Quarterly* 103 (Summer, 1988): 267-293.

SEE ALSO Constitutional interpretation; Judicial review; New Deal; Roberts, Owen J.; Salaries of justices; *Schechter Poultry Corp. v. United States*; *West Coast Hotel Co. v. Parrish.*

United States v. Cruikshank

CITATION: 92 U.S. 542
DATE: March 27, 1876
ISSUES: Federal enforcement of civil rights; states' rights
SIGNIFICANCE: Based on narrow interpretations of the Fourteenth and Fifteenth Amendments, the Supreme Court severely limited the authority of the federal government to protect the civil rights of African Americans.

Because state courts rarely prosecuted acts of violence against the freed slaves of the South, the Enforcement Act of 1870 made it a federal crime to engage in a conspiracy to deprive a citizen of constitutional rights. In Colfax, Louisiana, an armed group of white rioters killed about one hundred blacks gathered for a political meeting. Federal prosecutors used the Enforcement Act to prosecute and convict William Cruikshank and two others for participating in the Colfax massacre.

The Supreme Court unanimously held that the indictments were invalid. In a complicated ruling, Chief Justice Morrison R. Waite concentrated on the difference between the rights of state and national citizenship. Any assaults on the rights of state citizenship, which included participation in state politics, were not enforceable in federal courts. In addition, the due process and equal protection clauses of the Fourteenth Amendment authorized federal legislation relating only to actions by state officials, not to acts of private persons. Finally, in charging interference with a Fifteenth Amendment right to vote, the indictments failed to specify that the defendants had been motivated by the race of the victims.

The decision in *United States v. Cruikshank* left protection for most African American rights with the southern states, where few people sympathized with their cause. The decision reflected the national mood, which had become tired of federal intervention in southern politics.

Thomas Tandy Lewis

SEE ALSO Race and discrimination; Reconstruction; Second Amendment; *Slaughterhouse Cases*; State action; States' rights and state sovereignty; Waite, Morrison R.

Cruzan v. Director, Missouri Department of Health

CITATION: 497 U.S. 261

DATE: June 25, 1990

ISSUE: Right to die

SIGNIFICANCE: The Supreme Court ruled that the Fourteenth Amendment protects a competent adult's "liberty interest" in refusing unwanted medical treatment even if the result is death and that the U.S. Constitution permits, but does not require, state courts to demand "clear and convincing" evidence of the person's desire before terminating life-support services.

In 1983 Nancy Cruzan suffered brain injuries in an automobile accident that left her in a permanent "vegetative state," with no realistic hope for recovery. An implanted feeding tube provided her body with a constant source of nutrition and water. She was one of approximately ten thousand such cases in the United States. In 1987 Cruzan's parents sought permission to have the feeding tube removed, which would result in her death. Missouri's living will statute, however, required clear and convincing evidence that Nancy Cruzan herself would have wanted to have the tube removed. Because the parents could not produce the necessary evidence, the state courts rejected their request.

By a 5-4 vote, the Supreme Court upheld the constitutionality of the Missouri law. In the majority opinion, Chief Justice William H.

Rehnquist wrote that the requirement of clear and convincing evidence of a person's desire was reasonable in view of the state's interest in preserving human life. Not only was it possible for family members to be mistaken about what a person would desire, but there was also the real danger that some families might be motivated by a financial incentive to seek a person's demise. Rehnquist noted that the Court in *Jacobson v. Massachusetts* (1905) had balanced an individual's liberty interest in rejecting a medical procedure with the legitimate interests of the state.

Rehnquist was careful not to define the extent of a person's "right to die." Based on the Court's precedents as well as the common-law doctrine of informed consent, an 8-1 majority of the justices were willing to "assume" that the Constitution grants a competent person the right to refuse lifesaving nutrition. Justice Antonin Scalia was the only justice to reject this assumption. Rehnquist's opinion did not attempt to draw a distinction between artificial nutrition and more complex forms of medical procedures, nor did it distinguish between patients facing imminent death and patients whose lives might be preserved for many years. Thus, the decision allowed states a great deal of latitude in making laws about living wills and related matters.

The Missouri courts eventually ruled that new evidence provided enough justification to honor the request of the Cruzan family. In *Washington v. Glucksberg* (1997), the Court unanimously agreed that the Constitution does not guarantee any right to physician assistance in ending one's life.

Thomas Tandy Lewis

SEE ALSO Die, right to; Due process, substantive; Rehnquist, William H.; *Roe v. Wade*; Scalia, Antonin; *Washington v. Glucksberg*.

Benjamin R. Curtis

IDENTIFICATION: Associate justice (December 20, 1851-September 1, 1857)
NOMINATED BY: Millard Fillmore
BORN: November 4, 1809, Watertown, Massachusetts
DIED: September 15, 1874, Newport, Rhode Island
SIGNIFICANCE: Curtis was the major dissenting voice in *Scott v. Sandford* (1857), although he had a reputation as a supporter of slavery. He served as chief counsel defending President Andrew Johnson at his impeachment trial.

When Benjamin R. Curtis was a child, his father, an officer in the merchant marines, died, and his widowed mother operated a store and circulating library to send her son to Harvard. Curtis graduated in 1829 and attended Harvard Law School but left to practice law. Gradually gaining respect as a lawyer, Curtis turned to politics and was elected to the Massachusetts legislature in 1849. A dedicated Whig and supporter of Daniel Webster, Curtis was chosen by President Millard Fillmore to fill a vacancy on the Supreme Court in 1851. While on the Court, Curtis usually agreed with the majority, although he was a New England Whig among many southern Democrats.

In *Cooley v. Board of Wardens of the Port of Philadelphia* (1852), a case involving jurisdiction over interstate commerce, Curtis upheld Pennsylvania's right to determine and collect fees for pilotage in the port of Philadelphia. Curtis effected a compromise giving the federal government control over foreign and interstate commerce, while states had authority within their borders.

In 1855 Curtis wrote for a unanimous Court in *Murray's Lessee v. Hoboken Land and Improvement Co.*, defining and limiting the concept of due process of law by upholding the solicitor of the treasury's ability to demand payment of debts from a customs official without obtaining a court order.

Curtis is best remembered for his dissenting opinion in the case of Scott v. Sandford (1857). Dred Scott, a slave, had accompanied his surgeon-owner to posts in Illinois and the Minnesota territory. Upon the surgeon's death, Scott maintained that his residency in free lands entitled him to freedom. The Court decided against Scott. The case caused controversy as groups debated the issue of slavery, particularly whether it should be allowed in new territories.

Curtis had a reputation as a supporter of slavery or at least as a defender of the status quo to avoid quarreling among the states. His previous decisions had been instrumental in returning runaways to slavery. However, in the Scott case, Curtis dissented vehemently from the majority opinion, and his reputation gave added weight to his words. He rejected the majority opinion that African Americans were not citizens because in 1787 they were considered citizens eligible to vote in five states, and citizens of states are also citizens of the United States. Curtis added that a slave who had lived in a free territory was entitled to freedom. Relations with the rest of the justices immediately became strained, and Curtis resigned.

When President Andrew Johnson faced impeachment proceedings in 1868, Curtis served as his chief counsel, providing logical, lucid arguments instrumental in Johnson's acquittal.

Benjamin R. Curtis. (Albert Rosenthal/ Collection of the Supreme Court of the United States)

Curtis turned down offers of political appointments, continued his law practice, and taught at Harvard until his death.

Carol G. Fox

FURTHER READING

Bader, William H., and Roy M. Mersky, eds. *The First One Hundred Eight Justices.* Buffalo, N.Y.: William S. Hein, 2004.

Fehrenbacher, Don E. *Slavery, Law, and Politics.* New York: Oxford University Press, 1981.

Friedman, Leon, and Fred L. Israel, eds. *The Justices of the Supreme Court: Their Lives and Major Opinions.* 5 vols. New York: Chelsea House, 1997.

Huebner, Timothy S. *The Taney Court: Justices, Rulings, and Legacy.* Santa Barbara, Calif.: ABC-Clio, 2003.

SEE ALSO Resignation and retirement; *Scott v. Sandford*; Slavery.

United States v. Curtiss-Wright Export Corp.

CITATION: 299 U.S. 304
DATE: December 21, 1936
ISSUES: Presidential powers; foreign affairs
SIGNIFICANCE: The Supreme Court declared that the federal government possesses broad and inherent powers to deal with other countries and that the president exercises primacy in formulating and conducting foreign policy.

In 1934 Congress passed a joint resolution authorizing the president to prohibit the sale of arms to the warring nations of Bolivia and Paraguay. Congress also provided criminal penalties for violators. President Franklin D. Roosevelt quickly proclaimed an embargo. After the Curtiss-Wright Export Corporation was indicted for disobeying the embargo, it asserted that the congressional resolution was an unconstitutional delegation of legislative power to the president.

By a 7-1 margin, the Supreme Court found nothing unconstitutional about the government's arrangement. Justice George Suther-

321

land distinguished between two kinds of legislation, domestic and foreign, and held that the rule against delegation of duties applied only to the former. He theorized that the powers in foreign affairs derived less from the Constitution than from the inherent attributes of a sovereign country. In the international field, moreover, the president has primacy, and Congress "must often accord to the President a degree of discretion and freedom from statutory restriction which would not be admissible were domestic affairs alone involved."

There has been much controversy concerning *Curtiss-Wright*'s expansive views of inherent presidential powers in foreign affairs. The decision was cited by opponents of the War Powers Act of 1973 and by supporters of executive discretion in the Iran-Contra affair. Probably a majority of legal scholars believe that Sutherland's statements about presidential powers are inconsistent with constitutional principles of separation of powers. In *Regan v. Wald* (1984), the Court recognized that the conduct of foreign affairs is under the domain of both the legislative and executive branches.

Thomas Tandy Lewis

SEE ALSO Delegation of powers; National security; Presidential powers; Rules of the Court; Sutherland, George; War powers.

William Cushing

IDENTIFICATION: Associate justice (February 2, 1790-September 13, 1810)
NOMINATED BY: George Washington
BORN: March 1, 1732, Scituate, Massachusetts
DIED: September 13, 1810, Scituate, Massachusetts
SIGNIFICANCE: Cushing was the first appointee to the Supreme Court. Serving on the Court for almost twenty-one years, he was adept at disposing of cases quickly and tersely by focusing on one simple issue that could resolve each case.

After graduating from Harvard College in 1751, William Cushing taught grammar school for one year in Roxbury, Massachusetts. Turning his interests to law, he began his own law practice in 1755. In 1760 he moved to Maine to become a probate judge and justice of the peace. Cushing returned to Massachusetts in 1771 and was subsequently chosen as a justice in the Massachusetts superior court. After the American Revolutionary War began, he was elected to the Massachusetts superior court of judicature, and in 1779 he was elevated to the position of chief justice to replace John Quincy Adams. In 1786 Cushing maintained order and respect for the law in western Massachusetts by handling the armed rebels in Shay's Rebellion. Cushing's experience with regional disorders made him a strong supporter of the Constitution. He served as the vice president of the Massachusetts state convention that ratified the Constitution in 1788, presiding over

William Cushing.
(Library of Congress)

most of the proceedings because the president, John Hancock, was ill.

On September 24, 1789, Cushing was nominated to the Supreme Court by President George Washington. He was confirmed by the Senate two days later. Although he served more than twenty years on the Court, he wrote only nineteen opinions. His opinions were brief, careful, and straightforward. Because of his previous experience with the early jurisprudence of the American states, Cushing was chosen to write the decisions on the property rights of colonists who had remained loyal to Great Britain during the Revolutionary War. In 1793 he concurred with the majority in the extremely unpopular decision of the Court in the *Chisholm v. Georgia* case, in which the Court upheld the rights of the citizens of one state to bring original suits in the Court against another state. Due to potential economic damage that might occur, this decision led to the adoption of the Eleventh Amendment in 1798.

In 1796 Cushing demonstrated his support of the Federalist agenda in *Ware v. Hylton*. He voted with the majority in concluding that debts encumbered before the Revolutionary War were still valid and that treaties were the supreme law of the land. As a result, President Washington nominated Cushing as the successor to Chief Justice John Jay. Cushing was confirmed by the Senate but resigned after one week due to declining health. However, he kept his position on the bench as an associate justice. Cushing served on the Court the longest of any of the six original appointees, being the only one to serve under both Jay and Chief Justice John Marshall.

Alvin K. Benson

SEE ALSO *Chisholm v. Georgia*; Constitutional law; Eleventh Amendment; Opinions, writing of.

Peter V. Daniel

IDENTIFICATION: Associate justice (January 10, 1842-May 31, 1860)
NOMINATED BY: Martin Van Buren
BORN: April 24, 1784, Crows Nest, Virginia
DIED: May 31, 1860, Richmond, Virginia
SIGNIFICANCE: As a Supreme Court justice, Daniel was a defender of
  slavery and an opponent of corporations and federal authority.

Peter V. Daniel began practicing law in 1808, was elected to the Virginia house of delegates in 1809, and served as lieutenant governor from 1818 to 1835. In 1836 he was appointed a federal judge by President Andrew Jackson. On February 27, 1841, he was nominated to the Supreme Court by President Martin Van Buren. He was

Peter V. Daniel.
(Max Rosenthal/
Collection of the
Supreme Court of
the United States)

325

confirmed by the Senate on March 2 and took office in January of the next year.

At a time when corporations were asserting their legal rights, Daniel believed that the law should not recognize these rights at all. He also opposed expanding admiralty law, which granted the federal government authority over ocean transport, to include commerce on major rivers and lakes.

Although he opposed federal power, Daniel was a strong advocate of state authority. In *West River Bridge Co. v. Dix* (1848), a case involving the power of a state to purchase ownership of a bridge, he wrote the majority opinion in favor of the state. He was also a strong defender of slavery and its control by the states. In *Scott v. Sandford* (1857), he agreed with the majority that the federal government had no power to outlaw slavery in new territories.

Rose Secrest

SEE ALSO *Scott v. Sandford*; Slavery; Taney, Roger Brooke.

United States v. Darby Lumber Co.

CITATION: 312 U.S. 100
DATE: February 3, 1941
ISSUE: Regulation of manufacturing
SIGNIFICANCE: Using a broad interpretation of the commerce clause, the Supreme Court upheld a federal law mandating minimum wages and maximum hours for employees producing goods for interstate commerce.

The Fair Labor Standards Act of 1938, the last major piece of New Deal legislation, applied to employees engaged "in commerce" and "in the production of goods for commerce." Fred Darby, owner of a Georgia company making goods to be shipped out of state, was indicted for paying his employees less than the minimum wage. In his appeal, Darby referred to the precedent of *Hammer v. Dagenhart* (1918), which had held that the U.S. Congress, under the commerce clause and the Tenth Amendment, had no authority to regulate activities that were only indirectly connected to interstate commerce. By a 9-0 vote, the Court overturned *Hammer* and upheld the 1938 statute. Chief Justice Harlan Fiske Stone wrote that Congress possessed the comprehensive authority to regulate any intrastate activities that had either a direct or indirect effect on interstate commerce. Only the employees of companies engaging in purely local activities remained outside the protection of the federal minimum-wage law. Stone's landmark opinion specifically repudiated the doctrine of dual federalism, so that the Tenth Amendment would no longer serve as a significant restraint on federal supervision of anything relating to interstate commerce.

Thomas Tandy Lewis

SEE ALSO Commerce, regulation of; Federalism; *Hammer v. Dagenhart*; *Lopez, United States v.*; New Deal; States' rights and state sovereignty; Tenth Amendment.

David Davis

IDENTIFICATION: Associate justice (December 10, 1862-March 4, 1877)
NOMINATED BY: Abraham Lincoln
BORN: March 9, 1815, Cecil County, Maryland
DIED: June 26, 1886, Bloomington, Illinois
SIGNIFICANCE: One of President Abraham Lincoln's best friends, Davis is best known for writing the opinion in an 1866 Supreme Court case that limited the use of military authority over civilians in areas not threatened by military action.

Upon graduation from Kenyon College in Ohio in 1832, David Davis moved to Massachusetts and read law with a local judge, Henry W. Bishop. Davis attended Yale Law School and was admitted to the Illinois bar in 1835, establishing a private practice in Pekin. During this time, Davis met Abraham Lincoln, a member of the Illinois legislature, who became a lifelong friend. In 1836 Davis moved to Bloomington, Illinois, where he steadily built a reputable law practice.

In 1844 Davis won a seat in the Illinois legislature and served on

David Davis.
(Library of Congress)

the education committee. As an elected member of the Illinois Constitutional Convention in 1847, Davis was instrumental in changing the judicial system by advancing reforms so that judges were elected by the people instead of by the legislature. In 1848 Davis was elected as a circuit judge on the Illinois Eighth Circuit, a position he held for fourteen years. Both Lincoln and Stephen Douglas tried cases in his court.

Davis campaigned for Lincoln in his two losing bids for the U.S. Senate. At the 1860 Republican convention, Davis orchestrated the nomination of Lincoln for president of the United States. Subsequently, he advised Lincoln on campaign strategy. After Lincoln's election, Davis advised him in assembling the cabinet.

In 1862 President Lincoln nominated Davis to the Supreme Court. Davis never demonstrated a strong interest in legal scholarship and wrote few important Court opinions. His most noteworthy decision came in *Ex parte Milligan* (1866). The case involved a civilian,

Lambdin P. Milligan, who was tried by an Indiana military court and convicted of conspiracy during the Civil War. Eventually, Milligan appealed his case to the Supreme Court. Davis argued that constitutional rights do not cease to exist during wartime and that Milligan's rights had been violated when he was tried by a court that was not sanctioned by Congress and also when he was denied his right to trial by a jury. Davis concluded that the president of the United States had no power to mandate the trial of civilians by a military commission in areas where civilian courts were operating.

After serving on the Court for fourteen years, Davis became bored and wanted to return to the excitement of the political arena. In 1872 Davis had been an unsuccessful candidate for nomination for the president of the United States on the Liberal-Republican ticket. In 1877 he resigned his position on the Court when he was elected as a U.S. senator from Illinois. From 1881 to 1883 Davis served as president pro tempore of the Senate.

Alvin K. Benson

SEE ALSO Constitutional law; Jury, trial by; Military and the Court; *Milligan, Ex parte.*

William R. Day

IDENTIFICATION: Associate justice (March 2, 1903-November 13, 1922)
NOMINATED BY: Theodore Roosevelt
BORN: April 17, 1849, Ravenna, Ohio
DIED: July 9, 1923, Mackinac Island, Michigan
SIGNIFICANCE: The first of President Theodore Roosevelt's Supreme Court appointees, Day supported antitrust regulation and state power to regulate economic rights. In his most important opinion, he struck down the Keating-Owen Child Labor Act (1916).

Born in Ohio in 1849, William R. Day was descended from a family of judges. His grandfather and father served as justices on state supreme courts. Day followed in their footsteps, graduating from law school and running his own law practice. During his law career, he became friends with the Republican governor, William McKinley.

William R. Day
(Library of Congress)

When McKinley was elected president, he appointed Day to the State Department. McKinley's successor, Theodore Roosevelt, was soon faced with his first Supreme Court appointment and searched for a judge who would favor his antitrust policies. He settled on Day.

The justice did not disappoint him. In the first important antitrust case for the administration, *Northern Securities Co. v. United States* (1904), Day provided the critical fifth vote in support of the government's prosecution of the company. Throughout his career, the justice consistently supported government regulation of monopolies.

Day was also a swing vote on the critical legal issue of the day, economic rights. Although he was willing to uphold some state economic regulations, he consistently voted to strike down federal economic regulations. It was these contradictory beliefs that placed Day on different sides of important cases during his Court tenure. For example, Day dissented in *Lochner v. New York* (1905), where the Court struck down a state workday maximum-hour law as a violation of liberty of contract. He also disagreed with the Court's decision in *Coppage v. Kansas* (1915), in which a five-member majority struck down a state law prohibiting antiunion employment contracts.

Day did vote to limit federal power in prosecutions. He authored the Court's opinion in *Weeks v. United States* (1914). In *Weeks*, the Court created the federal exclusionary rule, which prohibited the use of any evidence in trial if that evidence had been obtained in violation of the Fourteenth Amendment. The exclusionary rule was used by subsequent Courts to overturn convictions in federal and state cases.

Day is probably best known for his opinion in *Hammer v. Dagenhart* (1918). In *Hammer,* Day wrote for a narrow majority in striking down the Keating-Owen Child Labor Act of 1916. The act prohibited the shipment across state lines of products made by children under the age of fourteen. Day stated that the regulation intruded upon the state power to regulate labor.

After the *Hammer* decision, Day served as a justice for four more years, but old age and ill health made him a less productive member of the Court. By 1922 he had become unable to complete his duties and, after consultation with his colleagues, decided to resign.

Douglas Clouatre

FURTHER READING

Bader, William H., and Roy M. Mersky, eds. *The First One Hundred Eight Justices.* Buffalo, N.Y.: William S. Hein, 2004.

Baker, Liva. *The Justice from Beacon Hill.* New York: HarperCollins, 1994.

Bickel, Alexander, and Benno Schmidt. *Judiciary and Responsible Government.* New York: Macmillan Press, 1984.

Ely, James W., Jr. *The Fuller Court: Justices, Rulings, and Legacy.* Santa Barbara, Calif.: ABC-Clio, 2003.

Friedman, Leon, and Fred L. Israel, eds. *The Justices of the United States Supreme Court: Their Lives and Major Opinions.* 5 vols. New York: Chelsea House, 1997.

Renstrom, Peter G. *The Taft Court: Justices, Rulings, and Legacy.* Santa Barbara, Calif.: ABC-Clio, 2003.

Shoemaker, Rebecca S. *The White Court: Justices, Rulings, and Legacy.* Santa Barbara, Calif.: ABC-Clio, 2004.

SEE ALSO Antitrust law; Exclusionary rule; *Hammer v. Dagenhart*; *Lochner v. New York.*

In re Debs

CITATION: 158 U.S. 564
DATE: May 27, 1895
ISSUES: Injunctions; Sherman Antitrust Act
SIGNIFICANCE: The Supreme Court upheld a federal injunction against a labor union in order to protect the U.S. mails and to preserve the orderly movement of interstate commerce. Also, the Court implicitly permitted lower courts to apply the Sherman Antitrust Act (1890) to labor unions.

During the famous Pullman strike in Chicago, members of the American Railway Union throughout the nation refused to handle trains carrying Pullman cars. When this resulted in firings, the union declared new strikes. President Grover Cleveland's administration sought and obtained a federal injunction against the strikers. The circuit court justified the injunction under the Sherman Antitrust Act

Eugene Debs, head of the Pullman union, was jailed for contempt of court when he refused to obey an injunction. (Library of Congress)

of 1890 and the authority of the federal government to deliver the mails. With the spread of violence, Cleveland sent federal troops to Chicago to preserve order. When Eugene Debs, president of the union, refused to honor the injunction, he was held in contempt and given a sentence of six months in jail. He appealed to the Supreme Court on a writ of habeas corpus.

Speaking for a unanimous Court, Justice David J. Brewer upheld the injunction and the contempt citation of Debs. Brewer reasoned that the national government possessed a broad constitutional mandate to remove obstacles to interstate commerce and movement of the mails and that it might choose to use either military power or the equity jurisdiction of the federal courts. By maintaining silence about the lower court's reliance on the Sherman Antitrust Act, Brewer's opinion left the door open for antitrust injunctions against union activities in interstate commerce. In *Loewe v. Lawlor* (1906), the Court explicitly ruled that the Sherman Antitrust Act applied to combinations of workers. The Clayton Act of 1914 exempted labor unions from antitrust injunctions, but the use of injunctions to stop strikes continued until the New Deal period.

Thomas Tandy Lewis

SEE ALSO Antitrust law; Bad tendency test; Brewer, David J.; Commerce, regulation of; Fuller, Melville W.; War and civil liberties.

DeJonge v. Oregon

CITATION: 299 U.S. 353
DATE: January 4, 1937
ISSUE: Freedom of assembly and association
SIGNIFICANCE: The Supreme Court, in overturning a conviction under a state criminal syndicalism law, incorporated the right of freedom of peaceable assembly and association to the states through the Fourteenth Amendment.

Chief Justice Charles Evans Hughes wrote the Supreme Court's unanimous opinion (Justice Harlan Fiske Stone did not participate) overturning the conviction of Dirk DeJonge under Oregon's criminal syndicalism law. DeJonge had helped run a meeting sponsored by the Communist Party to protest actions taken by police against workers. Although DeJonge, some of the other leaders, and about 15 percent of attendees were affiliated with communists, the meeting was entirely orderly. Minor Communist Party activities may have taken place, but no one advocated violence or criminal syndicalism. The prosecution relied heavily on party literature not used in the meeting but found elsewhere that tangentially associated the Communist Party with syndicalism.

The Oregon Supreme Court upheld DeJonge's conviction on grounds that merely participating in a totally peaceful meeting called by the Communist Party could still violate the law. The Court reversed the decision, saying lawful discussion in a peaceful assembly is not a crime. This decision first applied the freedom of association to the states under the Fourteenth Amendment's due process clause.

Richard L. Wilson

SEE ALSO Assembly and association, freedom of; *Brandenburg v. Ohio*; First Amendment; Fourteenth Amendment; Incorporation doctrine; *Schenck v. United States*.

Delegation of Powers

DESCRIPTION: The authorization by Congress of a transfer of its lawmaking power to another branch of government.

SIGNIFICANCE: By validating Congress's transfer of considerable lawmaking authority to executive branch agencies and to the president, the Supreme Court contributed to the growth of the federal government's administrative and regulatory power.

The Supreme Court has been called on several times to address the controversial issue of when, if ever, Congress may transfer, or delegate, legislative power to the executive branch. The controversy is rooted in the text of the Constitution, whereby the people have delegated the authority to Congress to exercise "all legislative powers."

According to one view, any subsequent delegation of those powers by Congress is unconstitutional and may lead to undemocratic government by unelected, and unaccountable, administrators. For political and practical reasons, this so-called "nondelegation" view has been generally rejected by the Court. With rare, but notable, exceptions, the Court has allowed Congress to authorize executive branch agencies to make law in the form of rules and regulations and to allow the president to make the rules that the president is constitutionally charged to execute.

EARLY RULINGS

In early cases, the Court attempted to respect the principle of nondelegation even while acknowledging that, for practical reasons, the executive and judicial branches had to be allowed to share some of the federal government's legislative responsibilities. Chief Justice John Marshall, writing for the Court in *Wayman v. Southard* (1825), distinguished powers that are "exclusively" legislative from those that are not and argued that Congress may let executive officials "fill up the details" of the nonexclusive powers. In 1892 the Court was asked to decide whether Congress could authorize the president to suspend trade with foreign countries when, in the president's judgment, it was necessary. Asserting that it is a "universally recognized" principle that Congress cannot delegate legislative power to the president, the Court nevertheless upheld this delegation of legislative responsibility to the president.

This ambivalence of the Court toward delegation continued into the twentieth century. As the responsibilities of the federal government grew, Congress created more administrative agencies and regulatory commissions to perform increasingly specialized tasks. The Federal Trade Commission (FTC), for example, was created by Congress to prohibit "unfair methods of competition." In *Federal Trade Commission v. Gratz* (1920), the Court upheld this broad delegation of rule-making authority, as it did repeatedly in similar cases in this period. However, unwilling to completely abandon the principle that legislative power was not to be delegated, the Court crafted the doctrine that delegation was permitted as long as the Congress provides an "intelligible principle" to guide the exercise of delegated powers.

RULINGS AFTER 1930

As part of a wide-ranging attack on the New Deal initiatives of President Franklin D. Roosevelt, the Court ruled in *Schechter Poultry Corp. v. United States* (1935) that Congress had not supplied an intelligible principle when delegating legislative authority to the president and to the National Industrial Recovery Administration. After this exceptional case, however, the Court began to issue a succession of rulings validating the delegation of legislative power. In *United States v. Curtiss-Wright Export Corp.* (1936), the Court held that Congress may delegate very broad foreign policy-making power to the president. By the end of the 1930's, a politically weakened Court retreated from the intelligible-principle standard, and congress proceeded to spawn numerous administrative agencies and commissions to deal with the demands of an increasingly complex industrial nation.

In domestic affairs, the Court ruled in *Yakus v. United States* (1944) that Congress could authorize an executive official, the price administrator, to set maximum prices on goods and services, guided only by the vague standard that the prices be "generally fair and equitable." In *Securities and Exchange Commission v. Chenery Corp.* (1947), the Court diluted the intelligible principle standard further by holding that as long as the administrators made a reasonable effort to acknowledge some limits to their discretionary power, the delegation was allowable. In 1970 Congress granted sweeping powers to the president to impose wage-and-price controls. Challenges to the Economic Stabilization Act of 1970 were rebuffed by the Court, even though the guidelines given by Congress to the president were stated in the most general of terms. By 1974 the Court was ready to declare, in *National Cable Association v. United States*, that the idea that there were meaningful limits on Congress's authority to delegate power has been "virtually abandoned by the Court for all practical purposes."

In the 1980's and 1990's the Court continued to allow the delegation of legislative powers, but it signaled that it would impose some constitutional limits. In 1984 Congress chose to create an independent sentencing commission to generate mandatory sentencing guidelines. This commission was to be composed of seven members, three of whom were federal judges. The commission was challenged as an unconstitutional delegation of legislative power to the judicial branch, but the Court upheld its creation in *Mistretta v. United States* (1989). In *Immigration and Naturalization Service v. Chadha* (1983), however, the Court ruled that the legislative veto, a procedure used by Congress to reassume rule-making authority after its delegation to an executive agency or official, was unconstitutional. In *Bowsher v. Synar* (1986), the Court also denied Congress the ability to delegate *to itself* what the Court considered to be an executive power. In this case, the comptroller general was considered to be a legislative officer charged by Congress to perform an executive function, namely, to execute budget cuts. In *Clinton v. City of New York* (1998), the Court ruled that Congress could not grant the president a line-item veto power whereby he could cancel selected items in spending bills.

Philip R. Zampini

FURTHER READING

Cann, Steven J. *Administrative Law.* 4th ed. Thousand Oaks, Calif.: Sage Publications, 2006.

Hall, Kermit L. *The Least Dangerous Branch: Separation of Powers and Court-Packing.* New York: Garland, 2000.

Lowi, Theodore. *The End of Liberalism.* 2d ed. New York: W. W. Norton, 1979.

Powers, Stephen. *The Least Dangerous Branch? Consequences of Judicial Activism.* Westport, Conn.: Praeger, 2002.

Warren, Kenneth F. *Administrative Law in the Political System.* 2d ed. Boulder, Colo.: Westview Press, 2004.

SEE ALSO *Clinton v. City of New York; Curtiss-Wright Export Corp., United States v.;* Elastic clause; New Deal; *Schechter Poultry Corp. v. United States;* Separation of powers.

Right to Die

DESCRIPTION: Constitutional right of individual persons to decline or discontinue life-sustaining medical treatment for themselves. This right does not include affirmatively committing suicide or obtaining medical help to do so.

SIGNIFICANCE: The Supreme Court has strongly suggested that this limited right exists. Patients may refuse medical procedures that would prolong their lives, but they cannot obtain medical assistance to hasten their deaths.

The federally guaranteed right to die is quite limited, which gives states great freedom to take different positions. The only action regarding the right to die that states may not take is to prohibit knowledgeable, competent patients from disconnecting their life-support system. In other words, the federal right provides only a minimum floor below which states cannot go.

Therefore, many states have voluntarily recognized some additional rights. For example, if the patient has become comatose or incompetent and cannot personally exercise his or her right to refuse treatment, most states will recognize some form of clear previous expression, advance directive, or living will. In the absence of such clear expression, many states will allow certain relatives, doctors, or guardians to make this decision based on the patient's "best interests" or his or her informal previous expression. However, some states rather severely restrict the conditions under which others may make the decision to remove life support for a patient or require extensive proof that it would accord with the patient's wishes. Whether the state may absolutely forbid such proxy decisions when the patient is comatose or incompetent is unclear. However, conversely, granting too much freedom to end the life of another may violate some notion of a right to life.

There are other state expansions of the minimum right to die. For example, if the main medical objective of administering known death-hastening pain-relieving medication is to alleviate otherwise intractable intense pain, pursuant to the patient's fully informed request, a number of states choose not to punish those who administer

338

this medication. These states regard this act as consistent with the federally guaranteed right to die, although they could probably prosecute those involved. This type of death is distinguished from common suicide—leaping off buildings, jumping in front of cars, employing poisons, weapons, or other equipment—and medically assisted suicide, which is illegal in most states and not within the federally guaranteed right to die.

THE CRUZAN CASE

The genesis of the constitutional right to die is the opinion in *Cruzan v. Director, Missouri Department of Health* (1990). The Supreme Court was faced with the case of a thirty-year-old woman in a "persistent vegetative state"—a coma—who was capable of some reflexes but no cognitive functions as the result of a severely brain-damaging automobile accident. Medical opinion was that she had virtually no chance of any significant recovery. She was apparently being kept alive by the medical administration of nutrition and hydration through tubes. There was evidence that, several years before the accident, at age twenty-five, she had told her roommate informally that if sick or injured she would not wish to continue her life unless she could live at least halfway normally.

Her parents, who had been appointed her guardians, wished to disconnect the life-support systems. The Missouri Supreme Court sustained an order preventing the disconnection. Because the patient had not executed a formal living will allowing disconnection pursuant to state law, the court held there must be other "clear and convincing evidence" of her wishes, which it found wanting. The Court was asked to overturn this ruling on the grounds that it violated the Constitution. It declined, ruling instead that the state court was within its constitutional rights.

THE RIGHT TO DIE

In the first part of its *Cruzan* decision, the Court assumed (but fell short of expressly holding) that the Constitution grants a competent, conscious adult a *personal* right to refuse life-sustaining hydration and nutrition. This followed, the justices intimated, from a long historical legal tradition recognizing bodily integrity, requiring consent to medical procedures, and allowing patients to refuse treatment. The legal community later regarded the first part of *Cruzan* as creating the right, personally, to refuse lifesaving treatment.

In *Washington v. Glucksberg* (1997), the Court interpreted this part of *Cruzan* as strongly suggesting that the protection of "liberty" in the due process clause of the Fifth and Fourteenth Amendments "protects the traditional right to refuse unwanted lifesaving medical treatment." It saw this right as analogous to other specific intimate personal liberties held protected by the clause in a string of previous cases: the freedom to marry, to have children, to direct their education and upbringing, to use contraception, to maintain bodily integrity, and to have an abortion.

However, the Court in *Cruzan* goes on to hold that even though the patient herself may have such a personal right, it does not follow that the parents may assert it for her. It held that the state's interests in preserving life and the element of personal choice, preventing potential abuses by surrogates, and allocating the risk of error sensibly loom comparatively larger on this question and justified Missouri in requiring a high standard of proof, although a state does not have to do so. Therefore, the Court upheld the order preventing disconnection.

The *Cruzan* opinion, recognizing the personal right but allowing restriction of surrogate assertion, is an evident compromise between conflicting interests: the individual interest in terminating a bad existence and the state's interest in preserving life.

PHYSICIAN-ASSISTED SUICIDE

The Court made two decisions relating to the right to die: *Washington v. Glucksberg* (1997) and *Vacco v. Quill* (1997). Both cases deal with whether there is a right to affirmative physician-assisted suicide such as lethal injections. Because of countervailing state interests and a desire to preserve the life-saving nature of the medical profession, the Court held that at least in the abstract, absent some compelling individual case, no such right exists. Nor is it a denial of constitutional equal protection of the laws to treat a patient who refuses life support more permissively than one who, in quite similar circumstances, seeks a doctor's assistance in dying. The Court justified its decision by pointing to the long historical, cultural, and legal distinction between passive measures such as refusal of treatment and active measures such as suicide.

The two 1997 cases were general challenges (by a group of physicians, a public interest group, and some by-then-deceased patients) to state laws against assisted suicide designed to prohibit physician-assisted suicide of terminally ill patients. Neither case was a specific challenge to a particular application of the prohibition to a terminally ill, intractably pain-wracked, motor-impaired patient who desired to commit suicide or had committed suicide with physician assistance.

In the context of the general challenge, the Court refused to invalidate state prohibitions against physicians assisting the suicide of terminally ill patients. However, several of the justices were willing to concede that a specially compelling individual case might arise in which a particular patient was in such dire straits that to deny him or her the right to physician-assisted suicide might violate his or her liberty protected by the Constitution. In other words, the justices suggested that some very particular application of the state law might be found unconstitutional.

However, until the Court makes such a ruling, the states are free to determine the legality of physician-assisted suicide and regulate it as they please. The justices apparently were reluctant to "freeze" the law by banning a certain kind of state provision for the entire nation at a time when states are experimenting and trying to find the right approach.

In 1994, Oregon passed the Death with Dignity Act, which authorized physicians to prescribe lethal doses of controlled substances to terminally ill patients in limited circumstances. In 2001, Attorney General John Ashcroft denounced Oregon's law and declared that it violated the federal Controlled Substances Act of 1970 (CSA). He further threatened to prosecute any physician who might make a prescription in order to assist a patient in committing suicide. The state of Oregon sued Ashcroft in federal court. Both the local district court and the Ninth Circuit held that the federal government had no authority under the CSA to regulate physician-assisted suicides, which were the kinds of medical decision that had traditionally been left up to the states.

In a 6-3 decision, the Supreme Court upheld the judgments of the lower courts in *Gonzales v. Oregon* (2006). Writing the official opinion for the Court, Justice Anthony M. Kennedy argued that Congress had enacted the Controlled Substances Act to prevent physicians from engaging in the traffic of illegal drugs, without any intent of defining the standards of medical practices. The CSA, therefore, did not authorize the federal government to decide on the legitimacy or illegitimacy of a state statute dealing with a medical practice desired by a patient. Although the Court's decision was controversial, Oregon's Death with Dignity Act was rarely applied by physicians, and it was not expected that the ruling would encourage many states to follow Oregon's lead in explicitly allowing physicians to help terminally ill patients to hasten their deaths.

Paul F. Rothstein
Updated by the Editor

FURTHER READING

Humphrey, Derek, and Mary Clement. *Freedom to Die: People, Politics, and the Right-to-Die Movement.* New York: St. Martin's Press, 1998.

McHugh, Paul R. "Dying Made Easy: Deaths of T. Youk and M. Schwartz from ALS." *Commentary* 107 (1999): 13.

Manning, Michael. *Euthanasia and Physician Assisted Suicide: Killing or Caring.* New York: Paulist Press, 1998.

Paris, John J. "Hugh Finn's 'Right to Die.'" *America* 179 (1998): 13.

Rosen, Jeffrey. *The Most Democratic Branch: How the Courts Serve America.* New York: Oxford University Press, 2006.

Rosenfeld, Barry. *Assisted Suicide and the Right to Die: The Interface of Social Science, Public Policy, and Medical Ethics.* Washington, D.C.: American Psychological Association. 2004.

Woodman, Sue. *Last Rights: The Struggle Over the Right to Die.* New York: Plenum Trade, 1998.

SEE ALSO *Cruzan v. Director, Missouri Department of Health*; Fundamental rights; Privacy, right to; Scalia, Antonin; States' rights and state sovereignty.

Dissents

DESCRIPTION: Disagreements with the outcome of a case before the Supreme Court and the treatment of the involved parties. These disagreements are usually expressed in the form of a written opinion added to the majority opinion.

SIGNIFICANCE: Although a dissenting opinion has no legal effect, it allows justices to call attention to perceived errors in the majority's reasoning and to suggest to potential opponents strategies for circumventing or overturning the majority result. Dissents may also influence the Court's final majority opinion.

Dissenting opinions were relatively rare in the first one hundred years of the Supreme Court's history and were far from the norm even in the early decades of the twentieth century. After the 1940's the number of dissents increased dramatically. Dissents should be distinguished from concurring opinions, in which a justice supports the majority outcome but offers a different rationale for reaching that outcome. Although dissenting opinions may affect the Court's decision making or the development of a law, they have no legal effect whatsoever. A rather cynical law professor was once asked by a first-year student how important dissents were and whether they should be studied. The professor responded that dissents were the equivalent of "judges baying at the moon." Court justices themselves are divided on the significance and effects of dissents.

HISTORY OF SUPREME COURT DISSENT

Before elevation of John Marshall to fourth chief justice in 1801, Court opinion procedures followed English practice as represented by the King's Bench. English judges delivered their opinions seriatim—each judge announcing his own opinion and the reasoning behind it. Unlike the King's Bench, Supreme Court justices delivered their opinions in reverse order of seniority, the most junior justice speaking first.

Marshall came to the bench with a powerful concern for the independence and authority of the judiciary, and he believed that the Court would command greater respect if it spoke with a single voice, presenting a united front to its opponents. Marshall therefore instituted the practice of issuing a single opinion and discouraged justices from writing dissenting opinions. Through most of his tenure, Marshall dominated the Court, for example, delivering twenty-four of the twenty-six opinions handed down between 1801 and 1805. Marshall's leadership skills, combined with the relative mediocrity of many of the justices who served with him during his thirty-four years on the Court, ensured that the norm of a single opinion for the Court and its corollary of no dissent became strongly embedded.

Although public regard for the Court increased, Marshall was not without his critics, and none perhaps was more vehement than Marshall's frequent political and personal opponent, his cousin President Thomas Jefferson. In an 1820 letter, Jefferson criticized Marshall's practice of issuing a single opinion and urged a return to seriatim opinions, denouncing the "crafty chief judge, who sophisticates the law to his own mind, by the turn of his own reasoning."

Marshall's dominance was not complete. There were dissents during Marshall's chief justiceship, most coming from Associate Justice William Johnson, characterized by a biographer as "the first dissenter." Johnson's first dissent was in *Huidekoper's Lessee v. Douglas* (1805). During Johnson's service on the Court, seventy dissenting opinions were filed, almost half written by Johnson. Marshall himself filed nine dissents and one special concurrence during his years on the Court.

During the tenure of Marshall's successor, President Andrew Jackson's appointee Roger Brooke Taney, dissents became more frequent. Taney was less obsessed with delivering the opinion of the Court himself than Marshall had been, and there were even instances of seriatim opinions. However, Marshall's norm of unity remained strong throughout the remainder of the nineteenth century, with concurring or dissenting opinions in only about 10 percent of the Court's decisions.

Marshall's norm held sway into the early decades of the twentieth century. Justice Oliver Wendell Holmes, who served on the Court from 1902 to 1932, is often referred to as the "Great Dissenter," but he dissented less frequently than his fellow justices did. Much of his reputation undoubtedly rests on the rhetorical quality of his dissents rather than their quantity, as is true of his frequent ally in dissent, Justice Louis D. Brandeis.

The turning point came in 1941 with the elevation of Associate Justice Harlan Fiske Stone to chief justice. Stone's predecessor, Charles Evans Hughes, was a stern taskmaster, and Stone resented Hughes's approach to presiding over the justices' conferences. Stone reacted by allowing extensive and often rambling discussion at conferences and tolerating dissent far more readily than Hughes. Stone's own rate of dissent was higher than that of any previous chief justice. High rates continued under Stone's successor, Fred M. Vinson. In the 1970's and early 1980's the number of dissenting opinions rose dramatically, but after the departure of Chief Justice Warren E. Burger in 1986, dissenters tended to join in a single dissenting opinion rather than write separate opinions. In the 1990's typically the senior justice in the minority assigned one of the dissenters to write a dissent for all to join.

The profound change in judicial norms regarding dissent is evident from a comparison of rates of dissenting opinions on the Warren E. Burger and William H. Rehnquist Courts with those of some of the most notable dissenters in earlier periods. According to one researcher, Brandeis averaged 2.9 dissents per term and Holmes 2.4. Justice William O. Douglas averaged 38.5 dissents per term during his time on the Burger and Rehnquist Courts. Second in line was Justice John Paul Stevens, who, in the period from 1975 to 1994, averaged 21 per term. Indeed, in the modern era, it is by no means rare for justices to dissent from denials of petitions for hearing and to file an opinion explaining their vote, an action considered unthinkable throughout the nineteenth century and into the early twentieth.

Scholars cite several reasons for the high dissent rates prevalent since the Stone Court. To some extent, the kinds of issues faced by the Court after 1937 may explain the erosion of consensual norms. The Court during the New Deal began to hear difficult cases dealing with the nature and scope of individual liberties. An increase in the number of law clerks assigned to each justice made it easier for justices to prepare separate opinions, while at the same time, the Court's dramatically increased caseload (a thousand cases per term during Stone's chief justiceship versus more than four thousand in the 1980's) heightens dissent because the justices no longer have time to engage in the extended discussions necessary for reaching a compromise opinion. Changes in the Court's jurisdiction during the early decades of the twentieth century also may have had an impact. As the Court gained more and more discretion over the cases it would hear and as its mandatory appellate jurisdiction was diminished, the easy cases that in the past would have produced unanimous decisions disappeared, leaving only the more difficult and divisive cases.

FUNCTIONS OF DISSENT

The battles that are fought in the conference room over difficult issues are hard and sometimes bitter. Indeed, in abortion, right to die, or capital punishment cases, the issues are quite literally matters of life and death. Not surprisingly therefore, one function of dissent is to allow expression of what a justice believes to be fundamental error by the majority. In the last decade of their tenure on the Court, both Justices William J. Brennan, Jr., and Thurgood Marshall knew that in most death penalty cases, they did not and probably never would have the votes to gain a majority for their view that the death penalty constitutes cruel and unusual punishment in violation of the Eighth Amendment. However, they regularly filed dissents in such cases. An opinion expressing their views was programmed into the Court's computer system and automatically added to every capital punishment case in which review was denied.

A dissent may result from a battle among the justices. In *Bowers v. Hardwick* (1986), five justices upheld the constitutionality of a Georgia antisodomy statute as applied to homosexual sex between consenting adults. The fifth vote in that case was supplied by Justice Lewis F. Powell, Jr., who had initially voted with the four dissenters. Justice Harry A. Blackmun was assigned to write for the majority, but when Powell switched his vote a few days after the conference, what was to have been the majority opinion overturning the Georgia statute became a dissent.

Justice Antonin Scalia argues that a dissent, threatened or actual, may serve to improve the quality of the majority opinion by forcing the author to think carefully about the argument and to remove any dubious assertions or reasoning. Scalia also believes that dissents

---

CHIEF JUSTICE CHARLES EVANS HUGHES ON DISSENT

There are some who think it desirable that dissents should not be disclosed as they detract from the force of the judgment. Undoubtedly, they do. When unanimity can be obtained without sacrifice or coercion, it strongly commends the decision to public confidence. . . .

Dissent in a court of last resort is an appeal to the brooding spirit of the law, to the intelligence of a future day, when a later decision may possibly correct the error into which the dissenting judge believes the court to have been betrayed.

—Charles Evans Hughes,
The Supreme Court of the United States (1928)

---

have several external functions. A dissent may augment rather than diminish the prestige of the Court, particularly if history judges the majority's decision harshly. The damage is mitigated if there is evidence that at least some of the justices saw the danger. In 1896 in *Plessy v. Ferguson*, seven justices voted to uphold separate but equal accommodations for blacks and whites. History's judgment of the Court would likely be much harsher were it not for the lone, eloquent dissent in that case by Justice John Marshall Harlan. In the *Bowers* case, later scholarly commentary was more favorable regarding Blackmun's position than that of the majority. After leaving the Court, Powell claimed that Blackmun's dissent in *Bowers* presented the better argument.

Other external consequences of a dissent, according to Scalia, are that it may help to change the law and to give the general public and the legal profession some sense of how the Court as a body thinks about fundamental issues of constitutional law. In the process, the Court is kept where, according to Scalia, it should be, "in the forefront of the intellectual development of the law."

IMPACT OF DISSENTS

Assessing the impact of dissenting opinions is even more difficult than determining the impact of Court decisions. Undoubtedly some of the internal and external consequences posited by Scalia do occur in some instances, but judging when and to precisely what effect is problematic. Blackmun's dissent in *Bowers* ultimately persuaded Powell, but only after Powell had left the Court.

Some argue that dissents undermine the legitimacy of the Court and may encourage noncompliance. The dissents by Holmes, Brandeis, and Stone that accompany some of the Court's anti-New Deal decisions in the early 1930's provided additional ammunition to President Franklin D. Roosevelt's supporters in the press and in Congress. In certain obvious landmark cases, the Court has gone to great pains to achieve unanimity. Chief Justice Earl Warren's prodigious efforts to produce a unanimous opinion in *Brown v. Board of Education* (1954) are well documented, but the unanimous opinion did not prevent massive resistance to desegregation in the states affected by the decision. In *United States v. Nixon* (1974), the justices consciously strove to produce a unanimous opinion in the face of suggestions from President Richard M. Nixon's attorney that the president would not comply with a fragmented decision. Ultimately, Nixon released the tapes as the Court ordered.

Philip A. Dynia

FURTHER READING

Two excellent studies of the workings of the Court provide detailed treatments of its decision-making process, particularly opinion writing: Lawrence Baum's *The Supreme Court* (8th ed. Washington, D.C.: Congressional Quarterly, 2004) and David M. O'Brien's *Storm Center* (7th ed. New York: W. W. Norton, 2005). O'Brien's study situates the Court in the larger context of the legal and political system of the United States. Slightly dated but eminently readable is Charles Evans Hughes's *The Supreme Court of the United States* (New York: Columbia University Press, 1928).

For a study of the Court and its procedures compared with courts in England and France, an indispensable source is Henry J. Abraham's *The Judicial Process* (7th ed. New York: Oxford University Press,

1998). On disagreements among the justices, an essential work is P. J. Cooper's *Battles on the Bench: Conflicts Inside the Supreme Court* (Lawrence: University Press of Kansas, 1995), as well as his and Howard Ball's *The United States Supreme Court from the Inside Out* (Englewood Cliffs, N.J.: Prentice-Hall, 1996). Also valuable is Donald E. Lively's *Foreshadows of the Law: Supreme Court Dissents and Constitutional Development* (Westport, Conn.: Praeger, 1992).

More general works on the Court's decision-making processes include H. W. Perry's *Deciding to Decide* (Cambridge, Mass.: Harvard University Press, 1991) and Bernard Schwartz's *Decision: How the Supreme Court Decides Cases* (New York: Oxford University Press, 1996). Another excellent and accessible discussion of the Court's procedures is Chief Justice William H. Rehnquist's *The Supreme Court: How It Was, How It Is* (New York: Morrow, 1987). Edward G. White's *Oliver Wendell Holmes, Jr.* (New York: Oxford University Press, 2006) is a full biography of the Supreme Court's most famous dissenter.

SEE ALSO Brandeis, Louis D.; Holmes, Oliver Wendell; Johnson, William; Marshall, John; Opinions, writing of; *Plessy v. Ferguson*; Seriatim opinions; Stone, Harlan Fiske.

Diversity Jurisdiction

DESCRIPTION: The authority of the federal courts to resolve disputes between citizens of different states or between a citizen and an alien when the total amount of damages in controversy exceeds seventy-five thousand dollars.

SIGNIFICANCE: Diversity jurisdiction, the requirements for which are clarified by the Supreme Court, accounts for a significant portion of the cases heard by the federal courts and was included in the Constitution to provide a forum in which litigants from different states could be assured of fairness.

Article III, section 2, of the U.S. Constitution grants authority to the federal courts to resolve disputes among citizens of different states. In the Judiciary Act of 1789, Congress provided that the federal courts had jurisdiction over cases between citizens of different states or between a citizen and an alien. Although the Constitution imposes no requirement as to a minimum amount of damages that must be involved in order to invoke diversity jurisdiction, Congress imposed a requirement that the amount in controversy, exclusive of interest and costs, must exceed a stated sum of damages. The requisite amount has increased over time and was set at seventy-five thousand dollars in the 1990's.

All cases brought under diversity jurisdiction can also be brought in a state court in which one of the litigants is situated. However, the framers of the Constitution created diversity jurisdiction out of a concern that state courts would be prejudiced against litigants from out of state. They believed that federal courts would serve as neutral forums in which citizens of one state would not be favored over those from another state. As Chief Justice John Marshall explained in *Bank of the United States v. Deveaux* (1809), "However true the fact may be, that the tribunals of the states will administer justice as impartially as those of the nation, to parties of every description, it is not less true that the Constitution itself either entertains apprehensions on this subject, or views with such indulgence the possible fears and apprehensions of suitors."

The Supreme Court has clarified the two requirements for diversity jurisdiction. The Court has strictly interpreted the requirement that the case involve citizens from different states, holding in the case of *Strawbridge v. Curtiss* (1806) that there has to be "complete diversity" so that all the plaintiffs must be citizens of different states than all the defendants. In addition, the Court has held that the citizenship of an individual is determined by the state of his or her domicile at the time the case is filed, while a corporation is considered to be a citizen of its state of incorporation and the state where it has its principal place of business. In determining the required jurisdictional amount, the Court held in *St. Paul Mercury Indemnity Co. v. Red Cab Co.* (1938) that the sum claimed by the plaintiff controls whether the requirement is met, as long as it made in good faith.

Kurt M. Saunders

FURTHER READING

James, Fleming, Jr., Geoffrey C. Hazard, Jr., and John Leubsdorf. *Civil Procedure.* 5th ed. Boston: Little, Brown, 2001.

Noonan, John Thomas. *Narrowing the Nation's Power: The Supreme Court Sides with the States.* Berkeley: University of California Press, 2002.

Wright, Charles A. *Law of Federal Courts.* St. Paul, Minn.: West Publishing, 1994.

SEE ALSO Appellate jurisdiction; Civil law; Judiciary Act of 1789; *Scott v. Sandford.*

Double Jeopardy

DESCRIPTION: Guarantee, stated in the Fifth Amendment, that if a person has been acquitted or convicted of an offense, he or she cannot be prosecuted a second time for that same offense.

SIGNIFICANCE: For nearly two centuries the Supreme Court decided very few double jeopardy cases, but in the last three decades of the twentieth century, it decided many.

The second clause of the Fifth Amendment, part of the Bill of Rights, states "nor shall any person be subject for the same offense to be twice put in jeopardy of life or limb." For the first part of the United States' existence, federal criminal cases were not appealed to the Supreme Court, so it had no federal double jeopardy cases. In addition, in *Barron v. Baltimore* (1833), the Court said that the provisions of the Bill of Rights limited the power of only the federal government and were inapplicable to the states. Consequently, there were no state court double jeopardy cases for the Court to review. Not until *Benton v. Maryland* (1969) did the Court conclude that the double jeopardy clause was applicable to the states, relying on the selective incorporation doctrine of the due process clause of the Fourteenth Amendment. After that time, so many, and sometimes contradictory, double jeopardy cases came before the Court that Chief Justice William H. Rehnquist referred to this area of the law as a Sargasso Sea—one in which even a skillful navigator could become entangled and lost.

THE BASIC PROTECTION

Jeopardy—the immediate threat of conviction and punishment—attaches in a criminal case when a jury is sworn in or, if there is no jury, when a judge begins to hear evidence. Whether jeopardy has attached is important because events occurring before that time, such as dismissal of the charges, will not preclude a subsequent prosecution; a dismissal of the charges after jeopardy has attached would preclude their being brought again.

A defendant who has been acquitted cannot be reprosecuted for that offense. Even with a relatively weak case, a prosecutor who could try the case multiple times might be able to perfect the presentation of witnesses and evidence so that eventually a jury would agree to convict. The Court found that such a result would be fundamentally unfair and would violate double jeopardy in *Ashe v. Swenson* (1970). After an acquittal, no matter how strong the state's evidence may have been, the defendant may not be forced to undergo the stress and expense of another prosecution for that crime, regardless of whether the verdict in the second case is a conviction or an acquittal.

Similarly, the Court ruled that a person cannot be tried again after having previously been convicted of the same offense in *Brown v. Ohio* (1977). However, in *United States v. Ball* (1896), the Court found that a necessary exception to this rule does allow the reprosecution of an individual whose conviction was reversed on appeal. There are many reasons why a conviction might be reversed, such as the improper admission of prejudicial evidence or inaccurate instructions to the jury. In these situations, after the reversal of the first conviction, the case could be retried without using the inadmissible evidence and with proper instructions to the jury, and the retrial would not be double jeopardy.

EXCEPTIONS

The doctrine protects against only successive criminal prosecutions or punishments; it does not prohibit a criminal prosecution after a civil action or a civil action after a criminal action. For example, property used in the commission of certain crimes, such as houses, cars, and other vehicles used in the manufacture and distribution of illegal drugs, is subject to forfeiture to the government. Such forfeiture actions usually are deemed to be civil rather than criminal punishments. Therefore, in *United States v. Ursery* (1996), the Court ruled that a person's having to forfeit his or her house and car to the government because they were used in a drug transaction is not the imposition of double jeopardy, although the individual had previously been criminally convicted and sentenced for the same drug transaction.

Similarly, those who have served the entire sentence for conviction of a sexual offense, such as rape or child molestation, may subsequently be adjudicated as sexually violent predators and ordered confined and treated until it is safe for them to be released. Because the subsequent adjudication is deemed civil and not criminal, the Court, in *Kansas v. Hendricks* (1997), found there is no double jeopardy, even if such sexual offenders might end up being confined for the rest of their lives.

The dual sovereignty doctrine is another major exception to the protection against double jeopardy. The basic guarantee is that the same sovereign, or government, will not prosecute or punish an individual twice for the same offense. In *Bartkus v. Illinois* (1959), however, the Court recognized that no double jeopardy violation occurs when different sovereigns prosecute an individual for the same offense. For these purposes, the federal government of the United States and the government of a given state, such as California, are deemed to be separate sovereigns. Likewise, according to *United States v. Wheeler* (1978), no double jeopardy takes place if an individual is tried for the same offense in a Native American court and in a federal court.

Cities and counties derive their governmental authority from that of the state in which they are located, so that neither a city nor a county is considered a separate sovereign from the state. Consequently, prosecutions for the same offense in, for example, Chicago municipal court and Illinois state courts would violate double jeopardy. In *Heath v. Alabama* (1985), the Court ruled that because the states are separate sovereigns from one another, prosecutions for the same offense by two separate states do not violate double jeopardy. With traditional crimes, such as murder or rape, it would be unusual for two states to have sufficient contact with the crime to have jurisdiction to prosecute it, but many conspiracies, especially those involving illegal drugs, have sufficient contacts with several states to confer jurisdiction on more than one. Nonetheless, dual sovereignty prosecutions involving two or more states are relatively rare.

William Shepard McAninch

FURTHER READING

Fireside, Harvey. *The Fifth Amendment: The Right to Remain Silent.* Springfield, N.J.: Enslow, 1998.

Garcia, Alfredo. *The Fifth Amendment: A Comprehensive Approach.* Westport, Conn.: Greenwood Press, 2002.

Lafave, Wayne, and Jerold Israel. *Criminal Procedure.* St. Paul: West Publishing, 1985.

McAninch, William. "Unfolding the Law of Double Jeopardy." *South Carolina Law Review* 44 (1993): 411.

Miller, Leonard G. *Double Jeopardy and the Federal System.* Chicago: University of Chicago Press, 1968.

SEE ALSO Bill of Rights; Fifth Amendment; Fundamental rights; Incorporation doctrine; *New York Times Co. v. Sullivan*; *Palko v. Connecticut.*

William O. Douglas

IDENTIFICATION: Associate justice (April 17, 1939-November 12, 1975)
NOMINATED BY: Franklin D. Roosevelt
BORN: October 16, 1898, Maine, Minnesota
DIED: January 19, 1980, Bethesda, Maryland
SIGNIFICANCE: An associate justice for nearly thirty-seven years, Douglas served longer on the Supreme Court than anyone else. As an associate justice, he always followed the Bill of Rights closely.

William O. Douglas was born in rural Minnesota but moved to Yakima, Washington, in 1904 with his newly widowed mother. Douglas, who contracted polio at age three, improved his health by becoming an outdoorsman and throughout his life was a naturalist and conservationist. After graduation from Whitman College in 1920, Douglas attended Columbia University Law School and was graduated second in his class in 1925. He then worked for a Wall Street law firm and taught at Columbia, leaving New York in 1932 to assume Yale University's Sterling Chair of Commercial and Corporate Law.

EARLY PUBLIC SERVICE

In 1934 Douglas, whose legal career focused on corporate reorganization and bankruptcy, joined the Securities and Exchange Commission (SEC). He was appointed SEC commissioner on January 21, 1936, and became chair of the SEC on September 21, 1937. The young lawyer continually impressed President Franklin D. Roosevelt, who considered him a possible candidate for the vice presidency in 1940 and again in 1944. On March 20, 1939, Roosevelt nominated Douglas to the Supreme Court, making him one of the youngest people ever nominated to such a position. Douglas was sworn in as an associate justice on April 17, 1939, at age forty-one.

President Harry S. Truman approached Douglas to become his running mate in 1948, but Douglas demurred. In the early 1950's he had considerable support as a possible Democratic candidate for the presidency but had little interest in leaving the Court to enter politics. In any case, his divorce from his first wife, Mildred, in 1953 diminished his appeal as a major political contender.

CAREER AS AN ASSOCIATE JUSTICE

Douglas was among the Court's most controversial associate justices. He married four women and divorced three of them. In 1966, at age sixty-eight, he married his fourth wife, who was so much younger than he that many conservative Americans considered him immoral. Personal matters had an effect on the public's perception of this gifted and intelligent jurist. He was frequently threatened with impeachment, the earliest threat coming in 1951 when he aroused public ire by advocating that the United States recognize communist China. In 1970 conservative members of the House of Representatives, rankled by Douglas's liberal decisions in court cases but also appalled by his personal antics, sought his impeachment.

A major factor in such efforts in the late 1960's and early 1970's was Douglas's dissent when the Court decided not to review several cases that challenged the legality of the Vietnam War. By that time, the nation was strongly divided by this conflict. The lines between liberals and conservatives were sharply drawn. Douglas, the ardent liberal, seemed to many in the opposition to be traitorous for suggesting that the Court consider the legality of the Vietnam engagement, which had already caused considerable social unrest in the United States.

Douglas was a strong advocate of enforcing and applying the Bill of Rights. He insisted that its guarantees be applied to people accused of crimes and tried in state courts. At this time, many courts in the South were particularly brazen in violating the rights of those who opposed segregation and who protested publicly for the rights of minorities, including the voting rights guaranteed them under the

William O. Douglas.
(Library of Congress)

Constitution but often denied them by specious state and local ordinances that dictated how precinct lines were drawn and that applied unreasonable literacy tests to African Americans, thereby disfranchising them.

In 1961 *Mapp v. Ohio* became one of the most important cases in Douglas's career as a jurist. Prior to *Mapp*, Douglas had argued that the Bill of Rights applied to individual states under the due process clause of the Fourteenth Amendment. *Mapp*, however, involved the search of Dollree Mapp's home without a proper warrant. The police were seeking someone suspected in a bombing, but Mapp refused to admit them without a warrant. When they returned three hours later with a paper purported to be warrant, they refused to allow Mapp to read the paper. When she attempted to grab it, they manhandled her and subsequently searched her house.

The police did not find their suspect. They did, however, find a stash of pornography in Mapp's basement and arrested her for possessing that material. Douglas argued that Mapp's Fourth Amendment rights, protecting her against unwarranted search and seizure, had been violated. Four other justices were persuaded by Douglas's argument and ruled that the state of Ohio had violated the defendant's constitutional rights.

DOUGLAS'S CONTRIBUTION

History has dealt kindly with the controversial rulings that originally brought the wrath of the community down on Douglas, who took courageous stands that were unpopular at the time. His flamboyant personal life also colored public images of him. After his death, most people who have viewed his career objectively have concluded that Douglas was a uniquely qualified jurist who fought strenuously to uphold the constitutional tenets of the fathers of the nation.

R. Baird Shuman

FURTHER READING

Ball, Howard, and Phillip J. Cooper. *Of Power and Right: Hugo Black, William O. Douglas, and America's Constitutional Revolution.* New York: Oxford University Press, 1992.

Belknap, Michal R. *The Vinson Court: Justices, Rulings, and Legacy.* Santa Barbara, Calif.: ABC-Clio, 2004.

Countryman, Vern. *The Judicial Record of Justice William O. Douglas.* Cambridge, Mass.: Harvard University Press, 1974.

Douglas, William O. *Nature's Justice: Writings of William O. Douglas.* Corvallis: Oregon State University Press, 2000.

Durum, James C. *Justice William O. Douglas.* Boston: Twayne, 1981.

Murphy, Bruce Allen. *Wild Bill: The Legend and Life of William O. Douglas.* New York: Random House, 2003.

Simon, James F. *Independent Journey: The Life of William O. Douglas.* New York: Harper & Row, 1980.

Urofsky, Melvin I. *The Warren Court: Justices, Rulings, and Legacy.* Santa Barbara, Calif.: ABC-Clio, 2001.

Wasby, Stephen L., ed. *He Shall Not Pass This Way Again: The Legacy of William O. Douglas.* Pittsburgh: University of Pittsburgh Press, 1990.

Yarbrough, Tinsley E. *The Burger Court: Justices, Rulings, and Legacy.* Santa Barbara, Calif.: ABC-Clio, 2000.

SEE ALSO Bill of Rights; Due process, procedural; Due process, substantive; Fourth Amendment; *Mapp v. Ohio*; Vietnam War.

Procedural Due Process

DESCRIPTION: Right not to be deprived by government of life, liberty, or property without notice and an opportunity to be heard according to fair procedures.

SIGNIFICANCE: The Supreme Court considers procedural due process to be one of the most fundamental constitutional rights.

The Supreme Court recognized that the constitutional right to procedural due process derives historically from the Magna Carta (1215), which prohibited the English monarch from depriving a certain class of subjects of their rights except by lawful judgment of their peers or by the law of the land. When the United States gained its independence, language modeled on the Magna Carta provision was included in some of the state constitutions. Soon after the ratification of the U.S. Constitution, the Fifth Amendment was adopted as part of the Bill of Rights. This amendment, applicable to the federal government, provided in part that "no person shall . . . be deprived of life, liberty, or property, without due process of law." In 1868 the Fourteenth Amendment formulated the same prohibition with regard to state—and, by implication, local—governments.

The due process clauses apply to criminal as well as civil procedures. However, because other constitutional protections are triggered in criminal matters by specific provisions of the Fourth, Fifth, Sixth, and Eighth Amendments, the Court has often invoked these more specific constitutional provisions in criminal procedure cases when it is unnecessary to address the more general requirements of the due process clauses.

BASIC PRINCIPLES

The Court ruled, in *Collins v. City of Harker Heights* (1992), that due process clauses provide a guarantee of fair procedure in connection with governmental deprivations of life, liberty, or property. In *Florida Prepaid Postsecondary Education Expense Board v. College Savings Bank* (1999), it held that procedural due process does not prevent governmental deprivation of life, liberty, or property; it merely prevents such deprivation without due process of law. Furthermore, the governmental deprivation must be deliberate. According to its finding in *Daniels v. Williams* (1986), a civil action against a governmental entity cannot be predicated on a due process theory if the governmental conduct at issue was merely negligent.

The two major components of fair procedure are notice and an opportunity to be heard. A primary purpose of the notice requirement is to ensure that the opportunity for a hearing is meaningful, as the Court determined in *West Covina v. Perkins* (1999). In both judicial and quasi-judicial proceedings, the Court determined that due process requires a neutral and detached judge in the first instance in *Concrete Pipe and Products of California v. Construction Laborers Pension Trust* (1993). However, where an initial determination is made by a party acting in an enforcement capacity, it found that due process may be satisfied by providing for a neutral adjudicator to conduct a *de novo* review (complete rehearing) of all factual and legal issues in *Marshall v. Jerrico* (1980).

The Court often (but not always) evaluates procedural due process issues by considering the three factors brought out in *Mathews v. Eldridge* (1976): the private interest affected by the official action; the risk of erroneous deprivation of such interest through the procedures used and the probable value, if any, of other procedural safeguards; and the relevant governmental interest.

CRIMINAL PROCEDURE

The Court applied the due process clauses in the criminal law area in cases in which other constitutional provisions do not apply. For example, the Court held that the adjudication of a contested criminal case in a mayor's court violates due process where the mayor's executive responsibilities may create a desire to maintain a high flow of revenue from the mayor's court in *Ward v. Village of Monroeville* (1972). It also held that a child in delinquency proceedings must be provided various procedural due process protections in *In re Gault* (1967).

The Court also made two rulings regarding placement in mental institutions. In *Vitek v. Jones* (1980), it held that a convicted felon serving a sentence in prison may not be transferred to a mental institution without appropriate procedures to determine whether he or she is mentally ill, and in *Foucha v. Louisiana* (1992), it determined that a person found not guilty of a crime by reason of insanity who is accordingly confined in a mental hospital is entitled to constitutionally adequate procedures to establish the grounds for continued confinement when the original basis for the confinement no longer exists.

OTHER APPLICATIONS

The Court applied the procedural component of the due process clause in many other contexts. For example, in *United States v. James Daniel Good Real Property* (1993), it held that, absent exigent circumstances, due process requires notice and a meaningful opportunity to be heard before the government can seize real property subject to civil forfeiture. In *Goldberg v. Kelly* (1970), the Court held that welfare recipients could not be deprived of their benefits without procedural due process protections. Similarly, in *Memphis Light, Gas and Water*

Division v. Craft (1978), the Court established federal due process procedures for termination of public utility service to customers in states that have a just cause requirement for such termination.

In *Cleveland Board of Education v. Loudermill* (1985), the Court determined that tenured classified civil servants were entitled to at least some procedural due process before termination, such as notice of allegations and opportunity to respond, coupled with a full post-termination hearing. However, it found that defamatory statements by governmental officials, in the absence of other governmental action, do not trigger due process analysis in *Paul v. Davis* (1976).

Alan E. Johnson

FURTHER READING

American Bar Association. *Due Process Protection for Juveniles in Civil Commitment Proceedings.* Chicago: American Bar Association, 1991.

Champion, Dean John. *The Juvenile Justice System: Delinquency, Processing, and the Law.* 4th ed. Upper Saddle River, N.J.: Prentice-Hall, 2003.

Cox, Steven M., John J. Conrad, and Jennifer M. Allen. *Juvenile Justice: A Guide to Theory and Practice.* 5th ed. New York: McGraw Hill, 2003.

Decker, John F. *Revolution to the Right: Criminal Procedure Jurisprudence During the Burger-Rehnquist Court Era.* New York: Garland, 1993.

Galligan, Denis J. *Due Process and Fair Procedures: A Study of Administrative Procedures.* New York: Oxford University Press, 1996.

Orth, John V. *Due Process of Law: A Brief History.* Lawrence: University Press of Kansas, 2003.

Roach, Kent. *Due Process and Victims' Rights: The New Law and Politics of Criminal Justice.* Toronto: Toronto University Press, 1999.

SEE ALSO *Adamson v. California*; Due process, substantive; Eighth Amendment; Fifth Amendment; Fourth Amendment; *Rochin v. California*; Self-incrimination, immunity against; Sixth Amendment.

Substantive Due Process

DESCRIPTION: The doctrine that the liberty protected by the due process clauses of the Fifth and Fourteenth Amendments encompasses more than the procedural rights owed by the government when it seeks to punish someone for a crime.

SIGNIFICANCE: Substantive due process has become the chief means by which the Supreme Court defines and extends the constitutional rights enjoyed by people in the United States.

One of the intents of the framers of the Fourteenth Amendment was to protect the property and contract rights of newly freed slaves from state law. The amendment states that the state shall not take away any person's life, liberty, or property without "due process of law." The phrase "due process" usually meant proper legal procedure, especially in criminal law.

However, in *Allgeyer v. Louisiana* (1897), the Supreme Court, most of whose members believed strongly in laissez-faire capitalism, decided that part of the "fundamental liberty" protected by the due process clause was a substantive right to make contracts. This new right was frequently used by the Court to strike down state economic regulations with which the justices disagreed. For example, in *Lochner v. New York* (1905), the Court declared unconstitutional a New York law restricting the number of hours per day that bakers could work because it interfered with the right of the bakers to contract with their employers for their services. Justice Oliver Wendell Holmes filed a powerful dissenting opinion in the case.

The Court also found a few other fundamental rights applicable to the states. In *Gitlow v. New York* (1925), for example, it held that freedom of speech, a First Amendment right, limited state governments. However, Holmes's reasoning in the *Lochner* dissent eventually prevailed. In 1936 the Court upheld a Washington state minimum-wage law in *Morehead v. New York ex rel. Tipaldo*. Soon after *Morehead*, several older, more conservative justices retired from the court. President Franklin D. Roosevelt appointed progressive justices, and a new era of judicial self-restraint began. To many observers, it appeared unlikely that substantive due process guarantees would surface again.

SUBSTANTIVE DUE PROCESS REBORN

The Court's interest in substantive liberty was rekindled in the 1960's. On November 1, 1961, the Planned Parenthood League of Connecticut opened a center in New Haven. On November 10, its executive director, Estelle Griswold, and its medical director, Dr. Harold Buxton, were arrested for violating the Connecticut birth-control statute. This law, which had been on the state's books since 1879, prohibited the use of birth-control devices and the provision of birth control information. Griswold and Buxton were the first people ever to have been charged under the statute. An earlier attempt to challenge the law had been defeated when the Court refused to take jurisdiction because no one had ever been prosecuted. Griswold and Buxton were convicted and appealed to the Court.

The Court's opinion in *Griswold v. Connecticut,* written by Associate Justice William O. Douglas for a 7-2 majority, struck down the Connecticut statute. Douglas reasoned that many constitutional provisions as well as many of the Court's cases had established a zone of privacy into which states are forbidden to intrude. The First Amendment, which protects speech and religion, also protects privacy in associations, the Third Amendment prevents the government from forcing the populace to house soldiers; and the Fourth Amendment limits "unreasonable" warrantless intrusions into the home.

The Fifth Amendment includes some substantive liberties. Finally, the Ninth Amendment establishes that there may be constitutional rights that are not explicitly set forth in the Constitution. Taken together, Douglas argued, these provisions establish a constitutional marital privacy right that the Connecticut birth-control statute infringed.

The two dissenters in the case, Associate Justices Hugo L. Black and Potter Stewart, argued that the decision would return the Court to the discredited era of substantive due process in which the justices had written their policy preferences into the Constitution. Black and Stewart pointed out that there was no explicit textual support in the Constitution for the new right of marital privacy. They were particularly perturbed by the majority's use of the Ninth Amendment, which seemed completely open ended to them and would give the Court limitless authority to define rights beyond the text of the Constitution.

The same right to receive and use contraceptive devices was extended to unmarried persons in *Eisenstadt v. Baird* (1972). In this case a Massachusetts statute was declared unconstitutional by the Court on two grounds: It unconstitutionally discriminated against unmarried people, and it collided with "a fundamental human right" to control conception.

ABORTION

The following year, conception and privacy rights were further extended by the Court in *Roe v. Wade* (1973). This famous case established that a pregnant woman has a constitutional right to an abortion on demand during the first trimester of pregnancy. Justice Harry A. Blackmun, writing for the seven-justice majority, argued that the Court's substantive due process cases had established a right of privacy that "is broad enough to encompass a woman's decision whether or not to terminate her pregnancy" and that outweighs the state's interest in protecting prenatal life, at least during the first trimester of pregnancy. Blackmun turned to historical medical and legal thinking about pregnancy and abortion to help define the extent of abortion rights. Some state regulation of abortions is permitted in the second trimester, and abortion may be prohibited altogether in the third.

The two dissenters, Justices William H. Rehnquist and Byron R. White, maintained that there is no "fundamental" right to an abortion on demand and referred to the historical tradition in England and the United States of prohibiting abortion. They argued that the Court should defer to the wishes of the majority, at least in the absence of a traditional fundamental right. *Roe v. Wade* is perhaps the boldest assertion of substantive due process rights by the Court. It has been immensely controversial and has resulted in a great deal of political action in opposition to the Court's decision and in occasional violence directed at abortion clinics, physicians, and patients. In the years since *Roe*, the Court has revisited the case often. Although the decree has been modified somewhat, the central holding—that a pregnant woman has a right to an abortion on demand in the first trimester—remains intact.

LIMIT ON NEW RIGHTS

At the end of the twentieth century, *Roe v. Wade* represented the high-water mark of the Court's protection of substantive liberties. The Court declined to extend the concept to protect homosexual sodomy in *Bowers v. Hardwick* (1986). A Georgia statute that prohibited anal or oral sex was challenged by Michael Hardwick, a gay man who had been threatened with prosecution under the law after he was found in bed with another man in the course of a police drug raid. In his opinion for the majority, Justice Byron R. White wrote that

> Sodomy was a criminal offense at common law and was forbidden by the laws of the original 13 States when they ratified the Bill of Rights. In 1868 when the Fourteenth Amendment . . . was ratified, all but 5 of the 37 States in the Union had criminal sodomy laws. In fact, until 1961, all 50 States outlawed sodomy, and today, 24 States and the District of Columbia continue to provide criminal penalties for sodomy performed in private and between consenting adults. . . . Against this background, to claim that a right to engage in such conduct is "deeply rooted in this Nation's history and tradition" or "implicit in the concept of ordered liberty" is, at best, facetious.

White also pointed out that *Griswold, Eisenstadt,* and *Roe* had all spoken to the right to decide whether or not to bear children. This crucial element is absent in *Bowers*. Four justices—Harry A. Blackmun, William J. Brennan, Jr., Thurgood Marshall, and John Paul Stevens—argued that the case was really about a "fundamental right to be let alone," and that the Court's earlier privacy decisions established just that. Although *Bowers* is a 5-4 decision, the issue did not appear again before the Court. The Georgia supreme court struck down the statute in question on independent state constitutional grounds in 1999.

The Court resisted attempts to get it to establish substantive rights to die or to assisted suicide. In *Cruzan v. Director, Missouri Department of Health* (1990), the Court refused to order the removal of life-support equipment from Nancy Cruzan, a young woman in a "persistent vegetative state" as a result of injuries suffered in an automobile accident. The majority, perhaps unwilling to further politicize the Court's work in the wake of the controversy surrounding *Roe v. Wade*, made it clear that it preferred to allow state governments to resolve these newly arising life and death questions. Similarly, in 1997 the court refused to hear a claim that an Oregon assisted-suicide law is unconstitutional.

The "new" substantive due process has allowed the Supreme Court to define new individual constitutional rights. So far these have been limited to substantive rights already found in the First Amendment and additional reproductive privacy rights. The doctrine is very controversial because every time the Court limits state power, it is acting in an antimajoritarian way. It is not clear to the public why the right to an abortion is somehow "fundamental" while the "bedroom privacy" argued for in the Georgia sodomy case is not. Nothing appears to illuminate these decisions besides the wishes of the justices. The Constitution itself neither explicitly establishes these rights nor implies them with any clarity. The absence of textual support for these decisions puts perception of the Court's legitimacy at risk.

Robert Jacobs

FURTHER READING

John V. Orth's *Due Process of Law: A Brief History* (Lawrence: University Press of Kansas, 2003) traces the concept of due process back from its early roots in English history through modern U.S. Supreme Court decisions. The property law and contract clause background of substantive due process is well discussed in *The Guardian of Every Other Right: A Constitutional History of Property Rights* by James Ely, Jr. (New York: Oxford University Press, 1992) and Polly J. Price's *Property Rights: Rights and Liberties Under the Law* (Santa Barbara, Calif.: ABC-Clio, 2003). *Private Property and the Limits of American Constitutionalism: The Madisonian Framework and Its Legacy* by Jennifer Nedelsky (Chicago: University of Chicago Press, 1990) provides less technical coverage of some of the same topics.

There is a vast literature on the "true" meaning of the Fourteenth Amendment and whether it does or does not "incorporate" the Bill of Rights. The classic argument for the incorporationist position is *The Supreme Court in United States History* by Charles Warren (Boston: Little, Brown, 1937), while the opposition is best represented by Charles Fairman's *The Fourteenth Amendment and the Bill of Rights: The*

Incorporation Theory (New York: Da Capo Press, 1970). A more recent work suggesting curtailing the judiciary's role is *The Fourteenth Amendment and the Bill of Rights* by Raoul Berger (Norman: University of Oklahoma Press, 1989). An argument supporting the Court's activities may be found in *Freedom and the Court: Civil Rights and Liberties in the United States* by Henry J. Abraham and Barbara A. Perry (8th ed. New York: Oxford University Press, 2003). Similarly, the legitimacy of the privacy decisions and the natural law threads of thought that produced them have engendered enormous comment. One balanced work is *The Supreme Court and the Second Bill of Rights: The Fourteenth Amendment and the Nationalization of Civil Liberties* by Richard C. Cortner (Madison: University of Wisconsin Press, 1981).

SEE ALSO Abortion; Birth control and contraception; Contract, freedom of; *Cruzan v. Director, Missouri Department of Health*; Due process, procedural; Fourteenth Amendment; *Griswold v. Connecticut*; Incorporation doctrine; Judicial activism; Judicial self-restraint; Privacy, right to; *Roe v. Wade*.

Duncan v. Louisiana

CITATION: 391 U.S. 145
DATE: May 20, 1968
ISSUE: Trial by jury
SIGNIFICANCE: With this decision, the Supreme Court applied the Sixth Amendment's right to jury trial to the states through the Fourteenth Amendment under the incorporation doctrine.

Justice Byron R. White, writing for a 7-2 majority, held that a jury trial is mandatory in a state court if the same offense would be entitled to a jury trial in federal court. Through this ruling, he applied a portion of the Sixth Amendment through incorporation under the Fourteenth Amendment.

The defendant had been convicted of a misdemeanor without benefit of a jury because Louisiana's laws did not mandate jury trials for minor offenses. The Supreme Court held that a portion of the

Bill of Rights must be considered part of due process if it is a part of the Anglo-American system of "ordered liberty," and juries were a part of that. This strengthened the theory of incorporation, which held that due process must include any feature without which one could not imagine civilized society existing. Justices John M. Harlan II and Potter Stewart dissented because they feared a further erosion of states' rights.

Richard L. Wilson

SEE ALSO *Batson v. Kentucky*; Due process, procedural; Incorporation doctrine; Jury, trial by; Sixth Amendment.

Gabriel Duvall

IDENTIFICATION: Associate justice (November 23, 1811-January 14, 1835)
NOMINATED BY: James Madison
BORN: December 6, 1752, Prince Georges County, Maryland
DIED: March 6, 1844, Prince Georges County, Maryland
SIGNIFICANCE: During his twenty-three-year tenure on the Supreme Court, Duvall sided with Chief Justice John Marshall on best-known decisions. Duvall favored a strong central government and nationalist interpretation of the Constitution.

Gabriel Duvall had a multifaceted career. He studied law and was admitted to the bar in 1778. He served as a soldier in the Maryland militia during the Revolutionary War. He was clerk of the Maryland House of Delegates in 1777 and was elected a member in 1787. He served until 1794 when he was elected to the U.S. House of Representatives; he was reelected in 1796 when he resigned to become chief justice of the General Court of Maryland. Duvall was then appointed comptroller of the treasury by President Thomas Jefferson, serving under Secretary of the Treasury Albert Gallatin until 1811, when he was nominated by President James Madison to the Supreme Court.

Most notable for agreeing with Chief Justice John Marshall and the minority in *Ogden v. Saunders* (1827), when the majority ruled

Gabriel Duvall.
(Library of Congress)

that states could discharge debts as long as they did not affect contracts predating state relief laws, Duvall also was noted for opposing Marshall in *Dartmouth College v. Woodward* (1819), which limited state legislative power. Duvall is also remembered for the unanimous opinion he wrote in *LeGrand v. Darnall* (1829), in which property left to a slave brought about the freeing of that slave. Duvall's health declined in later years. Upon hearing that President Andrew Jackson intended to appoint a fellow Marylander, Roger Brooke Taney, to the Court, Duvall resigned in January, 1835. He lived another nine years in retirement.

Gregory N. Seltzer

SEE ALSO Marshall, John; Slavery; Taney, Roger Brooke.

369

Eighth Amendment

DATE: 1791

DESCRIPTION: Amendment to the U.S. Constitution that forbids requiring excessive bail, imposing excessive fines, and inflicting cruel and unusual punishments.

SIGNIFICANCE: The three clauses of the Eighth Amendment are the only provisions in the Constitution that place substantive limits on the severity of punishments in criminal cases. The Supreme Court's role has been to interpret these clauses.

TEXT OF THE EIGHTH AMENDMENT

Excessive bail shall not be required, nor excessive fines imposed, nor cruel and unusual punishments inflicted.

The Eighth Amendment is derived almost verbatim from the English Bill of Rights (1689). Adopted in 1791 as part of the Bill of Rights, the amendment was intended to prohibit the abuse of federal government power, but the precise meaning of the amendment is unclear and requires interpretation by the Supreme Court.

The first two clauses of the Eighth Amendment (prohibiting excessive bail and fines) have not been applied to the states. Although the Court has never established an absolute right to bail, it has reviewed whether bail has been set higher than necessary to ensure that a defendant appears for trial.

The Court has taken a flexible interpretation of the cruel and unusual punishment clause, stating in *Trop v. Dulles* (1958) that punishments should be evaluated in light of the "evolving standards of decency" of a maturing society. The clause was formally applied to the states in *Robinson v. California* (1962). Barbaric punishments are prohibited, but the Court has refused to hold that the death penalty itself is cruel and unusual punishment. Punishments disproportionate to the crime, the treatment of prisoners, and conditions of confinement may also violate the Eighth Amendment.

John Fliter

FURTHER READING

Bedau, Hugo Adam, ed. *The Death Penalty in America: Current Controversies.* New York: Oxford University Press, 1997.

Foley, Michael A. *Arbitrary and Capricious: The Supreme Court, the Constitution, and the Death Penalty.* New York: Praeger, 2003.

Jowell, Jeffrey, and Dawn Oliver, eds. *The Changing Constitution.* 5th ed. New York: Oxford University Press, 2004.

Melusky, Joseph A., and Keith A. Pesto. *Cruel and Unusual Punishment: Rights and Liberties Under the Law.* Santa Barbara, Calif.: ABC-Clio, 2003.

SEE ALSO Bail; Bill of Rights; Capital punishment; Due process, procedural; *Furman v. Georgia*; *Payne v. Tennessee*.

Elastic Clause

DATE: 1789

DESCRIPTION: Last clause of Article I, section 8, of the U.S. Constitution, authorizing Congress to make all laws necessary and proper for exercising its enumerated powers and any other power granted by the Constitution to the national government.

SIGNIFICANCE: After an 1819 Supreme Court decision, the elastic clause provided the basis for the doctrine of implied powers, stretching the powers of the national government beyond those specifically granted by the Constitution.

In 1791, when advising President George Washington on the constitutionality of establishing a national bank, Thomas Jefferson and others opposed to a strong national government maintained that Congress was limited to exercising those powers expressly granted by the Constitution, for example, the power to coin money. All other powers were reserved for the states. Jefferson argued that the necessary and proper clause imposed additional limits on the powers of Congress. The clause limited any use of powers not expressly granted by the

Constitution except when such powers were absolutely necessary or indispensable to the exercise of an enumerated power. A national bank, for example, was unconstitutional both because the Constitution did not expressly delegate the power to create corporations to Congress and because a bank was not an indispensable means for achieving Congress's legitimate ends. A broader interpretation of the clause, Jefferson argued, would effectively create a national government with unlimited power.

Alexander Hamilton and others opposed Jefferson's strict construction of the clause, maintaining that the Constitution established an independent national government that, although exercising limited powers, was fully sovereign within the scope of its powers. Hamilton argued that the elastic clause had to be broadly interpreted as granting whatever additional powers would assist Congress in carrying out its enumerated powers. The clause allowed Congress to do not just what was indispensable but also whatever was convenient or helpful to achieving its ends. The incorporation of a bank, for example, was constitutional because it was a useful means for Congress to carry out its delegated power to collect taxes.

When the controversy over the incorporation of the Second Bank of the United States reached the Supreme Court in *McCulloch v. Maryland* (1819), Chief Justice John Marshall transformed Hamilton's loose construction of the clause into constitutional law. In his opinion, he stated that if the ends were legitimate and within the scope of the Constitution, all means that were appropriate and not prohibited, as well as consistent with "the letter and spirit" of the Constitution, were constitutional. His decision meant that the Constitution did not limit the federal government's powers to those expressly delegated, but included powers implied by Congress's freedom to choose the means by which it would carry out its responsibilities.

Joseph V. Brogan

FURTHER READING

Fisher, Louis. *The Politics of Shared Power: Congress and the Executive.* College Station: Texas A&M University Press, 1998.

Fried, Charles. *Saying What the Law Is: The Constitution in the Supreme Court.* Cambridge, Mass.: Harvard University Press, 2004.

Gunther, Gerald. *John Marshall's Defense of "McCulloch v. Maryland."* Stanford, Calif.: Stanford University Press, 1969.

Jowell, Jeffrey, and Dawn Oliver, eds. *The Changing Constitution.* 5th ed. New York: Oxford University Press, 2004.

Willoughby, Westel Woodbury. *The Supreme Court of the United States: Its History and Influence in Our Constitutional System.* Union, N.J.: Lawbook Exchange, 2001.

SEE ALSO Bill of Rights; *McCulloch v. Maryland*; Marshall, John; States' rights and state sovereignty; Tenth Amendment.

Eleventh Amendment

DATE: 1795

DESCRIPTION: Amendment to the U.S. Constitution that prohibits lawsuits in federal courts against states by citizens of other states or of foreign countries.

SIGNIFICANCE: This forty-three-word amendment has been interpreted by Supreme Court decisions to extend far beyond what it literally declares. In particular, it has been used to provide states with the common-law privilege of sovereign immunity, which means that they cannot be sued without their consent.

TEXT OF THE ELEVENTH AMENDMENT

The Judicial power of the United States shall not be construed to extend to any suit in law or equity, commenced or prosecuted against one of the United States by Citizens of another State, or by Citizens or Subjects of any Foreign State.

Ratified in 1795, the Eleventh Amendment was the first amendment added to the U.S. Constitution following the adoption of the Bill of Rights. It was adopted specifically to overrule a Supreme Court decision, *Chisholm v. Georgia* (1793). In that decision, the Court had ruled that a default judgment in favor of the plaintiff, who served as executor for the estate of a South Carolina merchant, was valid because the defendant, the state of Georgia, had refused to appear in its own defense at the trial. Georgia claimed that, as an independent and sovereign state, it enjoyed immunity from such litigation.

Article III, section 2, of the U.S. Constitution grants jurisdiction to federal courts in the case of controversies between a state and citizens of another state. In a 4-1 decision, with only justice James Iredell dissenting, the Court held that the plaintiff in *Chisholm* had the right to sue the state of Georgia and that the state of Georgia was legally remiss in not responding to that suit. Opinions by Justices John Jay and James Wilson reiterated the nationalist view that sovereignty rests in the people of the United States for the purposes of union. In regard to these purposes, Georgia, in the eyes of these justices, did not meet the criterion of being a sovereign state.

PASSAGE OF THE AMENDMENT

On March 4, 1794—within a year of the *Chisholm* decision—Congress drafted the Eleventh Amendment and urged its passage. By February 4, 1795, the legislatures of the requisite three-quarters of the states had ratified the amendment, which officially made it a law and a part of the U.S. Constitution. The only states not ratifying it were Pennsylvania and New Jersey. By an odd circumstance, however, the amendment was not officially declared a part of the Constitution until January 8, 1798, when President John Quincy Adams declared it to be in effect in a presidential message.

The date on which the Eleventh Amendment officially became a part of the Constitution is often given as January 8, 1798, although it is now conceded that presidents play no official role in the amendment process, so the Eleventh Amendment officially became a part of the Constitution after its ratification in 1795.

DOCTRINE OF SOVEREIGN IMMUNITY

Under the Eleventh Amendment, federal courts are prohibited from considering lawsuits brought against states by two specific classes of people: citizens of other states and citizens and subjects of foreign nations. As time passed, however, the Eleventh Amendment was interpreted more broadly than had probably been originally intended by its framers.

In *New Hampshire v. Louisiana* (1883), the Supreme Court ruled that one state could not sue another state if it did so in the interests of one or more of its citizens rather than in its own interest. A further extension of the Eleventh Amendment occurred in *Ex parte New York* (1921), when the Court found that the amendment applied to admiralty jurisdiction so that sovereign states, as defined by the Court, could not be sued in federal courts for events that took place in the waters that adjoined those states. In *Monaco v. Mississippi* (1934), the Court clearly found that foreign sovereigns could not sue sovereign states of the United States in federal courts.

The words of the Eleventh Amendment do not refer to any limitations on the right of state citizens to sue the state within which they reside. Nonetheless, in the controversial *Hans v. Louisiana* (1890) decision, the Court concluded that the Eleventh Amendment protects the states' sovereign immunity from all lawsuits, even those coming from citizens of the same state. The Court limited the effect of the *Hans* ruling somewhat in the case of *Ex parte Young* (1908), which allowed suits against state officers whenever they violated the U.S. Constitution. The theory behind the ruling was that the state was not being sued, although officials could be sued for acts committed in the name of the state. Many years later the *Young* ruling was itself limited in *Edelman v. Jordan* (1974), which held that the Eleventh Amendment bars suits against state officials for damage awards that would be paid out of the state treasury.

During the 1990's, the five conservative members of the Rehnquist Court wanted to adhere faithfully to the *Hans* precedent, while the four liberal members believed it had been wrongly decided. The Court voted five to four to restore *Hans* and reverse a 1989 precedent in *Seminole Tribe v. Florida* (1996), ruling that a state's sovereign immunity overrides power to regulate commerce. By a 5-4 vote in *Alden v.*

Maine (1999), the Court extended the protection of sovereign immunity to states sued in their own state courts for violations of federal law. The *Alden* ruling was based on the concept of sovereign immunity that existed in the English common law at the time the Constitution was adopted.

The same five-member majority ruled in *Kimel v. Florida Board of Regents* (2000) that the Eleventh Amendment barred state employees from suing state institutions under the Age Discrimination in Employment Act (1967). Then in *Federal Maritime Commission v. South Carolina State Ports Authority* (2002), the Court, again by a 5-4 majority, further shielded states from the obligation of having to answer private complaints before federal executive agencies.

The impact of sovereign immunity has been limited in practice because all of the states except for Virginia have waived much of their immunity. Virginia has thus become the only state that can almost never be sued by its own citizens. Even Virginia, however, can be sued in federal bankruptcy cases. This was decided in *Central Virginia Community College v. Katz* (2006), when the supervisor of a bankrupt estate sued a state-run college in federal court under the bankruptcy laws. The Supreme Court voted five to four to uphold the suit. Writing for the majority, Justice John Paul Stevens explained that because Article I of the Constitution authorized Congress to enact uniform bankruptcy laws, it could be assumed that the states had agreed to this limitation on their immunity when they ratified the Constitution. *Katz* is unique in being the only case in which the Court has permitted Congress to use one of its Title I powers as a justification for authorizing a person to sue a state.

EXCEPTIONS

Significant exceptions have been made to the states' immunity under the Eleventh Amendment. Immunity does not extend to the political subdivisions within the states, such as cities and counties. Although states may waive their sovereign immunity from suit, Congress may not assume they have done so unless the waiver is explicit. Congress, by virtue of its enforcement powers specified in section 5 of the Fourteenth Amendment, may enact statutes that authorize private causes of action against states for violating the provisions of the amendment, in particular the equal protection clause. Congress's power to abrogate under section 5, however, is limited. In *City of Boerne v. Flores* (1997), the Court specified that laws passed under section 5 must be narrowly tailored to address constitutional violations, thus giving Congress only limited power to enforce laws against discrimination based on age and disability.

Perhaps no amendment to the Constitution has been interpreted in as many various ways as the Eleventh. Some noted legal scholars have called for its restatement and simplification. Others have proposed that the amendment should be interpreted literally based on the simple declaration of its forty-three words. At present, however, citizens who think they have cause to take action against states must pursue political action or work within the framework of exceptions that has resulted from the Supreme Court's complex interpretations of the amendment. Since the *Seminole Tribe* decision of 1996, most of the major decisions under the Eleventh Amendment have been decided by 5-4 votes, which strongly suggests that the precedents are vulnerable to future reversals.

R. Baird Shuman
Updated by the Editor

FURTHER READING

Baum, Lawrence. *The Supreme Court.* 8th ed. Washington, D.C.: CQ Press, 2003.

Doernberg, Donald. *Sovereign Immunity or the Rule of Law.* Durham, N.C. Carolina Academic Press, 2006.

Noonan, John Thomas. *Narrowing the Nation's Power: The Supreme Court Sides with the States.* Berkeley: University of California Press, 2002.

O'Brien, David. *Constitutional Law and Politics, Volume One: Struggles for Power and Governmental Accountability.* 6th ed. New York: W. W. Norton, 2005.

Orth, John V. *The Judicial Power of the United States: The Eleventh Amendment in American History.* New York: Oxford University Press, 1987.

Symposium. "State Sovereign Immunity and the Eleventh Amendment." *Notre Dame Law Review* 75 (2000): 817-1182.

SEE ALSO Americans with Disabilities Act; Bill of Rights; *Chisholm v. Georgia*; Federalism; Peckham, Rufus W.; Separation of powers.

Oliver Ellsworth

IDENTIFICATION: Chief justice (March 8, 1796-December 15, 1800)
NOMINATED BY: George Washington
BORN: April 29, 1745, Windsor, Connecticut
DIED: November 26, 1807, Windsor, Connecticut
SIGNIFICANCE: Ellsworth helped author the Judiciary Act of 1789, which established the federal judicial system. As an associate justice, he favored the expansion of the powers of the federal courts, but illness and a diplomatic assignment prevented him from having much impact.

Intended by his father to have a career in the church, Oliver Ellsworth entered Yale in 1762 but left two years later to complete his college education at Princeton, where he earned a B.A. in 1766. Soon

Oliver Ellsworth.
(William Wheeler/
Collection of the
Supreme Court of
the United States)

after returning home, he gave up the study of theology for law. Admitted to the bar in 1771, he set up practice in Windsor, Connecticut. Four years later, he moved to Hartford, where he quickly rose to prominence and recognition as a leader of the Connecticut bar.

In 1777, Ellsworth was appointed state's attorney for Hartford County. He became a member of the Governor's Council within three years and a judge of the Connecticut superior court shortly thereafter. During the Revolutionary War, as a member of the Committee of the Pay Table, he supervised the state's war expenditures; in 1779, he was chosen to serve on the Council of Safety. Also in 1777, the Connecticut general assembly appointed him a delegate to the Continental Congress, where he served for six years. As a delegate, Ellsworth gained recognition for the Connecticut compromise, which established two legislative houses and, to create a balance between states with large and small populations, granted each state two senators. He also recommended that the words "United States" be used instead of the word "nation" to designate the government.

One of the first U.S. senators from Connecticut, he served in this capacity for seven years until appointed chief justice of the United States in 1796. In the Senate, Ellsworth had earned respect for drafting the Judiciary Act of 1789, which established the circuit and district court system, but his brief term as chief justice was fairly undistinguished. His decisions were more remarkable for common sense than for legal learning. Although he was known as a good lawyer, Ellsworth was more an advocate than a jurist. Noteworthy, however, is his decision on *Hylton v. United States* (1796), the first time the Supreme Court ruled on the constitutionality of an act of Congress.

In 1799 Ellsworth, although still chief justice, traveled to France, where he and other U.S. commissioners negotiated with Napoleon Bonaparte to avoid a war between the two countries. The combined effects of arduous travel and difficult negotiations broke his health, and he resigned from the Supreme Court in 1800, while still in France. After retiring to Connecticut in 1801, he served in that state's upper house and was appointed chief justice of Connecticut's highest court in 1807, the year of his death.

Bes Stark Spangler

FURTHER READING

Bader, William H., and Roy M. Mersky, eds. *The First One Hundred Eight Justices.* Buffalo, N.Y.: William S. Hein, 2004.

Brown, William Garrott. *The Life of Oliver Ellsworth.* New York: Macmillan, 1905. Reprint. New York: DaCapo Press, 1970.

Friedman, Leon, and Fred L. Israel, eds. *The Justices of the Supreme Court: Their Lives and Major Opinions.* 5 vols. New York: Chelsea House, 1997.

Harrington, Matthew P. *Jay and Ellsworth, The First Courts: Justices, Rulings, and Legacy.* Santa Barbara, Calif.: ABC-Clio, 2007.

SEE ALSO Chief justice; Jay, John; Judiciary Act of 1789.

Employment Discrimination

DESCRIPTION: Act of making decisions related to hiring and promoting workers based on non-job-related characteristics such as race, color, religion, national origin, gender, age, and disability.

SIGNIFICANCE: The Fourteenth Amendment of the Constitution prohibits state-sponsored discrimination, and Congress, through its authority to regulate interstate commerce, passed several important statutes preventing employment discrimination. Through the Supreme Court's power to interpret these statutes, it influences employment discrimination law and policy.

Title VII of the Civil Rights Act of 1964 (including its amendments) is the most important employment discrimination statute in U.S. law. It forbids employment discrimination on the grounds of race, color, religion, sex, or national origin by private companies (with at least fifteen employees), labor unions, employment agencies, and federal, state, and local governments. The statute also created the Equal Employment Opportunity Commission (EEOC) to investigate charges of discrimination, attempt to work an agreement, and if necessary file suit in federal court on behalf of the plaintiff. Congress also passed the Age Discrimination in Employment Act of 1967 and the Americans with Disabilities Act of 1990, which extend similar protections against age and disability discrimination in the workplace. Although some Supreme Court litigation addressed employment discrimination in religion, national origin, disability, and age, the bulk of the Court's influence was in the areas of race and gender.

RACE

Because racial discrimination has been so prominent in U.S. history, most of the Court's rulings involving Title VII concern race. In *Griggs v. Duke Power Co.* (1971), the Court had to decide whether African Americans could pursue a Title VII claim for employment practices that were not intended to discriminate but nevertheless put them at a disadvantage. The Duke Power Company used an examination as a standard for hiring and promotion. On this test, not directly related to job duties, blacks generally scored lower than whites. The Court ruled unanimously that even if there is no discriminatory intent, a practice that has a disparate impact on a protected class constitutes a Title VII violation. However, in *Wards Cove Packing Co. v. Atonio* (1989), the Court held that to establish disparate impact, plaintiffs needed to go beyond demonstrating that a particular practice caused a statistical disparity. Plaintiffs must also prove that the disparity did not result from a business necessity. The Civil Rights Act of 1991 reversed the Court's interpretation in *Wards Cove*, shifting the burden of proof to the employer to show that the employment practice is directly related to the position in question and is necessary for the normal operation of the business.

Furthermore, in *McDonnell Douglas Corp. v. Green* (1973), the Court addressed how to prove discriminatory intent (disparate treatment). McDonnell Douglas refused to rehire a black worker who had protested his layoff by criminally trespassing on McDonnell Douglas property. Although the Court sided with McDonnell Douglas, it did articulate a procedure for proving disparate treatment, which generally favors plaintiffs. First, the employee must show only that he/she is a member of a racial minority, applied and was qualified for the job, was rejected, and the position remained open. Then, the employer has a chance to provide a nondiscriminatory reason for its practice, but the plaintiff still has an opportunity to demonstrate that the employer's claim is a pretext for discrimination. In short, when a plaintiff alleges disparate treatment, the employer shoulders the burden of justifying the employment practice.

Not all racial employment discrimination litigation is based on Title VII. In *Johnson v. Railway Express Agency* (1975), the Court ruled that the Civil Rights Act of 1866 prohibited racial discrimination in private contracts, including discriminatory hiring. In *Patterson v. McLean Credit Union* (1989), the Court refused to apply this statute to racial harassment in the workplace. However, the Civil Rights Act of 1991 amended the 1866 act to cover racial harassment.

GENDER

Because gender discrimination is covered under Title VII, the landmark rulings for race apply to women as well, although there are several issues that are distinct for sex discrimination. First, Title VII allows for discrimination in cases in which it may be reasonably necessary for the operation of the business in question, thus establishing the bona fide occupational qualification exception. In upholding Alabama's exclusion of women from guard positions in maximum security prisons, the Court nevertheless articulated a stringent standard for allowing an occupational qualification exception in *Dothard v. Rawlinson* (1977). Any bona fide occupational qualification must be a "business necessity," which is usually difficult for an employer to establish. In *Automobile Workers v. Johnson Controls* (1991), the Court ruled that a battery manufacturer may not use the bona fide occupational qualification to exclude women of childbearing age from jobs that expose them to toxic materials that may damage a potential fetus.

Another gender discrimination issue concerns sexual harassment. In *Meritor Savings Bank v. Vinson* (1986), the Court ruled that sexual harassment did constitute sexual discrimination under Title VII. It decided further that a plaintiff could bring Title VII action even if she does not suffer any physical or psychological damage (*Harris v. Forklift Systems*, 1993) or is unable to establish employer negligence (*Burlington Industries v. Ellerth*, 1998).

OTHER CATEGORIES

In cases of discrimination against aliens under the Fourteenth Amendment, the Court has made a distinction based on the performance of essential government functions. For jobs not performing such functions, the Court has held that alien status is a suspect category, which means that any discrimination must be assessed by the strict scrutiny test. In the case of *Sugerman v. Dougall* (1973), for example, the Court found that a law prohibiting aliens from employment as civil servants violated the equal protection clause. The Court also struck down state laws prohibiting aliens from practicing law. In contrast, if the job performs an essential function, the Court has applied minimal scrutiny, asking if there is a rational basis for the requirement of citizenship. Under this standard, the Court has approved state laws barring aliens from employment as police officers (*Foley v. Connelie*, 1978) and as public school teachers when the applicants did not intend to become citizens (*Ambach v. Norwich*, 1979).

In Fourteenth Amendment cases involving discrimination based on age, the Court begins with the assumption that age is not a suspect category and therefore applies minimal scrutiny, making it highly unlikely that a plaintiff will prevail. The best-known decision is *Massachusetts Board of Retirement v. Murgia* (1976), in which the Court approved a state requirement that uniformed police officers must retire at the age of fifty. Older employees have had slightly better chances of prevailing when they have sued under the Age Discrimination in Employment Act (ADEA), which allows employers to take age into account when it is considered to be a bona fide occupational qualification (BFOQ). However, the Supreme Court has not ruled in favor of many plaintiffs under the ADEA. Rather, the Court has often accepted the BFOQ rationale for requiring early retirement in many positions, such as airline pilots. In addition, the Court recognized in *Hazen Paper Co. v. Biggins* (1993) that the ADEA does not prohibit employers from discriminating against older workers on grounds that are indirectly related to age, such as the increased costs of hiring older persons, so long as the employer does not directly discriminate against a person because of age.

Until the late twentieth century, there were few laws prohibiting discrimination based on disability. The most important federal statute in the area, the Americans with Disabilities Act of 1990 (ADA), requires employers to make reasonable accommodations to "otherwise qualified individuals" with disabilities so long as the accommodations do not impose an "undue hardship" on the employers. The law does not require employers to hire disabled persons who are less competent or qualified than other applicants. The importance of the ADA has been limited by Supreme Court decisions that have narrowly defined the term "disability" under the statute. The most consequential of these rulings was *Sutton v. United Air Lines* (1999), when the Court held that the ADA did not apply to persons with correctable physical conditions that do not substantially limit a major life activity. Thus, the Court held that an airline company may continue to enforce its policy of refusing to hire persons with bad vision that is correctable with glasses. The obvious problem with the decision was that a person with uncorrectable vision would not be "otherwise qualified" for the job.

Through 2006, Congress had never passed a federal law prohibiting employment discrimination based on sexual orientation. In fact, the military's "Don't ask, don't tell" policy technically bans gays and lesbians from enlisting in the armed forces if they openly reveal their orientation. The Court has never suggested that homosexuality might be a suspect classification. However, in *Romer v. Evans* (1996) the Court, applying the rational basis test, held that state constitutions and statutes may not prohibit local governments from passing ordinances that ban discrimination based on sexual orientation. Many states have added the classification of sexual orientation to their civil rights laws. The Court offended and angered supporters of gay rights in the case of *Boy Scouts of America v. Dale* (2000), when the justices voted five to four to allow the scouts, based on their right of expressive association, to refuse to allow gays to have leadership positions in the organization, regardless of what is declared in state antidiscrimination laws.

Steven C. Tauber
Updated by the Editor

FURTHER READING

Bloch, Farrell. *Antidiscrimination Law and Minority Employment.* Chicago: University of Chicago Press, 1994.

Epstein, Richard A. *Forbidden Grounds: The Case Against Employment Discrimination Laws.* Cambridge, Mass.: Harvard University Press, 1992.

Friedman, Joel William, and George M. Strickler. *Cases and Materials on the Law of Employment Discrimination.* Westbury, N.Y.: Foundation Press, 1997.

Hall, Kermit L. *Freedom and Equality: Discrimination and the Supreme Court.* New York: Garland, 2000.

Player, Mack A., Elaine W. Shoben, and Risa L. Liebowitz. *Employment Discrimination Law Cases and Materials.* St. Paul, Minn.: West Publishing, 1995.

SEE ALSO Affirmative action; Age discrimination; Americans with Disabilities Act; *Boy Scouts of America v. Dale*; Fourteenth Amendment; Gender issues; *Griggs v. Duke Power Co.*; Race and discrimination.

Employment Division, Department of Human Resources v. Smith

CITATION: 494 U.S. 872
DATE: April 17, 1990
ISSUE: Freedom of religion
SIGNIFICANCE: Narrowly interpreting the free exercise clause of the First Amendment, the Supreme Court ruled that the states were not required to make a religious exception for the use of illegal drugs.

Alfred Smith and another Native American were fired from their jobs after their employer discovered that they occasionally smoked the hallucinogenic drug peyote as a part of tribal religious ceremonies. The use of peyote was illegal in Oregon, and the state's policy was to deny unemployment benefits to anyone discharged for work-related misconduct. The two men argued that the denial of benefits unconstitutionally infringed on their right to religious freedom. Their lawyers referred to *Sherbert v. Verner* (1963), which had required states to justify any indirect restraints on religion according to the "compelling state interest" standard.

In the *Smith* case, however, the Supreme Court voted six to three to uphold Oregon's policy. Justice Antonin Scalia argued that states had no obligation to make exceptions for laws that were reasonable, secular in intent, and generally applicable to all persons. Such matters were left up to legislative discretion, even if an unfortunate consequence was an "incidental burden" on unconventional religious practices. Although Justice Sandra Day O'Connor joined the majority in upholding Oregon's policy, she joined the three dissenters in wanting to continue *Sherbert*'s standards of strict scrutiny. Religious leaders and civil libertarians were outraged at the *Smith* decision. In the Religious Freedom Restoration Act of 1993, Congress required courts to return to the standards of *Sherbert*, but the Court overturned this requirement in *Boerne v. Flores* (1997).

Thomas Tandy Lewis

SEE ALSO *Boerne v. Flores*; Fundamental rights; Judicial scrutiny; Religion, freedom of; *Sherbert v. Verner.*

Engel v. Vitale

CITATION: 370 U.S. 421
DATE: June 25, 1962
ISSUE: Establishment of religion
SIGNIFICANCE: The Supreme Court, by invalidating a nondenominational prayer, first banned prayers in public schools as an unconstitutional establishment of religion.

Justice Hugo L. Black wrote the 7-1 opinion, in which Justice Byron R. White did not participate. The Supreme Court invalidated a twenty-two-word nondenominational school prayer composed by New York's educational authority as an unconstitutional establishment of religion. Having previously applied the prohibition against the establishment of religion to the states under the Fourteenth Amendment in *Everson v. Board of Education of Ewing Township* (1947), the Court needed only to clarify what it meant by a "wall of separation between church and state." *Engel* raised the wall much higher.

Black provided a lengthy review of British and American history to justify his decision but did not cite any specific Court precedent. He opined that this decision would not block all public expression of religion but held that schools could not sponsor such expressions. Although the Court was supported by a number of groups that filed *amicus curiae* (friend of the court) briefs, when it sided with those who wanted a high wall, it provoked an intense reaction from many conservative religious groups. The storm of criticism did not deter the Court, which persisted in its position. Justice Potter Stewart was the lone dissenter, accusing the majority of misreading the First Amendment's religious clauses, which forbade only governmental establishment of an official church. To do otherwise was to open up unnecessary conflicts with the free exercise provision that Stewart thought was preeminent.

Richard L. Wilson

SEE ALSO *Abington School District v. Schempp*; *Everson v. Board of Education of Ewing Township*; Evolution and creationism; Religion, establishment of; *Wallace v. Jaffree*; Warren, Earl.

Environmental Law

DESCRIPTION: Legislation dealing with and often designed to protect the natural and physical surroundings—the air, earth, and water—in which humans, other animals, and plants exist, or with the plants and animals themselves.

SIGNIFICANCE: The Supreme Court often interpreted the wording of environmental laws and regulations, determined the intended environmental policy goals, ensured that agencies enforce these laws, and resolved conflicting interests among the state and national governments on environmental issues.

Recognizing that technical expertise is necessary to implement environmental public policies, legislators have delegated considerable policy-making power to administrative agencies. Federal environmental legislation is often written in very general terms to provide considerable discretion to administrative agencies in the administration and enforcement of environmental law. The agencies' use of this discretion is subject to challenge in the judicial system. Industry groups and environmental organizations often challenge the processes and rationale by which agency decisions are made and the agencies' interpretation of the words and concepts in the legislation. Judicial interpretation of constitutional provisions and legislative acts permitted the federal government and federal regulatory agencies increased authority in regulation of environmental issues. Requests to the court system for judicial administrative oversight and for interpretation of legislation have allowed industry and environmental organizations to delay implementation of administrative decisions, to obtain specific policy goals within the context of environmental legislation, and to encourage legislative amendments and administrative alterations to environmental legislation.

Until the late 1960's, control of land use, pollution, and environmental nuisances was limited to state and local laws implemented under the police powers of the state. These powers were upheld by the Supreme Court in *Euclid v. Ambler Realty Co.* (1926) and *Georgia v. Tennessee Copper Co.* (1902). Federal government regulation of the environment was limited because the Constitution included no specific grant of authority to the federal government to act in this area. The Court upheld the federal government's power to regulate treatment of migratory wildfowl by treaty in *Missouri v. Holland* (1920) and to regulate pollution in navigable waters in *United States v. Republic Steel Corp.* (1960). Federal environmental legislation was largely limited to conserving and protecting nationally owned park lands, forests, and prairies; to constructing harbor facilities; to constructing irrigation, power generation, and flood control structures on navigable waters; to promoting agricultural soil and water conservation issues; and to studying air and water quality conditions. In *Hodel v. Indiana* (1981), the Court permitted the federal government to use its commerce power to establish environmental regulations, thereby increasing the range of federal government activity in environmental regulation.

Beginning with the enactment of the National Environmental Policy Act (NEPA) of 1969, the federal government began taking responsibility for the quality of the natural environment and for setting standards for environmental quality. As each subsequent act was passed by the legislature, appeals were made to the courts to modify the impact of each of those acts. As a consequence of judicial decisions, agency administration and enforcement of the laws and the public policy impact of the laws were modified. Many of the acts were subsequently amended by the legislature to clarify the legislature's intent and to remedy omissions in the original legislation.

THE 1969 ACT

The NEPA was intended to force nonenvironmental agencies to include environmental considerations in making agency decisions by requiring environmental impact statements (EIS) for government projects and by allowing citizens to sue in federal court when government agencies failed to fully assess environmental impact. Citizens used the judicial process to delay permitting for private and governmental projects affecting the environment. These delaying actions raised the costs of the proposed projects but also provided the time and the incentive for industry and government to review and modify their original proposals to lessen unfavorable effects on the environment.

Subsequent suits brought to the Court gradually eroded the effectiveness of environmental impact statements. For example, in *Kleppe v. Sierra Club* (1976), involving the strip-mining industry, the Court postponed the need for an EIS until late in the proposed project's planning and limited the EIS to impact on the local area rather than an entire geographic region. In *Vermont Yankee Nuclear Power Corp. v. Natural Resources Defense Council* (1978), the Court held that the technical expertise of the Nuclear Regulatory Commission to manage nuclear power policy could not be challenged by the technical expertise of environmental experts, thus severely limiting the use of EIS by environmental cause organizations to ensure that environmental issues were considered in agency policy decisions. The Court also instructed lower courts that only arbitrary and capricious agency actions or actions clearly beyond agency statutory authority are to be invalidated.

Andrus v. Sierra Club (1979) exempted budget processes from EIS review and *Strycher Bay v. Karlen* (1980), *Baltimore Gas and Electric v. Natural Resources Defense Council* (1983), and *Metropolitan Edison Co. v. People Against Nuclear Energy* (1983) had the combined effect of reducing the substantive content requirements for environmental impact statements and limiting their effectiveness as vehicles for ensuring that environmental considerations would be included in government agency and private industry decision making.

WATER AND AIR POLLUTION CASES

The Federal Water Pollution Control Act of 1972 (also known as the Clean Water Act) gave the Environmental Protection Agency (EPA) authority to control private and state activities to reduce water pollution in an effort to make the waterways "swimmable and fishable" and free of manmade pollutants. The EPA set industry standards for the effluent permitted to flow into streams and pollution reduction standards for each pollution source discharging effluent into the streams. The EPA also set standards for use of the "best practicable" or "best available" technology for achieving required pollution reductions. In subsequent litigation, the Court required the EPA to provide numerous variances from EPA requirements and challenged the expertise of the EPA to classify pollutants or to set standards for their discharge into streams.

The Court also interpreted the wording in the 1972 act to erode previous federal common-law remedies available to downstream citizens affected by upstream pollution. In *Illinois v. Milwaukee* (1972) and *Middlesex County Sewerage Authority v. National Sea Clammers* (1981), the Court held that industries or agencies with EPA permits for effluent discharge could not be sued for the environmental damage their effluent caused downstream water users.

Other Court decisions effectively reduced the authority of the EPA to limit water pollution, prevented citizens from suing for damages, limited citizen standing to sue in order to require agencies to implement environmental protections, and provided public help for polluting industries and municipal governments at the expense of citizens living downstream.

The Clean Air Act Amendments of 1970 gave the EPA authority to set national ambient air quality standards similar to the clean water standards authorized under the Clean Water Act. The EPA chose to enforce those standards only in areas with high levels of air pollution. The Court ruled in *Sierra Club v. Ruckelshaus* (1972) and *Fri v. Sierra Club* (1973) that standards must also be set and enforced for areas with low pollution levels, thus requiring the EPA to either expand the scope of its activities or cease enforcing its standards in areas with substantial air pollution. Congress subsequently required the expansion of EPA activity in the 1977 amendments to the Clean Air Act.

The Court made other decisions concerning Clean Air Act enforcement that reduced the impact of the act and provided considerable relief to industry. In *Chevron U.S.A. v. Natural Resources Defense Council* (1984) and *Alabama Power v. Castle* (1979), the Court allowed industries to offset increases in air pollution in one area of their plants with reductions in other areas and permitted some increase in air pollution by individual industries in geographic areas where overall pollution was on the decline. In the 1990 Amendments to the Clean Air Act and other legislation, Congress began to micromanage air pollution public policy in response to the actions of the courts.

HAZARDOUS WASTE

Congress passed the Resource Conservation and Recovery Act (RCRA) of 1976 and the Comprehensive Environmental Response, Compensation, and Liability Act (also known as the Superfund Act) of 1980 to control the transportation and disposal of hazardous wastes and to identify and clean up abandoned hazardous waste dumps. The Superfund requirement that the costs of dump cleanup should be recovered from those who owned the site or profited from its operation brought numerous lawsuits. In *United States v. Monsanto* (1988) and *United States v. Northeastern Pharmaceutical and Chemical Co.* (1986), the Court established strict liability and joint liability of all concerned. The decision to assign joint liability for any entity that profited from the waste dump brought a flood of civil suits as industries, banks, insurance companies, and others argued as to how much of the costs of cleaning up abandoned dumps each should bear. The Court's subsequent interpretation of strict and joint liability resulted in banks, lending institutions, and governments becoming liable for cleanup costs simply because of loans, defaults on loans, confiscation of property for nonpayment of property taxes, and other "innocent" acts. Congress amended the Superfund Act with the Superfund Amendments and Reauthorization Act of 1986 in an effort to relieve innocent parties of the liabilities assigned by the courts.

OTHER JUDICIAL LIMITS

The Constitution's Fifth Amendment mandate that private property may not be taken for public use without just compensation (the takings clause) was applied by the Court in *Nollan v. California Coastal Commission* (1987) as a signal that government environmental regulations limiting an owner's land use must be substantially in the state interest. The Court invalidated state and local laws that interfered with federal regulations in *Burbank v. Lockheed Air Terminal* (1973) and that seek to regulate areas already regulated by the federal government in *Exxon Corp. v. Hunt* (1986) and *International Paper Co. v. Ouillette* (1987). In these and other cases, the Court held that federal law supplants and preempts state and local law on environmental issues on which the federal government chooses to act. In those cases in which federal laws contain nonpreemption provisions intended to allow states to enact complementary laws, the Court narrowly interpreted these nonpreemption provisions and restricted states from acting in areas in which comprehensive federal environmental laws and regulations already exist. The Court's use of the doctrine of federal preemption to invalidate state and local environmental laws when national legislation is enacted serves to erode the power of state and local governments within the federal system.

During most of the late twentieth century, the Court permitted Congress and federal agencies to increase the number of environmental issues addressed through law and regulation and generally upheld agency discretion in interpreting and applying rules and regulations.

At the beginning of the twenty-first century, the majority of the justices appeared to be increasingly skeptical about the advantages of strictly enforcing the environmental laws. Environmental activists were especially alarmed by the Court's 4-1-4 decision in *Rapanos v. United States* (2006), in which the Court came close to giving a narrow redefinition of the Clean Water Act in a way that would have severely restricted federal regulation over many wetlands of the country. One of the problems was the general wording of the Clean Water Act (CWA), which forbade the discharge of pollutants into "navigable waters," a term that the Army Corps of Engineers had long interpreted as including most wetlands, even those that are marginal and intermittent. When Kentucky entrepreneur John Rapanos wanted to fill in three wetland areas on his property in order to build shopping centers, he argued in court that only "actually navigable waters" can be regulated under the statute. A plurality of four justices agreed with him, holding that the term in the statute could only refer to "relatively permanent, standing or flowing bodies of water," and that to be called navigable waters there would have to be a surface connection of water. Four justices strongly disagreed with this analysis, and they wanted to continue the Corps's broader definition, which included occasional wetlands adjacent to tributaries of navigable waters. Justice Anthony M. Kennedy, the swing vote, took a position between the two camps. Since the Court did not render a majority judgment on most of the complex legal issues, the case was sent back to the Kentucky courts for additional analysis and research. Almost certainly the case would require a great deal of additional litigation before returning to the docket of the Supreme Court for a definitive judgment.

Gordon Neal Diem
Updated by the Editor

FURTHER READING

James P. Lester's text *Environmental Politics and Policy: Theories and Evidence* (Durham, N.C.: Duke University Press, 1995) describes the role and interrelationships among branches of government in environmental law. Two general works on land-use law that touch on environmental issues are David J. Frizell's *Land Use Law* (3d ed. Eagan, Minn.: Thomson/West Group, 2005) and Polly J. Price's *Property Rights: Rights and Liberties Under the Law* (Santa Barbara, Calif.: ABC-Clio, 2003).

Gregory McAvoy's *Controlling Technocracy: Citizen Rationality and the NIMBY Syndrome* (Washington, D.C.: Georgetown University Press, 1999) examines the so-called not-in-my-backyard attitude that often complicates environmental planning. Nancy K. Kubasek describes the administrative law and judicial adversary processes for resolving a variety of environmental disputes in a basic text aimed at an audience with little legal or scientific training in *Environmental Law* (Paramus, N.J.: Prentice-Hall, 1996). Stephen R. Chapman's *Environmental Law and Policy* (Paramus, N.J.: Prentice-Hall, 1998) describes the formulation, application, and interpretation of laws, rules, and regulations to resolve specific environmental problems.

Better Environmental Decisions: Strategies for Governments, Businesses, and Communities (Washington, D.C.: Island Press, 1998), edited by Ken Sexton and others, reviews a variety of decision-making styles, discusses some legal issues related to each, and recommends improvements for more effective decisions.

Other books describing environmental case law include Jeffrey Graba's *Environmental Law* (St. Paul, Minn.: West Publishing, 1994), Rosemary O'Leary's *Environmental Change: Federal Courts and the EPA* (Philadelphia: Temple University Press, 1995), Robert V. Percival's *Environmental Regulation: Law, Science, and Policy* (New York: Little, Brown, 1996), and Benjamin Davy's *Essential Injustice: When Legal Institutions Cannot Resolve Environmental and Land Use Disputes* (New York: Springer Verlag, 1997).

SEE ALSO Commerce, regulation of; Fifth Amendment; Takings clause; Zoning.

Epperson v. Arkansas

CITATION: 393 U.S. 97
DATE: November 12, 1968
ISSUE: Establishment of religion
SIGNIFICANCE: The Supreme Court found laws banning the teaching of evolution to be an unconstitutional establishment of religion.

The Supreme Court unanimously overturned an Arkansas Supreme Court ruling that upheld Arkansas "Monkey Law" statutes banning the teaching of evolution in public elementary schools, secondary schools, and universities. The Court held that Arkansas violated the freedom of religion mandate of the First Amendment as applied to the states by the Fourteenth Amendment under the incorporation doctrine. Justice Abe Fortas wrote the majority opinion, with Justices John M. Harlan II and Hugo L. Black concurring. In 1982 Arkansas responded by passing a new law that required all public schools to "balance" any teaching of evolution with the teaching of creation by a "supreme power." This was declared unconstitutional in a federal district court in *McLean v. Arkansas Board of Education* (1982). This case was very similar to one covering a Louisiana policy later declared unconstitutional by the Court in a 7-2 decision in *Edwards v. Aguillard* (1987).

Richard L. Wilson

SEE ALSO *Engel v. Vitale*; Evolution and creationism; *Lee v. Weisman*; Religion, establishment of; *Wallace v. Jaffree*.

Equal Protection Clause

DATE: 1868

DESCRIPTION: Provision of the Fourteenth Amendment to the U.S. Constitution that prohibits certain forms of discrimination.

SIGNIFICANCE: Though the Supreme Court initially gave the equal protection clause a narrow construction, in the last half of the twentieth century, the clause was reinvigorated and used first to eliminate official racial segregation and then to prohibit a variety of other forms of discrimination.

Thomas Jefferson securely linked the ideal of equality to the U.S. political tradition when he argued in the Declaration of Independence that "all men are created equal." However, his tribute to equality did not immediately find a home in the U.S. Constitution. No clause within the Constitution guaranteed equal treatment by the law, and in fact, the accommodation of slavery within the original constitutional text amounted to an obvious breach of the principle of equality. Not until after the Civil War (1861-1865), when the Reconstruction Congress attempted to secure the political and civil rights of the newly freed slaves, would "equality" enter the constitutional vocabulary. The ratification of the Fourteenth Amendment in 1868 added to the Constitution the principle that Jefferson had championed almost a century earlier. Section 1 of the amendment declared that no state "shall deny to any person within its jurisdiction the equal protection of the laws."

EARLY INTERPRETATIONS

In two early cases, the Supreme Court used the equal protection clause of the Fourteenth Amendment to unsettle official patterns of racial discrimination. *Strauder v. West Virginia* (1880) invalidated a state law that denied African Americans the right to sit on juries and thus submitted them to trial by juries in which people of their race could not sit. This disqualification from an important civil right, declared the Court, offended the equal protection clause. Later that decade, in *Yick Wo v. Hopkins* (1886), the Court held that the Fourteenth Amendment's equal protection guarantee extended beyond discrimination embedded in the text of laws to racial discrimination practiced in the administration of otherwise evenhanded laws.

In other cases, though, the Supreme Court minimized the transformative potential of the equal protection clause in ways that would endure well into the twentieth century. First, in the *Slaughterhouse Cases* (1873), the Court suggested that the clause, though written in general terms capable of application to many forms of inequality, nevertheless would probably not be applied to matters other than discrimination against African Americans. Second, in the *Civil Rights Cases* (1883), the Court limited the application of the clause to inequalities involving state action rather than private acts of discrimination. By this limitation, the Court deprived Congress of power under the Fourteenth Amendment to address private forms of racial and other impermissible discriminations.

Finally, in *Plessy v. Ferguson* (1896), the Court grafted onto the equal protection clause the separate but equal doctrine, which permitted states to maintain systems of racial segregation, even though the significance of these systems was to treat African Americans as second-class citizens and thus deprive them of equal treatment under the laws. The commutative effect of these interpretations of the equal protection clause by the Court was to diminish the clause's usefulness as a source of constitutional protection from invidious discrimination. Even in the 1930's, Justice Oliver Wendell Holmes observed that applications to invoke the equal protection clause were the "last resort of constitutional argument."

EMERGING STANDARDS OF REVIEW

Though an able commentator on the law of the times, Holmes could not see the future. Beginning in the 1940's, the Court, chastened perhaps by the alarming spectacle of Nazi racism toward Jews, reinvigorated the equal protection clause. It did so by establishing two broad categories of cases in which the clause would prove to be most protective against forms of official discrimination. The narrowing of the clause's potential reach in this fashion was necessary because laws routinely classify individuals differently for a variety of purposes and thus discriminate among individuals. State traffic laws allow seventeen-year-olds to obtain a driver's license but not eight-year-olds. State universities grant admission to those who have graduated from high school or obtained comparable credentials but refuse those who drop out early and never make up their educational deficits. In these and innumerable other respects, laws discriminate without offending typical notions of equality. The task of the Court, beginning in the 1940's, was to identify particular forms of discrimination that might be singled out as constitutionally troublesome in a sense not shared by the kind of routine discriminations that characterize ordinary law.

The Court first ventured that the equal protection clause would demand special scrutiny of discriminations that affected fundamental rights or interests. In *Skinner v. Oklahoma* (1942), the Court held that a law that provided for compulsory sterilization of certain habitual criminals but not others discriminated with respect to the fundamental right of procreation. In such cases, the Court determined, it would strictly scrutinize the asserted justifications for the discrimination. Finding such justification lacking in *Skinner,* the Court ruled that the sterilization law violated the Fourteenth Amendment's equal protection clause. In the years following *Skinner,* the Court determined that matters such as the right to vote, the right to privacy (concerning one's choice to use contraceptives), the right to travel, and the right to access to justice were sufficiently fundamental to subject acts of discrimination affecting these rights to more rigorous scrutiny.

As the Court was striving to identify particular rights or interests worthy of protection from discriminatory treatment, it also began to study whether particular grounds for discriminating among individuals might be subjected to corresponding rigorous review. For example, the equal protection clause clearly had its genesis in suspicion of laws that classified individuals on the basis of their race. In *Korematsu v. United States* (1944), the Court, in an opinion by Justice Hugo L. Black, codified this suspicion against racial classifications in principle, though the Court approved an act of racial discrimination that relocated people of Japanese ancestry to internment camps during World War II. At the level of principle, the Court was adamant: Racial classifications called for the most stringent review. In the application of this principle, though, the Court deferred to the military's judgment that the prevention of a West Coast invasion required the relocation of people of Japanese ancestry. This holding would be the last in which the Court upheld a law burdening a minority on account of race.

DESEGREGATION

After the Court gave a constitutional harbor to racial segregation through its adoption of the separate but equal doctrine, segregation in public schools and a variety of other public and private contexts became deeply entrenched in the South. In *Brown v. Board of Education* (1954), however, the Court repudiated the separate but equal doctrine and held that segregated public schools were inherently unequal. The following year, in *Brown v. Board of Education II* (1955), the Court ruled that desegregation efforts were to proceed "with all deliberate speed." However, the only haste exhibited with respect to desegregation by southern school districts was directed at eluding the Court's desegregation order. By 1964, ten years after the decision in *Brown,* only 2 percent of the schools segregated at the time of the decision had experienced any significant desegregation. The Court, in the meantime, summarily ruled that segregation in golf courses, state parks, beaches, and public transportation violated the equal protection guarantee.

In the 1960's and 1970's the Court presided over cases involving efforts of segregated school districts to frustrate desegregation efforts and of federal district courts to further them. In *Green v. County School Board of New Kent County* (1968), the Court made it clear that desegregation required not simply that school districts cease their previous segregation practices but that they dismantle the segregated school systems produced by those practices. Eventually, the Court approved radical strategies to secure desegregation. Most controversially, in *Swann v. Charlotte-Mecklenburg Board of Education* (1971), the Court upheld a district court order requiring widespread busing of students to create racially balanced schools. Importantly, though, the Court held that such remedies required a showing that a school district had engaged in illegal segregation practices—de jure segregation, or segregation by law. The existence in schools of segregation that could be traced to social practices rather than officially sanctioned practices—de facto segregation—was not sufficient to justify a federal court to order remedies such as busing.

SUSPECT AND QUASI-SUSPECT CLASSIFICATIONS

In the years that followed the Court's decisions in *Korematsu* and *Brown*, the Court ventured to determine whether other ways of classifying individuals should be treated with a constitutional suspicion comparable to that now applied to racial discrimination. Classification schemes treated to this kind of suspicion are referred to as "suspect classifications," and are presumptively invalid except in those cases in which the government demonstrates that the classification is necessary to achieve some compelling government interest. In its inquiry into whether other forms of classifications were suspect, the Court was guided by one of constitutional law's most famous footnotes: Footnote Four from the opinion of Justice Harlan Fiske Stone in *United States v. Carolene Products Co.* (1938). In an otherwise unremarkable decision, Justice Stone suggested for the Court that heightened scrutiny might be justified for laws reflecting prejudice against "discrete and insular minorities." In practice, the Court has identified race, religion, and national or ethnic origin as suspect classifications. Additionally, laws discriminating among individuals on the basis of whether they are U.S. citizens are suspect, except in a narrow range of cases involving citizenship requirements for voting or for holding positions closely related to democratic self-government.

The Court wrestled at length over the question of whether laws that classified individuals on the basis of their gender should receive the strict scrutiny applied to suspect classifications. Discrimination on the basis of gender classifies individuals according to an immutable characteristic, and the Court has often expressed its suspicion of using immutable traits as grounds for distinguishing among individuals. Nevertheless, whether men or women receive less favorable treatment under a particular gender classification, neither group can readily be identified as a discrete and insular minority. Accordingly, the Court eventually fashioned an intermediate level of scrutiny for gender classifications, more rigorous than the scrutiny applied to normal legislative classifications but not so rigorous as that applied to suspect classifications such as laws discriminating on the basis of race. Classification schemes subjected to this intermediate scrutiny are sometimes referred to as "quasi-suspect classifications." The Court included within this category both laws that discriminate on the basis of gender and those that discriminate on the basis of illegitimacy. The Court will uphold these kinds of laws only if they are supported by some important government purpose and the discrimination at issue is substantially related to achieving this important purpose.

OTHER CLASSIFICATIONS

The Court turned away a variety of other claims that particular forms of classifying individuals should be treated as suspect or quasi-suspect. For example, except in cases involving access to certain aspects of justice, the Court declined to treat with any special suspicion laws that classify individuals on the basis of wealth. Furthermore, the Court refused to recognize classifications on the basis of age as inherently suspect, leaving the protection of individuals from age discrimination to the political process.

Nevertheless, the Court did not automatically sustain classification schemes when they were neither suspect nor quasi-suspect. For a classification that is neither suspect nor quasi-suspect, the Court applies what it refers to as rational basis scrutiny. In these circumstances, classifications are upheld as long as they are rationally related to a legitimate government interest. Although the application of this standard of review normally upholds a government classification scheme, occasionally it does not. For example, in *Cleburne v. Cleburne Living Center* (1985), the Court declined to classify mental infirmity as a suspect or quasi-suspect category. Nevertheless, it declared unconstitutional a zoning ordinance that required a special permit for the operation of a group home for the mentally retarded on a particular site, even though the ordinance allowed a wide variety of other land uses on the site. The Court concluded that the negative reactions of nearby residents and the unsubstantiated fears of elderly residents concerning the mental retardation home were not legitimate justifications for discriminatory treatment of the home.

Similarly, in *Romer v. Evans* (1996), the Court invalidated a Colorado constitutional amendment that discriminated against homosexuals by providing that no state or municipal law could accord them any special protection from discrimination. Although the Court did not determine that sexual orientation was a suspect or quasi-suspect classification, a majority of the justices reasoned that the amendment reflected "bare animus" against gays and lesbians, and that this animus was not a legitimate basis for upholding the amendment from an equal protection challenge.

AFFIRMATIVE ACTION

In his well-known dissent to the opinion of the Court in *Plessy v. Ferguson* (1896), Justice John Marshall Harlan rejected the separate but equal doctrine embraced by the majority. Instead, in his view the equal protection clause mandated that the law be color-blind. Understood literally, this color-blind reading of the equal protection clause would prevent laws designed to benefit racial minorities as well as those designed to burden and harass them. Beginning in the 1960's and 1970's, though, many American observers contended that the legacy of past and continuing racial discrimination in the United States could not be rectified without taking affirmative steps. These affirmative actions typically consisted of laws and policies that singled out racial minorities for beneficial or even preferential treatment as a way of remedying past discriminatory laws and policies.

Beginning with the Court's decision in *Korematsu*, it was clear that laws intentionally burdening racial minorities would be subjected to strict scrutiny. More than forty years would pass before the Court finally concluded that laws that singled out racial minorities for beneficial treatment would also receive the same rigorous scrutiny. The path to this ultimate conclusion was neither direct nor widely supported. In its first important consideration of affirmative action plans, a majority of the Court concluded in *Regents of the University of California v. Bakke* (1978) that the equal protection clause prevented a state university from using racial quotas in its admissions process but permitted the university to consider race as one factor in striving to create a diverse student body. Therefore, while the university could not set aside a particular number of seats for minority students, it could treat minority status as one among several favorable factors in the admissions process. A few years later, in *Fullilove v. Klutznick* (1980), the Court upheld a challenge against a federal set-aside program that gave certain preferences to minority businesses in the award of federal contracts. In neither *Bakke* nor *Fullilove* did the Court determine the standard of review to be applied in affirmative action cases.

The final years of the twentieth century witnessed a conservative majority on the Court becoming increasingly hostile to affirmative action programs. In closely divided decisions, the Court eventually determined, first in *Richmond v. J. A. Croson Co.* (1989) and then in *Adarand Constructors v. Peña* (1995), that equal protection principles required that *all* racial classifications, including those intended to benefit racial minorities, be subjected to strict scrutiny. Though at least some forms of affirmative action might be justified as necessary to serve compelling governmental interests such as remedying past racial discrimination, it nevertheless appeared that many affirmative action programs would no longer survive challenge under equal protection.

Timothy L. Hall

FURTHER READING

An excellent introduction to this subject is Francis Graham Lee's *Equal Protection: Rights and Liberties Under the Law* (Santa Barbara, Calif.: ABC-Clio, 2003). A general treatment of the equal protection clause can be found in Darien A. McWhirter's *Equal Protection: Exploring the Constitution* (Phoenix, Ariz.: Oryx Press, 1995). For historical coverage of the idea of equality in U.S. history, see J. R. Pole's *Pursuit of Equality in American History* (2d ed. Berkeley: University of California Press, 1993) and Charles Redenius's *The American Ideal of Equality: From Jefferson's Declaration to the Burger Court* (Port Washington, N.Y.: Kennikat Press, 1981).

The Fourteenth Amendment: From Political Principle to Judicial Doctrine by William E. Nelson (Cambridge, Mass.: Harvard University Press, 1988) provides a useful analysis of the broader context of the equal protection clause in the Fourteenth Amendment. *The Civil Rights Era: Origins and Development of National Policy, 1960-1972,* by Hugh Davis Graham (New York: Oxford University Press, 1990), examines a crucial period in the enforcement of the equal protection guarantee through civil rights laws.

Particular treatments relating to racial equality include *African Americans and the Living Constitution,* edited by John Hope Franklin and Genna Rae McNeil (Washington, D.C.: Smithsonian Institution Press, 1995), and *Simple Justice: The History of "Brown v. Board of Education" and Black America's Struggle for Equality,* by Richard Kluger (New York: Alfred A. Knopf, 1976).

Useful sources for further reading concerning gender discrimination issues are Cathy Young's *Ceasefire! Why Women and Men Must Join Forces to Achieve True Equality* (New York: Free Press, 1999), and Robert Max Jackson's *Destined for Equality: The Inevitable Rise of Women's Status* (Cambridge, Mass.: Harvard University Press, 1998).

For treatments of the controversy regarding affirmative action, one may consult *Affirmative Discrimination: Ethnic Inequality and Public Policy* by Nathan Glazer (New York: Basic Books, 1975), *A Conflict of Rights: The Supreme Court and Affirmative Action* by Melvin I. Urofsky (New York: Scribner's Sons, 1991), and *The Color-Blind Constitution,* by Andrew Kull (Cambridge, Mass.: Harvard University Press, 1992).

SEE ALSO Affirmative action; Age discrimination; *Bolling v. Sharpe;* Civil Rights movement; Fourteenth Amendment; Fundamental rights; Gender issues; Guarantee clause; Incorporation, inverse; Judicial scrutiny; *Loving v. Virginia;* Privileges and immunities; Race and discrimination; Segregation, de jure.

Espionage Acts

DATE: 1917-1918

DESCRIPTION: Laws passed during World War I outlawing the unauthorized transmission of information that might injure the nation's defense and banning a wide range of expressions of opinion critical of governmental policies or symbols during wartime.

SIGNIFICANCE: Espionage act prosecutions led to the first significant attempts by the Supreme Court to interpret the free speech provisions of the First Amendment, including the original espousal of the clear and present danger test.

On June 15, 1917, two months after the United States entered World War I, Congress passed the Espionage Act. In addition to outlawing a wide variety of acts that fit the commonsense definition of "espionage," including the gathering, transmission, or negligent handling of information that might harm U.S. defense efforts, the law forbade, during wartime, the willful making or conveying of false information with intent to interfere with the nation's armed forces or to promote the success of its enemies, as well as willful attempts to cause insubordination, disloyalty, mutiny, or refusal of duty within the military or the obstruction of military recruitment or enlistment. In practice, this law was used as the springboard for massive prosecutions of antiwar speeches and publications of all kinds across the United States, based on the theory that many such viewpoints were false and, in any case, aimed at undermining recruitment or other aspects of the war effort.

Despite the sweeping language and even more sweeping prosecutions associated with the 1917 law, a far more draconian amendment to the Espionage Act, sometimes known as the Sedition Act, was enacted in 1918 in response to complaints that the original law was not stringent enough to suppress antiwar sentiment. The 1918 amendments outlawed virtually all conceivable criticism of the war, including any expressions of support for "any country with which the United State is at war" or that opposed "the cause of the United States therein." Also banned was the oral or printed dissemination of all "disloyal, profane, scurrilous, or abusive language" about the "form of government" of the country, the Constitution, the flag, the military, and military uniforms, as well as any language intended to bring any of the above into "contempt, scorn, contumely, or disrepute."

Under these laws, more than two thousand people were indicted for written or verbal criticism of the war and more than one thousand were convicted, resulting in more than one hundred jail terms of ten years or more. No one was convicted under the espionage acts during World War I for spying activities. The 1918 amendments to the Espionage Act were repealed in 1920. Although the original 1917 law remains in effect, it was virtually never used after World War I to prosecute expressions of opinion (partly because the 1940 Smith Act included more updated sedition provisions); it has, however, been used in cases involving alleged theft of information, including in the prosecutions of Julius Rosenberg and Ethel Rosenberg during the Cold War and the Vietnam War-era prosecution of Daniel Ellsberg for dissemination of the Pentagon Papers.

COURT RULINGS

The Supreme Court handed down six rulings concerning the constitutionality of Espionage Act prosecutions in 1919-1920, during a severe "red scare." In every case, it upheld lower court convictions. Although the Court's rulings no doubt reflected the anticommunist climate, they had long-term significance because they were the first cases in which the Court sought to interpret the free speech clauses of the First Amendment and thus helped shape decades of subsequent debate and interpretation of this subject. In *Schenck v. United States* (1919), the Court upheld the conviction (under the original 1917 law) of a group accused of seeking to obstruct enlistment in the armed forces by mailing antidraft leaflets. Despite the lack of evidence that Schenck's mailings had any effect whatsoever, the Court, in a famous ruling penned by Justice Oliver Wendell Holmes, rejected Schenck's First Amendment claims. Holmes wrote that although the defendants would have been within their constitutional rights in saying what they did in ordinary times, the character of "every act depends upon the circumstances in which it is done." Just as "the most stringent protection of free speech would not protect a man in falsely shouting fire in a theater and causing a panic," the question was always whether the expression was used in such circumstances and was of such a nature as to create a "clear and present danger" that it would cause the "substantive evils" that Congress has the right to prevent.

In *Abrams v. United States* (1919), a second landmark case (based on the 1918 amendment), the Court upheld the conviction of a group of defendants who had thrown from a New York City rooftop leaflets critical of U.S. military intervention against the new Bolshevik government in Russia. This case became known especially because of a dissent by Holmes, who essentially maintained that no clear and present danger had been demonstrated and that Congress could not constitutionally forbid "all effort to change the mind of the country." In words that became famous both for their eloquence and because, after 1937, most Court rulings in First Amendment cases reflected their sentiment more than those of the majorities in either *Abrams* or *Schenck*, Holmes declared that U.S. constitutional democracy was based on giving all thought an opportunity to compete in the free trade in ideas, and as long as that experiment remained part of the Constitution, Americans should be "eternally vigilant against attempts to check the expression of opinions that we loathe and believe to be fraught with death, unless they so imminently threaten interference with the lawful and pressing purposes of the law that an immediate check is required to save the country."

In the only significant Espionage Act case involving First Amendment claims to be decided by the Court after 1920, a Court majority reflected Holmes's *Abrams* dissent. In *Hartzel v. United States* (1944), involving a man who had mailed articles attacking U.S. policies during World War II to Army officers and draft registrants (circumstances almost identical to *Schenck*), the Court reversed Hartzel's conviction on the grounds that there was no proof he had willfully sought to obstruct the activities of the armed forces.

Robert Justin Goldstein

FURTHER READING

Chafee, Zechariah. *Free Speech in the United States.* New York: Atheneum, 1969.

Fialka, John. *War by Other Means: Economic Espionage in America.* New York: W. W. Norton, 1997.

Gannon, James. *Stealing Secrets, Telling Lies: How Spies and Codebreakers Helped Shape the Twentieth Century.* Washington, D.C.: Brassey's, 2001.

Hitz, Frederick P. *The Great Game: The Myth and Reality of Espionage.* New York: Alfred A. Knopf, 2004.

Jeffreys-Jones, Rhodri. *Cloak and Dollar: A History of American Secret Intelligence.* New Haven, Conn.: Yale University Press, 2002.

Owen, David. *Hidden Secrets: A Complete History of Espionage and the Technology Used to Support It.* New York: Firefly Books, 2002.

Polenberg, Richard. *Fighting Faiths: The Abrams Case, the Supreme Court, and Free Speech.* New York: Viking Penguin, 1987.

SEE ALSO Bad tendency test; First Amendment; *Schenck v. United States*; Sedition Act of 1798; Seditious libel; Smith Act; Speech and press, freedom of; War and civil liberties.

Everson v. Board of Education of Ewing Township

CITATION: 330 U.S. 1

DATE: February 10, 1947

ISSUE: Establishment of religion

SIGNIFICANCE: The Supreme Court upheld bus fare reimbursements for private school students in the first case to use the Fourteenth Amendment to apply the First Amendment's establishment of religion clause to the states.

Justice Hugo L. Black wrote the 5-4 opinion for the Supreme Court; Justices Robert H. Jackson, Felix Frankfurter, Wiley B. Rutledge, Jr., and Harold H. Burton dissented. On one level, all nine justices agreed that the establishment of religion clause applied to the states and that government should be neutral with respect to religion, neither aiding nor obstructing it. The disagreement was over whether the principle of neutrality toward religion was properly applied in this case.

New Jersey law authorized school boards to reimburse parents for the cost of bus transportation to attend school, whether public or parochial. Arch Everson was a local taxpayer in Ewing township who believed this violated the establishment clause. The four dissenting justices agreed with him, but the majority on the Court believed bus fare payment was remote from any religious purpose. They believed that the money for bus transportation would have been paid to all parents regardless of the kind of school their children attended. Depriving Roman Catholic parents of the payments forced them to pay taxes to support the transportation of other children while not receiving the benefit themselves. The larger point of this case was to establish that neither the state nor the federal government could support a religious institution, and on that point, all agreed.

Richard L. Wilson

SEE ALSO Burton, Harold H.; *Engel v. Vitale*; *Epperson v. Arkansas*; Religion, establishment of.

Evolution and Creationism

DESCRIPTION: Modern scientific theories of natural and human origins and religious beliefs about the world's creation.

SIGNIFICANCE: The battle between the teaching of evolution versus creationism entered the public schools and arrived before the Supreme Court, which found that the establishment clause forbids public schools from lending their authority to advance creationism.

The emergence of the theory of evolution as a scientific account of human origins has, since the nineteenth century, created conflicts with religious beliefs. Conservative Christians, in particular, have often viewed evolution as inconsistent with biblical teaching concerning creation. They viewed the gradual nature of the evolutionary process as contradicted by the biblical account of creation. They read the Bible as describing a relatively brief creation process—in some views, six literal days—and one not characterized by a progression from primitive to higher life-forms.

EARLY ATTEMPTS TO BAN THE TEACHING OF EVOLUTION

The debate between science and religion over natural origins inevitably arrived in the public schools. In areas controlled by conservative religious sensibilities, opponents of evolution were able, for a time, to prevent public school teachers from teaching the evolutionary account. As the twentieth century progressed, these prohibitions eventually took the form of law. The most celebrated attempt to enforce such a legal prohibition against teaching evolution was the Scopes trial in Tennessee in the 1920's. *State of Tennessee v. John Thomas Scopes* (1925), which eventually came to be known as the "Monkey Trial," involved the criminal prosecution of a Tennessee schoolteacher for teaching evolution in violation of a state law prohibiting such teaching. For eight scorching days in July of 1925, the trial pitted William Jennings Bryan as a special prosecutor for the state of Tennessee against Clarence Darrow as attorney for the defendant. Bryan secured a conviction in the case, and the presiding judge imposed a $100 fine on Scopes. However, in the court of public opinion, Bryan fared more poorly. During the trial, he agreed to be cross-examined by Darrow and, at least in the minds of many observers, allowed Darrow to tar him and other evolution opponents as unsophisticated religious fundamentalists. On appeal, the Tennessee appellate court affirmed the constitutionality of the Tennessee antievolution statute but held that a jury rather than a judge should have assessed the fine in the case. The state of Tennessee, its law thus vindicated, declined to prosecute the case again, and so Scopes and others who wished to take their challenge to the Supreme Court were frustrated.

Several decades would pass before the Court finally considered the constitutionality of laws prohibiting instruction concerning evolution. When it did, in *Epperson v. Arkansas* (1968), the Court found a law prohibiting the teaching of evolution to be a violation of the First Amendment's establishment clause. During the 1960's, the Court had begun to examine the influence of religion in the public schools, declaring unconstitutional school-sponsored prayers in *Engel v. Vitale* (1962) and *Abington School District v. Schempp* (1963). With these precedents in mind, the Court concluded that attempts to ban the teaching of evolution in public schools amounted to an impermissible intrusion of religion on the public school curriculum.

CREATION SCIENCE AND THE PUBLIC SCHOOL CURRICULUM

The battle that began as an attempt to keep evolution out of public schools metamorphosed over the next two decades into a rear-guard attempt to return creationism to the schools. In the early 1980's, for example, the Louisiana legislature passed the Balanced Treatment for Creation-Science and Evolution-Science in Public School Instruction Act. This law essentially provided that public schools that chose to teach "evolution-science" also had to teach "creation-science" and was justified by the legislature as necessary to preserve academic freedom. The Supreme Court disagreed, however.

By the time the matter arrived before the justices in the last half of the 1980's, the Court had interpreted the First Amendment's establishment clause as imposing a three-part requirement on state and federal laws. According to the three-part test adopted in *Lemon v. Kurtzman* (1971), laws had to have a secular purpose, a secular effect, and entail no excessive entanglement between government and religion.

The Louisiana law was challenged in *Edwards v. Aguillard* (1987), and a majority of the Court agreed that the law offended the establishment clause. According to the Court, the Louisiana statute stumbled over the first prong of the three-part *Lemon* test. In spite of the Louisiana legislature's assertion that the act was necessary to preserve academic freedom, a majority of the Court concluded that the act was, in fact, supported by an essentially religious purpose—that of restoring the religion-rooted view of natural origins represented by "creation-science" to the public school classroom. Finding that the law lacked any real secular purpose, therefore, the Court concluded that it violated the establishment clause.

Timothy L. Hall

FURTHER READING

Conkle, Daniel O. *Constitutional Law: The Religion Clauses.* New York: Foundation Press, 2003.

Ecker, Ronald L. *Dictionary of Science and Creationism.* Buffalo, N.Y.: Prometheus Books, 1990.

Gilkey, Langdon. *Creationism on Trial: Evolution and God at Little Rock.* Charlottesville: University Press of Virginia, 1998.

Hall, Kermit L. *Conscience and Belief: The Supreme Court and Religion.* New York: Garland, 2000.

Jurinski, James John. *Religion on Trial: A Handbook with Cases, Laws, and Documents.* Santa Barbara, Calif.: ABC-Clio, 2003.

Larson, Edward J. *Summer for the Gods: The Scopes Trial and America's Continuing Debate over Science and Religion.* New York: Basic Books, 1997.

_____. *Trial and Error: The American Legal Controversy over Creation and Evolution.* New York: Oxford University Press, 1985.

Webb, George Ernest. *The Evolution Controversy in America.* Lexington: University Press of Kentucky, 1994.

SEE ALSO *Abington School District v. Schempp*; *Engel v. Vitale*; *Epperson v. Arkansas*; First Amendment; *Lemon v. Kurtzman*; Religion, establishment of.

Exclusionary Rule

DESCRIPTION: Judicially created doctrine proscribing the admissibility at trial of evidence obtained illegally through violation of a defendant's constitutional rights.

SIGNIFICANCE: The Supreme Court ruling in 1914 excluded the use of physical evidence gathered through unreasonable search or seizure, and later rulings prohibited any evidence obtained in violation of the Fifth Amendment right against self-incrimination, the Sixth Amendment right to counsel, and Fifth and Fourteenth Amendment rights to due process of law.

The exclusionary rule, as applied to Fourth Amendment search and seizure provisions, originated with the Supreme Court's 1914 decision in *Weeks v. United States.* Although no emergency conditions existed, police officers had twice conducted nonconsensual, warrantless searches of Freemont Weeks's home, obtaining letters and documents that were later used as evidence against him over his objections at trial. Weeks was ultimately convicted, and the Supreme Court addressed his appeal. In a unanimous opinion, the Court noted that the Framers of the Constitution intended through the passage of the Bill of Rights to protect the American people from the general warrants that had been issued under the authority of the British government in colonial times. The Court declared that the courts, which are charged with the support of the Constitution, should not sanction the tendency of those who enforce the criminal laws of the country to obtain conviction by means of unlawful seizures. The Court concluded that if letters and private documents can be seized illegally and used in evidence against a citizen accused of an offense, the protection of the Fourth Amendment against unreasonable searches and seizures is of no value.

This newly minted rule was strengthened by *Silverthorne Lumber Co. v. United States* (1920), and *Agnello v. United States* (1925), which made clear that illegally acquired evidence could not be used by the government, regardless of the nature of the evidence. However, the mandatory exclusion of illegally obtained evidence pertained only to federal law enforcement and trials. Although the Court eventually agreed in *Wolf v. Colorado* (1949) that the due process clause of the Fourteenth Amendment prohibited illegal state governmental searches and seizures, it initially maintained that the states did not necessarily have to use the exclusionary rule as a method of enforcing that right. The states were allowed to come up with other safeguards to protect the constitutional rights of their citizens.

SILVER PLATTER DOCTRINE

The incorporation of the prohibitions of the Fourth Amendment into the due process clause of the Fourteenth Amendment did not secure compliance by state law-enforcement officers. In fact, because no real means of regulating unlawful state law-enforcement behavior existed, state law-enforcement agents cooperated with federal agents by providing them with illegally seized evidence, which was admissible in federal court because it was not obtained by federal agents. This practice became known as the "silver platter doctrine" because federal agents were being served up evidence like food on a platter.

The silver platter doctrine was denounced by the Court in *Elkins v. United States* (1960), which disallowed the admission of evidence obtained by state officers during a search that, if conducted by federal officers, would have violated a defendant's Fourth Amendment rights. The Court decided that it hardly mattered to victims of illegal searches whether their rights had been abridged by federal agents or by state officers, and that if the fruits of an illegal search conducted by state officers could no longer be admitted in federal trials, no incentive would exist for federal and state agents to cooperate in such abhorrent schemes.

Partially because of state law-enforcement officers' disregard for the Fourth Amendment's proscriptions, in *Mapp v. Ohio* (1961), the Court reconsidered its stance on extending the exclusionary rule to state action.

Mapp v. Ohio

In 1957 Cleveland, Ohio, police officers went to Dollree Mapp's home with the goal of finding and questioning a bombing suspect. When the officers requested entry, Mapp refused to let them in without a search warrant. The officers returned a few hours later and forcibly entered Mapp's house. A struggle ensued; officers handcuffed Mapp and carried her upstairs, then searched her entire house, including the basement. They found obscene materials during their search, and she was charged and convicted of possessing them. During her trial, no warrant was introduced into evidence. The Ohio supreme court upheld Mapp's conviction, although it acknowledged that the methods used to obtain the evidence offended a sense of justice.

In the *Mapp* majority opinion, the Court deplored the futility of protecting Fourth Amendment rights through remedies such as civil or criminal sanctions. It noted the failure of these remedies and the consequent constitutional abuses and suggested nothing could destroy a government more quickly than its failure to observe its own laws. The Court declared that if the Fourteenth Amendment did not bar improperly seized evidence, the Constitution would consist of nothing more than empty words. In addition, more than half of the states had already adopted the exclusionary rule through either statutory or case law. Therefore, the Court ruled that the exclusionary rule applied to the states as well as the federal government. This avoided the incongruity between state and federal use of illegally seized evidence. Through *Mapp*, the Court altered state criminal trial procedures and investigatory procedures by requiring local officials to follow constitutional standards of search and seizure or suffer exclusion of evidence at trial.

RATIONALE FOR THE RULE

Some legal experts theorize that the exclusionary rule is a natural outgrowth of the Constitution. The government cannot provide individual rights without protecting them, and the exclusionary rule provides this function. Therefore, the rule is an implicit part of the substantive guarantees of the Fourth Amendment prohibition against unreasonable search and seizure, the Fifth Amendment right against self-incrimination, the Sixth Amendment right to counsel, and the Fifth and Fourteenth Amendment rights to due process. The exclusionary rule also involves the concept of maintaining judicial integrity. The introduction into evidence of illegally gathered materials must be proscribed to maintain judicial integrity and deter police misconduct.

The most common reason invoked for assertion of the exclusionary rule is that it effectively deters constitutional violations and that this deterrent effect is crucial to the vitality of the constitutional amendments. Beginning with *United States v. Calandra* (1974), the Court viewed the rule as primarily a judicial creation designed to deter police misconduct. Therefore, the Court felt free to balance the costs of excluding evidence against the benefits of the rule's effect as a deterrent and produced an ever-expanding list of judicially acknowledged exceptions to the exclusionary rule.

EXCEPTIONS TO THE RULE

After 1961, when the Court held that the states must apply the exclusionary rule to state investigatory and trial procedures, the rule came under increasing attack by those who argued that it exacts too great a price from society by allowing guilty people to either go free or to receive reduced sentences.

The Court, reflecting societal division over the exclusionary rule, fashioned a number of exceptions to it. For example, in *Calandra*, the Court refused to allow a grand jury witness the privilege of invoking the exclusionary rule in refusing to answer questions that were based on illegally seized evidence, as any deterrent effect that might be achieved through application of the rule was too uncertain. For the same reason, the Court also held that illegally seized evidence may be admitted at trial in civil cases (*United States v. Janis*, 1976) and when it would "inevitably" have been discovered through other legal means (*Nix v. Williams*, 1984) as well as used to impeach a witness's credibility (*United States v. Havens*, 1978) and against third persons (*United States v. Paynor*, 1980).

However, what most eroded the exclusionary rule was the good-faith exception, first approved for criminal cases by the Court in *United States v. Leon* (1984). The good-faith exception permitted the use of illegally acquired evidence if the officers who seized it did so in good faith. In *Leon*, the Court found no reason to apply the exclusionary rule to a situation in which an officer relied on a search warrant issued by a neutral magistrate that later was found not to be supported by probable cause. The Court reasoned that in such a case, the exclusion of evidence would have no deterrent effect on police officers and would exact too great a price from society. In *Illinois v. Krull* (1987), the Court ruled that the exclusionary rule did not bar the admissibility of evidence seized in good-faith reliance on a statute, subsequently found to be unconstitutional, which authorized warrantless administrative searches.

In 1995 the Court again extended the good-faith exception when it held in *Arizona v. Evans* that the exclusionary rule does not require suppression of evidence seized in violation of the Fourth Amendment because of inaccurate information based on a court employee's clerical errors. In *Evans*, a police officer made an arrest following a routine traffic stop when his patrol car computer erroneously indicated there was an outstanding misdemeanor warrant for Evans's arrest. When the issue of suppression reached the Court, it again applied the rationale of *Leon*. There was neither any evidence that court employees were inclined to ignore or subvert the Fourth Amendment nor any basis for believing that application of the rule would have an effect on the future behavior of court employees. Therefore, the Court decided that it would not serve the purposes of justice to apply the exclusionary rule in *Evans*.

In *Hudson v. Michigan* (2006), the Supreme Court approved an exception to the exclusionary rule when it upheld the use of criminal evidence acquired from a search and seizure in which the police did not knock and announce their presence, contrary to the long-standing knock-and-announce rule. Writing for a 5-4 majority, Justice Antonin Scalia acknowledged that the police conducting the search were not faced with "exigent circumstances" that would have justified their entering the home without knocking. However, the Court found that suppression of the resulting evidence was too severe a penalty for the constitutional violation.

Scalia criticized the exclusionary rule for generating "substantial social costs which sometimes include setting the guilty free and the dangerous at large." The increasing professionalism of modern police, he also asserted, had advanced to the point that the need for the deterrence of the exclusionary rule was greatly diminished. In a dissenting opinion, Justice Stephen G. Breyer argued that the majority's decision had destroyed the major legal incentive for the police to comply with the knock-and-announce rule and that the reasoning behind the decision would make the Fourth Amendment unenforceable. Although the long-term implications of the *Hudson* ruling were unclear, observers agreed that the exclusionary rule was only a shadow of its earlier condition.

Rebecca Davis
Updated by the Editor

FURTHER READING

Joel Samaha discusses the history of the exclusionary rule, rationales that justify it, and its social costs and deterrent effects in *Criminal Procedure* (6th ed. Belmont, Calif.: Wadsworth, 2005). For basic information regarding the exclusionary rule and its exceptions, see David Savage's *The Supreme Court and Constitutional Rights* (Washington, D.C.: CQ Press, 2004), Louis Fisher's *Constitutional Rights: Civil Rights and Civil Liberties* (2d ed. New York: McGraw-Hill, 1995), Lee Epstein and Thomas G. Walker's *Constitutional Law for a Changing America: Rights, Liberties, and Justice* (5th ed. Washington, D.C.: CQ Press, 2004), Craig Ducat's *Constitutional Interpretation* (8th ed. Belmont, Calif.: Thomson/West, 2004), and Joan Biskupic's *The Supreme Court and*

Individual Rights (3d ed. Washington, D.C.: Congressional Quarterly, 1997).

Timothy Lynch's journal article "In Defense of the Exclusionary Rule" (*Harvard Journal of Law and Public Policy* 23 [2000]) is an advanced study of the exclusionary rule that should be understandable to undergraduate college students.

SEE ALSO Breyer, Stephen G.; Due process, substantive; *Ferguson v. City of Charleston*; Fifth Amendment; Fourteenth Amendment; Fourth Amendment; Fundamental rights; *Hudson v. Michigan*; Incorporation doctrine; *Mapp v. Ohio*; Search warrant requirement; Self-incrimination, immunity against; Sixth Amendment.

Executive Agreements

DESCRIPTION: International agreements made by presidents on their own constitutional authority or in cooperation with Congress.

SIGNIFICANCE: Executive agreements enhanced presidential leadership in foreign affairs and served as the form for key international commitments from the Yalta Agreement to the North American Free Trade Agreement. On several occasions, the Supreme Court was asked to rule on the constitutionality of an executive agreement.

Executive agreements vary widely in formality and importance. Many address routine economic, military, and political subjects such as postal regulations and trade agreements, and others, such as the Yalta Agreement in 1945, the Vietnam War peace settlement in 1973, and the North American Free Trade Agreement (NAFTA) in 1993, had significant international political and economic consequences.

Article I, section 10, of the U.S. Constitution implicitly recognizes executive agreements by its prohibition on states making agreements and compacts with foreign powers, but it does not indicate how executive agreements are related to treaties made by the president with the advice and consent of two-thirds of the Senate. The Supreme Court provided some assistance in *Weinberger v. Rossi* (1982) when it observed that the word "treaty" in international law referred to a compact between sovereign states, but the Constitution distinguished Article II treaties from those governed by Article IV, section 2, the supremacy clause, which also included executive agreements. As the Court said in *United States v. Pink* (1942), this meant that a state law inconsistent with an executive agreement had to yield, because the agreement, like a treaty, was the supreme law of the land. Executive agreements and treaties also have to comply with personal constitutional guarantees. In *Reid v. Covert* (1957), the Court held that an executive agreement providing for trial by courts-martial for U.S. military personnel and their dependents violated the constitutional right to trial by jury. However, the Court never clearly indicated how treaties and agreements differ or defined the president's sole power to make agreements without the Senate and to collaborate with both chambers.

SOLE EXECUTIVE AGREEMENT

Presidents have used their Article II power as commander in chief to make armistice and cease-fire agreements, enter into agreements to protect troops, control occupied areas, and arrange postwar territorial and political matters as at Yalta and Potsdam. Presidents have also construed their Article II diplomatic powers broadly to argue that their authority to settle claims lies within the penumbra of their power to recognize foreign governments. In 1933 President Franklin D. Roosevelt recognized the Soviet Union, established diplomatic relations, and negotiated a claims settlement agreement. In *United States v. Belmont* (1937) and *Pink*, the Court held that the Litvinov claims settlement agreement was a legally enforceable international compact that the president, as the sole organ of the federal government in foreign relations, had the authority to negotiate without consulting the Senate. In 1980 President Jimmy Carter negotiated the release of diplomatic personnel held hostage by Iran on the basis of an executive agreement that provided for the arbitration of claims, but in *Dames and Moore v. Regan* (1981), the Court was more cautious. *Pink* gave the president a measure of authority to enter into an agreement providing for claims settlement when it was necessary to resolve a major foreign policy dispute, but the Court emphasized that the crucial factor in upholding the agreement was a history of congressional acquiescence that had invited similar presidential actions.

CONGRESSIONAL-EXECUTIVE AGREEMENTS

Presidential collaboration with Congress is based on Article I's requirement that revenue bills originate in the House of Representatives and its grant to Congress of the power to oversee foreign commerce and, under the necessary and proper clause, to make all laws reasonably related to foreign commerce and to the president's foreign relations powers. Congress at times took the initiative and provided presidents with prior authorization to make agreements on postal rates, trademark and copyright regulations, foreign assistance, and reciprocal trade agreements. Presidents also took the initiative and negotiated agreements with foreign governments and then sought authorization from Congress in the form of a statute or a joint resolution. The Congress-initiated agreement has a long historical pedigree, but the use of the president-initiated agreement dates back to World War II (1941 1945) and takes its current form from the Trade Act of 1974. This act stipulated congressional involvement in the negotiation process and a fast-track approval procedure (limited debate, and a thumbs up or down vote with no amendments) that President Bill Clinton used with NAFTA.

Executive agreements initiated by presidents have become a largely interchangeable alternative to treaties. They substitute the one-third plus one Senate veto for a simple majority of both chambers, provide the House of Representatives with an equal voice, and eliminate the danger that the House may refuse to approve the appropriation of funds necessary to implement a treaty. The Court has not addressed the constitutional status of these agreements. If it does, its reliance in *Dames and Moore* on Justice Robert H. Jackson's concurring opinion in *Youngstown Sheet and Tube Co. v. Sawyer* (1952) could allow it to frame a decision in terms of whether the president's action was taken with the support of, in opposition to, or in the absence of congressional authorization. However, the Court is unlikely to address the larger issue of a president's use of an agreement instead of treaty because it is a political question inappropriate for judicial inquiry.

Presidents' use of executive agreements will continue to be defined by their relationship with Congress and by their awareness that the Senate has objected to extensive use of these agreements. The Bricker Amendment (1954), though it would have conferred explicit constitutional recognition on executive agreements, sought to curtail and regulate them by providing that they would be effective as internal law only if they were supported by legislation. Congress has also been troubled by covert agreements and in the Case Act (1972), required their publication. As a consequence, presidents' use of executive agreements will be shaped by their respect for the Senate and its treaty power, their awareness that treaties have greater dignity, and their knowledge that the constitutional status of agreements is beyond doubt.

William C. Green

FURTHER READING

Akerman, Bruce, and David Golove. *Is NAFTA Constitutional?* Cambridge, Mass.: Harvard University Press, 1995.

Antieau, Chester James. *Our Two Centuries of Law and Life, 1775-1975: The Work of the Supreme Court and the Impact of Both Congress and Presidents.* Littleton, Colo.: Fred B. Rothman, 2001.

Fisher, Louis. *Constitutional Conflicts Between Congress and the President.* 4th ed. Lawrence: University Press of Kansas, 1997.

Henkin, Louis. *Foreign Affairs and the Constitution.* New York: W. W. Norton, 1972.

Smith, Herbert Arthur. *The American Supreme Court as an International Tribunal.* Buffalo, N.Y.: William S. Hein, 2003.

Yates, Jeff. *Popular Justice: Presidential Prestige and Executive Success in the Supreme Court.* Albany, N.Y.: State University of New York Press, 2002.

SEE ALSO Executive privilege; Presidential powers; Treaties; *Youngstown Sheet and Tube Co. v. Sawyer*; World War II.

Executive Privilege

DESCRIPTION: Inherent power of the president to withhold information from Congress and the courts or to refuse to testify in a legislative or judicial proceeding.

SIGNIFICANCE: The Supreme Court recognized a constitutionally based limited privilege grounded in the doctrine of the separation of powers.

Presidential discretion to refuse to appear before a legislative or judicial proceeding is sometimes considered a separate category of executive discretion called executive privilege, or presidential privacy. According to William Safire, the phrase "executive privilege" was first used in the 1950's, but the concept dates back to the practice of the royal prerogative, privilege of clergy, and privileges of Parliament.

ORIGINS AND EARLY USES

Executive privilege is also considered an implied power under Article II of the U.S. Constitution. George Washington claimed the authority to withhold information from Congress during a 1792 congressional investigation into the St. Clair affair, in which General Arthur St. Clair, governor of the Northwest Territory, suffered a devastating defeat when ambushed by Indians in 1791. Although Washington gave the House of Representatives the documents it requested regarding the St. Clair expedition, the president argued that if he deemed it in the national interest, he could withhold the information.

Because of its opaque historical roots, disagreement exists regarding the meaning and scope of executive privilege, its application in U.S. government, and its constitutional basis. As a result of these disagreements, in the post-World War II period, federal courts frequently were asked to decide cases involving executive privilege. Constitutional scholars such as Raoul Berger represent one side of the debate that argues that executive privilege is a myth, not a constitutional reality. Proponents of a broad interpretation of executive privilege tend to be presidents and executive officials who argue for it in a particular political context rather than on principle. The debate over its application has been colored by the specific controversies that engendered its use. For example, President Dwight D. Eisenhower used executive privilege to prevent Defense Department officials from revealing information sought by the House of Representatives during the Army-McCarthy hearings in 1953-1954.

Only a president can invoke executive privilege because in the Constitution, all executive power rests in that office. Executive privilege is justified by the president's need to receive frank advice from advisers, to protect national security, and to check and balance the subpoena power of Congress and the courts. In each of these cases, the justification for keeping information within the executive branch is national interest or the public good, often in combination with national security. Although executive privilege has no textual mooring in the Constitution, it emanates from the principle of the separation of powers.

A LIMITED PRIVILEGE

The Supreme Court set limits to executive privilege in the landmark precedent *United States v. Nixon* (1974), which led to the resignation of President Richard M. Nixon. In the 8-0 decision written by Chief Justice Warren E. Burger, the Court ruled that the president may not give privileged status to information that is instrumental to a criminal investigation. Nixon's use of executive privilege regarding the Watergate tapes was considered inconsistent with the idea that this privilege exists to serve the national interest, not to protect the president from criminal prosecution or impeachment.

Although post-World War II presidents have tended to argue for an absolute privilege, the federal courts have rejected the idea based largely on the legitimate needs of the other branches of government to acquire information from the executive. The Court has accepted a constitutionally based limited privilege. The closest the Court came to accepting an absolute privilege power was in *Spalding v. Vilas* (1896) and *Barr v. Matteo* (1959). The Court's position, however, was reshaped by the Watergate affair, and the effects of the *United States v. Nixon* decision were apparent in *Butz v. Economou* (1978). In the *Butz* decision, the majority, represented by Justice Byron R. White, denied absolute immunity based in part on its inconsistency with the rule of law.

In the 1990's, the federal courts ruled that President Bill Clinton's use of executive privilege was unfounded because, as with Nixon, it was invoked to avoid criminal prosecution and impeachment, not to serve the needs of the nation. During the investigation involving the president and Monica Lewinsky by independent council Kenneth Starr, the Clinton administration attempted to expand the meaning and application of executive privilege to new areas of the president's life. Two such areas were the attempt to extend executive privilege to the president and his attorneys and to the Secret Service agents who protect the president. U.S. District Judge Norma Holloway Johnson and a three-judge appeals court panel rejected Clinton's claims of executive privilege in the Lewinsky investigation. Johnson ruled that White House attorney Bruce Lindsey and White House aide Sidney Blumenthal must testify before a federal grand jury. President Clinton's attorneys appealed the decision to the Supreme Court, but the Court refused to hear the case.

In a related matter, the Clinton administration argued that Secret Service agents are covered by "protective-function privilege" because requiring them to testify about the president before a federal grand jury or to be deposed by the independent council's office is incompatible with their duty to protect the president. Acceptance of this claim would have significantly expanded the extent of executive privilege. However, the Court also refused to hear this case, letting stand the lower court's decision to deny the president's claim of a protective-function privilege.

Michael P. Federici

FURTHER READING

Antieau, Chester James. *Our Two Centuries of Law and Life, 1775-1975: The Work of the Supreme Court and the Impact of Both Congress and Presidents.* Littleton, Colo.: Fred B. Rothman, 2001.

Berger, Raoul. *Executive Privilege: A Constitutional Myth.* Cambridge, Mass.: Harvard University Press, 1974.

Fisher, Louis. *Constitutional Conflicts Between Congress and the President.* 4th ed. Lawrence: University Press of Kansas, 1997.

Rozell, Mark J. *Executive Privilege: The Dilemma of Secrecy and Democratic Accountability.* Baltimore, Md.: Johns Hopkins University Press, 1994.

Safire, William. *Safire's New Political Dictionary.* New York: Random House, 1993.

Yates, Jeff. *Popular Justice: Presidential Prestige and Executive Success in the Supreme Court.* Albany, N.Y.: State University of New York Press, 2002.

SEE ALSO Advisory opinions; Burger, Warren E.; Executive agreements; Presidential powers; White, Byron R.

Federalism

DESCRIPTION: Political union and the resulting constitutional structures that configure relationships among the states and institutions of national governance.

SIGNIFICANCE: Problems of federalism involve questions of constitutional structure. The Supreme Court has expressed its position on relationships among institutions of national and state governance and enforced federal constitutional limitations against the states.

Even before the U.S. Constitution went into effect, there were serious debates about what type of political system it would create—and what type of union had already been formed. Part of the problem was multiple and shifting word usages. Those advocating the Constitution's ratification identified themselves as Federalists, described the new structures as partly federal, and claimed those structures were necessary to preserve the federal union. At the same time, members of the founding generation identified federalism with a confederation of sovereign states, as distinct from a consolidated or national government. Relying on these distinctions, James Madison in *The Federalist* (1788) No. 39, argued that the proposed Constitution was neither purely federal nor entirely national but instead included features of each.

Federalism in the American context has since become identified with this hybrid political system—especially the Constitution's configuration of national and state governing powers. Unlike the Articles of Confederation, the Constitution establishes a centralized government, which has institutions that directly represent the people and are capable, in turn, of acting directly on them. As a result of the Constitution's delegation of limited powers to these institutions, however, the states continue to hold independent governing powers. The states also play other important roles within the constitutional order, through, among other mechanisms, their equal representation in the Senate and their participation in constitutional amendment.

Not surprisingly, controversies involving problems of federalism survived the Constitution's ratification. Some such controversies—but certainly not all those of constitutional significance—have arisen in the context of litigation. Accordingly, the Supreme Court played an important role in the development of American federalism on several fronts. In the process, the Court articulated a range of competing conceptions of the constitutional design.

QUESTIONS OF FEDERAL JURISDICTION

One set of issues centered on problems of jurisdiction and matters of interpretive or decisional authority. Article III of the U.S. Constitution defines the jurisdiction of federal courts as including cases or controversies "between Citizens of a State and Citizens of another State." In *Chisholm v. Georgia* (1793), the Court held that this provision authorized federal courts to decide a suit against Georgia brought by two citizens of South Carolina. Two years later, Congress and the states overturned this holding by passing the Eleventh Amendment, which restricts federal courts from hearing suits against states brought by citizens of other states or by citizens of foreign nations. In subsequent decisions, the Court held that this amendment also bars suits against a state by its own citizens without its consent. However, the significance of these exceptions has been diluted by the Fourteenth Amendment, along with distinctions between the states and state officials. As explained below, a fertile area of constitutional litigation involves federal courts' enforcing the U.S. Constitution and federal laws against the states and state actors.

Article III delegates to federal courts the authority to decide some cases based on the identity of the litigants, as with lawsuits between citizens of different states. Federal courts also have authority to decide controversies based on the subject matter, including cases "arising under th[e] Constitution, the Laws of the United States, and Treaties." Especially during the republic's first 100 years, substantial conflict surrounded the Court's assertions of appellate power to review decisions by state courts in cases raising such "federal questions." Most prominently, in *Martin v. Hunter's Lessee* (1816), a civil case, and *Cohens v. Virginia* (1821), a criminal case, the justices insisted that they had final authority to review decisions by state courts. In both contexts, state courts denied that the Supreme Court had authority to review or reverse their decisions.

Challenges of federal authority by state judges, legislatures, and others continued through the antebellum period and into the twentieth century. The Court responded to one such challenge in *Ableman v. Booth* (1859), in the context of efforts by the Wisconsin Supreme Court to authorize the release of prisoners from a local jail based on the state judges' position that the federal Fugitive Slave Act of 1850 was unconstitutional. In response, Chief Justice Roger Brooke Taney unflinchingly reasserted the Supreme Court's interpretive supremacy. He claimed that "no power is more clearly conferred by the Constitution and laws of the United States, than the power of this court to decide, ultimately and finally, all cases arising under such Constitution and laws." (Ironically, however, the Court's position on the constitutional status of slavery was soon overruled by the Civil War and Reconstruction amendments.)

Almost one hundred years later, Chief Justice Earl Warren echoed Taney's position on the preeminence of the Court's interpretive powers in *Cooper v. Aaron* (1958). In that case, the justices sought to overcome resistance to their previous ruling in *Brown v. Board of Education* (1954). Collapsing the constitutional text into its interpretation by the justices, Warren proclaimed that "the interpretation of the Fourteenth Amendment by this Court in the Brown Case is the supreme law of the land, and Article 6 of the Constitution makes it of binding effect on the States."

EARLY VIEWS OF FEDERAL-STATE RELATIONS

Woven through these cases raising questions of jurisdictional and decisional authority were controversies over the scope of Congress's powers (or federal powers more generally) and their relationships to state powers, along with efforts to enforce other limitations on the states. Among other things, the Supreme Court justices took positions on the constitutional status of slavery, the scope of the Constitution's delegation of commercial powers and their negative implications, implied powers, and taxing and spending powers. The Tenth Amendment was at the center of these debates because it both presupposes that federal powers are intrinsically limited and refers to reserved powers of "the states" and "the people." The Fourteenth Amendment was also centrally relevant, as it was the vehicle for the Court's applying much of the Bill of Rights to the states, along with additional guarantees of due process and equal protection.

During the republic's early years, the federal government's role was relatively limited compared to that of the states. Nevertheless, in cases such as *McCulloch v. Maryland* (1819) and *Gibbons v. Ogden* (1824), Chief Justice John Marshall offered a vigorous conception of federal powers and emphasized the supremacy of delegated over reserved powers. He presumed that federal powers were intrinsically limited and thus were consistent with the states' continuing to have substantial regulatory autonomy. However, he did not regard state powers as affirmative limitations on congressional powers or as capable of interfering with their exercise. Therefore, he claimed that state powers must give way to legitimate assertions of federal power.

Taney, Marshall's successor, developed the idea of state police powers and placed greater emphasis on the limited scope of federal powers. Beneath the surface if not always transparently, there was recurring concern during Taney's tenure with problems of slavery. In some contexts, he and his colleagues treated federal and state powers as potentially overlapping, as with powers of commercial regulation in general. At the same time, the justices treated some federal and state governing powers as mutually exclusive and reciprocally limiting. Taney relied on a version of the latter approach, characteristically dual federalist, in *Scott v. Sandford* (1857). Among other things, he argued that limitations on Congress's powers relating to slavery corresponded to—and protected—powers reserved exclusively to the states.

The predominant view during the antebellum period, as articulated by Chief Justice Marshall in *Barron v. Baltimore* (1833), was that federal judges lacked authority to enforce the Bill of Rights against the states. Other parts of the constitutional text, such as Article I, section 10, imposed limitations directly on the states. The Court interpreted some constitutional delegations of power to Congress as preempting state regulations within certain "spheres." However, the Court, along with Congress, allowed large measures of state autonomy. Accordingly, dual federalism largely prevailed in both theory and practice.

CONSTITUTIONAL TRANSFORMATIONS

The Civil War and Reconstruction substantially altered these relationships between institutions of federal and state governance, along with their respective relationships to the people at large. During the war itself, governing power became increasingly centralized, supporting further consolidations of national power after the war. These tendencies were exacerbated, moreover, by problems of reconstruction. The Thirteenth, Fourteenth, and Fifteenth Amendments altered representational structures, imposed additional limitations on the states, and otherwise sought to reduce state autonomy and enhance national powers.

During these transformative periods, the Court's role was mixed. In *Ex parte Merryman* (1861), the Taney Court denied that President Abraham Lincoln had authority to suspend the writ of habeas corpus. However, the president refused to comply with this decision, and in the *Prize Cases* (1863), a majority of the justices upheld Lincoln's blockade of Southern ports. After the war, in *Ex parte Milligan* (1866), the Court reasserted itself, with Salmon P. Chase as chief justice, by invalidating the military trial of a civilian when civil courts were open. In *Mississippi v. Johnson* (1867), *Georgia v. Stanton* (1868), *Ex parte McCardle* (1869), and *Texas v. White* (1869), however, the justices refrained in various contexts from taking a position on the validity of military reconstruction. In the last of these cases, Chase supported the cause of the Union by proclaiming that "the Constitution in all its provisions looks to an indestructible Union composed of indestructible states." Thus, he denied that states could legitimately secede from the Union, claimed that the war had altered relationships between the rebellious states and the Union, and affirmed congressional power to restore republican governments in the South.

The judges initially interpreted the Thirteenth, Fourteenth, and Fifteenth Amendments as supporting Congress's power to secure civil rights from abridgment by the states or individuals. However, soon the justices joined a broader retreat from Reconstruction, as signaled by the opinions in *Slaughterhouse Cases* (1873) and *Civil Rights Cases* (1883). Justices Samuel F. Miller and Joseph P. Bradley wrote the respective majority opinions. In the former case, the Court upheld a monopoly on the slaughtering of meat in New Orleans; in the latter, it invalidated the Civil Rights Act of 1875. From opposite directions, these two decisions perpetuated models of dual federalism.

DUAL FEDERALISM

In *Slaughterhouse Cases*, Miller claimed that the "one pervading purpose" of the Thirteenth, Fourteenth, and Fifteenth Amendments was "the freedom of the slave race, the security and firm establishment of that freedom, and the protection of the newly-made freeman and citizen." Though he suggested that other races might benefit from their guarantees, Miller denied that these amendments "radically changed the whole theory of the relations of the State and Federal governments to each other and of both these governments to the people." More specifically, he denied that the privileges or immunities clause of the Fourteenth Amendment "was intended to bring within the power of Congress the entire domain of civil rights heretofore belonging exclusively to the States." Nor did that clause "constitute this court a perpetual censor upon all legislation of the States, on the civil rights of their own citizens." He staked out corresponding positions on the Thirteenth Amendment and the Fourteenth Amendment's due process and equal protection clauses.

In *Civil Rights Cases*, Bradley likewise argued that the Fourteenth Amendment did not "invest Congress with power to legislate upon subjects which are within the domain of State legislation." In his view, the amendment provided remedies for abridgments of rights by states, not individuals. Relying on the Tenth Amendment, a majority of the justices claimed that the law regulating individual actions exceeded Congress's delegated powers.

Although the Court would subsequently adhere to aspects of the majority opinions in these two cases, many of the dissenters' arguments would eventually prevail in one form or another. The dissents of Justices Stephen J. Field and Bradley in *Slaughterhouse* anticipated judicial enforcement of commercial rights as limitations on the states in reliance on the due process clause of the Fourteenth Amendment. Federal judges went even further by relying on that clause as the primary vehicle for enforcing much of the Bill of Rights against the states, making prescient Justice Noah H. Swayne's characterization of the amendment as "a new Magna Charta." Justice John Marshall Harlan's dissent in the *Civil Rights Cases* likewise anticipated national regulation of individual actions. Relying on the Fourteenth Amendment and Article I's delegation of commercial powers, Congress in the twentieth century would assert—and the justices would uphold—sweeping national civil rights legislation, economic regulations, and other expansions of national power.

In the meantime, the Court enlisted the Fourteenth Amendment, along with the Fifth and Tenth, to promote economic laissez-faire. *Lochner v. New York* (1905) and *Hammer v. Dagenhart* (1918) epitomize the restrictive decisions of this era. Both dealt with matters of federalism: the first through the justices' invalidation of a state law in reliance on the U.S. Constitution; the second because the majority relied on dual federalist premises to strike down an act of Congress. In *Lochner*, the Court held that a state maximum-hour workday law for bakers deprived them of liberty without due process of law in violation of the Fourteenth Amendment's due process clause; and in *Hammer*, they argued that a federal law regulating child labor exceeded Congress's powers, conflicted with the Fifth Amendment, and encroached on powers reserved exclusively to the states. The combined result of such decisions was to treat a wide range of commercial transactions (but not all) as beyond the legitimate reach of governmental restriction, federal or state.

THE MODERN ERA

Controversy over this issue erupted during the New Deal. In response to intense pressure from President Franklin D. Roosevelt, Congress, state legislatures, and various constituencies, the Court shifted its posture in the late 1930's and early 1940's. *West Coast Hotel Co. v. Parrish* (1937) and *United States v. Darby Lumber Co.* (1941) both signaled and epitomized this change, often described as "revolutionary." In *West Coast*, the Court employed deferential reasoning to uphold a state minimum-wage, maximum-hour law, and in *Darby*, it affirmed Congress's powers to regulate terms of employment. In the process, the Court rejected dual federalist premises: Instead of presuming that federal and state powers were mutually exclusive and reciprocally limiting, they treated such powers as substantially overlapping, in many ways complementary, but with federal powers supreme.

The Court did not, however, entirely withdraw from enforcing constitutional limitations on the states. On the contrary, *United States v. Carolene Products Co.* (1938) suggested that the Court would continue to enforce enumerated rights, seek to guard political processes, and ensure fidelity to requirements of equal protection. Such efforts and their extensions gained momentum through the Civil Rights and women's movements and social change more generally, culminating in Warren and post-Warren Court precedents such as *Brown v. Board of Education* (1954), *Mapp v. Ohio* (1961), *Miranda v. Arizona* (1966), *Griswold v. Connecticut* (1965), and *Roe v. Wade* (1973).

Chief Justice Earl Warren's successors, Warren E. Burger and William H. Rehnquist, led modest retreats from these overall trends toward the Court's upholding greater concentrations of central governing power along with increased supervision of state actions. For example, in *National League of Cities v. Usery* (1976), the Court invalidated provisions in the Fair Labor Standards Act (1938) as they applied to the states. However, a majority of the justices overruled this decision nine years later in *Garcia v. San Antonio Metropolitan Transit Authority* (1985). Once again invoking principles of federalism, the Court in *United States v. Lopez* (1995) invalidated a federal law limiting possession of guns near schools. For the first time since 1937, a majority of the justices held that Congress had exceeded its commercial powers. Then in *Seminole Tribe v. Florida* (1996) and again in *Kimel v. Florida Board of Regents* (2000), the Rehnquist Court revitalized the doctrine of the states' "sovereign immunity" under the Eleventh Amendment, which severely restricted Congress's power to mandate lawsuits against the states without their consent. In another decision that expanded states' rights, *Printz v. United States* (1997), the justices held that Congress could not command state and local officials to enforce a federal law.

Cases from the founding period exemplify ways that constitutionalism in the United States rests on a premise that the states and the people may act through representational structures in some capacities while acting independently of them in others. Principles of federalism are at the heart of these interactions, forming and being reformed by ongoing commitment to constitutional governance. Rather than being settled by more than two hundred years of practice, these principles have remained radically contestable.

Wayne D. Moore

FURTHER READING

A good starting point is Robert F. Nagel's *The Implosion of American Federalism* (New York: Oxford University Press, 2002), a wide-ranging exploration of the subject of federalism that pays special attention to the role of the Supreme Court. Other up-to-date studies of the subject include Ralph A. Rossum's *Federalism, the Supreme Court, and the Seventeenth Amendment: The Irony of Constitutional Democracy* (Lanham, Md.: Lexington Books, 2001), Kermit L. Hall's *A Nation of States: Federalism at the Bar of the Supreme Court* (New York: Garland, 2000), and *The Supreme Court's Federalism: Real or Imagined?* (Thousand Oaks, Calif.: Sage Publications, 2001), edited by Frank Goodman.

Two other useful and up-to-date historical surveys of the topic are Robert Sutton's *Federalism* (Westport, Conn.: Greenwood Press, 2002) and Christopher N. May's *Constitutional Law: National Power and Federalism* (New York: Aspen, 2004).

Federalism is placed in its historical and theoretical context in *A Nation of States: Essays on the American Federal System* (Chicago: Rand McNally, 1963), edited by Robert A. Goldwin; Raoul Berger's *Federalism: The Founders' Design* (Norman: University of Oklahoma Press, 1987); and *How Federal Is the Constitution?* (Washington, D.C.: American Enterprise Institute for Public Policy Research, 1987), edited by Robert A. Goldwin and William A. Schambra. Similar treatments of federalism can be found in Wayne D. Moore's *Constitutional Rights and Powers of the People* (Princeton, N.J.: Princeton University Press,

1996) and Daniel J. Elazar's *Covenant and Constitutionalism: The Great Frontier and the Matrix of Federal Democracy* (New Brunswick, N.J.: Transaction, 1998).

For a progressive approach to federalism, see the essays in "Constructing a New Federalism: Jurisdictional Competence and Competition," Symposium Issue, *Yale Law and Policy Review/Yale Journal on Regulation* (1996).

SEE ALSO *Civil Rights Cases*; Eleventh Amendment; Fourteenth Amendment; *Gibbons v. Ogden*; Judiciary Act of 1789; New Deal; Reconstruction; *Shipp, United States v.*; *Slaughterhouse Cases*; States' rights and state sovereignty; Tenth Amendment.

Ferguson v. City of Charleston

CITATION: 532 U.S. 67
DATE: March 21, 2001
ISSUES: Search and seizure; gender issues
SIGNIFICANCE: The Supreme Court held that the Fourth Amendment prohibits hospitals from testing pregnant women for illegal drugs without their consent if the purpose is to notify the police of illegal behavior.

A public hospital of Charleston, South Carolina, reacting to the growing number of "crack babies," instituted a program of automatically testing maternity patients for cocaine and other illegal drugs, and then alerting the police when the test results were positive. The police used the threat of prosecution to coerce the women into substance abuse treatment. A small number of noncooperative women were prosecuted. In a suit against the city, Crystal Ferguson and nine other plaintiffs alleged that the tests were unconstitutional in the absence of either a warrant or informed consent. The city argued that the program was justified by the "special need" of preventing pregnant women from endangering their fetuses.

By a 6-3 vote, the U.S. Supreme Court agreed with the plaintiffs. Writing for the majority, Justice John Paul Stevens explained that the "special needs" exception to the Fourth Amendment, which the Court had allowed to protect the public safety in special circumstances, did not apply to programs which were so directly connected to law enforcement. While the ultimate goal of the program might have been to coerce the women into treatment, the immediate objective of the searches was to obtain evidence of wrongdoing that would be admissible in criminal prosecutions. The question of whether any of the ten plaintiffs had voluntarily consented to the tests was left to the lower courts to decide.

Thomas Tandy Lewis

SEE ALSO Fourth Amendment; Gender issues; Search warrant requirement; Stevens, John Paul.

Stephen J. Field

IDENTIFICATION: Associate justice (May 20, 1863-December 1, 1897)
NOMINATED BY: Abraham Lincoln
BORN: November 4, 1816, Haddam, Connecticut
DIED: April 9, 1899, Washington, D.C.
SIGNIFICANCE: For thirty-four years, Field used his position as a Supreme Court justice to effect a broad interpretation of the Constitution in restricting government regulation of property rights.

Born in Connecticut, Stephen J. Field was the son of a clergyman. His brother, David Dudley Field, was a prominent Democratic politician and lawyer in New York. Stephen followed a less conventional path. After earning his law license, he moved to California in 1849 at the height of the gold rush. There he established his reputation as a judge on the state supreme court, creating legal order out of the chaos of the booming state.

His prominent position earned him the attention of President Abraham Lincoln when the U.S. Congress created a tenth seat on the Supreme Court. Lincoln recognized the political rewards of appointing a prowar Democrat from one of the fastest expanding states in the union. The president also knew he would receive the grati-

Stephen J. Field.
(Library of Congress)

tude of the powerful David Dudley Field if his brother Stephen were appointed.

Upon his confirmation to the Court in 1863, Field performed as Lincoln had hoped, supporting the Civil War effort and the expansion of presidential power during the era. He was less friendly to executive prerogatives in the postwar period; in *Ex parte Garland* (1867) and *Cummings v. Missouri* (1867), he voted to strike down loyalty oaths for former confederates seeking political office.

ECONOMIC RIGHTS

Field was also protective of individual economic rights. He broadly interpreted the newly ratified Fourteenth Amendment, arguing that the equal protection, due process, and privileges and immunities clauses protected property owners from state economic regulation. His support for property rights was seen in the first of the *Legal Tender Cases* (1870) as he voted to strike down the federal government's issuing of paper money to finance the Civil War. Field agreed that the inflation created by the printing of money represented the government taking property without compensation. In the second of the

435

Legal Tender Cases (1871), Field dissented as the Court reversed course and upheld the Legal Tender Act.

Field's support of economic rights continued. In the *Slaughterhouse Cases* (1873), a narrow 5-4 majority ruled that the Fourteenth Amendment did not prevent the government from granting monopolies. Field dissented on the basis that the amendment's privileges and immunities clause protected the right of an individual to work at a trade without government interference.

The philosophy was reiterated by Field over the next quarter century. Dissenting from such cases as *Munn v. Illinois* (1877), which upheld the regulation of grain elevators, Field maintained the broad view that the Fourteenth Amendment could be used to protect the property rights of individuals and corporations.

Field continued to air his views before the Court, vigorously dissenting whenever the Court upheld state regulation of business. Eventually his dogged determination and changes in the Court's personnel produced a shift in doctrine. In *Santa Clara County v. Southern Pacific Railroad Co.* (1886), the Court ruled that corporations were recognized as persons under the Fourteenth Amendment. This advanced Field's argument that the amendment should protect corporate property rights. It also opened the door for the Court to use the due process clause of the Fourteenth Amendment to protect those rights.

THE TERRY AFFAIR

Before Field could witness his final victory, he was embroiled in a personal controversy that made him the only justice to ever experience an assassination attempt. The Terry affair, as it became known, centered on a former California judge, David S. Terry. When Field made a ruling detrimental to Terry's wife, the California judge threatened the justice's life. In response, the federal government provided a marshal as Field's personal bodyguard when he traveled to California. That marshal, David Neagle, and Field were confronted by Terry. A struggle followed, and Neagle shot Terry dead. Neagle was arrested, producing a legal case that made its way to the Supreme Court. With Field not participating, the justices ruled in *In re Neagle* (1890) that the marshal could not be prosecuted under state law because he was acting under the direction of federal law in protecting Field.

The Terry affair did not dampen Field's determination to use the Constitution to protect property rights. It was during the 1890's that Field's views took center stage, dominating the Court's decisions. Between 1895 and 1897 Field's colleagues followed his lead in striking down laws that restricted economic liberty.

FIELD'S SUCCESS

In *United States v. E. C. Knight Co.* (1895), the Court narrowed the scope of antitrust laws, preventing the government from breaking up monopolies that involved the manufacturing of goods. This prevented antitrust prosecutions of corporate monopolies, a result favored by Field. In *Pollock v. Farmers' Loan and Trust Co.* (1895), the Court struck down the federal income tax as unconstitutional. Field wrote a separate opinion in the case, denouncing the income tax as a move toward communism and warning against legislation that might cause class warfare. Finally in one of the last decisions in which Field participated, *Allgeyer v. Louisiana* (1897), the Court recognized a freedom to contract. In *Allgeyer,* a unanimous Court agreed that the Fourteenth Amendment protected an individual's right to make contracts without government interference.

Field's victory in *Allgeyer* marked the end of his judicial career. Throughout the 1890's his mental abilities had declined, and he was unable to fully function on the Court. He retired on December 1, 1897, having served longer than any other justice up to that time. During his thirty-four years, he was able to move the Court toward a dynamic reading of the Fourteenth Amendment that protected economic rights. His career marked the success of a man whose strength of character and determination allowed him to reshape American law.

Douglas Clouatre

FURTHER READING

Bader, William H., and Roy M. Mersky, eds. *The First One Hundred Eight Justices.* Buffalo, N.Y.: William S. Hein, 2004.

Ely, James, Jr. *The Chief Justiceship of Melville Fuller.* Columbia: University of South Carolina Press, 1995.

_____. *The Fuller Court: Justices, Rulings, and Legacy.* Santa Barbara, Calif.: ABC-Clio, 2003.

Friedman, Leon, and Fred L. Israel, eds. *The Justices of the United States Supreme Court: Their Lives and Major Opinions.* 5 vols. New York: Chelsea House, 1997.

Gillman, Howard. *The Constitution Besieged.* Durham, N.C.: Duke University Press, 1993.

Huebner, Timothy S. *The Taney Court: Justices, Rulings, and Legacy.* Santa Barbara, Calif.: ABC-Clio, 2003.

Kens, Paul. *Justice Stephen Field.* Lawrence: University of Kansas Press, 1997.

Lurie, Jonathan. *The Chase Court: Justices, Rulings, and Legacy.* Santa Barbara, Calif.: ABC-Clio, 2004.

Swisher, Carl Brent. *Stephen J. Field: Craftsman of the Law.* Hamden, Conn.: Archon Books, 1963.

SEE ALSO *Allgeyer v. Louisiana*; Civil War; Fourteenth Amendment; Loyalty oaths; Presidential powers; *Slaughterhouse Cases.*

Fifteenth Amendment

DATE: 1870

DESCRIPTION: Amendment to the U.S. Constitution forbidding discrimination in voting rights on the basis of race, color, or previous condition of servitude. Section 2 gives enforcement power to Congress.

SIGNIFICANCE: The Supreme Court decided many cases involving discrimination in access to voting, especially after the passage of the Voting Rights Act of 1965. The law and the Court's interpretive decisions ended racially discriminatory voting restrictions in the United States.

The original U.S. Constitution tied the right of individuals to vote in federal elections to state election laws. A person who was eligible to vote in elections for the lower house of the state legislature was entitled to vote in federal elections. The result was that eligibility to vote was determined by state, not federal, law. If a national decision on voting rights was to be made, a constitutional amendment such as the

Twenty-Fourth, which ended poll taxes, was required.

In 1868, after the Northern victory in the Civil War, the Fourteenth Amendment established citizenship and civil rights for the newly freed slaves. On February 3, 1870, the Fifteenth Amendment was adopted to prevent state governments from denying freed slaves the right to vote. Its language however, is much broader, because it prohibits denial of the right to vote "on account of race, color, or previous condition of servitude." Section 2 of the amendment gives Congress the power to enforce its terms by remedial legislation.

DISCRIMINATORY LAWS

Immediately after the ratification of the amendment, Congress passed the Enforcement Act of 1870, which made it a crime for public officers and private persons to obstruct the right to vote. Enforcement of this law was spotty and ineffective, and most of its provisions were repealed in 1894. Meanwhile, beginning in 1890, most of the states of the former Confederacy passed laws that were specifically designed to keep African Americans from voting. Literacy tests were a major disqualifier because at that time more than two-thirds of adult African Americans were illiterate. At the same time, white illiterates were allowed to vote under grandfather clauses, property qualifications, and "good character" exceptions, from which African Americans were excluded. Racially discriminatory enforcement of voting qualifications became the principal means by which African Americans were barred from the polls.

TEXT OF THE FIFTEENTH AMENDMENT

Section 1. The right of citizens of the United States to vote shall not be denied or abridged by the United States or by any State on account of race, color, or previous condition of servitude.

Section 2. The Congress shall have power to enforce this article by appropriate legislation.

In the absence of a statute, the only remedy for these discriminatory practices was case-by-case litigation. The Supreme Court, in case after case, struck down the discriminatory state practices. Grandfather clauses were invalidated in *Guinn v. United States* (1915). The state-mandated all-white primary was outlawed in *Nixon v. Herndon* (1927); party-operated all-white primaries were forbidden by *Smith v. Allwright* (1944) and *Terry v. Adams* (1953). The Court held in *United States v. Thomas* (1959) that phony polling place challenges to African Americans seeking to vote—by the time the challenges had been resolved, the polls had closed—were improper under the Fifteenth Amendment. Racial gerrymandering was forbidden by *Gomillion v. Lightfoot* (1960). In that case, Alabama had redefined the shape of the city of Tuskegee so as to exclude all but four or five of its four hundred African American voters, thus denying this group the opportunity to influence city government. The Court also dealt with discriminatory administration of literacy tests in several cases, most important, *Schnell v. Davis* (1949), in which Justice William O. Douglas, writing for the Court, remarked that "the legislative setting and the great discretion it vested in the registrar made it clear that . . . the literacy requirement was merely a device to make racial discrimination easy."

VOTING RIGHTS ACT OF 1965

The mass disenfranchisement of African Americans could not be reached efficiently or fully by means of individually brought cases. Although some of the discriminatory state practices were halted, every voting registration decision could be made on the basis of race if voting registrars wished to do so. Against this background, Congress passed the Voting Rights Act of 1965. Section 2 of the Fifteenth Amendment provided constitutional authority for this law, which was aimed at "ridding the country of racial discrimination in voting," according to the statute's preamble. The law forbade a number of discriminatory practices. Literacy tests were "suspended" for five years in areas where voting discrimination had been most flagrant. To deal with voting discrimination through outright intimidation and violence, the law provided for federal voting registrars and protection by federal marshals.

The first important cases arising under this law came to the Court in 1966. In *South Carolina v. Katzenbach* (1966), the Court held unanimously that the most important provisions of the Voting Rights Act were constitutional. Chief Justice Earl Warren wrote that "the record here showed that in most of the States covered, various tests and devices have been instituted with the purpose of disenfranchising Negroes, have been framed in such a way as to facilitate this aim, and have been administered in a discriminatory fashion for many years. Under these circumstances, the 15th Amendment has clearly been violated." Because Congress's power under the amendment is remedial, this finding of fact was necessary to invoke federal power. The broad construction of Congress's power to deal with discrimination in voting in *South Carolina v. Katzenbach* established an important precedent to which the Court consistently adhered.

Congress renewed the Voting Rights Act in 1970 and extended the literacy test ban to the entire country. The extension reached New York State's English-language literacy test, which had the practical effect of disenfranchising many Puerto Rican voters. The English-language literacy test had been in place long before any substantial Puerto Rican migration to New York City had taken place. The extension was upheld by the Court in *Oregon v. Mitchell* (1970). Although the justices disagreed on some aspects of the new law, they were unanimous in upholding the constitutionality of the literacy test ban, even though there was no showing that New York had attempted to discriminate against Puerto Ricans. However, in *Rome v. United States* (1980), the Court became enmeshed in the question of the extent to which Congress may control state and local government under the Fifteenth Amendment. The question arose as to whether the remedial power reached only deliberate attempts by states and municipalities to deny Fifteenth Amendment voting rights or whether it was the effect of state practices on African American—and by extension, other minority group—voting that authorized federal action. The Court has not fully settled this extraordinarily complex constitutional question. Congress renewed and further extended the requirements of the Voting Rights Act again in 1982, this time for a period of twenty-five years.

The effect of the Court's Fifteenth Amendment decisions coupled with the broader provisions of the Voting Rights Act has been immense. In 1961 only 1.2 million African Americans were registered to

Commemorative print celebrating ratification of the Fifteenth Amendment. (Library of Congress)

vote in the South—one-quarter of voting-age blacks. By 1964 nearly 2 million were registered. In 1975 between 3.5 and 4 million blacks were registered to vote in the South. By the end of the century, although electoral turnout among African Americans and other persons of color in the United States was still lower than that of whites, the gap had nearly been closed. Today, formal legal discriminatory barriers to voting no longer exist.

Robert Jacobs

FURTHER READING

One possible starting point for further study is Robert E. DiClerico's *Voting in America: A Reference Handbook* (Santa Barbara, Calif.: ABC-Clio, 2004), a handy general reference work that covers the entire history of voting-rights issues in America. A study that focuses on the role of the Supreme Court in the extension and protection of voting rights is Charles L. Zelden's *Voting Rights on Trial: A Handbook with Cases, Laws, and Documents* (Santa Barbara, Calif.: ABC-Clio, 2002).

Jack Greenberg's *Race Relations and American Law* (New York: Columbia University Press, 1959) offers a good place to start for a comprehensive view of the constitutional rules before the passage of the Civil Rights Act of 1964 and the Voting Rights Act of 1965. John Braeman's *Before the Civil Rights Revolution: The Old Court and Individual Rights* (New York: Greenwood Press, 1988) discusses the developing jurisprudence of the Court in the area of civil rights.

For insight into the inner workings of the Warren Court, Bernard Schwartz's *Inside the Warren Court* (Garden City, N.Y.: Doubleday, 1983), with Stephen Lesher, is based not only on the documentation but also on personal acquaintance. *Compromised Compliance: Implementation of the 1965 Voting Rights Act* (Westport, Conn.: Greenwood Press, 1982) by Howard Ball, Dale Krane, and Thomas P. Lauth contains one of the first important discussions of the remedial versus effects morass in which the Court finds itself.

Using cases, Daniel Hays Lowenstein's *Election Law* (Durham, N.C.: Carolina Academic Press, 1995) analyzes how the Supreme Court has treated questions regarding electoral structures and processes. J. Morgan Kousser's *The Shaping of Southern Politics: Suffrage Restriction and the Establishment of the One-Party South, 1880-1910* (New Haven, Conn.: Yale University Press, 1974) and *Colorblind Injustice: Minority Voting Rights and the Undoing of the Second Reconstruction* (Chapel Hill: University of North Carolina Press, 1998) analyze the right to vote in the South, covering the Reconstruction era in the first volume and the post-World War II years in the second.

Michael Dawson's *Behind the Mule: Race and Class in American Politics* (Princeton, N.J.: Princeton University Press, 1994) examines voting rights in connection with race as does Abigail M. Thernstrom's *Whose Votes Count? Affirmative Action and Minority Voting Rights* (Cambridge, Mass.: Harvard University Press, 1987).

SEE ALSO *Cruikshank, United States v.*; Fourteenth Amendment; Grandfather clause; Hunt, Ward; Poll taxes; Race and discrimination; Reconstruction; Slavery; *Smith v. Allwright*; Thirteenth Amendment.

Fifth Amendment

DATE: 1791

DESCRIPTION: Amendment to the U.S. Constitution and part of the Bill of Rights that provides a right to avoid self-incrimination, a right to a grand jury indictment in capital or infamous crime cases, a right to be free from double jeopardy, and a right to just compensation for property taken by the government.

SIGNIFICANCE: The Supreme Court has used the Fifth Amendment to protect citizens against government coercion.

The Fifth Amendment includes more than just a right against self-incrimination, yet it is virtually synonymous with the right against self-incrimination. This right reflected the framers' judgment that in a society based on respect for the individual, the government shouldered the entire burden of proving guilt and the accused need make no unwilling contribution to his or her conviction.

The Fifth Amendment is restricted on its face to "criminal cases." However, the Supreme Court ruled that the Fifth Amendment applies to criminal and civil cases and extends to nonjudicial proceed-

---

TEXT OF THE FIFTH AMENDMENT

No person shall be held to answer for a capital, or otherwise infamous crime, unless on a presentment or indictment of a Grand Jury, except in cases arising in the land or naval forces, or in the Militia, when in actual service in time of War or public danger; nor shall any person be subject for the same offence to be twice put in jeopardy of life or limb, nor shall be compelled in any criminal case to be a witness against himself, nor be deprived of life, liberty, or property, without due process of law; nor shall private property be taken for public use without just compensation.

---

ings, such as legislative investigations and administrative hearings. The protection of the clause extends only to people, not organizations such as corporations or unions, and is applicable to witnesses as well as to the accused.

The self-incrimination clause is violated if evidence compelled by the government incriminates the person who provides it. Given these standards, self-incrimination violations occur most commonly during police interrogations and government hearings. Although the purpose of the clause is to eliminate the inherently coercive and inquisitional atmosphere of the interrogation room, a person may voluntarily answer any incriminating question or confess to any crime, subject to the requirements for waiver of constitutional rights, even if his or her statements are intended as exculpatory but lend themselves to prosecutorial use as incriminatory.

A DEFINITION

The Court first addressed the meaning of the self-incrimination clause in *Twining v. New Jersey* (1908). The question was whether the right against self-incrimination was "a fundamental principle of liberty and justice which inheres in the very idea of free government" and therefore should be included within the concept of due process of law safeguarded from state abridgment. The Court decided against the right. It reaffirmed this position in *Palko v. Connecticut* (1937), in which the Court held that the right against compulsory self-incrimination was not a fundamental right; it might be lost, and justice might still be done if the accused "were subject to a duty to respond to orderly inquiry."

The Court abandoned this position in its 1966 decision in *Miranda v. Arizona*, a tour de force on self-incrimination. The opinion announced a cluster of constitutional rights for defendants held in police custody and cut off from the outside world. The atmosphere and environment of incommunicado interrogation was held to be inherently intimidating and hostile to the privilege against self-incrimination. To prevent compulsion by law-enforcement officials, before interrogation, people in custody must be clearly informed that they have the right to remain silent and anything they say may be used in court against them and that they have the rights to consult an attorney, to have a lawyer present during interrogation, and to have a lawyer appointed if they are indigent.

When Chief Justice Warren E. Burger replaced Earl Warren in 1964 and Justice Harry A. Blackmun replaced Abe Fortas in 1970, they joined Byron R. White, John M. Harlan II, and Potter Stewart in support of a narrow application of *Miranda*. These five justices constituted the majority in *Harris v. New York* (1971), indicating the beginning of a contracting trend for *Miranda*. Chief Justice Burger held that the prosecution is not precluded from the use of statements that admittedly do not meet the *Miranda* test as an impeachment tool in attacking the credibility of an accused's trial testimony.

The erosion of *Miranda* continued in several rulings in the 1970's. In *Michigan v. Tucker* (1974), the Court held that failure to inform a suspect of his or her right to appointed counsel before interrogation was only a harmless error in the total circumstances of the case. Then one year later in *Oregon v. Haas* (1975), the Court reaffirmed *Harris* and allowed the use of a suspect's statements for impeachment purposes though they had been made before arrival of counsel that he had requested before making any statements. And the next year in *Michigan v. Mosley* (1976), the Court did not construe *Miranda* as invoking a "proscription of indefinite duration on any further questionings . . . on any subject." This ruling approved an interrogation process in which a suspect had initially used the shield of Miranda rights to remain silent but several hours later in a different room was administered the Miranda rights again and proceeded to respond to questions about a different crime.

By the mid-1980's it was clear that the Court under Chief Justice William H. Rehnquist would continue to construe *Miranda* very narrowly. In *New York v. Quarles* (1984), for example, the Court held that when a danger to public safety exists, police may ask questions to remove that danger before reading Miranda warnings. Answers given to the police may be used as evidence. In *Illinois v. Perkins* (1990), the Court ruled that Miranda warnings are not required when a suspect is unaware he or she is speaking to the police and gives a voluntary statement. The case concerned a jailed defendant who implicated himself in a murder when talking to an undercover agent placed in his cell. Justice Anthony M. Kennedy wrote in the opinion, "*Miranda* forbids coercion, not mere strategic deception." Finally, in *Arizona v. Fulminante* (1991), the Court admitted that the defendant's confession was coerced by the threat of physical attack. However, the Court held that if such testimony is erroneously admitted as evidence, a conviction need not be overturned if sufficient independent evidence supporting a guilty verdict is also introduced.

At the turn of the century, the Court's decision to maintain the precedent with continued narrow application of *Miranda* appeared well entrenched. The majority of the justices appeared to be comfortable with that approach, and changes appeared unlikely.

DOUBLE JEOPARDY CLAUSE

Also under the Fifth Amendment, a person shall not be subject "for the same offense to be twice put in jeopardy of life or limb." The underlying premise of the double jeopardy clause is to prohibit the government from making repeated attempts to convict an individual Acquittal acts as an absolute bar on a second trial. The meaning of acquittal, however, often divides the Court

The Court ruled that there is no double jeopardy in trying someone twice for the same offense if the jury is unable to reach a verdict—in *United States v. Ball* (1896), the jury is discharged—in *Logan v. United States* (1892), or an appeals court returns the case to the trial court because of defects in the original indictment—in *Thompson v. United States* (1894). The Court also unanimously ruled in three cases—*Jerome v. United States* (1943), *Herbert v. Louisiana* (1926), and *United States v. Lanza* (1922)—that a person may be prosecuted for the same act under federal law and state law. The theory is that the person is being prosecuted for two distinct offenses rather than the same offense.

The double jeopardy clause also prohibits prosecutors from trying defendants a second time for the express purpose of obtaining a more severe sentence. However, in 1969 the Court decided that there is no constitutional bar to imposing a more severe sentence on reconviction (after the first conviction is thrown out), provided the sentencing judge is not motivated by vindictiveness. In North Carolina v. Pearce; Chaffin v. Stynchcombe (1973), it ruled that the guarantee against double jeopardy requires that punishment already exacted must be fully credited to the new sentence.

The double jeopardy clause also bars multiple punishments for the same offense. In *United States v. Ursery* (1996) and *Kansas v. Hendricks* (1997), the Court narrowly construed this right. The latter case involved a challenge to a statute that permitted the state to keep certain sexual offenders in custody in a mental institution after they had served their full sentence. The Court ruled that the civil confinement was not a second criminal punishment but a separate civil procedure, thus not a violation of the double jeopardy clause.

RIGHT TO A GRAND JURY

The Fifth Amendment also provides that "no person shall be held for a capital, or otherwise infamous crime, unless on a presentment or indictment of a grand jury, except in cases arising in the land or naval forces, or in the militia, when in actual service in time of war or public danger." The grand jury procedure is one of the few provisions in the Bill of Rights that has not been incorporated into the due process clause of the Fourteenth Amendment and applied to the states. Instead the Court ruled that states may prosecute on a district attorney's "information," which consists of a prosecutor's accusation under oath in *Hurtado v. California* (1884) and *Lem Wood v. Oregon* (1913).

The Court held in *Costello v. United States* (1956) that, unlike in a regular trial, grand juries may decide that "hearsay" evidence is sufficient grounds to indict. In 1992 the Court issued an opinion in *United States v. Williams* (1992) indicating that an otherwise valid indictment may not be dismissed on the ground that the government failed to disclose to the grand jury "substantial exculpatory evidence" in its possession. In 1974 the Court decided in *United States v. Calandra* that witnesses before a grand jury may invoke the Fifth Amendment privilege against self-incrimination. This privilege is overridden if the government grants immunity to the witness. Witnesses who then refuse to answer questions may be jailed for contempt of court. Witnesses may not refuse to answer because questions are based on illegally obtained evidence.

THE TAKINGS CLAUSE

Finally, the Fifth Amendment provides that private property shall not "be taken for public use, without just compensation." This is referred to as the takings clause, or the just compensation clause. The Court incorporated the takings clause under the due process clause of the Fourteenth Amendment in *Chicago, Burlington, and Quincy Railroad Co. v. Chicago* (1897); therefore, states are also forbidden from taking private property for public use without just compensation. Not every deprivation of property requires compensation, however. For example, the Court held in *United States v. Caltex* (1952) that under conditions of war, private property may be demolished to prevent use by the enemy without compensation to the owner. When compensation is to be paid, a plethora of 5-4 decisions by the Court—including *United States v. Fuller* (1973) and *Almota Farmers Elevator and Wholesale Co. v. United States* (1973)—demonstrate fundamental disagreements among the justices about the proper method of calculating what is "just."

Court decisions in the early and mid-1990's underscore the complexity and reach of the takings clause. Several cases broadened the powers of the states, and others expanded property rights. In *Yee v. Escondido* (1992), a unanimous Court held that a rent-control ordinance did not amount to a physical taking of the property of owners of a mobile home park. A more significant ruling, *Lucas v. South Carolina Coastal Council* (1992), narrowed the rights of states to rely on regulatory takings that completely deprive individuals of the economic use of their property. To be exempt from compensating a property owner, a state must claim more than a general public interest or an interest in preventing serious public harm.

The Court broadened property rights by holding that land-use requirements may be "takings." The decision in *Dolan v. City of Tigard* (1994) dealt with the practice of local governments giving property owners a permit for building a development only on the condition that they donate parts of their land for parks, bike paths, and other public purposes. These conditions are valid only if the local government makes "some sort of individualized determination that the required dedication is related both in nature and extent to the impact of the proposed development." This 5-4 decision underscores the Court's inability to reach agreement on constitutional principles under the Fifth Amendment.

Susan L. Thomas

449

FURTHER READING

General works on the Fifth Amendment include Alfredo Garcia's *The Fifth Amendment: A Comprehensive Approach* (Westport, Conn.: Greenwood Press, 2002), Harvey Fireside's *The Fifth Amendment: The Right to Remain Silent* (Springfield, N.J.: Enslow, 1998), and Burnham Holmes's *The Fifth Amendment* (Englewood Cliffs, N. J.: Silver Burdett Press, 1991). David Bodenhamer's *Fair Trial: Rights of the Accused in American History* (New York: Oxford University Press, 1992) presents a useful account of double jeopardy and self-incrimination rights.

Also recommended is Anthony Lewis's *Gideon's Trumpet* (New York: Vintage, 1989). A well-written and thorough account of the takings clause is found in Richard Epstein's *Takings: Private Property and the Power of Eminent Domain* (Cambridge, Mass.: Harvard University Press, 1985). A more scholarly account is James Ely's *The Guardian of Every Other Right: A Constitutional History of Property Rights* (New York: Oxford University Press, 1992).

SEE ALSO *Adamson v. California*; *Barron v. Baltimore*; *Bolling v. Sharpe*; *Chicago, Burlington, and Quincy Railroad Co. v. Chicago*; Double jeopardy; *Gideon v. Wainwright*; *Griswold v. Connecticut*; Incorporation doctrine; *Kelo v. City of New London*; *Palko v. Connecticut*; Self-incrimination, immunity against; Takings clause.

First Amendment

DATE: 1791

DESCRIPTION: Amendment to the U.S. Constitution and part of the Bill of Rights that guarantees freedom of speech, freedom of the press, religious liberty, separation of church and state, and the rights to peaceably assemble and to petition the government for redress of grievances.

SIGNIFICANCE: The wellspring of individual rights protected by the U.S. Constitution, the First Amendment presented the Supreme Court with endless challenges to decide the limits of governmental power and the scope of personal liberties.

TEXT OF THE FIRST AMENDMENT

Congress shall make no law respecting an establishment of religion, or prohibiting the free exercise thereof; or abridging the freedom of speech, or of the press, or the right of the people peaceably to assemble, and to petition the Government for a redress of grievances.

Although the First Amendment, together with the other nine amendments known as the Bill of Rights, became part of the U.S. Constitution on December 15, 1791, the Supreme Court took little note of it until the beginning of the twentieth century. This was not for lack of federal laws impinging on free speech, from the Sedition Act of 1798 and the Comstock Act of 1873 to the Alien Immigration Act of 1930 and a wide variety of postal regulations. However, the Court never found that any of these laws violated the First Amendment. Indeed, in 1907 the Court upheld the conviction of an editor for contempt, rejecting a defense based on the First Amendment on the grounds that it only prohibited prior restraint.

It was almost inevitable that the Court and the First Amendment would travel together through U.S. constitutional law, frequently crossing paths, sometimes diverging, often forced by circumstances to retrace the same ground. Each clause of the First Amendment invites, indeed demands, judicial interpretation.

FREEDOM OF SPEECH

Beginning at the end of World War I, the Court tackled the task of devising a series of tests to determine whether particular speech was constitutionally protected. The Court could not merely cite the general language of the First Amendment; it had to apply those opaque terms to the real world of real cases.

The first test was articulated by Justice Oliver Wendell Holmes in 1919 in a series of cases challenging the convictions of antiwar activists under the Espionage Act of 1917. The clear and present danger

451

test looked at whether the speech posed a real and immediate risk of a substantive evil that Congress had a right to prevent. Holmes captured the test in a powerful, albeit often misquoted, metaphor that persists to this day: "The most stringent protection of free speech would not protect a man in falsely shouting fire in a theatre and causing a panic."

Later in 1919, Holmes and his ally, Justice Louis D. Brandeis, dissented in *Abrams v. United States,* arguing for greater constitutional protection for controversial or even subversive speech. The majority of the Court continued to use the clear and present danger test to uphold the punishment of such speech.

Six years later, the majority of the Court tightened the noose on free speech by focusing on whether the expression had a bad tendency. Over bitter dissent from Holmes and Brandeis, the Court upheld a conviction under the New York State Criminal Anarchy Act, stating that a "single revolutionary spark may kindle a fire," and therefore the state may "suppress the threatened danger in its incipiency."

In 1951 the Court used a slightly reformulated test to uphold the convictions of eleven members of the Communist Party under the Smith Act (1940). Chief Justice Fred M. Vinson, writing for the Court, asked "whether the gravity of the 'evil' discounted by its improbability" would justify government limits on speech.

In 1964 Justice William J. Brennan, Jr., introduced a test that was far more protective of free speech. In the landmark case of *New York Times Co. v. Sullivan,* the Court held that false criticism of public officials was constitutionally protected unless it was made with knowledge that it was false or in reckless disregard of the truth. Instead of tilting the constitutional balance in favor of the government, the *Sullivan* test gave the advantage to the speaker.

The Holmes-Brandeis view in favor of more robust protection for free speech was finally vindicated in 1967 in *Brandenburg v. Ohio,* in which the Court declared that mere advocacy of the use of force or violation of the law could no longer be punished unless "such advocacy is directed to inciting or producing imminent lawless action and is likely to produce such action."

THE RELIGION CLAUSES

As in the field of free speech, the perplexing issues surrounding freedom of religion have required the Court to fashion several constitutional tests to ensure the free exercise of religion, without establishing a state-sponsored religion. As the twentieth century ushered in an era of secularization, the dominance of religion in public life began to be seen as inconsistent with the First Amendment's promise of neutrality when it came to religious faith. Religion was seen as a part of the private sphere of life, leaving the public sphere, including most visibly public schools, free of religious symbols, let alone indoctrination.

In several decisions spanning more than twenty years, from *Everson v. Board of Education of Ewing Township* in 1947 to *Lemon v. Kurtzman* in 1971, the Court developed the test that any governmental action touching on religion would survive invalidation under the establishment clause only if it had a secular purpose that neither endorsed nor disapproved of religion, had an effect that neither advanced nor inhibited religion, and avoided creating a relationship between religion and government that entangled either in the internal affairs of the other. The *Lemon* test has been criticized across the political and constitutional spectrum, but it has provided lower courts and legislators with some level of guidance in dealing with such issues as prayer in schools and financial aid to religious institutions.

Meanwhile, the Court had to interpret the free exercise clause of the First Amendment in numerous cases in which believers claimed a right to ignore laws that required them to perform an act that violated their religious beliefs or that prohibited them from performing an act that was required by their religious beliefs.

Beginning in 1879 in *Reynolds v. United States* and for almost a hundred years, the Court dealt with most free exercise cases by upholding laws that punished *actions* but struck down laws that punished *beliefs*. However, the easy dichotomy began to break down when, in *Sherbert v. Verner* (1963), the Court ordered a state to pay unemployment benefits to a Seventh-day Adventist even though she would not make herself available for work on Saturday (her Sabbath). In 1972, in *Wisconsin v. Yoder*, the Court held that the Amish were not required to send their children to public school past the eighth grade in violation of their religious beliefs.

By the 1980's, the pendulum had begun to swing against religious liberty as the Court issued a succession of decisions ruling against a Native American who sought to prevent the government from assigning his daughter a social security number, an Orthodox Jew who sought to wear a yarmulke in violation of Air Force uniform regulations, a Native American tribe that sought to prevent construction of a federal highway that would interfere with their worshiping, and two Native Americans who sought unemployment compensation after they were fired from their jobs for smoking peyote as part of tribal religious rituals.

The Court has found the religion clauses of the First Amendment fraught with interpretative dangers. The Court is frequently criticized either for going too far in promoting religion or for exhibiting hostility toward religion. That alone may be evidence that the Court is doing its job as conceived by the Founders.

THE RIGHT TO PEACEABLY ASSEMBLE

Although freedom of speech and freedom to worship protect highly personal rights, the First Amendment's guarantee of the right "of the people peaceably to assemble," protects the right of association. These are the rights of the people as a community to join together to achieve certain political, social, economic, artistic, educational, or other goals.

For the Court, interpreting the right to assemble has been even more difficult than construing other aspects of the First Amendment, because by its very nature, assembly involves both speech *and* conduct. At first blush, the First Amendment has nothing to do with conduct. However, when the Court is confronted with cases involving public demonstrations, protests, parades, and picketing, it is apparent that these activities are intended to send a message—and communicating messages is clearly protected by the First Amendment.

However, blocking traffic, littering the streets, or physically obstructing others from going about their business is not protected by the First Amendment. Consequently, when it comes to freedom of assembly, the Court has used a balancing test, seeking first to determine whether the law regulating assembly is in fact a ruse to suppress a particular viewpoint, and if not, whether the law serves a compelling state interest unrelated to the suppression of free speech.

For example, in 1940 in *Thornhill v. Alabama*, the Court struck down a state law that prohibited all picketing. Although the First Amendment does not afford an absolute right to picket, the Court overturned the statute because instead of regulating specific aspects of labor demonstrations, it prohibited "every practicable method whereby the facts of a labor dispute may be publicized."

Closely aligned with freedom of assembly is freedom of association or the right of the people to form and join organizations in order to educate themselves and influence public policy on important issues of the day. Even during the hysteria of the Cold War in the 1950's, the Court held in *Yates v. United States* (1957) that when membership in the Communist Party involved nothing more than the advocacy or teaching of the abstract doctrine of the forcible overthrow of the government (as contrasted with the advocacy or teaching of direct action to achieve that end), convictions under the Smith Act were unconstitutional.

In 1958, in *National Association for the Advancement of Colored People v. Alabama*, the Court found that the forced disclosure of an organization's membership list violated the members' rights to pursue their lawful interests and to freely associate with like-minded persons. Although freedom of association is not expressly set forth anywhere in the Constitution, the Court nevertheless found freedom of association to be an integral part of the First Amendment.

THE RIGHT TO PETITION THE GOVERNMENT

The least controversial (and least litigated) right in the First Amendment is the right "to petition the government for redress of grievances." Aside from a doomed attempt in 1836 by the House of Representatives to impose a gag rule against the receipt of petitions from abolitionists who opposed slavery, Congress has not had the temerity to even attempt to restrict this quintessential right to write to your Congressperson, thereby sparing the Court the task of striking down such legislation.

Stephen F. Rohde

FURTHER READING

Steven H. Shiffrin and Jesse H. Choper's *The First Amendment: Cases, Comments, Questions* (St. Paul, Minn.: West Publishing, 1996) provides a basic introduction to the First Amendment. Henry Julian Abraham and Barbara A. Perry's *Freedom and the Court: Civil Rights and Liberties in the United States* (8th ed. Lawrence: University Press of Kansas, 2003) is a comprehensive overview of the Supreme Court's approach to civil rights and liberties that includes an excellent chapter on the Court's First Amendment jurisprudence.

The First Amendment: The Legacy of George Mason (London: Associated University Presses, 1985), edited by T. Daniel Shumate, focuses on the origin and meaning of the amendment. Louis E. Ingelhart's *Press and Speech Freedoms in the World, from Antiquity Until 1998: A Chronology* (Westport, Conn.: Greenwood Press, 1998) covers the concept of freedom of speech and press from ancient times until the modern period, and Margaret A. Blanchard's *Revolutionary Sparks: Freedom of Expression in Modern America* (New York: Oxford University Press, 1992) covers the concept from the beginning to the end of the twentieth century.

The First Amendment and the freedoms of association and assembly are examined in *Freedom of Association* (Princeton, N.J.: Princeton University Press, 1998), edited by Amy Gutmann, and Paul L. Murphy's *Rights of Assembly, Petition, Arms, and Just Compensation* (New York: Garland, 1990). The First Amendment and religion are examined in *Toward Benevolent Neutrality: Church, State, and the Supreme Court*, edited by Ronald B. Flowers and Robert T. Miller (Waco, Tex.: Baylor University Press, 1998), *The Believer and the Powers That Are: Cases, History, and Other Data Bearing on the Relation of Religion and Government*, by John Thomas Noonan, Jr. (New York: Macmillan, 1987), and *Religious Liberty in the Supreme Court: The Cases That Define the Debate over Church and State*, edited by Terry Eastland (Grand Rapids, Mich.: Wm. B. Eerdmans, 1995).

The Bill of Rights, edited by Thomas Tandy Lewis (2 vols. Pasadena, Calif.: Salem Press, 2002), is a compact reference work on the Bill of Rights that devotes nearly half its space to the First Amendment.

SEE ALSO Assembly and association, freedom of; Bad tendency test; Brandeis, Louis D.; *Brandenburg v. Ohio*; Brennan, William J., Jr.; Censorship; Dissents; *Everson v. Board of Education of Ewing Township*; Fourteenth Amendment; Holmes, Oliver Wendell; Incorporation doctrine; *Lemon v. Kurtzman*; *National Association for the Advancement of Colored People v. Alabama*; *New York Times Co. v. Sullivan*; Religion, establishment of; Religion, freedom of; *Reynolds v. United States*; *Wisconsin v. Yoder*.

Flag desecration

DESCRIPTION: Act of physically "harming" the U.S. flag, usually through such means as burning or tearing; at times the term was also applied to verbal criticism of the flag or what it represents.

SIGNIFICANCE: The Supreme Court upheld the right, under the First Amendment, of people to both verbally and physically assault the flag and, in so doing, helped define and extend the meaning of constitutionally protected symbolic speech.

The U.S. flag, a symbol of the nation, is displayed widely in front of government buildings, private homes, and commercial enterprises and used extensively as a design springboard for clothing, advertising, and a wide variety of other products. However, it attracted little interest and received little public display for more than eighty years after its original adoption as a symbol of the nation by the Continental Congress on June 14, 1777. Only the outbreak of the Civil War (1861-1865) transformed the flag into an object of public adoration—although only, of course, in the North.

The newly found Northern love for the flag continued after the Civil War, but the flag's growing popularity was not accompanied by any sense that it should be regarded as a sacred object or relic. During the nation's rapid postwar industrialization, as the modern advertising industry developed, the flag became increasingly popular as a decorative accompaniment in the commercialization of a wide range of products. Gradually, after 1890, Union veterans and members of patriotic hereditary groups such as the Sons of the American Revolution began to protest alleged commercial debasement of the flag, which they declared would ultimately cause the significance of both the flag and patriotism to degrade among the general public. After about 1900 the supposed threat to the flag shifted from commercialization to that allegedly posed by its use as a means of expressing political protest by political radicals, trade union members, and immigrants (who were often indiscriminately lumped together).

Between 1897 and 1932 veterans and hereditary-patriotic groups lobbied for stringent laws to "protect" the flag from all forms of alleged "desecration" (the harming of sacred religious objects) and succeeded in obtaining passage of flag desecration laws in all forty-eight states, with thirty-one states acting between 1897 and 1905 alone. The laws generally outlawed attaching anything to or placing any marks on the flag, using the flag in any manner for advertising purposes, and physically or verbally "harming" flags in any way, including, typically, publicly mutilating, trampling, defacing, defiling, defying, or casting contempt on the flag. The term "flag" was generally defined to mean any object of any form, size, or material that resembled the U.S. flag.

EARLY COURT RULINGS

The earliest state flag desecration laws were quickly and, at first, successfully challenged in local and state courts as illegally restricting property rights by adversely affecting commercial interests. However, in *Halter v. Nebraska* (1907), the Supreme Court upheld Nebraska's law in sweeping terms that made clear the futility of any further legal challenges for the foreseeable future. In a case involving sales of Stars and Stripes beer, which had pictures of flags on the bottle labels, the Court declared that the state was entitled to restrict property rights for the valid and worthy purpose of fostering nationalism. In a ruling that did not address free speech rights, the Court declared that "love both of the common country and of the State will diminish in proportion as respect for the flag is weakened," that advertising usage of the flag tended to "degrade and cheapen it in the estimation of the people," and that the state was entitled to "exert its power to strengthen the bonds of the Union and therefore, to that end, may encourage patriotism and love of country among its people."

The Court did not consider another flag desecration case until 1969, and during the interim period, the constitutionality of flag desecration laws was essentially considered beyond review by the lower courts. The Court revisited the issue during the Vietnam War, when flags were widely burned or used in other unorthodox ways to express political dissent (resulting in hundreds of flag desecration prosecutions).

In *Street v. New York* (1969), the Court relied heavily on its rulings in *Stromberg v. California* (1931) and *West Virginia State Board of Education v. Barnette* (1943) to strike down flag desecration provisions that outlawed *verbal* disrespect for the flag as violating the First Amendment. The Court, by a 5-4 vote, overturned Street's flag desecration conviction on the grounds that because he had been charged under a provision of New York's law outlawing casting contempt on the flag by words or acts and evidence concerning his statements had been introduced at trial, he might have been convicted for his words alone. Any such conviction, in the absence of any evident threat to the peace or incitement to violence, was held to violate the First Amendment because "it is firmly settled that under our Constitution [1789] the public expression of ideas may not be prohibited merely because the ideas are themselves offensive to some of their hearers," even opinions about the flag "which are defiant or contemptuous." The Court completely avoided addressing the constitutionality of laws that banned *physical* flag desecration on the grounds that there was no need to decide the case "on a broader basis than the record before us imperatively requires." Aside from *Street*, the Court in 1974 overturned convictions in two other Vietnam-era flag desecration cases, *Goguen v. Smith* and *Spence v. Washington*, which were both decided on narrow grounds that again avoided directly addressing the validity of state interests in protecting the physical integrity of the flag in light of First Amendment questions.

A TEXAS FLAG BURNING

In *Texas v. Johnson* (1989), which arose from a 1984 Dallas flag-burning incident, the Court directly faced the question of physical desecration of the flag, ruling by a 5-4 vote that Texas's venerated objects law had been unconstitutionally applied to Johnson. Texas advanced two interests as overriding Johnson's First Amendment rights, but the Court dismissed them. First, it found that the state's interest in maintaining order was not implicated because no disturbance of the peace occurred or threatened to occur because of Johnson's act. Second, regarding a need to preserve the flag as a national symbol, the Court held that because Johnson's guilt depended on the communicative nature of his conduct, the Texas statute violated the main principle behind the First Amendment, that the government cannot ban the expression of an idea because society finds that idea offensive or disagreeable. Citing its holding in *Street* that a state cannot criminally punish a person for speech critical of the flag, the Court declared flatly that Texas's attempt to distinguish between written or spoken words and nonverbal conduct "is of no moment where the nonverbal conduct is expressive, as is here, and where the regulation of that conduct is related to expression, as it is here."

Furthermore, the Court declared that the government cannot ban expression of ideas that it does not like because the expression takes a particular form; therefore, the state cannot criminally punish a person for burning a flag in political protest on the grounds that other means of expressing the same idea were available. The Court concluded that the principles of freedom reflected in the flag would be reaffirmed by its decision: "We do not consecrate the flag by punishing its desecration, for in doing so we dilute the freedom that this cherished emblem represents."

Johnson touched off an intense and massive uproar across the United States. Virtually every member of Congress endorsed resolutions condemning the ruling. To circumvent the ruling, most Democrats maintained that an ordinary law would suffice, but President George H. W. Bush and most Republicans maintained that a constitutional amendment would be required. The Democratic congressional leadership noted that *Johnson* struck down a Texas statute that forbade flag desecration likely to cause "serious offense" to observers, rather than, as the Court noted at one point, "protecting the physical integrity of the flag in all circumstances" and argued that the court might uphold such a "content neutral" law.

THE 1989 FLAG PROTECTION ACT

Whether due to a perceived cooling of public sentiment, to increasing signs of growing opposition to a constitutional amendment, or to increased acceptance of the argument that trying a statute first was preferable to a constitutional change, by October, 1989, the drive for a constitutional amendment, seemingly unstoppable in late June after President Bush endorsed it, was sputtering. On October 19, the constitutional amendment failed to reach the two-thirds majority it required in the Senate. However, both houses of Congress passed the proposed statutory alternative, the Flag Protection Act of 1989.

The Flag Protection Act provided penalties of up to one year in jail and a one thousand dollar fine for anyone who "knowingly mutilates, physically defiles, burns, maintains on the floor or ground, or tramples upon any flag of the United States" with "flag" defined as "any flag of the United States, or any part thereof, made of any substance, of any size, in a form that is commonly displayed." Although the stated purpose of the act was to end flag burnings, its immediate impact was to spur perhaps the largest single wave of such incidents in U.S. history, as flags were burned in about a dozen cities shortly after the law took effect in late October.

Acting under an extraordinary expedited review procedure mandated by the act, the Court struck down the Flag Protection Act by a 5-4 vote in *United States v. Eichman* on June 11, 1990. The *Eichman* ruling essentially underlined *Johnson*, finding that the government's interest in protecting the flag's position as a symbol of the United States and certain ideals did not justify the infringement on First Amendment rights. Although conceding that the new law, unlike the Texas statute in *Johnson*, did not explicitly place content-based limits on the scope of prohibited conduct, the Court held that the Flag Protection Act still suffered from the same fundamental flaw as the Texas law, namely that it could not be justified without reference to the content of the regulated speech. The Court added, "Punishing desecration of the flag dilutes the very freedom that makes this emblem so revered, and worthy of revering."

The *Eichman* decision sparked an immediate renewal of calls by President Bush and others for a constitutional amendment. However, the proposed amendment was defeated in both houses of Congress in 1990. After Republicans gained control of both houses of Congress in 1994, the amendment was passed by the required two-thirds majority in the House in 1995, 1997, and 1999. However, in the Senate, it failed to gain a two-thirds vote (by three votes) in 1995 and was not taken up during the 105th Congress (1997-1998).

Robert Justin Goldstein

FURTHER READING

Curtis, Michael, ed. *The Flag Burning Cases.* Vol. 2 in *The Constitution and the Flag.* New York: Garland, 1993.

Goldstein, Robert Justin. *Burning the Flag: The Great 1989-1990 American Flag Desecration Controversy.* Kent, Ohio: Kent State University Press, 1996.

_____, ed. *Desecrating the American Flag: Key Documents of the Controversy from the Civil War to 1995.* Syracuse, N.Y.: Syracuse University Press, 1996.

_____. *Flag Burning and Free Speech: The Case of "Texas v. Johnson."* Lawrence: University Press of Kansas, 2000.

_____. *Saving "Old Glory": The History of the American Flag Desecration Controversy.* Boulder, Colo.: Westview Press, 1995.

Miller, J. Anthony. *"Texas v. Johnson": The Flag Burning Case.* Springfield, N.J.: Enslow, 1997.

Welch, Michael. *Flag Burning: Moral Panic and the Criminalization of Protest.* New York: Aldine de Gruyter, 2000.

SEE ALSO National security; Speech and press, freedom of; Symbolic speech; *Texas v. Johnson; Virginia v. Black.*

Florida v. Bostick

CITATION: 501 U.S. 429
DATE: June 18, 1991
ISSUE: Search and seizure
SIGNIFICANCE: The Supreme Court held that the Fourth Amendment allows the controversial police practice of randomly approaching individuals in public places and asking them for permission to search their belongings, as long as the request is not coercive in nature.

It is an elementary principle of law that persons may waive their constitutional rights. In *Schneckloth v. Bustamonte* (1973), the Court held that, when a suspect is not in custody, the evidence obtained in a consensual search may be used in a criminal trial even when the suspect did not know that he could refuse to agree to the search. Encouraged by this ruling, some police officers routinely boarded buses or trains and asked individual passengers for permission to search their luggage. Using this technique, two officers found cocaine in a bag belonging to Terrance Bostick. The police claimed that they advised Bostick of his right to refuse the search, but he denied that he gave his permission. After the trial court denied Bostick's motion to suppress the evidence, the Florida supreme court held that Bostick had been unconstitutionally seized because a "reasonable person" would not have felt free to leave the bus to avoid police questioning.

By a 6-3 vote, the Supreme Court reversed the judgment. Justice Sandra Day O'Connor's majority opinion quoted earlier decisions holding that the police did not need reasonable suspicion in order to ask questions of a person in a public place and that such questioning did not constitute a seizure. Because there were many circumstances preventing Bostick from leaving the bus, O'Connor concluded that the legal issue was not whether a reasonable person would have felt free to leave but rather whether a reasonable person would have felt free to refuse to submit to the search. The "reasonable person test," moreover, presupposes "an innocent person." Thus, the Court remanded the case to the state courts for a reexamination of "all the circumstances" of the search in order to decide whether Bostick had given his consent voluntarily.

Expanding upon *Bostick* in *Ohio v. Robinette* (1996), the Court ruled that the police are not required to inform motorists who are stopped for other reasons that they are "free to go" before their consent will be recognized as voluntary.

Thomas Tandy Lewis

SEE ALSO Automobile searches; Fourth Amendment; O'Connor, Sandra Day; Search warrant requirement; *Terry v. Ohio*.

Abe Fortas

IDENTIFICATION: Associate justice (October 4, 1965-May 14, 1969)
NOMINATED BY: Lyndon B. Johnson
BORN: June 19, 1910, Memphis, Tennessee
DIED: April 5, 1982, Washington, D.C.
SIGNIFICANCE: Associate justice and nominee for chief justice who re-
    signed from the Supreme Court in disgrace.

A gifted student, Abe Fortas received a scholarship to study at Yale
Law School. After graduating in 1933, Fortas taught at Yale and
worked for various New Deal government agencies. He worked full-
time for the U.S. government from 1941 to 1946, when he went into
private practice. Fortas earned recognition as a brilliant legal mind
and as an advocate of liberal causes. He successfully argued the case
of *Gideon v. Wainwright* (1963) before the Supreme Court, guaranteeing the indigent a right to counsel in state criminal cases.

Fortas was a close friend of Lyndon B. Johnson, and when Johnson
became president in 1963, he relied heavily on Fortas for counsel.

Abe Fortas.
(Library of Congress)

Johnson wanted Fortas to serve on the Supreme Court, both as an advocate for his Great Society programs and as a source of information concerning the attitudes and opinions that prevailed among the justices. Fortas also had the support of Justice William O. Douglas, whom he had known since his days as a Yale law student. In order to create a vacancy on the Court, Johnson offered Justice Arthur J. Goldberg the United Nations ambassadorship. Goldberg accepted and Johnson nominated Fortas. During his confirmation hearings, Fortas downplayed his close relationship with the president, and he received little opposition from the Senate, which quickly confirmed his nomination.

As an associate justice, Fortas served as an advocate for liberal issues. He provided the fifth and crucial vote in the ruling in the 1966 case of *Miranda v. Arizona*, which required that suspects be informed of their constitutional rights when arrested. Fortas wrote the majority opinion in the 1967 case *In re Gault*, which concerned the rights of juveniles accused of a crime. In his opinion, Fortas argued that accused juveniles possessed most of the rights of adults. He also wrote the majority opinion in the 1969 case *Tinker v. Des Moines Independent Community School District*, in which wearing an armband as a sign of protest was protected as a First Amendment right.

THE NOMINATION

During his years on the Court, Fortas remained in close contact with President Johnson, offering him advice on both foreign policy and domestic issues. In 1968 when Chief Justice Earl Warren resigned, Johnson sought to provide a defense against possible future conservative attacks on his liberal programs by nominating Fortas for the vacant position. In order to gain support for the Fortas nomination from southerners who were less than enthusiastic at the notion of a liberal Jewish chief justice, Johnson planned to nominate Texas judge William H. Thornberry to take Fortas's position as associate justice.

The Fortas nomination proved to be a disaster for the Democratic Party. Because Johnson was a lame duck, Republicans had everything to gain by slowing the nomination process in the hope that a Republican would be elected to the White House in the upcoming election. Southerners were not mollified by the Thornberry nomination, and several southern senators voiced their antagonism toward Fortas. Senate hearings revealed the depth of opposition to the nomination. Senators expressed their concern that Fortas's close relationship with the president had constituted a violation of the separation of powers. In addition, Fortas was criticized for his liberal positions.

The September, 1968, revelation that Fortas had received $15,000 from wealthy private individuals for teaching a seminar at American University made little difference, as opposition to Fortas had become so intense that he had no chance of being confirmed. Although the Senate Judiciary Committee approved his nomination, Senate Republicans began a filibuster. Fortas asked Johnson to withdraw his nomination, and Johnson complied with his request on October 1.

Fortas's trials were not yet over. On May 5, 1969, *Life* magazine reported that while serving as associate justice, Fortas had accepted $20,000 from the Wolfson Family Foundation for assisting with foundation efforts. Fortas had returned the money after Louis Wolfson was indicted on stock fraud charges. Nonetheless, Fortas's relationship with Wolfson showed a lack of judgment and pointed to possible ethical violations. Fortas quickly issued an unconvincing statement regarding his dealings with Wolfson. He did not reveal that he and Wolfson had originally signed a contract ensuring him $20,000 a year for life, and $20,000 a year to his wife should she survive him.

Fortas's enemies, including members of President Richard M. Nixon's administration who hoped to create a vacancy on the Court, went into action. Members of Congress began discussing impeachment. Fortas struggled to retain his position on the Court; however, his fate was sealed when the Justice Department learned of the lifetime contract with Wolfson. On May 14, 1969, Fortas resigned. He continued to practice law after his resignation. In 1982, the final year of his life, he argued a case before the Court.

Although widely recognized as an outstanding lawyer, Fortas showed considerable lack of judgment during his tenure on the Court. His relationship with Johnson went beyond offering advice—at times Fortas shared confidential information regarding the operations of the Court. Always concerned with money, he engaged in financial dealings that raised doubts about his ability to serve as an impartial jurist.

Thomas Clarkin

FURTHER READING

Bader, William H., and Roy M. Mersky, eds. *The First One Hundred Eight Justices.* Buffalo, N.Y.: William S. Hein, 2004.

Kalman, Laura. *Abe Fortas: A Biography.* New Haven, Conn.: Yale University Press, 1990.

Murphy, Bruce Allen. *Fortas: The Rise and Ruin of a Supreme Court Justice.* New York: William Morrow, 1988.

Shogan, Robert. *A Question of Judgment: The Fortas Case and the Struggle for the Supreme Court.* Indianapolis, Ind.: Bobbs-Merrill, 1972.

Urofsky, Melvin I. *The Warren Court: Justices, Rulings, and Legacy.* Santa Barbara, Calif.: ABC-Clio, 2001.

SEE ALSO *Epperson v. Arkansas; Gideon v. Wainwright;* Goldberg, Arthur J.; Nominations to the Court; *Tinker v. Des Moines Independent Community School District.*

Fourteenth Amendment

DATE: 1868

DESCRIPTION: Amendment to the U.S. Constitution that provides legal protections for individuals against actions by state governments.

SIGNIFICANCE: The Supreme Court has used the due process and equal protection clauses of this amendment to expand both the number and breadth of rights protecting individuals. More than any other amendment, the Fourteenth has provided the basis for the range of rights that Americans have come to take for granted in the twenty-first century.

The Fourteenth Amendment was ratified after the Civil War (1861-1865) to provide protection for individuals, particularly African Americans newly freed from slavery, against actions taken by state governments. Before ratification of the amendment, the rights provisions within the Constitution were aimed at preventing the federal government from violating individuals' legal protections. There were serious concerns that the former Confederate states might undertake actions that would threaten the liberty of individuals, especially African Americans, who resided within those states.

The amendment guarantees three primary rights: due process of law, equal protection of the law, and privileges or immunities of citizens. Section 5 of the amendment also grants Congress the power to enact legislation to enforce the rights specified in the amendment. Because the words describing Fourteenth Amendment rights are so vague, the Supreme Court has had to use its interpretive powers to give meaning to the rights contained within it.

The Court's first major interpretation of the Fourteenth Amendment was in the *Slaughterhouse Cases* (1873), in which butchers in New Orleans complained that they had been denied due process, equal protection, and privileges or immunities of citizenship when the state of Louisiana gave one company an exclusive monopoly to slaughter livestock. The Court found that there was no Fourteenth Amendment violation. The justices declared that the equal protection clause was intended to protect newly freed African Americans, not occupational groups such as butchers. They said that the due process clause did not apply and that the privileges or immunities clause was similarly inapplicable. Although the Court's initial interpretation of the Fourteenth Amendment did not identify any specific protections provided for citizens, subsequent cases began to identify how the Fourteenth Amendment protected rights.

Due Process Clause

During the twentieth century, the Supreme Court began to use the Fourteenth Amendment's due process clause as the mechanism for applying the protections of the Bill of Rights against the states. Through a process that scholars call "incorporation," the Court gradually decided that many provisions of the Bill of Rights, which protect individuals against actions by the federal government, should be incorporated in the due process clause in order to provide protection for individuals against actions by state and local governments. Some justices argued that the Court should declare that all rights from the Bill of Rights are contained in the Fourteenth Amendment due process clause. However, most justices preferred to examine each right individually to determine whether that particular right should be applied to state governments.

Beginning with the Court's decision in *Gitlow v. New York* (1925), which determined that the First Amendment's protection for freedom of speech applied to the states through the Fourteenth Amendment's due process clause, the justices examined specific rights from the Bill of Rights in a series of cases extending through the 1960's. By the time the Court declared in *Duncan v. Louisiana* (1968) that the Sixth Amendment's right to trial by jury was incorporated into the due process clause, the Court had applied nearly the entire Bill of Rights to the states through the incorporation process. Along the way, the Court incorporated the Fifth Amendment privilege against self-incrimination, the Sixth Amendment right to counsel, the Eighth Amendment prohibition on cruel and unusual punishments, and other important rights. Only a few rights remained unincorporated and still applicable against the federal government only. These rights include the Second Amendment right to bear arms, the Fifth Amendment right to a grand jury, and the Seventh Amendment right to a jury in civil cases. In effect, the Fourteenth Amendment's due process clause served as the vehicle for expanding the scope of constitutional rights so that citizens would enjoy the same protections against all levels of government.

In the late nineteenth century and early twentieth century, the Court used the due process clause as a general source of protection for economic liberty. It relied on the Fourteenth Amendment to strike down a variety of state laws seeking to regulate businesses and enhance social welfare. For example, in *Lochner v. New York* (1905), the Court struck down a state law regulating bakers' working hours on the grounds that the law violated the due process-based right for workers to freely contract to provide their labor as they wished for their employers. Historians view the Court's decisions as primarily advancing the interests of businesses rather than those of the individual workers whose rights were supposedly violated by the economic regulation and social welfare laws. These decisions viewed the right to due process as a substantive right rather than as merely a guarantee that the government would follow certain processes before affecting individuals' lives and property. The Court's use of substantive due process theories to protect economic rights disappeared in the late 1930's as the Court's composition changed and other political actors, especially President Franklin D. Roosevelt, grew more vocal in their criticism of Court decisions blocking economic legislation intended to alleviate the effects of the Great Depression.

The due process clause has also been interpreted to provide other protections for individuals. For example, in *Brown v. Mississippi* (1936), police officers' actions in torturing suspects to obtain confessions were found to violate the suspects' right to due process of law. In other words, the torture deprived the suspects of the proper processes due to them in the criminal justice system. In addition to decisions to ensure procedural fairness in criminal justice, due process has also been referred to by the Court as the source of other personal rights not explicitly specified in the Constitution, such as a right for competent adults to decline unwanted medical care, as in *Cruzan v. Director, Missouri Department of Health* (1990).

EQUAL PROTECTION CLAUSE

Initially, the Court did not interpret the equal protection clause as a strong vehicle for eliminating discrimination. In *Plessy v. Ferguson* (1896), for example, the Court found no violation of equal protection when Louisiana mandated that African Americans ride in separate railroad cars. Because the Court found no equal protection problem with racial segregation, various states imposed segregation on many facets of their societies. During the mid-twentieth century, the Court began to shift its interpretation of the equal protection clause. Eventually this provision of the Fourteenth Amendment was used in *Brown v. Board of Education* (1954) to declare that racial segregation in public schools violated the Constitution. In subsequent decisions, the Court interpreted the clause to bar other forms of racial discrimination by the government.

In interpreting and applying the equal protection clause, the Court developed a special analytical approach that requires the government to show compelling reasons for any policy or program that involves racial discrimination. The only time that state governments have been able to successfully justify treating people differently with regard to their race has been in cases concerning affirmative action programs that seek to remedy the country's long history of discrimination by giving extra consideration to school and job applicants who are members of racial groups that have been victimized by discrimination. In *Regents of the University of California v. Bakke* (1978), for example, although the Court ruled against racial quotas and ordered that Bakke, a white applicant, be admitted, it held that a university could give members of racial minorities groups extra consideration in the admissions process for medical school without violating the equal protection clause.

The Court rejected efforts to apply the equal protection clause to private discrimination, even when state support arguably existed for that discrimination. For example, in *Moose Lodge v. Irvis* (1972), the Court refused to accept the argument that the state's granting of a liquor license to a club that denied membership to African Americans meant that state action was a component of the discrimination and therefore prohibited by the equal protection clause.

During the 1970's, the Court expanded the applicability of the equal protection clause by interpreting it to prohibit many kinds of discrimination by gender in government policies and programs. In its interpretation of the Fourteenth Amendment, the Court did not provide the same level of protection against gender discrimination that it provided against racial discrimination. Therefore, in *Rostker v. Goldberg* (1981), the Court held that the Selective Service program, which registers young men and not women for a potential military draft, is permissible despite its different treatment of men and women. The Court rejected equal protection claims based on other alleged forms of discrimination, such as a claim that the equal protection clause bars discrimination by government based on people's wealth in *San Antonio Independent School District v. Rodriguez* (1973). The Court has interpreted the equal protection clause to provide protection against discrimination based on race, gender, national origin, and a few other categories only. In most instances not involving one of these categories, the government may treat people differently as long as there is a rational basis for distinguishing people as part of a legitimate governmental program.

Because the Fourteenth Amendment was the first constitutional provision explicitly aimed at giving individuals protection against state actions, the due process and equal protection clauses of the Fourteenth Amendment have been relied on by the Court for broadly expanding the scope and reach of constitutional rights. The Court paid little attention to the privileges or immunities clause until its decision in *Saenz v. Roe* (1999), which used the clause to protect citizens' right to travel, including a right for people moving to new states to be treated equally with established residents in receiving benefits from social welfare programs. The rediscovery of the privileges and immunities clause opens further possibilities for the Fourteenth Amendment's use as a vehicle for the expansion of constitutional rights.

Christopher E. Smith

FURTHER READING

The history of the Fourteenth Amendment and its role in expanding the scope of rights is examined in Michael Kent Curtis's *No State Shall Abridge: The Fourteenth Amendment and the Bill of Rights* (Durham, N.C.: Duke University Press, 1986). The incorporation process is analyzed in Henry J. Abraham's *Freedom and the Court* (5th ed. New York: Oxford University Press, 1988). Raoul Berger's *Government by Judiciary: The Transformation of the Fourteenth Amendment* (Cambridge, Mass.: Harvard University Press, 1977) provides a critique of the Court's expansion of constitutional rights.

The Court's use of the due process clause to protect economic liberties is analyzed in Howard Gillman's *The Constitution Besieged: The Rise and Demise of "Lochner" Era Police Powers Jurisprudence* (Durham, N.C.: Duke University Press, 1993). Richard Kluger's *Simple Justice* (New York: Random House, 1975) provides a detailed account of the Court's use of the equal protection clause to attack racial discrimination.

A comprehensive presentation of the Court's interpretation of the Fourteenth Amendment is contained in William B. Lockhart, Yale Kamisar, Jesse H. Choper, and Steven H. Shiffrin's *The American Constitution* (6th ed. St. Paul, Minn.: West Publishing, 1986). The justices' voting records on Fourteenth Amendment issues are analyzed in Thomas R. Hensley, Christopher E. Smith, and Joyce A. Baugh's *The Changing Supreme Court: Constitutional Rights and Liberties* (St. Paul, Minn.: West Publishing, 1997).

SEE ALSO Affirmative action; *Brown v. Mississippi*; Citizenship; Due process, procedural; Due process, substantive; Equal protection clause; Incorporation, inverse; Incorporation doctrine; Privileges and immunities; Race and discrimination; *San Antonio Independent School District v. Rodriguez*; *Slaughterhouse Cases*.

Fourth Amendment

DATE: 1791

DESCRIPTION: Amendment to the U.S. Constitution and part of the Bill of Rights that protects people against unreasonable searches and seizures.

SIGNIFICANCE: In the early 1900's the Supreme Court began expanding the applications of the Fourth Amendment, balancing the rights of the accused against the safety of other people.

The Framers of the Bill of Rights were concerned with the old English practice of issuing general warrants and writs of assistance. These two legal tools authorized searches with few stipulations on searching agents, allowing searches day or night on bare suspicion. Authorized by the monarch, they were valid for the duration of his or her lifetime. They were not required to name a specific person or place but could be stated in more general terms. No oath before a magistrate was necessary to secure a warrant, and probable cause was not required. Every-

---

TEXT OF THE FOURTH AMENDMENT

The right of the people to be secure in their persons, houses, papers, and effects, against unreasonable searches and seizures, shall not be violated, and no Warrants shall issue, but upon probable cause, supported by Oath or affirmation, and particularly describing the place to be searched, and the persons or things to be seized.

thing was left to the discretion of the holder of the warrant. The result was harassment. The colonists were victims of these general warrants and writs of assistance and purposely set out to outlaw them.

James Madison revised his initial draft of the Fourth Amendment, changing the word "secured" to "secure" and adding the clause "against unreasonable searches and seizures." Although Madison's goal was to eliminate general warrants and writs of assistance, scholars believe these alterations made the meaning of the amendment ambiguous. The Fourth Amendment outlaws only unreasonable searches and seizures, logically allowing those deemed reasonable. The Framers envisioned that searches conducted with a warrant, which required specifics such as who is to be searched, what is to be seized, and when, were constitutionally permissible. The warrant clause stipulated what was expected of police when conducting searches. However, left unanswered were the questions of whether there are times when it is reasonable to search without a warrant, what constitutes probable cause, and whether the amendment restricts only police or other governmental agents with searching authority.

The Court in *Wolf v. Colorado* (1949) made clear that search warrants had to be supported by probable cause and issued by a neutral and impartial magistrate. However, often searches are conducted without a search warrant.

EXCEPTIONS TO THE WARRANT REQUIREMENT

The Court created a number of exceptions to the search warrant requirement. Using the reasonableness clause of the amendment rather than the warrant provision, the Court rejected the idea of a bright-line rule in favor of a more fact-bound, case-by-case approach. The police do not need a warrant for searches incident to arrest; stop-and-frisk situations; when illegal or stolen items are in plain view during a legal search; administrative, consensual, and border searches; and searches involving exigent circumstances such as automobile searches.

When an individual is arrested on probable cause, a police officer is permitted to conduct a warrantless search of the person. This exception to the warrant requirement, search incident to arrest, rests on the understanding that the arresting officer must have the power to disarm the accused and preserve any evidence. Protecting the officer's safety and retaining probative evidence is reasonable. The officer may search not only the person but the areas of immediate control. In *Chimel v. California* (1969), the Court reasoned that the scope of a search incident to arrest included wherever the arrestee might reach to grab a weapon or piece of evidence.

If in the course of a valid search, an officer comes on stolen or illegal items in plain view, they may be seized and used as evidence. This inadvertent windfall is permissible and reasonable under the Fourth Amendment as long as the officer happens on the evidence in the course of conducting a legal search. Related is the plain feel exception. In *Minnesota v. Dickerson* (1993), the Court held that if an officer feels what seems to be contraband or evidence of a crime when patting down the outside of a suspect's clothing, the items can be seized.

In *Terry v. Ohio* (1968), the Court allowed for searches on the street that did not meet the standard of probable cause. In this case, it upheld the brief detention of a suspect for weapons on the grounds of reasonable suspicion rather than probable cause. Only a limited frisk was permitted with the lowered standard of cause. If the pat-down yielded a basis for an arrest, however, a full search incident to arrest could follow.

The Court has applied the Fourth Amendment to the increasing problems arising in a mobile society. Planes, buses, trains, and boats all raise exigency concerns because of the highly mobile nature of the place to be searched and the futility of the police in executing search warrants on moving objects. The most common exigent circumstance is created by the automobile. As early as 1925 in *Carroll v. United States*, the Court made clear that the automobile would not be afforded the same level of privacy rights protection as an individual's home or person. Stopping an automobile and searching it on the street without a warrant was reasonable. However, the particulars of the car have generated a volume of litigation aimed at answering questions such as whether the police can lawfully open the glove box, the trunk, or containers in the automobile or search the driver, passengers, and their personal items. Given the lower expectation of privacy in automobiles, the Court in *Michigan Department of State Police v.*

Sitz (1990) allowed roadblocks to briefly stop all drivers to catch those driving under the influence of drugs and alcohol.

Employees of other governmental agencies, such as housing, fire, health, welfare, and safety inspectors, also have searching capabilities. These agents have a lesser standard than probable cause and often invoke an element of surprise, such as unannounced inspections of restaurants. Related to these types of searches are those to ensure safety in the workplace or school by drug-testing employees and students. In *National Treasury Employees Union v. Von Raab* (1989), the Court upheld suspicionless mandatory urinalysis testing for promotion on the grounds of safety (the employees would have access to firearms and secure information). By 1995 in *Vernonia School District v. Acton*, the Court upheld the right to drug-test all student athletes without requiring suspicion of individuals.

The courts have long recognized that individuals and items entering the United States may be searched at the international border without warrant or probable cause. The Court has placed some limits on these searches, such as the level of intrusion. Strip searches, for example, must be justified by real suspicion. In an attempt to stop the influx of illegal drugs, law enforcement developed the drug courier profile, a composite of variables that indicates the likelihood an individual is trafficking drugs. In *United States v. Sokolow* (1989), the Court upheld the use of the profile as a basis for detaining and searching individuals both at the border and within the continental United States.

In *Schneckloth v. Bustamonte* (1973), the Court acknowledged the use of consent searches, noting that individuals may waive their Fourth Amendment rights and allow a search without a warrant or probable cause. The key to the validity of such searches is that they must be voluntary; an individual must knowingly and freely consent to be searched. The waiver must be uncoerced, given without trickery or fear or promise of reward. Consent can be withdrawn at any time, and a refusal to give consent cannot then be used to establish probable cause.

The Fourth Amendment also applies to wiretapping and other forms of police surveillance. The Court in *Katz v. United States* (1967) reasoned that a person's expectation of privacy includes the seizure of intangible items such as words.

EXCLUSIONARY RULE

The Fourth Amendment describes the right to be secure against unreasonable searches and seizures without mentioning a remedy. The common-law remedy for search and seizure violations was a suit of trespass. This was used until *Weeks v. United States* (1914) when the Court adopted the exclusionary rule, which excludes illegally seized evidence from trials. The twofold purpose of the rule is to preserve the integrity of the judiciary and deter police misconduct. *Weeks* mandated the application of the exclusionary rule to searching agents of the federal government. In 1949 in *Wolf*, the Court incorporated the Fourth Amendment, thereby requiring states not to abridge the search and seizure rights of their citizens, yet allowing them to choose the remedy. This choice was eliminated in *Mapp v. Ohio* (1961) when the Court incorporated the remedy of exclusion from trials for all Fourth Amendment violations, by either state or federal officials.

Mapp's scope was limited by the Court. In *Linkletter v. Walker* (1965), the Court refused to apply the exclusionary rule retroactively. The exclusion remedy was limited in scope so that it did not include grand jury proceedings in *United States v. Calandra* (1974). The Court ruled in *United States v. Havens* (1980) that illegally seized evidence could be used to impeach the credibility of the defendant at trial and in *Nix v. Williams* (1984) that it could also be admitted into evidence if the police would have eventually discovered the evidence by lawful means. In 1984 in *United States v. Leon* and *Massachusetts v. Sheppard*, the Court allowed the use of illegally obtained evidence if the police error was made in objective good faith. The Court was unwilling to exclude reliable probative evidence when the error made by the police was unintentional and made in the course of attempting to follow the law.

Priscilla H. Machado

FURTHER READING

Otis H. Stephens and Richard A. Glenn's *Unreasonable Searches and Seizures: Rights and Liberties Under the Law* (Santa Barbara, Calif.: ABC-Clio, 2004) covers the subject of Fourth Amendment jurisprudence through two centuries of American history. Samuel Dash's *The Intruders: Unreasonable Searches and Seizures from King John to John Ashcroft* (New Brunswick, N.J.: Rutgers University Press, 2004) takes an even deeper historical approach, tracing protection against unreasonable searches back to early English history. Paula Franklin's *The Fourth Amendment* (New York: Silver Burdett Press, 2001) describes the origins of the Fourth Amendment as a check on police abuses.

William W. Greenhalgh's *The Fourth Amendment Handbook: A Chronological Survey of Supreme Court Decisions* (2d ed. Chicago: Criminal Justice Section, American Bar Association, 2003) is a professional handbook for lawyers. Another good historical treatment of the Fourth Amendment is Nelson B. Lasson's *The History and Development of the Fourth Amendment to the United States Constitution* (Baltimore, Md.: Johns Hopkins University Press, 1937). Several classic and often-cited works about the Fourth Amendment are Jacob W. Landynski's *Search and Seizure and the Supreme Court* (Baltimore, Md.: Johns Hopkins University Press, 1966), Wayne LaFave's *Search and Seizure: A Treatise on the Fourth Amendment* (Mineola, N.Y.: Foundation Press, 1978), Erwin N. Griswold's *Search and Seizure: A Dilemma of the Supreme Court* (Lincoln: University of Nebraska Press, 1975), and Telford Taylor's *Two Studies in Constitutional Interpretation* (Columbus: Ohio State University Press, 1969).

A general treatment of Fourth Amendment rights can be found in David M. O'Brien's *Constitutional Law and Politics: Civil Rights and Liberties* (6th ed. 2 vols. New York: W. W. Norton, 2005).

Some law review articles debating the policy implications of the Fourth Amendment and its remedy are Anthony Amsterdam's "The Supreme Court and the Rights of Suspects in Criminal Cases," *New York University Law Review* 45 (1970): 785, Yale Kamisar's "Is the Exclusionary Rule an 'Illogical' or 'Unnatural' Interpretation of the Fourth Amendment?" *Judicature* 62 (1978): 67, and Malcolm Wiley's "Constitutional Alternatives to the Exclusionary Rule," *South Texas Law Journal* 23 (1982): 531. Warren E. Burger expressed his views on the Fourth Amendment in "Who Will Watch the Watchman?" *American University Law Review* 14 (1964): 1.

SEE ALSO Automobile searches; Bill of Rights; *Chimel v. California*; Exclusionary rule; *Ferguson v. City of Charleston*; *Hudson v. Michigan*; *Katz v. United States*; *Kyllo v. United States*; *Mapp v. Ohio*; Search warrant requirement.

Felix Frankfurter

IDENTIFICATION: Associate justice (January 30, 1939-August 28, 1962)
NOMINATED BY: Franklin D. Roosevelt
BORN: November 15, 1882, Vienna, Austria
DIED: February 22, 1965, Washington, D.C.
SIGNIFICANCE: During his twenty-three years as an associate justice, Frankfurter, a dedicated liberal in his personal life, was a major advocate of judicial self-restraint. As a justice, he attempted to decide cases procedurally rather than to reconstruct the judicial system.

Felix Frankfurter was twelve when he arrived in the United States from his native Austria. He learned English quickly and in 1902 was graduated third in his class from the City College of New York. Four years later, he received a law degree with highest honors from Harvard University. He soon left the private practice of law to take a position as assistant to Henry L. Stimson, U.S. attorney for New York's southern district. In 1914 he became a faculty member at Harvard Law School.

During World War I (1917-1918), Frankfurter became a legal adviser on industrial matters to Secretary of War Newton D. Baker. In 1917 he served as secretary and later as counsel to President Woodrow Wilson's Mediation Commission. The following year, he chaired the War Labor Policies Board. These government appointments gave Frankfurter the opportunity to deal with a broad variety of circumstances involving labor unrest. They also brought him to the attention of a broad range of government officials, some of whom were distressed by his liberal stands in relation to matters involving labor but many of whom admired his ability to deal objectively with controversial situations.

Frankfurter was Woodrow Wilson's legal adviser at the Paris Peace Conference in 1919, after which he resumed his teaching career at Harvard. During the next decade, he was instrumental in founding the American Civil Liberties Union and helped to launch the *New Republic*, a magazine of political opinion. He was highly visible as a liberal activist, writing an impassioned article for the March, 1927, issue of *The Atlantic Monthly* in which he called for a new trial in the famous

Sacco-Vanzetti case, whose defendants were both sentenced to death for a murder committed during a payroll robbery even though their trial was tainted in several ways.

When Franklin D. Roosevelt became president in 1933, Frankfurter became a frequent legal adviser to him. The president's respect for Frankfurter grew through the years, and Roosevelt became increasingly dependent upon him for legal guidance as he proceeded with implementing the New Deal.

APPOINTMENT TO THE COURT

On January 5, 1939, Roosevelt nominated Frankfurter to serve as an associate justice of the Supreme Court. The nomination was unanimously confirmed in the Senate and, on January 17, 1939, Frankfurter was sworn in. The United States was in the midst of the New

Felix Frankfurter.
(Library of Congress)

Deal, and Washington officials rejoiced at the appointment of a liberal activist who had proved his mettle as a champion of civil liberties. The *Nation* magazine proclaimed that Frankfurter's whole life had been a preparation for service on the Court.

Even the conservative press applauded the appointment, acknowledging Frankfurter's even-handedness in judicial matters. Frankfurter's qualifications as a jurist could hardly be questioned. Few feared that his decisions would reflect narrow prejudices or unbalanced partisanship.

FRANKFURTER AS A JUSTICE

Frankfurter, the quintessential liberal when appointed to the Court, in time came to be known as one of the Court's staunch conservatives. This transformation occurred because the Court, during the Roosevelt administration, came to be dominated by liberals who viewed it as their duty to promote liberal goals through their decisions. Some of these liberals felt hostility toward Frankfurter and considered him a turncoat.

Frankfurter believed fervently in Justice Oliver Wendell Holmes's dedication to judicial self-restraint, which grew out of the Court's tendency, when it was dominated by conservatives at the beginning of the twentieth century, to vote against cases brought before it that promoted progressive social legislation. During Frankfurter's term, the Court had a majority of liberal justices, and he feared that it was becoming more concerned with making law than with interpreting the Constitution as it related to the cases brought before it. Because he realized the necessity of the separation of powers that characterizes democratic societies, Frankfurter frequently voted with the conservative minority rather than with the liberal majority, often casting the deciding vote in 5-4 decisions.

Frankfurter's greatest contribution as a justice was to maintain to the best of his ability the separation of powers that assures government by the people rather than government by the government. Ironically, it was Frankfurter's deep-seated liberalism that forced him into taking conservative stands. He recognized that a Court dominated either by liberals or conservatives bent on changing society rather than on interpreting the law as it is set forth in the Constitution overstepped its authority, taking on duties specifically assigned by the Constitution to the legislative branch of government. The Constitution is, after all, the U.S. government's contract with its citizens.

Frankfurter's transformation into a judicial conservative did not represent a contradiction in his thinking. Rather, it was totally consistent with his most closely held beliefs. He never at any point in his life failed to support the concept of government by the people.

R. Baird Shuman

FURTHER READING

Baker, Leonard. *Brandeis and Frankfurter: A Dual Biography.* New York: Harper & Row, 1984.

Belknap, Michal R. *The Vinson Court: Justices, Rulings, and Legacy.* Santa Barbara, Calif.: ABC-Clio, 2004.

Burt, Robert A. *Two Jewish Justices: Outcasts in the Promised Land.* Berkeley: University of California Press, 1988.

Parrish, Michael. *Felix Frankfurter and His Times: The Reform Years.* New York: Free Press, 1982.

_____. *The Hughes Court: Justices, Rulings, and Legacy.* Santa Barbara, Calif.: ABC-Clio, 2002.

Renstrom, Peter G. *The Stone Court: Justices, Rulings, and Legacy.* Santa Barbara, Calif.: ABC-Clio, 2001.

Simon, James F. *The Antagonists: Hugo Black, Felix Frankfurter and Civil Liberties in Modern America.* New York: Simon & Schuster, 1989.

Urofsky, Melvin I. *Felix Frankfurter: Judicial Restraint and Individual Liberties.* Boston: Twayne, 1991.

_____. *The Warren Court: Justices, Rulings, and Legacy.* Santa Barbara, Calif.: ABC-Clio, 2001.

SEE ALSO Judicial self-restraint; New Deal; Political questions; *Rochin v. California*; Separation of powers.

Full Faith and Credit

DESCRIPTION: A clause in the U.S. Constitution stating that states in the United States must recognize the validity of judicial decisions and legislative acts originating within other states.

SIGNIFICANCE: Although the original clause is somewhat unclear, the Supreme Court has interpreted it as meaning that judgments rendered in one state have conclusive effect in other states and that federal and state courts must grant full faith and credit to one another.

The full faith and credit clause, Article IV, section 1, of the U.S. Constitution, mandates that each state must give at least the same effect to the laws and court judgments of another state as would that other state. Although this clause covers "public acts" and "records" as well as judicial proceedings, it is most often applied to the recognition of court judgments from other states.

Not all state court judgments are entitled to full faith and credit. Every state that is asked to recognize another state's court judgment must determine what effect, if any, the judgment would have in the state that rendered it. Generally, if that judgment is not a final judgment on the merits, it is not entitled to full faith and credit. For example, a judgment based on a procedural error is not a "judgment on the merits." Likewise, a judgment rendered by a state court that lacked jurisdiction over the subject matter of the lawsuit or over the parties to the lawsuit is not entitled to full faith and credit in another state. To be a final judgment on the merits, a court judgment must have been entered by a state court that had the power to hear the particular dispute and based on the substantive law applicable to the dispute. After determining the effect and validity of a particular state court judgment in the state that rendered it, then the other state must give the same force and effect to that court judgment.

The application of the full faith and credit clause can lead to peculiar results. In *Fauntleroy v. Lum* (1908), an arbitration decision was entered against Lum to pay off a gambling debt. Under Mississippi law at the time, gambling was illegal. However, Lum failed to raise this defense, and the arbitrators were convinced that Lum's debt was

483

not an illegal gambling debt. The plaintiff, Fauntleroy, then found Lum in Missouri and requested the Missouri state court to give full faith and credit to the Mississippi arbitration decision. Justice Oliver Wendell Holmes, in writing the opinion for the Supreme Court, ruled that because the Mississippi arbitration decision is a final judgment on the merits under Mississippi law, then Missouri must give the Mississippi arbitration decision full faith and credit. Justice Holmes also stated that full faith and credit applies even if the Mississippi arbitration decision is contrary to Mississippi law.

Early in the twenty-first century, the emotional debate over same-sex marriages often involved the full faith and credit clause. When the high court of Massachusetts held in 2004 that gays and lesbians must be given the same rights of marriage as heterosexual couples, opponents of same-sex marriage feared that federal or state courts might interpret the clause to mean that such marriages would be recognized outside the states in which the marriages were contracted. Congress, however, had already passed the Defense of Marriage Act of 1996, which specified that other states would not be required to recognize a same-sex marriage or a domestic partnership.

By 2006, at least twenty states had passed similar laws, and most of them had either constitutional provisions or statutes defining marriage as exclusively a union between one man and one woman. In 2006, conservatives in Congress attempted, but failed, to pass a constitutional amendment banning same-sex marriages. Opponents of the amendment argued that the amendment would have no effect, because the courts had long recognized a "public policy exception," which allowed states not to recognize marriages inconsistent with strong public policies, as in the case of polygamous marriages. Proponents of the amendment, however, replied that it was impossible to be certain about how activist liberal judges might rule in the future. The emotional and sometimes acrimonious debate over the issue promised to continue for many years.

Michael Flynn
Updated by the Editor

SEE ALSO Comity clause; Privileges and immunities; States' rights and state sovereignty.

Melville W. Fuller

IDENTIFICATION: Chief justice (October 8, 1888-July 4, 1910)
NOMINATED BY: Grover Cleveland
BORN: February 11, 1833, Augusta, Maine
DIED: July 4, 1910, Sorrento, Maine
SIGNIFICANCE: Fuller was a gifted judicial administrator who managed the Supreme Court efficiently for twenty-two years; however, his legal impact was limited and many of his most important decisions were later overturned.

Melville W. Fuller's parents divorced shortly after his birth, and Fuller grew up in the household of his maternal grandfather, Chief Justice Nathan Weston of the Maine Supreme Judicial Court. After graduating from Bowdoin College in 1853, he read law for a year in an uncle's law office, then attended lectures at Harvard Law School for six months. Fuller moved to Chicago in 1856, where he practiced law for thirty-two years. An enthusiastic supporter of Stephen

Melville W. Fuller.
(Albert Rosenthal/
Collection of the
Supreme Court of
the United States)

Douglas, Fuller became active in Democratic Party affairs in 1858. As his legal reputation grew, he began to specialize in appellate work, especially in the field of commercial law. Fuller was admitted to practice before the Supreme Court in 1872, thereafter frequently arguing cases before the Court. In 1888 President Grover Cleveland chose Fuller, a committed Democrat who shared Cleveland's conservative economic and social views, to be the new chief justice.

Fuller proved a particularly effective administrator. Although the majority of the justices were Republicans, Fuller's Court never divided along party lines. Fuller's impartiality and friendly personality permitted him to manage court conferences efficiently, preventing serious disputes from breaking out between the justices. Several of his colleagues called him the best presiding judge they had ever known. In 1891, Fuller successfully lobbied Congress to pass the Circuit Court of Appeals Act, which established, for the first time, nine intermediate federal courts and curtailed appeals to the Supreme Court. Between 1890 and 1892 the number of new cases facing the Court fell from 623 to 290. The act reduced the justices' onerous circuit court duties and permitted the Court to concentrate on the most significant constitutional issues.

A CONSERVATIVE JUSTICE

Fuller was more successful as an administrator than in the decisions that he authored or joined; his opinions dealing with the most important constitutional issues were later either modified or overturned. In Fuller's view, the principal purpose of government was the protection of property rights. He was comfortable with large corporations and supportive of the expanding industrial capitalism of the late nineteenth century.

Fuller's conservative bias colored two major rulings that he wrote in 1895. In *United States v. E. C. Knight Co.* (1895), Fuller eviscerated the Sherman Antitrust Act of 1890, which attempted to ban monopolies in restraint of trade. He held that the E. C. Knight Company, which controlled more than 90 percent of U.S. sugar refining, did not violate the act. Congress could regulate only interstate commerce, and Fuller ruled that manufacturing companies did not engage in commerce. Thus, even if a manufacturing company shipped to every state in the Union, the Sherman Antitrust Act did not affect it. As long as this restricted definition of commerce held, only collusive actions by railroads could be successfully prosecuted under the act. However, later Court decisions would severely modify and ultimately abandon Fuller's interpretation of the act.

Fuller wrote the majority opinion in *Pollock v. Farmers' Loan and Trust Co.* (1895), in which the Court found a federal income tax to be unconstitutional. This reversed precedents going back to 1796 that had been accepted by the Court in validating the income tax imposed during the Civil War years. Fuller's decision immediately evoked a furious political response. In 1896 the Democratic Party platform repudiated both Cleveland and Fuller, calling for a reversal of the Court's ruling. The Progressive movement of the early twentieth century made annulment of the decision a major goal, leading, in 1913, to the ratification of the Sixteenth Amendment to the Constitution granting Congress the power to tax income.

Fuller consistently ruled against labor unions. In 1905 he joined the Court majority in *Lochner v. New York*, rejecting a New York law that set maximum work hours for bakers as an unreasonable interference with the right of free contract. Fuller was willing to apply the Sherman Act against labor unions, voting, in *In re Debs* (1895), to uphold the criminal conviction of labor leader Eugene Debs for interfering with commerce during the Pullman Strike. In 1908 he wrote the opinion in *Loewe v. Lawlor*—the Danbury Hatters' case—ruling that a labor boycott in support of a strike violated the Sherman Act. The decision did not explain why hat making, unlike sugar refining, was involved in commerce. Legislation and judicial decisions subsequently reversed both *Lochner* and *Loewe*.

Constitutional issues involving civil rights did not engage Fuller's concern. He rejected Justice John Marshall Harlan's thesis that the rights guaranteed in the Fourteenth Amendment applied to the states. The Court did not agree with Harlan that freedom of speech was protected against state infringement by the amendment. The Fuller Court ignored acts discriminating against African Americans in the fields of education and voting rights and refused to assert federal jurisdiction in cases in which states were accused of violating the constitutional rights of African Americans. Fuller voted with the majority in *Plessy v.*

Ferguson (1896), accepting the separate but equal doctrine as justification for racial segregation. This, and other civil rights decisions of the Fuller court, would later be overturned by the Court.

In 1892 Fuller declined an offer from President Cleveland to become secretary of state, on grounds that leaving the chief justiceship for another office would be detrimental to the reputation of the Court. Fuller accepted an appointment to the Venezuelan Boundary Arbitration Commission in 1897 and served on the Permanent Court of Arbitration at The Hague from 1900 until his death. By 1910 Fuller's health was failing; he died of a heart attack while at his summer home in Maine.

Milton Berman

FURTHER READING

Bader, William H., and Roy M. Mersky, eds. *The First One Hundred Eight Justices.* Buffalo, N.Y.: William S. Hein, 2004.

Ely, James W., Jr. *The Chief Justiceship of Melville W. Fuller, 1888-1910.* Columbia: University of South Carolina Press, 1995.

————. *The Fuller Court: Justices, Rulings, and Legacy.* Santa Barbara, Calif.: ABC-Clio, 2003.

Friedman, Leon, and Fred L. Israel, eds. *The Justices of the Supreme Court: Their Lives and Major Opinions.* 5 vols. New York: Chelsea House, 1997.

King, Willard L. *Melville Weston Fuller: Chief Justice of the United States, 1888-1910.* New York: Macmillan, 1950.

SEE ALSO *Debs, In re*; Harlan, John Marshall; Income tax; *Lochner v. New York*; *Plessy v. Ferguson*.

Fundamental Rights

DESCRIPTION: Notion that a select number of constitutional rights are so essential to American traditions of liberty and justice that they deserve special recognition and protection.

SIGNIFICANCE: The Supreme Court utilized the doctrine of fundamental rights as a basis for deciding which provisions of the Bill of Rights should be binding on the states through the Fourteenth Amendment. Moreover, since the 1950's the Court has applied "strict scrutiny" standards when examining governmental restrictions on those rights deemed to be fundamental.

When making his proposal for a Bill of Rights in 1789, James Madison did not declare that all of his suggested amendments were of equal significance. Indeed, he wrote of his special concern for his rejected proposal that would have prohibited the states from violating "the equal rights of conscience, nor the freedom of speech, or of the press, or the trial by jury in criminal cases." He clearly considered these particular rights to be more basic than some of the other provisions, such as those enumerated in the Third and Seventh Amendments.

The term "fundamental rights" entered American jurisprudence in Justice Bushrod Washington's circuit court opinion in *Corfield v. Coryell* (1823), which focused on Article IV's entitlement of "privileges and immunities of Citizens in the several states." Influenced by the natural law tradition, Washington wrote that this entitlement included a few rights that were "in their very nature, fundamental; which belong of right, to the citizens of all free governments." While he wrote that it was impossible to list all fundamental rights, he gave a few examples, such as the rights to own property and to travel through the states.

John Bingham and the other framers of the Fourteenth Amendment often quoted *Corfield* when discussing the privileges or immunities clause which they inserted into the new amendment. Although it is doubtful that most framers expected the clause to make each and every provision in the Bill of Rights binding on the states, many of them suggested that it would prohibit the states from violating the more fundamental of these rights, such as the First Amendment's guarantee of

489

free speech. The Supreme Court, however, gave an extremely restrictive interpretation to the clause in the *Slaughterhouse Cases* (1873), an interpretation that has never been directly overturned.

During the years from 1897 to 1937, the majority of the justices consistently held that the freedom to enter into contracts was one of the fundamental rights guaranteed by the Fifth and Fourteenth Amendments. They based this right on a substantive interpretation of the due process clause, as in *Adkins v. Children's Hospital* (1923), which overturned a federal minimum wage requirement as an unconstitutional infringement on a protected liberty. Beginning in 1937, however, a majority of the justices accepted that government might restrict the freedom of contract in order to promote reasonable public interests. At the same time, liberal members of the Court became increasingly concerned for the civil liberties enumerated in the first eight amendments. For a number of years, the judges argued about which, if any, of these rights should be incorporated into the Fourteenth Amendment, thus making them applicable to the states. In a seminal case, *Palko v. Connecticut* (1937), Justice Benjamin Cardozo argued for the incorporation of those rights that were "fundamental," either because they were "of the very essence of a scheme of ordered liberty," or because they were "principles of justice so rooted in the traditions and conscience of our people as to be ranked fundamental." In subsequent years, the majority of the justices would endorse some variation of Cardozo's approach to incorporation.

A related question was whether the Court should use the same standards of scrutiny when considering fundamental rights as when considering less essential rights. In the famous Footnote Four of *United States v. Carolene Products Co.* (1938), Justice Harlan Fiske Stone suggested that it might be appropriate to utilize a heightened level of scrutiny when examining three kinds of policies: those that appear to contradict explicit constitutional prohibitions; those that appear to interfere with political processes, such as limitations on the right to vote; and those that are discriminatory against racial or religious minorities. Years later, the footnote's advocacy of a double standard would provide ammunition for proponents of liberal judicial activism.

During World War II, beginning with *Murdock v. Pennsylvania* (1943), the Court's majority accepted the doctrine of "preferred freedoms," extending special judicial protections for the freedoms of the First Amendment. Similarly, in *Korematsu v. United States* (1944), in approving Japanese internment, the majority opinion declared that public policies discriminating on the basis of race were "immediately suspect," therefore requiring "the most rigid scrutiny." Ironically, judges in both federal and state courts were soon quoting *Korematsu* as a binding precedent, holding that the Constitution protects a fundamental right against invidious discrimination on the basis of race.

Building on these precedents, the Warren Court established the use of the "strict scrutiny" standard whenever examining a public policy with a suspect classification of persons, or a public policy restricting a fundamental right. When dealing with the second category, the justices first asked whether the policy could be justified by a compelling public interest, and then they demanded the government to show that it could not achieve its purpose with a policy that was less restrictive of the fundamental right.

A good example of the Warren Court's approach to protecting fundamental rights is *Sherbert v. Verner* (1963), which overturned a state's unemployment compensation law that only indirectly placed a burden on a religious practice. In *Griswold v. Connecticut* (1965), moreover, the Court declared that the right of privacy was a fundamental right, even though privacy is not mentioned in the Constitution. The Court also held that the right of interstate movement was fundamental in *Shapiro v. Thompson* (1969). These seminal precedents prepared the way for the monumental *Roe v. Wade* (1973) case, in which the justices expanded the right of privacy to include a woman's fundamental right to terminate an unwanted pregnancy.

By the 1970's, the Court was crystallizing its jurisprudence into three levels, or standards, of judicial assessment: strict scrutiny, intermediate (or "heightened") scrutiny, and minimal scrutiny. The Court applied the demanding standard of strict scrutiny to cases involving restrictions on fundamental rights, which included the right to equality based on race and sometimes alienage, as well as the right to vote, the right to travel, the right to reproductive freedom, and selective rights in the first eight amendments. For governmental deprivations or restrictions in these areas to be approved, government had to show that the restriction is narrowly tailored to attain a "compelling" governmental interest. The intermediate standard was applied to gender, illegitimacy, and for many years affirmative action programs. It required government policy to be "substantially" related to an "important" governmental interest. Ordinary scrutiny was applied to cases involving indigence, age, homosexuality, education, housing, and welfare. This standard only required "reasonable" policies based on a "legitimate" government interest.

After William H. Rehnquist became chief justice in 1986, the Court's conservative majority overturned several precedents concerning fundamental rights and strict scrutiny. In *Planned Parenthood v. Casey* (1992), for example, the Court endorsed a more permissive "undue burden" standard for evaluating restrictions on the abortion rights of women. In *Employment Division, Department of Human Resources v. Smith* (1990), likewise, the majority of the justices announced that they would no longer use the standard of strict scrutiny when examining legislation of general applicability that placed an incidental burden on religion practices. In affirmative action cases, however, the Court ruled in *Richmond v. J. A. Croson Co.* (1989) and *Adarand Constructors v. Peña* (1995) that "any preference based on racial or ethnic criteria must necessarily receive a most searching examination." When the Court approved such a preference in *Grutter v. Bollinger* (2003), it was only the second time (the first being *Korematsu*) that the opinion for the Court unambiguously approved a suspect classification when explicitly applying strict scrutiny assessment.

Thomas Tandy Lewis

FURTHER READING

Abraham, Henry, and Barbara Perry. *Freedom and the Court: Civil Rights and Liberties in the United States.* 8th ed. Lawrence: University Press of Kansas, 2003.

O'Brien, David M. *Constitutional Law and Politics.* Vol. 2, *Civil Rights and Civil Liberties.* 6th ed. New York: W. W. Norton, 2005.

SEE ALSO Bill of Rights; Black, Hugo L.; Cardozo, Benjamin N.; Due process, substantive; *Gratz v. Bollinger/Grutter v. Bollinger*; Harlan, John M., II; Incorporation doctrine; *Palko v. Connecticut.*